BUTLER'S
LIVES OF THE SAINTS

NEW

FULL EDITION

SEPTEMBER

BUTLER'S
LIVES OF THE SAINTS

NEW FULL EDITION

Patron
H. E. CARDINAL BASIL HUME, O.S.B.+
Archbishop of Westminster

BUTLER'S LIVES OF THE SAINTS

NEW
FULL EDITION

SEPTEMBER

Revised by
SARAH FAWCETT THOMAS

BURNS & OATES

THE LITURGICAL PRESS
Collegeville, Minnesota

First published 2000 in Great Britain by
BURNS & OATES
Wellwood, North Farm Road,
Tunbridge Wells, Kent TN2 3DR

First published 2000 in North America by
THE LITURGICAL PRESS
St John's Abbey, Collegeville,
Minnesota 56321

ISBN 0 86012 258 1   Burns & Oates
ISBN 0-8146-2385-9   The Liturgical Press

Library of Congress Catalog Card Number: 95-81671

Typeset by Search Press Limited
Printed in the United States of America

CONTENTS

Contents

PREFACE

The revision of the Calendar in 1969 is now popularly seen as a process of downgrading. Saints are said to have been "demoted" or dropped. But apart from a few cases where this is literally true—St Eustace and St Catherine of Alexandria are notable examples—the reality is rather different. Apart from the relatively few saints who remain in the universal Calendar and are celebrated throughout the Catholic Church on their feast-day, there is a huge company of saints who have been not so much downgraded as localized—given back, in other words, to the localities where their cult is traditional.

That being said, the September list offers no escape from the fact that most saints in the Roman Calendar are, broadly speaking, European. Given the history of Christianity so far, this is probably inevitable. Having made a great swathe round the Mediterranean, the Roman Empire fanned out through the territories to the north. Christianity followed the same route, its progress much helped by local peoples, who were the first to be converted. Even today, when it has crossed every cultural barrier and the number of non-European Christians far exceeds the number of those in Europe, Rome is still the centre of the largest Christian grouping.

This prompts a variety of thoughts: on the significance, for our understanding of the saints, of time and place; on the effect of these on the type of information we have about the saints; and on the paucity of acknowledged saints from areas such as black Africa and Australasia, where Christianity has nevertheless put down roots and where the Church is vibrant and active.

In the early years, when Christianity was spreading through the countries clustered around the Mediterranean and their immediate hinterland, the first to be venerated as saints were the martyrs—those who sacrificed their lives for their beliefs. Only later, when the persecutions ceased and Christianity became tolerated and even established, did the Church begin to venerate those who lived heroically according to the same beliefs. When Christianity was introduced to the great non-European cultures, such as those of Japan, China, and later, Korea, it was understandably seen as a threat to the established order, and the pattern repeated itself. (It is worth mentioning here that the Korean Church, as the entry for the Martyrs of Korea on the 20th records, has the distinction of having been founded by a layman. But to the disappointment of many Korean Catholics, the earliest generation of martyrs was not included in the 103 who were canonized in 1984, all of whom suffered after the arrival of the French missionaries with whom they are commemorated.) The first saints in these and other areas of the Far East were the martyrs—those who bore witness with their lives to their newfound faith. But somehow, in these countries, the second stage has been slow to happen. This is partly because of the innate European bias of the selection of saints, although genuine attempts have been and are being made to correct this and the sheer force of numbers is in favour of change. But it is partly also because the coming of Christianity to these countries coincided with a tightening-up of the rules for the recognition and veneration of saints. Europe has so many saints because prior to the seventeenth century so many popular cults were approved without an elaborate process of proof.

The fact that all these saints exist does not necessarily mean, however, that we know a great deal about them personally. Hagiography for many today is synonymous with a suspension of the critical faculties. It is understood to mean the presentation of individuals in a manner that may not deny their fallibility but glosses over it in order to show what holy persons they were. The accusation has not always been justified. In the Gospels the very human failings of the earliest saints are not glossed over. St Peter denies Christ three times and loses his temper with the servant of the man sent to arrest his master; St Thomas is an extreme sceptic; and several disciples fall asleep when they are supposed to be keeping watch. The almost perfect modern hagiographer, Friedrich von Hügel (*almost* perfect because his written style is so dense and cumulative that for most he is probably unreadable), had a similar approach. In his hugely detailed work, *The Mystical Element of Religion*, which is subtitled "as studied in St Catherine of Genoa and her friends," he is not afraid to draw attention in a quite explicit way to Catherine's weaknesses, but he does so not in order to do her down but to emphasize her extraordinary achievement.

Not all the saints are what we would describe as instantly attractive and likable people. St Jerome (30th) provoked the fierce loyalty of some, but many found him thoroughly difficult and unlikable, especially during the first half of his life. Catherine of Genoa (15th), already mentioned, had a melancholic temperament and was almost devoid of humour. These are normally regarded as negative qualities, but we need to acknowledge their existence if we are to appreciate what these and other saints made of the raw material that was dealt out to them. The truth is that on average it will have been no worse or better than the raw material that is dealt out to the rest of us. It is what they made of it, under grace, that is a source of wonder and should, as von Hügel appreciated, excite our admiration.

This is, of course, a peculiarly modern approach to the matter. Hagiography is affected by time and place. Fifteen hundred years ago, what people wanted were stories of miracles, and stories of miracles were by and large what they got. Miracle stories and entire legends were transferred from one saint to another. The literal truth did not matter. The aim was to show that a particular individual was a man or woman of God. We of today are fortunate that the letters of St Jerome and St Gregory the Great (3d) or the vignette of St Satyrus (17th) by his brother, St Ambrose (7 Dec.), have survived from that early period to satisfy our intense interest in the individual. But these are exceptional cases. We can hazard a guess about the personalities of those who, like St Gerard of Csanad (24th), St William of Roskilde (2d), and so many of the Celtic saints, were prepared to leave home and country, the stability and comfort of the familiar, in order to preach the gospel to uncivilized and frequently ungrateful peoples. But they will have been as distinct and different as any members of any group anywhere, so it can never be more than a guess.

We depend, of course, on information. The sort of information that survives, like the form in which it does so, varies greatly from period to period and place to place. Where some of the earlier saints are concerned, the sources have less to tell us about the individual concerned and more about the beginnings of a particular national church or a monastic foundation. St Unno (17th) and Bd Eskil of Lund (6th) were involved in the Christian beginnings of Denmark and Sweden respectively, and we know a certain amount about their successes and failures in this connection. But we know nothing about the sort of people they were.

In more recent times information has been quite plentiful and detailed, thanks to improved methods of communication, preservation, and so on. As far as groups of martyrs are concerned—and there are two such in this month: the Martyrs of September (2d), a particular group from among the many who died during the French Revolution; and the Martyrs of Korea (20th)—individual delineation of character is not expected. But when it comes to individuals, the information available is different in kind. We know a good deal more about St Peter Claver (9th), St Robert Bellarmine (17th), or Bd Jacques Laval (9th), about St Emily de Rodat (19th), St Teresa Couderc (26th), St Vincent de Paul (27th), or Bd Frederick Ozanam (8th), and even about someone as early as Hildegard of Bingen (17th) than we do about earlier saints, including those for whom the sources are relatively good. But only too often there are elements missing, as if mentioning their dark side might take away from their claim to sanctity or even just be disrespectful. It is so difficult to discover, for example, how Bd Bernardino of Feltre (28th) experienced the following he had and—let it be said—the power he wielded. Most of us might reasonably feel that it would go to our head. So how he learned to deal with his reactions is something we need to have some idea of if he is to be a useful model for us. What we want is more biographers like von Hügel who are not afraid to look at the dark side in order to appreciate how "costly" is the achievement of the saints.

So many people have shown interest in my part in this project, and I thank them all for their support. My particular thanks go to Paul Burns for trusting me with a second volume, and to David Farmer, who was again so generous with his time and his knowledge, particularly about the early English saints. I would also like to thank Dr Richard Sharpe, who spent time on the Celtic entries and made good many serious deficiencies in that area; John Harwood, who did the same for the Russian and Eastern entries; Sr Winifred Morley, R.C.; Dr Marie Henry Keane, O.P.; Fr Henry Pass C.S.Sp.; Fr Jack Clancy, C.Ss.R.; and Br Thomas More, O.F.M. Cap., who provided useful information, respectively, on St Teresa Couderc, St Hildegard of Bingen, Bd Jacques Laval, Bd Caspar Stanggassinger, Bd Ignatius of Santhià; Desmond Sullivan; Christa Pongratz-Lippitt, who provided the entry on Bd Anton Schwartz (15th), beatified in June 1998, at very short notice; and above all Tony, who supported me throughout with his ideas, his talent for cooking, and his great good humour.

28 August 1998, Feast of St Augustine

Sarah Fawcett Thomas

Abbreviations and Short Forms

A.A.S.	*Acta Apostolicae Sedis, Commentarium officiale.* Rome, 1908-.
AA.SS.	*Acta Sanctorum*, 64 vols. Antwerp, also Rome and Paris, 1643-. (Page and volume numbers may vary in different editions.)
AA.SS. O.S.B.	L. D'Achéry and J. Mabillon. *Acta Sanctorum Ordinis Sancti Benedicti*, 9 vols. 1668-1701.
Anal.Boll.	*Analecta Bollandiana.* 1882-.
A.N.C.L.	*Ante-Nicene Christian Library.* 1864-.
Anstruther	G. Anstruther, O.P. *The Seminary Priests*, 4 vols. Ware, Ushaw, and Great Wakering, 1968-77.
Baudot et Chaussin	J. Baudot and P. Chaussin. *Vies des Saints et des Bienheureux*, 13 vols. (J. Dubois and P. Antin vols. 7ff.). Paris, 1935-59.
Bede, *H.E.*	The Venerable Bede, *Historia Ecclesiastica*, ed. L. Sherley-Price and D. H. Farmer. London, 1955; rev. ed., 1990.
B.H.L.	*Bibliotheca Hagiographica Latina Antiquae et Mediae Aetatis.* 1898-1901; suppl., 1911
Bibl.SS.	*Bibliotheca Sanctorum*, 13 vols. Rome, 1960-70. Suppl. 1 (*Prima Appendice*). Rome 1987.
C.M.H.	*Commentarius Perpetuus in Martyrologium Hieronymianum*, ed. H. Delehaye, P. Peeters, *et al.*, in *AA.SS.*, 64.
C.S.E.L.	*Corpus Scriptorum Ecclesiasticorum Latinorum.* Vienna, 1866-.
D.A.C.L.	H. Cabrol and H. Leclerq (eds.). *Dictionnaire d'archéologie chrétienne et de liturgie*, 15 vols. Paris, 1907-53.
D.C.B.	W. Smith and H. Wace (eds.). *Dictionary of Christian Biography*, 4 vols. London, 1877-87.
D.H.G.E.	A. Baudrillart *et al.* (eds.). *Dictionnaire d'histoire et de géographieecclésiastiques.* Paris, 1912-.
D.N.B.	*Dictionary of National Biography.* Oxford, 1995.
Dict.Sp.	M. Viller *et al.* (eds.). *Dictionnaire de spiritualité.* Paris, 1937-.
D.T.C.	A. Vacant, E. Mangenot, and E. Amman (eds.).

	Dictionnaire de théologie catholique, 15 vols. Paris, 1903-50.
E.E.T.S.	Early English Text Society.
E.H.D.	D. C. Douglas *et al.* (eds.). *English Historical Documents*. 1953-.
F.E.	L. Duchesne, *Fastes épiscopaux de l'ancienne Gaule*, 3 vols. 2d ed., Paris, 1907-15.
H.S.S.C.	F. Chiovaro *et al.* (eds.). *Histoire des saints et de la sainteté chrétienne*, 12 vols. Paris, 1972-88.
Jöckle	C. Jöckle. *The Saints*. 1995.
K.S.S.	A. P. Forbes (ed.). *Kalendar of Scottish Saints*. Edinburgh, 1872.
L.B.S.	
Léon, *Auréole*	J. Léon de Clary, O.F.M., *L'auréole séraphique*. Eng. trans. *Lives of the Saints and Blessed of the Orders of St Francis*, 4 vols. Taunton, 1887.
Liber Pontificalis	L. Duchesne (ed.). *Liber Pontificalis*. Paris, 1886.
M.G.H.	G. Pertz *et al.* (eds.). *Monumenta Germaniae Historiae*, 64 vols. Hanover, 1839-1921. The *Scriptores* series is split into sub-series, including *Auctores antiquissimi*, *Scriptores rerum merovingicarum*, and *Scriptores*.
M.M.P.	R. Challoner. *Memoirs of Missionary Priests*. London, 1741-2. New ed. by J. H. Pollen, London, 1924.
N.C.E.	*New Catholic Encyclopedia*, 14 vols. New York, 1967.
O.D.C.C.	F. L. Cross and E. A. Livingstone (eds.). *The Oxford Dictionary of the Christian Church*. 3d ed.; Oxford and New York, 1997.
O.D.P.	J. N. D. Kelly. *The Oxford Dictionary of Popes*. Oxford, 1986.
O.D.S.	D. H. Farmer. *The Oxford Dictionary of Saints*. 4th ed., Oxford and New York, 1997.
P.G.	J. P. Migne (ed.). *Patrologia Graeca*, 162 vols. Paris, 1857-66.
P.L.	J. P. Migne (ed.). *Patrologia Latina*, 221 vols. Paris, 1844-64.
Propylaeum	H. Delehaye (ed.). *Propylaeum ad Acta Sanctorum Decembris: AA.SS. 65*. Brussels, 1940.

S.C.	Sources Chrétiennes. Paris, 1940-.
Sozomen	Sozomen. *Historia Ecclesiastica.* In vol. 2 of P. Schaff and H. Wace (eds.). The Nicene and Post-Nicene Christian Fathers. 1887-1900; 2d series rp., Grand Rapids, Michigan, 1979.
V.S.H.	C. Plummer (ed.). *Vitae Sanctorum Hiberniae*, 2 vols. Oxford, 1910; 2d ed., 1968.

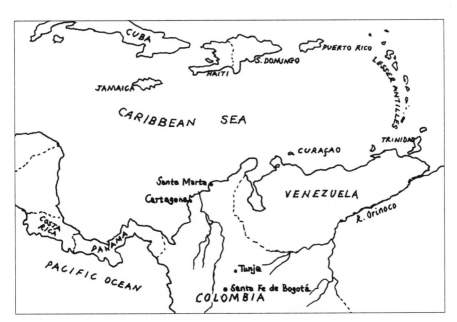

NORTHERN SOUTH AMERICA AND THE CARIBBEAN:
Places associated with St Peter Claver (9th)

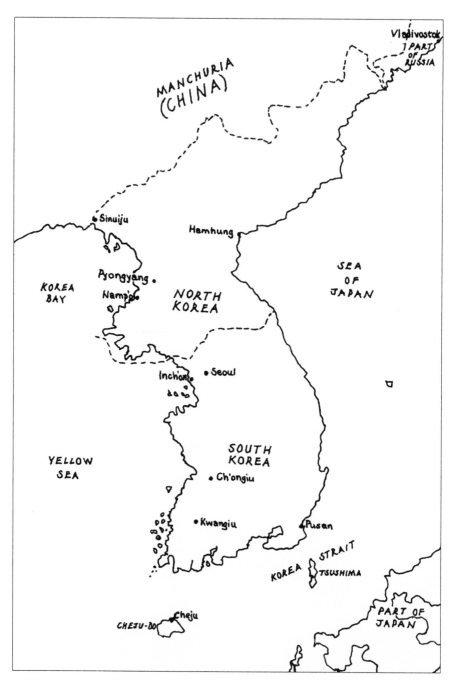

KOREA: see SS ANDREW KIM, PAUL CHONG, AND COMPANIONS,
Martyrs of Korea (20th)

xvi

1

St Verena (? Fourth Century)

St Verena is one of those saints about whom nothing at all is known apart from the simple fact of their existence. She is mentioned by name in the Roman Martyrology, which says she died at Aquae Durae near Constance, as well as in the additions to the *Hieronymianum* and in the ninth-century Munich martyrology, but that is all. The details are supplied by two Lives, a *Vita I* written by Hatto III, abbot of Reichenau, in about 888, and a *Vita II*, which was put together between 1000 and 1010. Both were "inspired" by the cult that had grown up at the tomb of a woman from Zurzach, a village on the Rhine northwest of Zurich. The cult itself is described in *Miracula Sanctae Verenae*, which appeared in 1010.

As told by her biographers, Verena's life was one of almost constant movement. Although it is impossible to date the details, it is likely that she lived in the fourth century. According to the legend she came originally from Egypt. Having become a Christian, she spent some time at the Thebaid under the direction of St Victor, who was one of her relatives. The first Life says that she then attached herself to the Theban Legion (22 Sept.), following it to Italy, where she stayed, thus escaping the massacre at Agaunum. When she heard what had happened to the Christian soldiers of the legion, she travelled to Agaunum to venerate their relics and search for Victor. She then moved on to Solothurn, where she lived for a while in the house of a local man who may or may not have been a Christian; in either case the biographers are at pains to point out that for all the women who knew her Verena remained a model of chastity and self-denial. People will still point to the cave where she lived subsequently and from which she would set out on her countless charitable errands among the local peasants—she is said to have been particularly concerned about their personal cleanliness. It is the second Life that moves her on from Solothurn to Koblenz and from there to Zurzach, where a cell was built specially for her. Here, it is said, she finally settled down, devoting her energies to work with the poor and the sick, especially lepers. After her death, which is supposed to have taken place in Zurzach, a cult developed around her tomb, and the monastery that was built over it in the tenth century became a place of pilgrimage.

Linked in both the written and the oral tradition with the Theban Legion, Verena is also linked with the very beginnings of Christianity in Switzerland. She is one of the most widely venerated of the Swiss saints, and many dedications survive to this day. In art she is usually represented as a mature woman holding a pitcher and some bread, or later a comb, all symbols of her charitable work.

AA.SS., Sept., 1, pp. 157-75; *M.G.H., Scriptores*, 4, pp. 457-60; *Bibl.SS.*, 12, 1033; J. Bütler, *Die Thebäische Legion* (1957). There is a full bibliography in A. Reinle, *Die heilige Verena von Zurzach* (1948), which is in turn reviewed in *Anal.Boll.* 69 (1980), pp. 412-5.

St Simeon Stylites the Elder (390-459)

Simeon was the first of the stylites, or pillar saints, of whom he is also the best known. Several Lives were written, but they tend to disagree on the details and almost certainly exaggerate when it comes to describing his way of life. From what can be pieced together it seems that he was born in Cilicia, near the border with Syria, the son of a shepherd. As a young man he had a dream or vision which inspired him to become a servant in a nearby monastery. He stayed here for two years before moving on to the monastery ruled by Heliodorus at Eusobona (Tell'Ada, near Antakya). His austerities were extreme, and when a rope of twisted palm leaves he was wearing somehow ate into his flesh he nearly died. It took three days of careful work softening and separating the leaves before it could be removed, and when he recovered, the abbot dismissed him.

Simeon went next to Telanissos (Dair Sem'an), where he is supposed to have spent his first Lent fasting totally from both food and drink. On Easter Sunday the other monks found the emergency supplies of bread and water they had left for him untouched. The unconscious Simeon they revived with the Eucharist and a few lettuce leaves.

After three years at this hermitage he took himself off to the top of a mountain, made an enclosure, and chained himself to the rock. Eventually the vicar of the patriarch of Antioch told him measures like this were unnecessary and that the grace of God and his own determination were all he needed to persevere in the way of life he had chosen. Simeon accepted the truth of this but still felt he had to resolve the problem created by the many people who came to visit him, seriously interrupting his solitude.

It was at this point that he embarked on an unusual and hitherto completely unknown way of life. Having built a pillar some nine feet high with a diameter of about six feet, he set himself up on top of it. For the remainder of his life, he lived successively on three or four different pillars—the sources disagree about their number and their dimensions. His austerity, always remarkable, became extreme during Lent, which he spent fasting totally, lying down to pray when he no longer had the physical strength to stand.

How much of this is exaggeration is not known. However, as he should perhaps have foreseen, his new way of life did not protect him from visitors. Rather, it attracted them, and soon he was giving twice-daily homilies. His preaching had curiously little in common with the obsessive fanaticism of his life style. In moderate and gentle terms he urged people to act with justice and sincerity toward others and to cultivate the inner life of prayer. He seems also to have kept sufficiently abreast of what was going on to champion the teaching of the Council of Chalcedon (451). His strongest words were in denunciation of usury and swearing. People of all walks of life came to consult him personally, including the emperors Theodosius II (408-50), Marcian (450-7), and Leo I (457-74), and many others corresponded with him by letter.

Simeon had been living on pillars for thirty-seven years when he died on 1 September 459. This extraordinary and from certain points of view appalling way of life must have evoked some of the same responses then as it does now (there is evidence that some Egyptian monks sent him a writ of excommunication but withdrew it when they heard of his charity and other virtues). But at the same time the challenge it represented to prevailing values commanded enormous respect, and his body was taken to burial accompanied by all the bishops of the province and many of the laity. The ruins of the church and monastery that were built near his pillar can still be seen. There is an extensive iconography, but almost exclusively in the East. The earliest representations come from Syria, a good example being a fifth- or sixth-century figure in bas-relief, now in the Louvre, from Gibrin, near Aleppo. The stylite tradition started by Simeon was continued by St Daniel (11 Dec.) and St Simeon the Younger (24 May).

AA.SS., Jan., 1, pp. 261-86; Theodoret, *Historia Religiosa*, 26. For near-contemporary Lives see H. Lietzmann, *Das Leben des heiligen Simeon Stylites* (1908); P. Peeters, "S. Siméon Stylite et ses premiers biographes," in *Anal.Boll.* 61 (1942), pp. 29-71; A. Leroy-Molinghen, "A propos de la Vie de Syméon Stylite," in *Byzantion* 34 (1964), pp. 375-84. For a study of the stylite movement see H. Delehaye, *Les Saints Stylites* (1923), pp. 584-96. Also *Bibl.SS.*, 11, 1116-38; *O.D.S.*, pp.436-7. On the iconography see J. Lassus, *Histoire de l'iconographie des stylites* (1969).

St Lupus of Sens, *Bishop* (623)

The earliest Latin Life of St Lupus (Loup, Leu), originally believed to be an eighth-century work, is now thought to date from the ninth century. Since it is regarded as unreliable, the most that can be said about Lupus for certain is that he succeeded St Artemius (28 Apr.) as bishop of Sens when the latter died in 609 and became a victim of the secular and ecclesiastical power struggles of the day. Filling in the details, the Life says he was the son of an *Orléanais* nobleman and a brilliant student. It portrays him as a humble, prayerful man who carried out his pastoral duties with great zeal. He was also said to have helped actively to maintain public order in times of political unrest.

On the death of Thierry II of Burgundy and Orleans (595-613), who in the last year of his life became king of Austrasia, Lupus supported the right of Thierry's son, Sigebert II, to succeed him. His troubles began when Sigebert died in that same year and Clotaire II (613-29) absorbed Burgundy to become king of all the Franks. When Clotaire's minister, Duke Farulf, marched on Sens, he and his men were frightened off when Lupus rang the church bell. But Lupus omitted to buy his own safety from Farulf, who immediately began to accuse him falsely to the king. In this he was aided and abetted by Medegislus, abbot of Saint-Rémi in Sens, who had his eye on the bishopric. Although Medegislus did not get what he wanted—the people of Sens killed him in his own church for his treachery—Clotaire believed Lupus' detractors, and the bishop was sent to Ausenne, a small village on the river near Blangy-sur-Bresle. He lost no time in evangelizing the pagans of the area, and even the governor and some members of the army were converted after he restored the sight of a blind man. News of this reached Clotaire, who realized that he had done Lupus a great wrong. Responding to an appeal from St Winebald (8 May), abbot of Troyes, and the people of Sens, he asked the bishop's forgiveness and restored him to his diocese. Lupus showed no resentment but continued to govern the diocese as though nothing had happened.

Lupus died in 623, allegedly at Briénon-sur-Armençon, where there is still a fountain named after him. He was buried, as he had requested, in the basilica of St Columba in Sens. This was renamed SS Columba and Lupus, and a monastery grew up around it. Over two centuries later, in 853, the relics were transferred to a new basilica that had been built. He is mentioned in the completer manuscripts of the *Hieronymianum* and in the martyrology of Wandelbert (*c.* 850), and for a while the cult, which is ancient, was widespread and popular. Some of the thirty or so place names in France that use the name Loup or Leu refer to another saint of the same name, St Lupus of Troyes (29 July). Nevertheless, not a few, including Saint-Loup-de-Naud (Seine-et-Marne) and Saint-Leu-d'Esseront, refer to today's saint. In quite another context Marcel Proust used the name for one of the central characters—Robert de Saint-Loup—of *A la recherche de temps perdu*. Lupus' archiepiscopal ring, one of the many in legend supposed to have been dropped in water and recovered from the belly of a fish, is preserved in the treasury of Sens Cathedral, along with another jewel said to have dropped miraculously into the chalice while he was celebrating Mass at Ordon (today Saint-Loup-d'Ordon).

For the Latin Life see *M.G.H., Scriptores merov.*, 4, pp.176-8. On the date of the Life see G. Vielhaber in *Anal.Boll.* 26 (1907), pp. 43-4. Also *Bibl.SS.*, 8, 388-9; *AA.SS.*, Sept., 1, pp. 248-66; Baudot et Chaussin, 9, pp. 22-4; H. Bouvier, *Histoire de l'Eglise de Sens*, 1, pp. 101-6; *F.E.*, 2, p. 396-400.

St Drithelm (*c.* 700)

What is known of this Northumbrian saint is recorded by Bede, who associates him with what he calls "a memorable miracle, like to those in former days." Drithelm was a good man, married, with a family. In about 693 he fell ill and one evening appeared to have died. Next morning, to the consternation of those present, all of whom fled except his wife, he sat up and announced that because of things he had just "seen" he would live a different sort of life in the future. Having taken time to pray in the village church, he divided his property into three—for his wife, his children, and the poor. He then went and told his story to King Aldfrith, at whose request he was accepted at Melrose Abbey by the then abbot, St Ethelwald (12 Feb.). His account of what happened that night sounds like a precursor of *La Divina Commedia* and is interesting for what it tells us of the afterlife beliefs of the time. He died and was met by "one with a shining countenance and bright garments," who took him on a journey to the mouth of hell and the gate of heaven. He was allowed to enter neither, though he did visit the ante-chambers to both. After this his guide, who had abandoned him briefly at the mouth of hell to give him a taste of what eternal separation from God would be like, told him that he must now return to his earthly life and live "in righteousness and simplicity" in order to win "a place among the blessed souls."

Drithelm spent the rest of his life as a monk at Melrose, on the banks of the Tweed, where his rigorous penances included standing in the river to recite the divine office while ice floated around him. Many were inspired by his example, including an Irish monk named Haemgisl (or Aemgilus) of whom Bede wrote: "He is still living and leading a solitary life in Ireland where he supports his declining years with coarse bread and cold water. He often went to Drithelm and heard of him all the particulars of what he had seen when separated from his body." It was in fact from Haemgisl that Bede got the story of the vision. Although there is no record of any formal cult of St Drithelm, Alcuin mentions him in his poem about the saints of York, and he features in Bishop Challoner's *Memorials of Ancient British Piety*. Bede's account in the *Historia Ecclesiastica* made him popular, it seems, and his story in turn helped to popularize Bede's book.

Bede, *H.E.*, 5, 21; Aelfric, *Homily* (ed. B. Thorpe, 2, 1846), pp. 348-56; *Bibl.SS.*, 4, 836-8; *O.D.S.*, pp. 136-7; S. J. Seymour, *Irish Visions of the Other World* (1930), pp. 154ff.

St Giles, *Abbot (c. 710)*

St Giles (Gilles, Aegidius) is one of those saints whose immense popularity was based on something other than certain information about the facts of his life. He was one of the best-loved and most widely known saints of the Middle Ages. Yet all that can be said about him for certain is that he was probably born in the first half of the seventh century—dates from the sixth to the eighth century are given; that he built a monastery on land given him for the purpose in about 673 by a King Wamba (or Flavius) at what is now Saint-Gilles, near Arles, in Provence; and that his shrine there became a place of pilgrimage, both as a stopping place on the routes to Compostela and the Holy Land and in its own right.

The legend that grew up around him was recorded in a tenth-century biography that made free use of material from the Lives of other saints and is definitely not trustworthy as far as the facts are concerned. According to the legend Giles was an Athenian by birth and became celebrated after the death of his parents for his generous almsgiving and his miracles—he was said to have cured a sick beggar by giving him his cloak, in a gesture reminiscent of that of St Martin of Tours (11 Nov.). Wary of this publicity, as of the prosperity that had prompted him to give away his temporal goods in the first place, he set sail from Athens, travelling westward until he reached Marseilles. Having spent two years with St Caesarius (27 Aug.) in Arles (this is a major inconsistency, since Caesarius died in 542), he became a hermit in a wood near Nîmes, not far from the mouth of the Rhône. At this point the biography includes a story that is told of a number of saints. Living alone in the wood, Giles was nourished by the milk of a hind, which was eventually pursued by King Wamba (or Flavius) and his hunting party. On this occasion and the next the hind took refuge in Giles' cave, and the dogs gave up the chase. Intrigued, the king, accompanied by a bishop, followed the huntsmen, one of whom shot into the bushes as the hind disappeared. Going in to investigate further, they found that Giles and not the hind had been wounded by the arrow. Giles accepted their apologies but refused the help and gifts they offered. The king nevertheless continued to visit him and eventually agreed that the money he was offering could be used to found a monastery, provided Giles was its first abbot.

As soon as it was built near Giles' cave, the monastery attracted a community and, according to the legend, the attention of another ruler (wrongly identified as Charlemagne, who was not born until about 742). From Orleans, the latter sent for Giles, but although he took his spiritual advice, he was too ashamed to confess a particularly serious sin that he had on his conscience. The situation was resolved on the following Sunday while Giles was celebrating Mass. As he prayed for the king during the Canon, "an angel of the Lord . . . laid upon the altar a scroll on which was written the sin the king had committed." He understood that, at his intercession, the king would be forgiven provided he did penance and did not sin in the same way in the future. When Mass was over he showed the scroll to the king who immediately acknowledged his sin and did penance.

Toward the end of his life, it is said, Giles travelled to Rome, where he commended his monastery to the pope. The pope in return gave it his protection and granted certain privileges. He also gave Giles two carved doors made of cedar wood, which Giles threw into the Tiber. His motive for doing this is not made entirely clear, but the doors were transported down the river to the sea and were waiting on a beach near the monastery when Giles arrived back in France. Having been warned beforehand in a dream, Giles died on 1 September.

Besides being inconsistent and anachronistic, the legendary account clearly relates to a number of papal Bulls that favour the monastery at Saint-Gilles and are known to have been forgeries. There is no denying, however, that St Giles was extraordinarily popular. He was, for example, the only non-martyr to be included among the Fourteen Holy Helpers (8 Aug.), a group of saints (the names tended to vary from place to place) whose collective cult spread from the Rhineland in the fourteenth century. Once his shrine at the monastery became an important centre of pilgrimage, he was soon being invoked as the patron of beggars, lepers, the physically handicapped, nursing mothers, shepherds, blacksmiths, and horses. There is strong evidence to show that, thanks in part to the Crusaders, his cult spread from Provence (*provincia sancti Aegidii*) to other parts of Europe. At least fifteen places in France take their name from him, as does one of the quarters of Brussels. In Britain, where no less than 162 churches were dedicated to him in England alone, the most notable dedications are St Giles' Cathedral in Edinburgh, St Giles, Cripplegate, in London, and St Giles, Oxford. In Oxford, one of two St Giles' Day fairs still survives, though not in its traditional form; the other, now discontinued, was in Winchester. At least twenty-four hospitals were named after him.

Despite the popularity of the cult, the monastery never really recovered from the damage done to it during the campaign against the Albigensians in the thirteenth century, and by the end of the Middle Ages it had been reduced to poverty. It has to be said that this was partly the fault of the monks, who became too reliant on offerings at the shrine. The relics of the saint did not suffer, because the canons of Saint-Sernin in Toulouse obtained most of them in the thirteenth century and the rest went to other places in France, Belgium, and Germany.

For the text of the Latin Life see *AA.SS.*, Sept., 1, pp. 284-304, and *Propylaeum*, p. 373. See also G. Iaris (ed.), *La Vie de Saint Gilles par Guillaume de Berneville* (1881); *H.S.S.C.*, 4, p. 276; *O.D.S.*, pp. 205-6; *Bibl.SS.*, 4, 958-60.

Representations in art are widespread. He is shown variously as an abbot with a staff, as on screens at Hempstead and Smallburgh in Norfolk; with his hind, as on a misericord in Ely Cathedral or in a painting by the Master of St Giles (National Gallery, London); or receiving the angel's scroll during Mass, as in a second painting by the Master of St Giles, also in the National Gallery. The sarcophagus of the emperor Charlemagne at Aix-la-Chapelle is decorated with scenes from the legend. And there are cycles of his life in stained glass in the cathedrals of Chartres and Amiens, and in fresco in the crypt of the church at Saint-Aignan-sur-Cher.

Bd Joan Soderini (1301-67)

The extant information about Joan is unreliable, partly because it is not contemporary and partly because it may have been doctored to meet comparisons with St Juliana Falconieri (19 June). The second edition of the *Annales* of the Servite Order, published in 1719, refers to what it describes as an untrustworthy piece of hagiography called *Giornale e Ricordi*. How widely known this was we do not know, but it probably reflects the sixteenth-century tradition about Joan. The various elements of this were brought together in Michele Poccianti's

Chronicon (1567), which was used as a principal source by anyone who wrote about Joan from then on.

The story that emerges is that Joan (Giovanna) was born into the noble Soderini family in Florence in 1301 and was related in some way to Juliana. The description of her as a well-behaved and pious only child is stereotypical, and the reports of her early revelations may well have been retrospective. When her parents, following the custom of the time, arranged a marriage for her, Joan announced that she wanted to become a nun. Despite their reluctance, her parents eventually gave their consent, and she joined the *mantellate*, the Servite Third Order, which had been recently established in Florence by Juliana Falconieri. Joan soon became known for her great austerity and spirit of prayer, her equable and cheerful manner, and the wholeheartedness with which she took part in the work of the house, notably the care of the sick. One of her patients was Juliana Falconieri herself, whom she nursed devotedly through her long and painful last illness. When Juliana died in 1341, Joan succeeded her as prioress and, despite severe trials and temptations, served the community in the spirit of her much-loved mentor until she herself died, according to Poccianti on 1 September 1367. She was buried in the church of the Annunziata in Florence, and her tomb immediately became a place of pilgrimage.

How far the details and even the dates are to be relied on is unclear. The canonization of Juliana in 1737 prompted a member of the Soderini family to seek approval for Joan's cult. Despite the weakness of the documentation, it was approved by Pope Leo XII (1823-9) in 1828.

See *AA.SS.*, Oct., 12, pp. 398-404; A. Giani, *Annales Ordinis Servorum* (1719), 1, pp. 320-1; *Monumenta O.S.M.*, 11 (1910), pp.43-4 (contains text of *Giornale e Ricordi*); L. Raffaelli, *La beata Giovanna Soderini* (1927); *Bibl.SS.*, 11, 1270.

ST SIMEON STYLITES THE ELDER (p. 2, above)
Silver pillar, gold scourges, on black field

2

St Antoninus, *Martyr* (Fourth Century)

There are numerous martyrs named Antoninus, but there seems to be no doubt about the authenticity of the cult of this one. In the past he has been confused with at least two of the others, including "Antoninus, a boy" mentioned in the Roman Martyrology with the martyr-bishop of Alexandria, St Aristaeus. However, he is almost without doubt the Antoninus who, according to the same martyrology, died at Pamiers and whose feast is kept in the East on 9 November. He is also a patron of Palencia in Spain, which received some of his relics.

According to the Eastern legend, he was a Syrian stonemason who zealously rebuked his fellow-citizens for worshipping stone images. Having spoken his mind, he then went off to live under the guidance of a local hermit named Theotimus. Two years later, against the hermit's advice, he returned to the town. When he discovered that the people were still worshipping their idols he went straight to the temple and tore down the image of the god. The angry people drove him out of the town, and he took refuge in Apamaea. Thinking to do him a favour, the local bishop asked him to build a church. This so angered the non-Christians in the local population that they gathered in protest and killed Antoninus, who is thought to have been about twenty at the time.

According to the Armenian synaxary, the bishop had a church built over Antoninus' burial place in Apamaea. Although this was destroyed during the seventh century, leaving no trace, it is mentioned in the Acts of a Syrian synod which took place in 518. As for the movement of his relics, the existence of legendary accounts to explain it suggests that this began to take place at a fairly early stage. For example, at Saint-Antonin-de-Rouergue (Tarn-et-Garonne) in the eleventh century there was a monastery that claimed to have his head and part of his body. They reached the monastery, it was said, via the rivers Ariège, Garonne, Tarn, and Aveyron in a boat miraculously navigated by an angel.

See *Bibl.SS.*, 2, 79-81; *AA.SS.*, Sept., 1, pp. 340-56; *C.M.H.*, pp. 484-6; H. Delehaye, "Saints et reliquaires de l'Apamée," in *Anal.Boll.* 53 (1934), p. 225. See also C. Daux, "La Barque légendaire de Saint Antonin, apôtre et martyr de Pamiers," in *Revue des questions historiques* 67 (1900), pp. 402-56.

St Nonnosus (? Sixth Century)

So little information has survived about Nonnosus that he is not especially interesting in himself. What is interesting is the light thrown by what information there is on the method of St Gregory the Great (3 Sept.), who is its sole source, and also on the history of the cult. In 593 Gregory was asked by some of his friends to create a compendium of the miracle stories associated with Italian saints. One of the people he approached for help was Maximian, bishop of Syracuse, whom he asked in particular for information on "the abbot Nonnosus" (*"de domno Nonnoso qui iuxta domnum Anastasium de Pentumis fuit"*). Maximian passed on to Gregory, who on his own admission had already been told but had forgotten (*"oblivione mandavi"*), the details. These had been acquired from an old monk who, like Nonnosus, had lived at the monastery of Suppentonia near Civitacastellana under the abbot Anastasius and was a friend of his.

Gregory, who describes Nonnosus as a humble and particularly good-natured person, says that he was for a time prior of the monastery at Mount Soracte during the régime of an extremely strict and austere abbot. Three miracles were attributed to him while he was there. The first, similar to one attributed to St Gregory the Enlightener (30 Sept.), involved the removal of a rock so large that even fifty pairs of oxen could not shift it from some land on which he wanted to cultivate a garden. Second, through his prayers he reunited the shattered fragments of a glass lamp he had dropped, which spared him the admonitions of the severe abbot. A similar miracle is attributed to St Donatus, a martyr-bishop of Arezzo. The inspiration for the third miracle seems to have been the prophet Elisha. One year, the olive crop of the monastery failed. The abbot told the monks to go out and work for the peasants round about in return for oil. Fearful that this would disturb the recollection of the monks, Nonnosus asked the abbot to counter his order and tell the monks instead to gather in their meagre harvest. A little of the oil pressed was put into each of the available receptacles. Nonnosus spent the night in prayer, and in the morning they were all full.

Gregory does not say when Nonnosus died, but he was buried at Mount Soracte. When the area was laid waste by the Saracens at the end of the ninth century, his remains were taken to Suppentonia, and from there, in the middle of the eleventh, to Freising. They came to light in 1161, in the course of some renovations, and were reburied in the cathedral crypt. Much later, in 1708, by which time no one could remember where they were, they came to light again. This time they were placed in a fine sarcophagus in the cathedral crypt as part of a week-long festival in honour of the saint. At some unknown date the head was taken to Bamberg, where it is still the object of devotion. St Nonnosus is venerated by sufferers from diseases of the kidneys, who for centuries have carried out the so-called *reptatio per cryptam* or *Durchschlüpfsbrauch*. This strange little ritual involves crawling three times round the sarcophagus on all fours while praying for the saint's help.

St Nonnosus' name does not appear in any of the ancient martyrologies. He is first mentioned in a twelfth-century Austrian collection of legends. The cult, which seems to have been strong in Bavaria, was renewed on Mount Soracte between 1655 and 1658, thanks to the efforts of a Cistercian named Andrea di San Bonaventura. In 1661 some of the relics were returned to Mount Soracte.

AA.SS., Sept., 1, pp. 409-39; *Bibl.SS.*, 9, 1047-50; *Anal.Boll.* 82 (1963), pp. 256-7; Gregory the Great, *Epistolae*, 3, 50; *idem, Dialogues*, 1, 7. The *Durchschlüpfsbrauch* is described in *Anal.Boll.* 56 (1937), p. 453.

St Agricolus of Avignon, *Bishop* (*c.* 630-*c.* 700)

Although he lived and died in the seventh century, the earliest written information about St Agricolus dates from the sixteenth, which is when a cult began to grow up. According to these late sources (which, coming so long after the event, are not reliable) he was born in about 630. His father, Magnus, was, according to the same sources, a Gallo-Roman senator who, after the death of his wife, became a monk at Lérins and later bishop of Avignon. When he was fourteen Agricolus followed his father to Lérins, where he quickly made progress intellectually and spiritually and was ordained to the priesthood. Then, after sixteen years spent as a monk at Lérins, he went at his father's request to Avignon as archdeacon. He soon became known for the quality of his preaching, his administrative ability, and not least, his practical concern for the poor and the sick. In 660 Magnus made him his coadjutor, and ten years later, when Magnus died, he succeeded to the see. As the number of worshippers had significantly increased, one of the things he did as bishop was to build at his own expense a new church within the city walls and call in monks from Lérins to run it. He died on 2 September, probably in 700, and was buried in the cathedral. Locally, people pray to him for fine weather and also in times of drought, when the reliquary containing his head is carried in procession.

See: *AA.SS.*, Sept., 1, pp. 450-5; *Bibl.SS.*, 1, 612-3; S. L. Duprat, *Les origines de l'église d'Avignon* (1909), pp. 73ff. Bibliography in *D.H.G.E.*, 1, 1019.

Two pictures of St Agricolus survive, both showing him as a bishop. One, dating from 1360, is the right-hand section of a triptych in the Musée Turpin de Crissé in Angers; the other, now in the Louvre, is a late-fifteenth-century altar frontal from the priory of Boulbon, near Tarascon.

St Wulfsindis (Seventh Century)

All that is known for certain about Wulfsindis is that she lived sometime during the sixth and seventh centuries and that she was one of the earliest popular saints of Bavaria. It is true that at least nine sources testify to her existence. These include the necrology of the monastery of Wessobrunn (*c.* 939), an addition to a Wessobrunn manuscript of the martyrology of Notker, and later, a document which states that sometime before 772 Duke Taxilon of

Bavaria gave to the monastery of Wessobrunn some land at Reisbach "where St Wulfsindis is buried." But the cult and all evidence of it died out, until it was revived in the middle of the eighteenth century by the historian of Wessobrunn, Celestin Leuthner.

Leuthner himself was forced to admit that there were no longer any traces of a cult at Reisbach; and no one knew where Wulfsindis was buried. Yet, pleased no doubt to have a local saint, people grasped at the slim results of Leuthner's research and the cult burgeoned. Reisbach became a place of pilgrimage, and an entire legend was woven round the simple fact of Wulfsindis' existence. She was, it was said, the daughter of a pagan nobleman, who killed her because of her Christian faith. Or she was tied to a horse by an army officer whose proposal of marriage she had spurned and dragged to her death. In the place where, according to tradition, she died there is a fountain which is said to have healing properties, especially for diseases of the eye. Until 1816 a column marked the exact spot, but in that year a chapel was built in her honour. The fact that no remains were ever found, despite repeated searches, until as late as 1893, produced the legend that they disappeared during the Thirty Years War. The cult has persisted in Reisbach, where Wolfsinde is a popular name, and on the Sunday before her feast there is a solemn procession in her honour.

C. Leuthner, *Historia Monasterii Wessofontani* (1753); C. Schreiber, *Wallfahrten durchs deutsche Land* (1928); A. Rosenthal-Dürr, *Die heilige Wolfsindis, eine volkstümliche Heilige in Niederbayern in Legende und Kult* (1951); R. Baurreiss, *Kirchengeschichte Bayerns* (1958).

St William of Roskilde, *Bishop* (*c.* 1070)

There is no separate Life of William of Roskilde, and the sources that mention him are not very satisfactory. Historians of Denmark maintain that he was an English priest who served as chaplain to King Cnut when the latter ruled in England (1016-35). In this capacity he would accompany the king to Denmark, and it was during such a journey that he realized just how widespread ignorance and superstition were in much of the country. Christianity had been introduced there during the ninth century, but there were still large areas where it had not taken hold. He remained behind to preach the gospel and was eventually promoted to the see of Roskilde on the island of Sjælland. Roskilde at that time was the seat of the Danish kings, which it remained until 1216. It was a bishopric from 1060 and the capital of Denmark until 1443.

Most of the details that have survived about William's life relate to his dealings with the Danish king Svend II Estridsen (1047-74), whose conduct in the early years of their acquaintance he was always trying to reform. On one occasion the king had some supposed criminals put to death without trial, and in a church, which violated the law of sanctuary. William is supposed to have barred the king's way as he attempted to enter the church next day, telling him he could come in only when his sin in shedding blood unjustly had been absolved. When several courtiers drew their swords to threaten William he uncovered his neck, saying he was ready to die in defence of the church of God. But Svend confessed to his crime and later gave the church at Roskilde some land as a peace-offering. After this the two men enjoyed a firm friendship and worked together to promote religion in the area.

When Svend died in 1074 he was buried in the abbey he had founded at Ringsted until a tomb could be prepared for him in the cathedral at Roskilde, the burial place of the Danish kings. A tomb was prepared at the same time for William, who is said to have died as the king's body was being transferred from Ringsted to Roskilde. King and bishop were buried together at Roskilde. St William appears in Danish calendars on this day, although there is no other trace of a liturgical feast in his honour.

Saxo Grammaticus, *Gesta Danorum* (*c.* 1200); *Bibl.SS.*, 7, 482.

St Brocard (*c.* 1230)

The first superior of the Frankish hermits on Mount Carmel—and in the eyes of many the founder of the Carmelite Order—was St Berthold (29 Mar.), who was introduced into Carmelite literature in about 1400. When he died, he was succeeded by a Frenchman named Brocard, or Burchard, who decided that his first task should be to establish a fixed rule of life for the hermits. To this end, in 1205 he approached the Latin patriarch of Jerusalem, St Albert (14 Sept.), who over the next five years produced a short written Rule, which Brocard imposed on his community. It obliged them to live alone in separate cells, to recite the divine office and meet for Mass daily, to practise poverty, chastity, and obedience, to observe long periods of silence, and to work with their hands.

The hermits, who had begun to spread throughout Palestine, ran into trouble after the Fourth Lateran Council (1215)—to which, ironically, Albert of Jerusalem would have taken Brocard as an expert on Islam and Eastern affairs in general had he himself not been murdered before the council assembled. The council issued a decree against the formation of new religious Orders, and the hermits were attacked on the ground that by obtaining approval for their Rule from the legate rather than from the Holy See, they had contravened this canon. According to Carmelite tradition, Pope Honorius III (1216-27) was about to suppress the Order when he had a vision in which Our Lady warned him not to. He finally approved the Rule on 30 January 1226. Brocard guided the community with patience and prudence throughout this difficult period and remained prior until he died in about 1230. Few details of his life have been recorded, but he is said miraculously to have restored a Muslim emir to health and converted him to the Christian faith. In art he is represented in a Carmelite habit, as for example on the confessional in the Augustinian church in Ghent.

See B. Zimmerman, *Monumenta historica Carmelitana*, pp. 276-9; *AA.SS.*, Sept., 1, pp. 567-82; Lezana, *Annales*, 4, p. 244; *Speculum Carmelitanum*, 2, p. 661; *Bibl.SS.*, 3, 345.

The Martyrs of September (1792)

The martyrs of the French Revolution are commemorated collectively on 2 January. Today's feast commemorates a very specific group, all of whom died in four prisons in Paris on 2 and 3 September 1792. The Church names and venerates 191 individuals, the overwhelming majority of whom were members of the clergy. But their deaths need to be seen in the wider context of a series of unbridled atrocities which claimed the lives of many times that number, including others unnamed who died for their faith and more than forty young people under the age of eighteen. Because the massacre took place outside the law official archives were almost non-existent, and such as there were did not survive the fire at the Hôtel de Ville in Paris in 1871. The most important sources of information were eyewitnesses, in particular those few priests who managed to escape.

With its promulgation of the Civil Constitution of the Clergy on 12 July 1790 the Constituent Assembly effectively alienated any support the Church might have given to the Revolution. Declaring the French clergy to be public servants, independent of the Holy See, it required each one to take an oath of allegiance to the Constitution. Initially any cleric who refused to swear was to be deprived of all he possessed, but later on, in 1792, the penalty became death by execution. Some, including four bishops and a number of priests, mostly from non-urban areas, seeing in it no threat to faith and morals, took the oath; they were described as *assermentés*. The majority, interpreting it as a political move against the Roman Church and an attempt to create a national, schismatic Church in its place, refused; they were the *réfractaires* or *insermentés*. This left the Church weakened because divided, although the hierarchy immediately condemned the decree as unlawful. This condemnation was confirmed, but not until ten months later, on 10 March 1791, by Pope Pius VI (1775-99), who described the decree as "heretical, contrary to Catholic teaching, sacrilegious, and opposed to the rights of the Church."

Throughout 1791 pressure was put on the *réfractaires* to take the oath. Some went abroad, and of those who left their parishes not a few came to Paris, where they lived anonymously among the Lazarists, the Sulpicians, and others. The anti-religious attitude of the Legislative Assembly hardened, and on 29 November it decreed that any priest who did not take the oath within eight days would be assumed to have *mauvaises intentions vers la Patrie*—in other words, to be a traitor. By April 1792 that assumption was being made about every priest, regardless of his views. France had declared war on a coalition headed by the Austrian emperor, Joseph II (1780-90), and Frederick Wilhelm II (1786-97), king of Prussia, and the pope had been persuaded by *emigrés* priests in Rome to declare in favour of the coalition.

Classified now as enemies of the Revolution, clerics figured prominently alongside the members of the aristocracy and others who were arrested in large

14

numbers during the last two weeks of August 1792. On the 23rd the fortress at Longwy surrendered to the coalition armies, and on the 30th Verdun was under threat. This, combined with the peasant uprising in the Vendée against the Revolution, further unsettled an already volatile situation. The mood in Paris, where the monarchy had been abolished earlier in the month, was a mixture of panic, terror, and triumphalism. There was martial euphoria when the Provisional Executive Council called for thirty thousand volunteers. But at the same time people became convinced that, once the troops left, Paris would be defenceless against a mass breakout from the prisons. Nothing can justify what happened next, but some of the blame surely lies with the inflammatory language and *laissez-faire* attitude of the leaders of the Revolution. On Sunday, 2 September, Marat claimed rhetorically in *L'Ami du Peuple*: "Citizens, the enemy is at the gates! . . . Not a single enemy must remain in Paris to enjoy our defeat!"

That same afternoon, twenty-four priests who had been marked for deportation were mobbed by a hostile crowd as they went under armed escort from the *mairie* to the Abbaye prison. At this point the situation was contained, but when they reached the prison a larger crowd called for "judgment." This was administered in summary fashion by the notorious Stanislas Maillard, who had made a name for himself at an earlier stage of the Revolution and now led a thuggish company of para-militaries. When the priests refused to take the oath of allegiance to the Constitution they were handed over to the crowd, which literally hacked the majority to death. Five survived to give an eyewitness account of what had happened, including the Abbé Roch, Ambroise Sicard, whose imprisonment showed how arbitrary the arrests had become: he had come from Bordeaux to Paris in 1789, and as the founder and director of a school for deaf-mute children he was immensely popular with the working people of the city. Among the nineteen who died was the king's confessor, Alexandre Lenfant, a former Jesuit (the Society was suppressed between 1759 and 1814) who had befriended and helped the royal family.

Later that day similar carnage took place at the Carmelite church in the rue de Rennes, where 150 bishops and priests and one layman were being held ("there's nothing more to do here," Maillard is reported to have said after the massacre at the Abbaye, "so let's go to the Carmelites"). Several bishops and some of the priests were saying Vespers in a chapel when the organized gang of thugs broke into the garden and murdered the first priest they met. The archbishop of Arles, Jean-Marie du Lau, came out of the chapel, followed by Bishop François Joseph de la Rochefoucauld of Beauvais and his brother, Bishop Pierre Louis de la Rochefoucauld of Saintes, to find out what the disturbance was. The archbishop of Arles was summarily executed as soon as he admitted his identity, and in the bout of shooting that followed the bishop of Beauvais' leg was shattered. At this point even the perpetrators of the crime seem to have been shocked by its random quality, and a "judge" was appointed to pass sentence. As he sat in a passage between the church and the sacristy the prisoners, including some who had tried desperately to escape, were brought before him in pairs. Not one was prepared to take the oath, and each was hacked to death as he moved on down the stairs. When the bishop of Beauvais' name was called, he replied: "I do not refuse to die with the others but I cannot walk. Please be kind enough to carry me where you wish me to go." This silenced his accusers, but it did not save him. At a very late stage in the proceedings there were some acquittals, and a few people managed to escape, but by the end of the day ninety-five people had died. These included the one layman, Charles de la Calmette, Comte de Valfons, and his confessor, Jean Guilleminet; the superior general of the Maurist Benedictines, Ambroise Augustin Chevreux, and two other monks; François Louis Hébert, confessor to Louis XVI; Jacques Friteyre-Durvé and fourteen other former Jesuits; and Jacques Galais, who, as the one responsible for the feeding arrangements in the prison, handed the "judge" 325 francs he owed the caterer. Also among the victims were three Franciscans, one Christian brother, thirty-eight members of the seminary of Saint-Sulpice, six diocesan vicars-general, three deacons, and an acolyte. The massacre continued during the night, with no attempt on the part of the authorities to put a stop to it. At the prison of La Force, where many aristocrats and a few clerics were being held, no one survived to give an account of what happened.

The Lazarist seminary of Saint-Firmin was also being used as a prison, and it was here, at about 5:30 in the morning of the following day, 3 September, that the marauders went next. Their first victim was a former Jesuit, Pierre Guérin. When he refused to take the oath he was thrown from the nearest window and stabbed in the courtyard below. His brother Robert also died, as did five other former Jesuits. The superior of the seminary, Louis Joseph François, widely loved in Paris, was offered the chance to escape, but he refused to desert his fellow-prisoners. He died, as did Ivo Guillon de Keranrun, vice-chancellor of the university of Paris, and three laymen.

All in all, about fourteen hundred people—half the prisoners in Paris—died during the September massacres. The decree of beatification for 191 described as the Martyrs of September was promulgated on 1 October 1926. L'Abbaye and La Force no longer exist. Saint-Firmin has been converted into an office building, while the old Carmelite convent is now occupied by the Institut Catholique.

The following died at the Abbaye: Daniel André des Pommerayes; Louis Benoist; Antoine du Bonzet; Jean Capeu; Armand Chapt de Rastignac; Claude Fontaine; Pierre Gervais; Santino Huré; Charles Hurtel; Louis Hurtel; Alexandre Lenfant; (?) Laurent; Louis le Danois; Thomas Monsaint; François Pey; Jean Rateau; Marc Royer; Jean Guyard de St-Clair; Jean Simon; Pierre Vitalis.

The following died at the Carmelite church: Vincent Abraham; André Angar; Jean Aubert; François Balmain; Jean Bangue; Louis Barreau de la Touche;

Louis Barret; Joseph Bécavin; Charles Béraud du Péron; Jacques Bonnand; Louis Boubert; Jean Boucharène du Chaumeils; Jean Bosquet; Jean Burté; Claude Dumas (Cayx); Jean Charton de Millon; Claude Chaudet; Ambroise Chevreux; Nicholas Clairet; Claude Colin; Bernard de Cucsac; François Dardan; Guillaume Delfaut; Mathurin Deruelle; Gabriel Desprez de Roche; Thomas Dubray; Thomas Dubuisson; François Dumasrambaud de Calendelle; Henri Ermès; Armand de Foucaul de Pontbriant; Jacques Friteyre-Durvé; Claude Gagnières des Granges; Jacques Galais; Pierre Gauguin; Louis Gaultier; Georges Girauld; Jean Goizez; André Grasset de Saint-Sauveur; Pierre Guérin; Jean Guilleminet; François Hébert; Jacques Hourrier; Jean-Baptiste Jannin; Jean Lacan; Pierre Landry; Claude Laporte; Pierre de la Rochefoucauld-Bayers; François de la Rochefoucauld-Maumont; Jean du Lau; Mathurin La Villecrohain; Robert le Bis; Guillaume Leclercq; Olivier Lefèvre; Urbain Lefèvre; François Lefranc; Charles Le Gué; Jacques Lejardinier Deslandes; Jacques Lemeunier; Vincent le Rousseau de Rosencoat; François Londiveau; Louis Longuet; Jacques de Lubersac; Henri Luzeau de la Moulonnière; Gaspard Maignien; Jean Marchand; René Massey; Louis Mauduit; François Méallet de Fargues; Jacques Menuret; Jean Morel; Jean Nativelle; René Nativelle; Auguste Nézel; Antoine Nogier; Joseph Pazery de Thorame; Julien Pazery de Thorame; Pierre Pazery de Thorame; Pierre Ploquin; Jean Pontus; René Poret; Julien Pouain-Delaunay; Pierre Psalmon; Jean Quéneau; Etienne de Ravinel; Augustin Robert de Lézardière; Claude Rousseau; François Salins de Niant; Jean Samson; Jean Savine; Jean Séguin; Jean Tessier; Loup Thomas (Bonnotte); François Vareilhe-Duteil; Pierre Vervier; Charles de la Calmette.

The following died at La Force: Jean Bottex; Michel de Lugardette; Hyacinthe Le Livec de Trésurin.

The following died at Saint-Firmin: André Alricy; René Andrieux; Pierre Balzac; Jean Benoit (Vourlat); Jean Bernard de Cornillet; Michel Binard; Nicholas Bize; Claude Bochaot; Jean Bonnel de Pradal; Pierre Bonzé; Pierre Briquet; Pierre Brisse; Charles Carnus; Jean Caron; Bertrand de Caupenne; Nicholas Colin; Sébastien Desbrielles; Jacques Dufour; Dionysius Duval; Jean Duval; Joseph Falcoz; Gilbert Fautrel; Eustache Félix; Filibert Fougères; Louis François; Pierre Garrigues; Nicholas Gaudreau; Etienne Gillet; Georges Giroust; Joseph Gros; Jean Gruyer; Pierre Guérin du Rocher; Robert Guérin du Rocher; Ivo Guillon de Keranrun; Julien Hédouin; Pierre Hénocq; Eligius Herque (du Roule); Pierre Joret; Gilles Lanchon; Jacques de la Lande; Louis Lanier; Jean de Lavèze-Bellay; Michel Leber; Pierre Le Clercq; Jean Legrand; Jean Le Laisant; Jean Le Maître; Jean Leroy; Martin Loublier; Claude Marmotamt de Savigny; Claude Mayneaud de Bizefranc; Henri Milet; François Monnier; François Mouffle; Joseph Oviefre; Jean Philippot; Claude Pons; Pierre Pottier; Jacques Rabé; Pierre Regnet; Ivo Rey de Kervisic; Louis Rigot; Nicholas Roussel; Pierre Saint-James; Jacques Schmid; Jean Seconds; Pierre de Turmenyes; René Urvoy; Charles Véret; Nicholas Verron; Jan de Villette.

17

For the beatification brief see *A.A.S.* 18 (1926), pp. 415-25. On the massacres in the context of the Revolution in general see Simon Schama, *Citizens* (1989); A. Latreille, *L'Eglise catholique et la révolution française* (1946-50); H. Daniel-Rops, *L'Eglise des révolutions* (vol. 6 of *Histoire de l'Eglise du Christ*, 1960); C. S. Phillips, *The Church in France 1789-1848* (1929); J. Le Goff and R. Remond (eds.), *Histoire de la France religieuse*, 3 (1991)—see especially bibliography, p. 537. On the September Massacres in particular see Lenotre, *Les massacres de Septembre* (1907); P. Caron, *Les massacres de Septembre* (1935); H. Leclercq, *Les Martyrs*, 11. There are also books devoted to individual martyrs.

ST GREGORY THE GREAT
The IHS (for the Host) and lions "guardianship" are taken to refer to
"St Gregory's Mass," while the three "bends" (diagonal stripes)
refer to his establishement of a monastery, the primacy of his office,
and his reform of church music. All in red on gold field.

3

ST GREGORY THE GREAT, *Pope and Doctor* (*c.* 540-604)

The second of only three holders of the office to be called "the Great"—the others were Leo I (440-61; 10 Nov.) and Nicholas I (858-67; 13 Nov.)—Gregory I was one of the most influential popes and one of the most significant writers of the Middle Ages. His father, Gordianus, was a Roman senator, and his wealthy patrician family, possibly related to the *gens* Anicia, had already given the Church two popes, St Felix II (483-92; 1 Mar.) and St Agapitus I (535-6; 22 Apr.). Gregory's education, which probably included a thorough grounding in the law as well as in Latin and Greek, would have been the best that was available at the time. When he had completed his studies, in about 573, he entered the service of the State, acquiring some administrative experience during a two-year stint as *praefectus urbis*, or administrator, of the city of Rome. At the same time he gained knowledge and understanding of human problems and an insight into Church-State relations. After his father died in 573, he turned the vast family properties he had inherited in Italy and Sicily over to the Church. Having given generously to the poor, he founded six monasteries, mainly in Sicily, and a seventh in the family mansion on the Coelian Hill in Rome. The latter he dedicated to St Andrew, and in 574 he joined it himself as a monk.

This was to be the happiest period of his life and one to which he would look back with nostalgia in later years. The only negative aspect was the chronic ill health he suffered from then on as a result of his austerities. But the peace was not to last. In 578 Pope Benedict I (575-9) called him away from the monastery to appoint him as one of the seven deacons of Rome. Then, in December 579, when the city was under siege from the Lombards, he was sent by Benedict's successor Pelagius II (579-90) as *apocrisiarius* (nuncio) to the court of the emperor Tiberius II (578-82) in Constantinople in the hope that Tiberius might provide military and material support.

Whatever his personal feelings in the matter, he acquitted himself with distinction. Although in his official residence he continued to live as a monk with a small community of monks from St Andrew's who had accompanied him, his life was anything but enclosed. Through discussions with the patriarch he became an expert on the Eastern Church, and taking his diplomatic duties seriously, he familiarized himself with the court and cultivated the acquaintance of influential individuals. He even became the godfather of the eldest son of the emperor Maurice (581-602). He also found time to form friendships that would last throughout his life, notably with St Leander (27 Feb.), brother of St Isidore of Seville (6 Oct.), who at the time was the representative in Constantinople of Spain's Visigothic monarch. Yet he remained suspicious of all things Eastern—except, it seems, the retsina, supplies of which were shipped to him after his return to Rome—and could not understand Westerners who adopted Eastern ways when they were there. His two areas of failure seem to have been his relationship with the patriarch, Eutychius, with whom he eventually became involved in a doctrinal dispute, and his attempt to obtain the support, military and material, for which he had gone in the first place.

When he was recalled to Rome in 585 or 586 he became abbot of his monastery, where he took up residence once again. However, his principal role seems to have been as a personal adviser to Pelagius II (579-90), to whom he gave invaluable support when he was trying to end the schism with Venetia-Istria occasioned by the affair of the so-called Three Chapters. This was an edict, published in 543, in which the emperor Justinian (527-65) took it upon himself to condemn the writings of Theodore of Mopsuestia and others on the two natures in Christ. The pope of the time, Vigilius (537-55), had cravenly signed the edict, but, initially at least, his successor, Pelagius I (556-61), had opposed it. Then, before he was elected pope, Pelagius suddenly accepted the condemnation both of the Three Chapters and of the Council of Chalcedon. This *volte-face* caused so much anger in the sees of northern Italy that they withdrew from communion with him. His two immediate successors, John III (561-74) and Benedict I (574-9), had other things on their minds, so the situation remained more or less unchanged when Pelagius II became pope in November 579. Pelagius, advised by Gregory, began to correspond on the subject with the bishop of Aquileia, and Gregory himself wrote the third of the pope's letters. But even this document, which was as conciliatory in tone as it was well argued theologically, failed to convince the northern Italians.

Toward the end of 589 the Tiber burst its banks, destroying the grain store, and as a direct consequence of this the city was ravaged by the plague. In the February of the following year Pelagius fell victim to the plague and died. The cardinals managed to meet to elect a successor and were unanimous in their choice of Gregory. Gregory, whose ambition it was to remain as far as possible a simple monk, was genuinely horrified and even went so far as to write to the emperor Maurice asking him to withhold his approval. Meanwhile he turned his attention to the urgent needs of the plague-ridden city. In addition to practical help he organized a triduum of processions during which people recited litanies and prayed to be delivered from the plague. In the end he was compelled to submit to the clerical and popular choice and was consecrated on 3 September 590.

It is clear from his letters, particularly his early letters, as pope, how loth he was to leave his monastery completely. He admitted to Leander of Seville:

In the position I now occupy I am so battered by the waves of life that I despair of bringing safely to port the weather-beaten old bark of which God, in his hidden wisdom, has given me charge. Sometimes the waves come at us from the front, sometimes their foaming mass swells up beside us, and sometimes the tempest pursues us from behind. . . . Weeping I remember that I have lost the peaceful shore of my retreat, with a sigh I look at the land onto which I am prevented from stepping by the violence of the winds.

But it is also clear from his achievements that, far from allowing his feelings to stand in his way, he ruled from the start with confidence, decisiveness, and authority. One of his first acts was to provide food for the people of Rome, who were by then suffering the effects not only of the plague but of famine. This required skillful organization and large funds. In order to find the latter, he reorganized estates owned by the Holy See—known collectively as the "patrimony of Peter"—in North Africa, Dalmatia, southern Gaul and Sicily, as well as in Italy. To each he appointed a manager whom he expected to carry out his task efficiently and humanely and to report back to him personally.

In addition to the famine and the plague there was the threat to Rome of the Lombard presence to the north. Because the exarch of Ravenna, the emperor's representative in Italy, refused to intervene, Gregory decided to deal with the situation himself, and in 592 concluded a peace treaty with Ariulf, duke of Spoleto. When the exarch broke this treaty in the following year and the Lombard king, Agilulf (590-616), marched on Rome, Gregory rallied some sort of defence and managed to save the city by agreeing to pay Agilulf an annual tribute. In default of any other effective government he undertook many of the tasks of a civil leader, negotiating treaties, appointing generals, and so on. His goal was twofold: peace and the conversion to orthodox Christianity of the Arian Lombards. If neither proved easy to obtain, it was not for want of effort on his part.

In the ecclesiastical sphere Gregory was equally energetic and determined, centralizing the administration and rooting out corruption. Making better use of metropolitans, he improved Rome's overall grasp of what was happening in the Western Church. His relations with individual churches were on the whole good and fruitful. North Africa gave him a certain amount of trouble, partly because of its tradition of independence and partly because of a revival of Donatism. But in Spain he met with cooperation from two sources: from the Visigothic king, Recarred (586-601), who in 589, with his subjects, converted from Arianism to orthodox Christianity; and from his close friend, Leander, who had by then succeeded his brother Isidore as bishop of Seville. In Gaul he re-established the papal vicariate in Arles and maintained a friendly if somewhat unlikely correspondence with Brunhild (613), the fearsome wife of Sigebert, king of Austrasia (561-75). In Italy he imposed rules for the election and conduct of bishops, directed priests to obey the celibacy laws, and deposed those who failed to do so. If he had a flaw it was that he was not a politician and does not appear to have appreciated the deviousness of the political mind. He saw his role as one of service, but it does not seem to have occurred to him that the structures he put in place for service might later be abused by people with less noble ideals.

One of his most notable and memorable initiatives was to send missionaries to convert the Anglo-Saxons. He had the vision to realize that the future lay beyond Rome, and from the start he seems to have masterminded the enterprise. He corresponded about it in advance and even arranged for the liberation of some Anglo-Saxon slaves so that they could be trained as monks (hence the saying which is famously attributed to him, *Non Angli sed angeli*). When the decision had finally been taken to go ahead, he picked a team of forty-one missionaries headed by St Augustine (27 May), prior of the monastery of St Andrew, and they left Rome in 596. Even when they had been in England for a while and had achieved some success, Gregory kept a close eye on what was going on. He would offer advice when Augustine needed it; he responded in 601 to their appeal for reinforcements by sending a group of monks headed by SS Mellitus (24 Apr.) and Paulinus (10 Oct.); and he wrote to the king and queen of Kent to explain what was going on. This close cooperation continued after Gregory's death, giving the English Church a particularly close relationship with the papacy. The first Life of Gregory was written in England. Bede (25 May), St Aldhelm (23 May), and an anonymous monk of Whitby refer to Gregory variously as "the apostle of the English," "our father and apostle in Christ," and "he from whom we have received the Christian faith, he who, as their teacher and apostle, will present the English people to the Lord on the day of judgment."

Gregory's relationship with the East, where the situation left plenty of room for friction, was rather different. He constantly found it necessary to uphold the primacy of Rome, objecting in particular to the patriarch of Constantinople's use of the title "ecumenical patriarch." This, he said, made an unacceptable challenge to the unique position of the pope. He also regarded it as pompous, preferring to style himself *servus servorum Dei*, which has persisted as the descriptive title of the pope. He has been justifiably criticized in this connection for his readiness to support Phocas (602-10), the Thracian centurion who toppled the emperor Maurice (582-602) in 602 and consolidated his position by murdering him and his entire family. Maurice, who took the view that Gregory was quibbling over a mere title, had consistently backed the Eastern bishops against Gregory. This so irritated Gregory that when Phocas, for reasons of his own, conferred the title on him as Western patriarch, he was able to overlook the means by which Phocas came to power.

Gregory's other achievements are many and various. As the first pope who was a monk, he was a fervent admirer of St Benedict of Norcia (11 July) and did all he could to encourage the spread of monasticism. One of his greatest interests was the liturgy, and his contribution to its development was considerable, though scholars disagree as to exactly how considerable. He composed some of the prayers in the so-called Gregorian Sacramentary, but there is no doubt that this did not reach its final form until after his death. He concerned himself particularly with liturgical music, and it seems likely that he played an important part in the codification and adaptation of the plainchant with which his name has always been associated.

He also found time to do a prodigious amount of writing, much of which has survived. His main aim was to present the Faith in a way that could be easily understood. In his *Homilies on the Gospels* and the *Moralia* on the book of Job (written at the request of Leander of Seville), he managed to introduce people unfamiliar with the Graeco-Roman world to the thinking of such important writers as Origen, St Augustine of Hippo (28 Aug.), and St Ambrose (7 Dec.). *Pastoral Care*—which Alfred the Great (871-99) subsequently translated into Old English—helped more than any other book to give the medieval episcopate its characteristic form, while the *Dialogues* (Lives of the saints) encouraged a preoccupation with the miraculous at a time when the place of secondary causes in the Christian world-view was not yet understood. Both enjoyed enormous popularity, and most Anglo-Saxon libraries would have had a copy. But Gregory's letters are probably his most interesting written legacy. There are 854 of them, addressed to people in all works of life on a wide variety of subjects.

One of the strongest influences in Gregory's writing is the *Rule of St Benedict*. In fact, his monastery probably followed the Rule of St Basil, so strictly speaking he was not, as he has traditionally been thought to be, a Benedictine. But there is no denying that he was Benedictine in his spirit and outlook, and he had a stronger influence than almost anyone else on the spirit of medieval monasticism.

Despite a worsening of the gastritis from which he had suffered throughout his life, and of his arthritis, he continued to the end to dictate letters and care for the needs of the Church. He died in 604, when he was about sixty-five, and was buried in St Peter's. The epitaph they gave him was "God's Consul," and very soon afterwards he was proclaimed a saint. From early times his feast was celebrated universally, and in England, where numerous churches, ancient and modern, are dedicated to him, it was given a high rank from the first. He was especially venerated in the East, and also in Ireland, where he was given an Irish royal genealogy, and an apocryphal *Liber de Gradibus Coeli* was attributed to him.

Early Lives: *Liber Pontificalis* (ed. Duchesne), 1, p. 312; Monk of Whitby (ed. B. Colgrave), *The Earliest Life of Gregory the Great* (1968); Bede, *H.E.*, 2, pt. 1; Paul the Deacon (ed. H. Grisar), in *Zeitschrift für katholische Theologie* 11 (1887), pp. 158-73, and in *P.L.*, 75, pp. 59-242. Modern Lives: F. H. Dudden (1905); P. Battifol (1928; Eng. trans., 1929); Abbot Snow (1932); J. Richards, *Consul of God* (1980); Carole Straw, *Gregory the Great* (1988). Works: *P.L.*, 75-8; critical editions of some of the scriptural works in *C.C.*, Series Latina, 144 (1963), 142 (1971), and of the *Registrum Epistolarum* (ed. P. Ewald and L. M.

Hartmann) in *M.G.H., Epistolae*, 1 and 2—see also D. Norberg, *In Registrum Gregorii Magni Studia Critica* (1939). On his spiritual teaching see C. Butler, *Western Mysticism* (1922, 1966); V. Recchia, *L'esegesi di Gregorio Magno al Cantico dei Cantici* (1967). On his monasticism see K. Hallinger, "Papst Gregor der Grosse und der hl. Benedikt," in *Studia Anselmiana* 12 (1957), pp. 231-319; G. Ferrari, *Early Roman Monasteries* (1957). See also E. Spearing, *The Patrimony of the Roman Church in the Time of Gregory the Great* (1918); E. H. Fisher, "Gregor der Grosse und Byzanz," in *Zeitschrift der Savigny-Stiftung für Rechtsgeschichte* 67 (1950), pp. 15-144; N. Sharkey, *Saint Gregory the Great's Concept of Papal Power* (1950); J. Ryan, "The Early Irish Church and the See of Peter" in *Medieval Studies presented to Aubrey Gwynn* (1961); R. A. Markus, *From Augustine to Gregory the Great* (1983); W. D. McCready, *Signs of Sanctity* (1989); R. Godding, *Bibliografia di Gregorio Magno* (1990); E. Duffy, *Saints and Sinners. A History of the Popes* (1997); *O.D.C.C.* (1997), pp. 706-7 (good bibliography).

The iconography is enormous. The earliest pictures of St Gregory can be found in liturgical books of the early Middle Ages, where he is shown as pope, writing at the dictation of the Holy Spirit, who appears in the form of a dove. Later, on Norfolk screens and pulpits, he appears with SS Ambrose, Jerome (30 Sept.), and Augustine of Hippo as one of the Four Latin Doctors of the Church. Later still, he is used to illustrate the efficacy of prayer in freeing souls from purgatory—the emperor Trajan, for example, is shown being released by Gregory's prayers. These themes were developed during the fifteenth century, as in the sculptures by Luigi Capponi in the church of St Gregory in Rome. Then, in the fifteenth and sixteenth centuries the so-called Mass of St Gregory theme became popular. This was not based on any known incident in his life but shows him celebrating Mass while the crucified Christ appears to confirm the ministers' faith in the Real Presence. There is an illumination showing a procession during the plague at the beginning of his reign in *Les Très Riches Heures du Duc de Berry* (Musée Condé, Chantilly).

St Phoebe (First Century)

Apart from those who died as martyrs, New Testament Christians were not normally mentioned in the Martyrology until Ado began to include them in the ninth century. St Phoebe comes into this category. At the end of his letter to the Christians of Rome, St Paul (29 June) sends individual greetings to a number of people whom he mentions by name. But before that he "commends" Phoebe to them all, in a way that suggests that she was probably the bearer of the letter: "I commend to you Phoebe, a deaconess of the church at Cenchrae, that you may receive her in the Lord as befits the saints, and help her in whatever she may require from you, for she has been a helper of many and of myself as well." Cenchrae was the small port city east of Corinth, where Paul wrote the letter in about 57. Nothing more is known about Phoebe, except in an interesting footnote to the story of Paul. Some scholars have concluded, from a remark made by Clement of Alexandria and from a phrase in one of the genuine but interpolated letters of St Ignatius of Antioch (17 Oct.), that the two had been married but that after Paul's conversion Phoebe ministered to him as a "sister."

See Rom. 16:1ff; *AA.SS.*, Sept., 1, pp. 602-5; *Enciclopedia Cattolica*, 9, 1316; H. Quentin, *Les Martyrologes historiques*, p. 665.

St Macanisius, *Bishop* (514)

Macanisius (Aengus, Mac Nisse) is one of the few disciples of St Patrick (17 Mar.) whose Life has come down to us. The problem is that it is a late one, probably written for the diocese of Connor after the Norman invasion, and contains a great deal of material that is fantastical or inconsistent or both. He is said to have been born in Ireland and baptized by St Patrick (17 Mar.), who eventually made him a bishop (though this is not confirmed by the earlier Patrician documents). At some point, presumably after this, he went on pilgrimage to the Holy Land, calling in at Rome on the way back. When eventually he returned to Ireland, he established a church and monastery which developed into the diocese of Connor, of which he is honoured as the founder and first bishop. The original foundation may in fact have been not at Connor itself but at nearby Kells. Here, according to one account, he changed the course of a river for the convenience of his monks (miraculously, according to the legend, though the same story is told of not a few Celtic saints). It is also said that while he was travelling through Munster with Patrick and St Brigit (1 Feb.) Macanisius had a vision of angels at Lynally in Co. Offaly, but he opposed Patrick's suggestion that they establish a monastery there on the ground that another bishop would do so in sixty years' time. This prophecy was fulfilled in the person of St Colmán Elo (26 Sept.). Macanisius is said to have had such respect for the scriptures that he would not put his book of the Gospels in a wallet while he was travelling but insisted on walking on all fours so that he could carry it on his back. Various dates are given for his death, most usually 507, 509, and 514. His name appears in the *Félire* of Oengus, and his feast is celebrated throughout Ireland.

For the Latin legend see *AA.SS.*, Sept., 1, pp. 622-6; J. O'Hanlon, *Lives of the Irish Saints* (1875), 9, p. 62ff. See also *Bibl.SS.*, 8, 454; J. F. Kenney, *Sources of the Early History of Ireland* (1929); W. Stokes (ed.), *The Tripartite Life of St Patrick* (1887)—in which Macanisius is the boy who carries Patrick's books.

St Remaclus, *Bishop* (*c.* 675)

There seems to be no doubt about the existence of St Remaclus, and several legends and places connected with his name still survive in the diocese of Liège. But the ninth-century *Vita prima Remacli*, the principal document on which other Lives, including the tenth-century *Vita secunda*, were based, has been shown to be unreliable. So it is not easy to establish the facts of his career, although *Miracula sancti Remacli*, a collective work by the monks of Stavelot, which was finished in the early eleventh century, provides many anecdotes as well as important insights into ninth- and tenth-century customs. There is also the so-called *Vita tertia*, dating from the fifteenth century, which summarizes the earlier versions.

Remaclus was born, probably in Aquitaine, at the end of the sixth century or the beginning of the seventh. Having spent some time under the direction of St Sulpicius (29 Jan.) in Bourges, he became a priest. He left Bourges when St Eligius (1 Dec.) asked him to become the first abbot of a monastery he had founded at Solignac, near Limoges. This appointment led to his being chosen as abbot of Cugnon in what is now Luxembourg, but he had not been there long when the king of Austrasia, Sigebert III (634-56), called him to court as an adviser.

It was on his advice that Sigebert founded the double abbey of Stavelot-Malmédy in the Ardennes in order to further the evangelization of what was still a pagan district. Initially the monks followed the Rule of St Columbanus (21 Nov.), but Remaclus subsequently moved over to that of St Benedict (11 July). The claim that he was at some stage bishop of Tongres-Maastricht seems to be unfounded, though it is more than likely that he was a missionary monastic bishop. For his monks, for the king's household, and for the ordinary men and women with whom he came in contact, he was an outstanding example of everything he preached. Many people were encouraged to change their way of life as a result of their association with him. He died on 3 September, sometime between 671 and 676, and was buried at Stavelot. His cult developed quickly, and many churches were anxious to acquire relics. This was particularly true in Belgium on account of his association with Stavelot-Malmédy, but it was not long before it spread to Cologne, Caen, and elsewhere.

St Remaclus is a patron of Tongres, Liège, Stavelot, and Malmédy. He is sometimes represented in art with a wolf. This is a reference to a legend that tells how a wolf, which ate the saint's ass, became his faithful companion.

B.H.L., 1, pp.113-41, lists the medieval biographies; for the more important, see *AA.SS.*, Sept., 1, pp. 692-5. On the unreliability of the sources see G. Kurth in *Bulletin de la Commission royale d'histoire de Belgique*, III, 4/3 (1876), pp. 355-68. See also *Bibl.SS.*, 11, 96-8; L. J. Van Der Essen, *Etude critique sur les vies des saints mérovingiens*, pp. 96-105; *Revue bénédictine*, 60, pp. 120-47. Künstle, p. 512.

St Aigulf, *Martyr* (*c*. 630-76)

Two sources of information about St Aigulf have survived. There is a somewhat fulsome Life written during the ninth century by a monk of Fleury named Adrevaldus and a shorter but nevertheless earlier anonymous account, which is much preferred by scholars. Aigulf was born of poor parents in Blois in about 630. When he was about twenty, he became a monk at Fleury, then in the fervent early years of its foundation. In about 670, after he had been a monk for some twenty years, he was sent as abbot to the monastery at Lérins, where, with the passage of time and pressure from the Moors, discipline had broken down. Inevitably there were some members of the community who resisted the reforms Aigulf introduced. However, two of them carried their resistance too far, appealing to the local governor against the abbot. When the governor sent a company of soldiers to keep order the monks persuaded them to kidnap Aigulf and his principal supporters and take them off to sea. The entire party eventually went ashore on the island of Capraia, between Corsica and Tuscany. Here, four of the monks, including Aigulf, were put to death after their eyes and tongues had been torn out. It has been suggested, not unreasonably, that they are more likely to have been killed by pirates or marauding Moors, but whatever is the truth, the surviving monks escaped and took the news to Lérins.

AA.SS., Sept., 1, pp. 747-55, contains both Adrevaldus's Life and the older, more reliable one. See also *Bibl.SS.*, 1, 634-5; *D.H.G.E.*, 1, 1141-2.

Bd Guala of Brescia, *Bishop* (1244)

In 1217 St Dominic (8 Aug.) went to Bergamo to find recruits for his new Order. The first to offer themselves and receive the habit were Guala Romanoni, who was already in his late thirties, and his brother Roger. Guala, whose name is Lombard in origin, was born into a noble family, according to his biographers, in about 1180. He was already a priest when he met Dominic, and probably a canon of the cathedral, living by a rule. It was not a happy situation, because the community he was living in had been formed by the unsuccessful merger of two. So Dominic's recruiting drive came just at the right time. Once committed, Guala went on with Dominic to Bologna to establish the friars there, and then to Brescia, where Dominic, who clearly appreciated his wisdom and experience, soon appointed him prior.

Guala was still prior in Brescia on 6 August 1221 when Dominic was struck down by his last illness. As he prayed in church for Dominic's recovery, Guala had a dream or vision, in which he saw two ladders coming down from heaven, one with Christ and the other with Mary at the top. Angels moved up and down the ladders, and at their foot was a figure dressed in the Dominican habit, his face covered with his hood as if for burial. Eventually the ladders were drawn up, and the Dominican was taken by the angels to the feet of Christ. Realizing what this must mean, Guala went as fast as he could to Bologna, only to learn that Dominic had died at the very time when he was having his dream. The incident is referred to in the third antiphon for Lauds in the Office of St Dominic: *Scala caelo prominens fratri revelatur, per quam pater transiens sursum ferebatur* ("A brother is shown a ladder suspended from heaven, by means of which our dying father was carried up"). When this was sung for the first time after the canonization of St Dominic in 1234, Guala was present in the choir at the friary in Bologna and intoned it himself.

His impressive personal qualities, as well as his ability as a preacher and his administrative talents, had meanwhile been recognized outside the Order. He carried out a number of delicate diplomatic missions for Pope Honorius III (1216-27) and his successor, Gregory IX (1227-41). One of the first acts of the latter was to appoint Guala as inquisitor, and over the years he made use of the

Dominican's gifts as a mediator and peacemaker. In 1229, when the bishop of Brescia became patriarch of Antioch, Gregory chose Guala to succeed him. It was not an easy assignment. Lombardy was caught up in the struggle between the Holy See and the emperor, Frederick II, and as a result Brescia was in a bad way, riven by political and ecclesiastical factions. Between 1232 and 1235 it fell to Guala to sort out a long-standing conflict between the pro-imperial Ghibillene faction and the papal legate. And meanwhile the diocese itself, with a lax clergy on the one hand and a high concentration of Cathars on the other, was in bad need of reorganization and moral reform. Too full of integrity for the first, too moderate for the second, Guala could be popular with no one.

Except the people. Much loved by them and especially by the poor, who appreciated his simplicity and his commitment, Guala remained in Brescia carrying out his duties for about ten years. In the end, however, he was forced to go into exile. Some have argued that the odds were so stacked against him that when Gregory died in 1241 he lost his one reliable source of support and was unable to govern. Others take the view that he was undermined by the combined opposition of the clergy and the commune and by an unsatisfactory papal legate. He certainly did not make things easy for himself when, in 1238, he removed his own possessions and any papers connected with diocesan property to a safe place in Bergamo. He rightly assumed that the clergy and the commune wanted to get their hands on the diocesan property, but from then on their aim was to get rid of him. Finally, in 1242, he retired to a monastery of the Vallombrosan Benedictines at Astino, where he remained for over a year, praying and studying. For the last year of his life he returned to Brescia, although he lived not in the city but at Val Canonica, where the people elected him mayor. It was there that he died on 3 September 1244. In 1245 his remains were taken to Astino, but today they are venerated in the cathedral in Bergamo. For a long time there was no public cult, although Guala's sanctity was recognized, and in the portrait in the church of St Dominic in Brescia (since destroyed) he had a halo. His cult was confirmed in 1868 by Pope Pius IX (1846-78).

See *AA.SS.*, Sept., 1, p. 773; T. Masetti, *Memorie storiche del B. Guala Romanoni* (1868); a French Life by J. Kuczynski (1916)—this effectively disposes of the idea that Guala prompted Pope Gregory IX to enforce the death penalty for heretics throughout Lombardy (cf. *Anal.Boll.* 38 [1920], p. 223); J. Procter, *Short Lives of the Dominican Saints* (1901), pp. 247-9; *Bibl.SS.*, 7, 412-9.

Apart from the portrait of Guala in the bishop's palace in Brescia, in the friary of San Matteo in Siena there are Francesco Traini's illustrations of episodes from the life of St Dominic, in some of which Guala figures.

Bd Antony Ixida and Companions, *Martyrs* (1570-1632)

Antony was born in 1570, at Shimabara, a town east of Nagasaki on the southern Japanese island of Kyushu. Christianity had been brought to Japan by St Francis Xavier in 1549, and Antony's Catholic parents presumably belonged to the first or second generation of converts. When he was old enough they sent him to study grammar, music, and Japanese literature at the Jesuit seminary in Arima, near Osaka. In January 1589 he was received into the Society of Jesus, after which he worked for a while as a catechist. After his ordination, sometime in 1608, he went to Hiroshima, working there and in the outlying areas to bring Christianity to the people.

In 1616, for reasons that are not clear, he was sent to prison for three years. This he took as an opportunity to preach the gospel to his fellow-prisoners. Once he had served his sentence, he went off to Nagasaki. Here he managed to carry out his apostolate for another dozen years or so by working clandestinely. On 6 January 1629 he was re-arrested and taken before the governor, who tried to persuade him to recant. When he refused, the governor subjected him and five others to tortures that had made many other Christians recant: they were placed in sulphurous boiling water at Ungen (with a doctor on hand to make sure they did not die). On 5 June 1631 he was back in Nagasaki, where he spent the next nine months supporting and encouraging others in their faith. At the end of that year he was re-arrested and returned to prison. In the long months that followed he was strengthened by the visits of Thomas of St Augustine, a Japanese priest who came in disguised as one of the governor's servants. Then, on 3 September, he was burned at the stake, along with five others: John Jerome Jo, a Japanese priest; three Augustinians, Bartolomeo Guttierrez, Vincenzo Carvalho, and Francisco de Gesú; and Gabriele della Maddalena, a Franciscan tertiary. They were beatified by Pope Pius IX (1846-78).

L. Profillet, *Le Martyrologe de l'Eglise de Japon, 1549-1649* (1897); R. H. Drummond, *A History of Christianity in Japan* (1909); J. Monsterleet, *Storia della Chiesa in Giappone* (1959), pp. 109-12; N. S. Fujita, *The Catholic Mission in pre-modern Japan* (1991). See also *Bibl.SS.*, 7, 1002; *O.D.C.C.*, pp.865-6.

Martyr's palm

4

St Marcellus, *Martyr* (*c.* 178)

Although the various *acta* that record the martyrdom of St Marcellus together with Valerian (15 Sept.) are of rather dubious worth, there is no doubt about the fact of the martyrdom and of the cult to which it gave rise. Only one set mentions them both, but an inscription in a church near Bagnols (Gard), which couples together certain relics of the two, seems to suggest that this is authentic. Their cult definitely developed early and was indirectly validated by Gregory of Tours (17 Nov.). According to a reliable contemporary account that has come down via Eusebius, in 177 many Christians in Lyons died for their faith, along with their bishop, St Pothinus (2 June). Marcellus, a priest, managed to escape first to Tournus and then to Chalon-sur-Saône, where he stayed briefly, converting his pagan host before he moved on. Travelling north, he fell in with the governor, Priscus, who invited him to a celebration at his house. When Marcellus realized that there were about to be some religious rites, he excused himself on the ground that he was a Christian. With that, angry onlookers seized him and would have killed him there and then, but Priscus tried to persuade him to worship the image of Saturn. When he refused, he was buried up to his waist on the bank of the Saône and died of exposure and starvation three days later. In the third century a basilica dedicated to Marcellus was the focus of a popular cult. This cult became more widespread when the monastery that had been built alongside the basilica came under the aegis of Cluny in 1050. There are traces of the cult as far afield as Cologne, Trier, and Worms in Germany and Seville and Toledo in Spain.

The *acta* are printed in *AA.SS.*, Sept., 2, pp. 187-202. See also *Bibl.SS.*, 6, 664; H. Quentin, *Martyrologes historiques*, pp. 179-80; P. Bernard, *Les origines et les premiers siècles de l'Eglise chalonnaise* (1922); A. Troubnikoff, *Les martyrs de Lyon et leurs temps* (1966); *O.D.S.*, pp. 314-5.

St Marinus (? Fourth Century)

Nothing certain is known about this saint, who nevertheless lives on in the name—San Marino—of the tiny republic which is supposed to have grown up over the site of his hermitage. His name first crops up in the eighth century in the *Liber Pontificalis*, which mentions a *castellum Sancti Marini*. Then toward the end of the ninth century there is a reference to *Sancti Marini monasterio*. It was after that, probably in the course of the next two centuries, that the legend developed.

30

This states that Marinus was born on the Dalmatian coast and was a stonemason by trade. Hearing that the walls of Rimini were to be rebuilt, he went there with St Leo (1 Aug.), another stonemason, in search of work. After some years' hard work in the quarries on Monte Titano (now in San Marino), where they helped and encouraged Christians who had been sentenced to hard labour for their refusal to deny their faith, Leo, who had been ordained priest by the bishop of Rimini, St Gaudentius (14 Oct.), went to live in Montefeltro (the cathedral there is dedicated to him). Marinus, who had been ordained deacon, returned for a while to his work at the quarry but eventually became a hermit on the slopes of the mountain. An expanded version of the legend suggests that a woman arrived from Dalmatia claiming to be his deserted wife, and it was her importunacy that drove him into the hills. The monastery founded on the site once occupied by Marinus' cell and a chapel dedicated to St Peter (29 June) is supposed to have expanded into the Republic of San Marino.

It was in the sixteenth century, when Marinus' bones were found and recognized, that interest began to grow. By the end of that century there were eight dedications in the area, of which three remain. There was another recognition of the bones in 1713; then in 1774 a lay society with Marinus as protector was approved, and in 1778 Pope Pius VI (1775-99) approved the Mass and Office of "St Marinus, deacon and confessor." In 1940 there was something of a clash between San Marino scholars and Cardinal Ildefonsus Schuster (30 Aug.), the then archbishop of Milan. The cardinal claimed that Marinus' bones had been found with others, including those of St Leo, in a sarcophagus in the church of San Stefano Maggiore in Milan.

For the legend see *AA.SS.*, Sept., 2, pp. 208-20. See also *Bibl.SS.*, 8, 1175-80; L. A. Gentili, *Compendio della vita di S. Marino* (1864); M.-P. Aebischer, *Essai sur l'histoire de Saint-Marin des origines à l'an mille* (1962).

St Boniface I, *Pope* (422)

Boniface, a Roman by birth, was the son of a priest named Iucundus. He became a priest himself and during the reign of Pope St Innocent I (401-17; 28 July) travelled several times to Constantinople on papal business. When Innocent's successor, Pope St Zosimus (26 Dec.), died on 26 December 418, a small faction made up of the deacons of Rome and some of the priests took over the Lateran and elected the archdeacon, Eulalius, to succeed him. However, on the same or the following day, in the basilica of Theodora, most of the senior clergy of Rome and many members of the laity elected the by now elderly Boniface. Both were consecrated on 29 December, Eulalius in the Lateran by the bishop of Ostia, whose traditional task it was to ordain the Bishop of Rome, Boniface in the church of San Marcello, in the presence of nine bishops.

The matter was further complicated by the fact that in his report to the emperor Honorius (395-423), who was then in Ravenna, Symmachus, the pagan prefect of Rome, came out in favour of Eulalius. Boniface was told to leave Rome, which he did, under protest. But he made use of powerful friends at court, including the emperor's redoubtable sister, Galla Placidia, to persuade Honorius to reconsider the matter. No conclusion was reached at a synod held in Ravenna, so Honorius called another. It would be held in Spoleto on 13 June 419, and bishops from Africa and Gaul would attend; in the meanwhile both Boniface and Eulalius were to retire from Rome, leaving the bishop of Spoleto to preside over the Easter ceremonies on 30 March. Boniface obeyed but was recalled to Rome and recognized as pope on 3 April, after Eulalius had so angered the government by his refusal to obey that he was finally banished from the city for good. By this stage Boniface was seriously ill and fearful that, were he to die, the trouble might well erupt again. So he asked Honorius to help maintain peace in the event of an election. Honorius, possibly intervening more immediately and more thoroughly than Boniface had anticipated, decreed that if two men were elected both would be disqualified—the government would recognize only a unanimously elected candidate.

Despite his age and failing health, Boniface ruled firmly, making a number of significant decisions. By restoring metropolitan rights to Marseilles, Narbonne, and Vienne and thus supporting the rights of bishops, he repaired some of the damage Pope Zosimus had done in making Arles a papal vicariate. On the other hand he managed to reassert papal authority in the vicariate of Thessalonika, where the eastern emperor, Theodosius II (408-50), had attempted to transfer jurisdiction to Constantinople. In Africa his intervention had mixed results. He managed to soothe the feelings of the bishops, which had been ruffled by Zosimus' legate over the case of a deposed priest. But then he ruffled them himself by rehabilitating a deposed bishop before he had heard the case against him. He was a staunch supporter of orthodoxy and in particular of St Augustine (28 Aug.) in the dispute with the Pelagians. He passed on to Augustine two letters in which the Pelagian leaders slandered him, Augustine, in order to give him the opportunity to answer them himself. As a mark of respect and gratitude Augustine dedicated to Boniface the treatise he wrote in reply to his critics.

Little of Boniface's own writing has survived apart from one or two letters, but from the available evidence he appears to have been a kind and humble man. He died on 4 September 422. He was buried in the cemetery of Maximus on the via Salaria in a chapel he had built near the tomb of St Felicitas (6 Mar.), to whom he had a strong devotion.

P.L., 20, 745-92; *Liber Pontificalis*, 1, pp. 227-9; *O.D.P.*, pp. 40-1; *D.C.B.*, 1, p. 327ff.; *D.H.G.E.*, 9, 895-7; *Bibl.SS.*, 3, pp. 328-30; *N.C.E.*, 2, p. 668ff. The official documents are in *Collectio Avellana* (*C.S.E.L.*, 35, pp. 59-83). See also E. Duffy, *Saints and Sinners: A History of the Popes* (1997), pp. 31, 33.

St Ultán of Ardbraccan, *Bishop* (657)

Altogether about eighteen Ultáns are named in the medieval Irish martyrologies. Of these, only two—St Ultán of Fosse or Péronne (2 May) and St Ultán of Ard Breccáin (now Ardbraccan, near Navan in Co. Meath)—are well known. No formal Life, Latin or Irish, of this Ultán has survived, so any details depend on such disparate sources as a notice in the *Félire* of Oengus and a Latin verse tribute to him. According to medieval Irish genealogists, he was the son of Rónán mac Findtáin, although he is usually referred to as Ultán Moccu Conchubir (of the people of Conchobor). He is supposed to have been bishop of Ard Breccáin and from that centre to have evangelized and ministered to the Dál Conchubir branch of the Desi of Meath. He was known in the Irish tradition for his learning and particularly for his knowledge of history and literature. He is said to have been head of the monastic school at Ard Breccáin, where he used his learning to educate in particular students who could not otherwise have afforded it. One of his many students was Tiréchán, to whom he was very helpful when the latter was gathering material for his annotations on the Life of St Patrick (17 Mar.) in the *Book of Armagh*.

The claim that he was the maternal uncle of St Brigid of Kildare (1 Feb.) can be ruled out immediately: she died in the first half of the sixth century, he in the second half of the seventh. But he was supposedly responsible for much of the material on her that has survived, including a Life, a Latin poem, and an Irish poem; and with four others he contributed to *Brigit bé bithmaith*, one of the oldest hymns in Irish. A poem in honour of St Brigid, beginning "*Christus in nostra insula*," is often attributed to him, but it is probably by someone else.

Little more is known about him. His ability to write was accompanied by artistic talent, and he is said to have illuminated his own manuscripts. According to the legend he was always concerned for children and their needs and was known to assume responsibility for up to 150 sick, orphaned, or unhappy children at a time. No details have survived about the circumstances of his death, which the medieval annalists put in 657, the *Annals of Ulster* in 663.

For the Latin poem see E. Dummler, *Poetae Latini medii aevi*, 1, p. 589. Also J. H. Bernard and R. Atkinson, *The Irish Hymnorum* (Henry Bradshaw Society, 1898); J. O'Hanlon, *Lives of the Irish Saints*, 9, p. 83ff.; *Bibl.SS.*, 12, 802-3.

St Ida of Herzfeld (*c.* 766-825)

The extant Life of Ida, written by a monk of Werden named Uffing, dates from a century and a half after her death and is full of improbable miracles. It is possible, nevertheless, to piece together some details about her life. A great-granddaughter of Charles Martel (688-741), she was brought up at the court of Charlemagne (768-814). The only one of five brothers and sisters not to become a religious, she was happily married to Eckbert of Saxony, with whom she had five children. Of these, three entered religion (one, like two of his uncles, became abbot of Corvey, while another became abbess of Herford). While she was still very young, she lovingly nursed Eckbert through a long and painful illness, from which he eventually died. Left now to herself, she provided for her children and then embarked on a life of prayer and strict self-denial. When her son, Warin, inspired by his mother's example, went to be a monk at Corvey, Ida moved from her home in Hofstadt castle to nearby Herzfeld. There she built a small chapel for her own use in a church she and her husband had built and meanwhile used most of the revenues from her estate to help the poor. She remained at Herzfeld, doing good works, for the rest of her life. As a reminder of her eventual death and of her duty to her neighbour, she is said to have had a stone coffin which she made sure was filled up daily with food for the poor. Toward the end of her life she suffered a persistent and painful illness, which she bore with great patience. She is thought to have died on 4 September 825, although some give 813 as the date. She was buried near her husband at Herzfeld in the cemetery of the convent she founded there. In 980 her relics were translated, and her tomb became a place of pilgrimage. She is invoked particularly by women who are pregnant.

For the Life see *AA.SS.*, Sept., 2, p. 255. For a more modern treatment see A. Husing, *Die hl. Ida, Gräfin von Herzfeld* (1880), and a booklet by J. Hérold (1925). See also *Bibl.SS.*, 7, 637-8.

St Irmgard of Cologne (*c.* 1085)

Irmgard (Irmgardis, Irmengarda), variously known as Irmgard of Cologne, Süchteln, and Aspel, was born sometime at the beginning of the eleventh century. The few details of her life that have come down to us relate to land concessions and the building of a church. Her father, Godizo of Aspel, in the Lower Rheinland, was related to St Henry II (1002-24; 13 July) and his wife St Cunegund (3 Mar.). When he and her mother died, Irmgard built a church over their tomb at Rees and dedicated it to Our Lady. Then on 15 February 1041 one of Henry's successors, Henry III (1039-56), made over to her large tracts of land in what are now Belgium and the Netherlands. She was still at Aspel in 1049, because there are records to show that in that year Pope St Leo IX (1048-56; 19 Apr.) visited her there. Shortly after this she is supposed to have left Aspel and gone to live as a hermit it Süchteln. She went once, if not twice, on pilgrimage to Rome before she died in Cologne on 4 September, probably but not definitely in 1085. The cult flourished in Aspel, Cologne, Rees, and Süchteln, and Irmgard was certainly being celebrated with the title of saint by 1319. In art she is represented as a noblewoman with a crown on her head and the model of a church in her hand. There is a view that Irmgard and a member of the Luxembourg royal family named Irmentrude were the same person—Irmentrude is mentioned frequently in eleventh-century Rhenish charts.

AA.SS., Sept., 2, pp. 270-8; P. Noremberg, *Die heilige Irmgardis von Süchteln* (1894), which airs the Irmentrude theory; I. Kleinermanns, *Die heilige Irmgardis von Aspel und ihre Beziehungen zu Rees, Süchteln und Köln* (1900); J. Deilmann, *Die heilige Irmgardis, Gräfin von Aspel* (1928); M. A. Goldmann, *Die heilige Irmgard von Aspel* (1940); *Bibl.SS.*, 7, 905; Baudot et Chaussin, 10, p. 77.

St Rosalia (1166)

Although churches in Sicily were being dedicated in honour of St Rosalia from the thirteenth century, she is not mentioned in any of the early martyrologies, and the first extant life dates from the sixteenth century. Most of what is known about her has been pieced together from local tradition, inscriptions, and paintings. According to these, she was born into a noble family near Palermo and received a thorough Christian education. At an early age she left home and went to live as a hermit in a cave at San Stefano Quisquina, near Bivona. An inscription found on the walls of this cave, ostensibly in her own hand, reads: "*Ego Rosalia Sinibaldi Quisquine et Rosarum domini filia amore Domini mei Iesu Christi in hoc antro habitare decrevi*" ("I, Rosalia, daughter of Sinibaldus, Lord of Quisquina and Rosae, have decided to live in this cave for the love of my Lord Jesus Christ"). After she had lived here for a while, Rosalia moved back to the Palermo area and into a stalagmitic grotto on the slopes of Monte Pellegrino. This was where she died, and her remains were eventually covered completely by the limestone deposits of the stalagmites. Meanwhile her cult flourished. The people of Palermo immediately honoured her as a saint, and from the end of the twelfth century many churches and chapels were dedicated to her in Sicily and southern Italy.

However, it was in 1624, when it had already begun to wane, that the cult really took off, and Rosalia was named principal patron of Palermo. There appear to be two versions of what happened. According to the first, in October 1623 during an epidemic of the plague, she appeared to a grief-stricken hunter named Vincenzo Bonello, who, having lost his wife to the plague, had come to Monte Pellegrino to commit suicide. The second has it that she appeared to a woman who was herself a victim of the plague and told her to make a pilgrimage to Monte Pellegrino. In either case, a search was made on Monte Pellegrino for her bones. Bones were indeed found, but there was no indication as to whom they belonged, and a first commission of doctors could not even identify them as those of a human body. However, when on 11 February 1625 a second commission of doctors and theologians authenticated them as those of Rosalia, they were placed in a reliquary and carried in procession to the cathedral. In the following year a church was built over her hermitage on Monte Pellegrino. Her name was included in the Roman Martyrology by Pope Urban VIII (1623-44)—in fact it appeared twice, once on this day, said to be that of her death, and once on 15 July, the day on which her relics, including a terracotta crucifix, a silver Greek cross, and some prayer beads as well as the bones, were said to have been found.

In Palermo 4 September is today still marked by a popular *festa* in her honour, and the people look for rain on the preceding days. The sanctuary on Monte Pellegrino, with its church, hostel, and shop, is still a place of pilgrimage throughout the year.

The Benedictines have claimed Rosalia as a member of their Order, but a similar claim made by the Greek religious who once flourished in Sicily is probably stronger. The Byzantine abbey of San Salvatore in Messina used to possess a wooden cross (now in Palermo) which bore the inscription: "I, Sister Rosalia Sinibaldi, place this wood of my Lord, whom I have ever followed, in this monastery."

Numerous minor biographies exist in Italian, but the best account is still that of the Bollandists in *AA.SS.*, Sept., 2, pp. 278-414. See also D. M. Sparacio, *S. Rosalia, vergine panormitana* (1924); *Bibl.SS.*, 11, 427-33; G. Farnedi, *Guia ai Santuari d'Italia* (1996), pp. 364-5.

In art, St Rosalia is most frequently represented with a crown of roses, as by van Dyck in the Museo Nazionale in Palermo. She is sometimes shown in an Augustinian habit. On the iconography see P. Collura, *Santa Rosalia nella storia e nell'arte* (1977).

Bd Catherine of Racconigi (1486-1547)

The primary source of information about this interesting but relatively little-known mystic is an account by two men who knew her well, Giovanni Francesco Pico della Mirandola, and a Dominican, Pietro Martire Morelli. Unfortunately, both seem to have accepted literally and without question everything she told them about herself and her experiences, so it is difficult to get at the reality behind the extravagant miracles and the stock hagiographical details they record. The story as it survives is as follows. Daughter of Giorgio Mattei and Billia Ferrari, Catherine (Caterina) was born at Racconigi, then a village, now a small town, south of Turin, in 1486. The circumstances of her birth, which seems to have taken place in a tumble-down shed or hovel, were, in retrospect, symbolic of the material side of her life. The family was very poor, and her life at home was dogged by constant deprivation and ill health. Her spiritual gifts by contrast were considerable, though even these led to the added burden of misunderstanding. By and large, though, her vivid spiritual life and its consolations seem to have compensated for her physical misery. We are told, for example, that when, as a child of nine, she broke down one day in tears of exhaustion over her work, she was visited and comforted by the Child Jesus. Later, when she was fourteen, she made a vow of virginity after an experience in which she believed that the Holy Spirit, through the intercession of St Stephen (26 Dec.), had taken possession of her in a special way. After this she suffered the pains of Christ's passion, although without any visible evidence.

Some of things said of her closely resemble things said of St Catherine of Siena (29 Apr.), and the lessons of her Office draw the connection: "Between Racconigi and Siena there is only the difference of canonization." But the resemblance should not be pushed too far. Like her namesake, Catherine became a Dominican tertiary, but not until she was twenty-eight, and even then she continued to live in the world and work hard for her family. In her prayer she offered herself constantly to God on behalf of others, be they souls in purgatory or victims of the wars that plagued Italy at this time. One of the wondrous qualities attributed to her was an ability to move at high speed over great distances in order to bring spiritual help to people who needed it—though perhaps that was just a way of saying that you could always rely on her to be there when she was needed.

In the last years of her life she suffered a long illness that she would certainly have regarded as an answer to her prayer. Her suffering was exacerbated by loneliness as her friends deserted her, and she died at Carmagnola on 4 September 1547 without the help of a priest. Five months later, after many miracles had been reported, her body was taken to Garezzo, where a cult, confirmed in 1810, continues to flourish. In Racconigi a chapel was built in her honour.

There are various editions of the account by Pico della Mirandola and Morelli. The best note is probably that by M. C. de Ganay in *Les Bienheureuses Dominicaines* (1913), pp. 475-501. For a fuller biography see I. Taurisano, *Catalogus hagiographicus O.P.* (1918); and modern Lives by J. Christophe (1947); G. Capello (1947); A. Ferraris (1947). See also *Bibl.SS.*, 3, 992-3; *Miscellanea di storia ecclesiastica e di teologia* 2 (1904), pp. 185-91.

5

St Bertinus, *Abbot* (*c.* 698)

Bertinus was a monk at the abbey of Luxeuil when he was asked to go, with St
Mommolinus (16 Oct.) and St Bertrand, to assist St Audomarus (or Omer, 9
Sept.), who had just been made bishop of Thérouanne. The work that faced
them was not easy. The Morini, who lived in the area, had been evangelized
about a century earlier, but the faith had not taken root, so the missionaries
were forced to put up with abuse and ill treatment verging on persecution.
However, despite discomfort, fatigue, and reverses of every kind they persevered, and eventually their efforts began to bear fruit. Their first monastery—
subsequently called the Old Monastery—was built on the banks of a river at
what is now the village of Saint-Momelin.

As the plot was narrow as well as marshy, it soon became inadequate for the
numbers who came to take the habit. Fortunately a convert named Adroald
had recently given Audomarus a plot of land at Sithiu (later Saint-Omer), on
the river Aa. Audomarus gave this to the missionaries with instructions to
build another monastery. The first abbot was Mommolinus, who had already
been abbot of the Old Monastery. Bertinus (who is said to have been chosen by
Audomarus as abbot of the original settlement but refused on the ground that
he was the youngest of the three) succeeded him when he went to be bishop of
Noyon in about 660. Under his leadership the monastery, dedicated at first to
St Peter but subsequently renamed Saint-Bertin, flourished. Although Bertinus
is numbered among the Benedictine saints, it is likely that during his lifetime it
followed the Rule of St Columbanus (23 Nov.), the founder of Luxeuil. The
land on which the monastery was built was singularly unforgiving: flat, low-
lying, and water-logged (the monks had to reach it by boat, and not for nothing
is the boat Bertinus' emblem in art). The monks nevertheless worked hard to
drain it and then, along with the gospel, passed their draining and building
techniques on to the Morini.

Work among the latter was not always rewarding, and Bertinus derived his
greatest comfort from the fervour of his monks. He also seized every opportunity to lay down more roots. In 663 he collaborated with Audomarus in building
a church on a hill near Sithiu, which he dedicated to Our Lady and which
afterwards became the cathedral of the diocese of Saint-Omer. When he was
given a plot of land at Wormhout near Dunkerque, he immediately founded a
cell there and put St Winnoc (6 Nov.) in charge. Exactly when he died is
uncertain, but he is known to have lived to a great age. He was buried in the

chapel of St Martin at Sithiu, and there is documentary evidence to show that by 745 he was already being referred to as a saint.

See *M.G.H., Scriptores merov.*, 5, where the Lives of St Bertinus are discussed—the oldest (ninth-century) ties in with the Lives of SS Audomarus and Winnoc. See also *H.S.S.C.*, 4, 212-7; *Bibl.SS.*, 3, 101-2.

The iconography, which is not extensive, relates mostly to the founding of the monastery at Sithiu. Two shutters of a lost altarpiece by Simon Marmion survive. One, now in Berlin, shows the death of St Bertinus, the other, in the National Gallery, London, shows his soul being carried up to God. See Künstle, 2, pp. 134-5.

Bd Gentilis, *Martyr (c. 1290-1340)*

Gentilis was born into the noble Finiguerra family at Matelica near Ancona in about 1290. Little is known about him for certain, and the first to mention him was Bartolomeo da Pisa, half a century after his death. According to the accounts that have survived he joined the Friars Minor and, once professed and ordained, was sent to the friary at Monte Alvernia, where he twice served as guardian. The setting of the friary and its strong associations—St Francis (4 Oct.) received the stigmata here on 14 September 1224—had a profound effect on him. He learned to love silence and solitude while at the same time developing a great yearning to evangelize the East and the Islamic world.

Eventually he was sent to Egypt, but this was not a great success. He spoke no Arabic, and his inability to learn it meant that he was unable to do anything very useful. He was about to return to Italy in despair when he was encouraged by a dream, or vision, to persevere. Soon after this he met Marco Comaro, the Venetian ambassador to the court of Persia, who invited him to accompany him across Arabia to Persia. On the way Gentilis tended the ambassador through a dangerous illness, assuring him that he would live to become doge of Venice. Together they visited the shrine to St Catherine of Alexandria on Mount Sinai, then a popular place of pilgrimage despite its inaccessibility. Sometime during the journey Gentilis disappeared mysteriously for a week. On his return word went round that he had been miraculously transported back to Italy so that he could fulfill a promise to his father that he would be with him when he died.

Once they reached Persia, Gentilis travelled northward as far as Trebizond (modern Tabriz), preaching as he went, and he is said to have made many converts. The date and exact place of his death are unknown, and although he is listed as a martyr it is not at all certain that he was put to death for the Faith, and on this account his name has been dropped from the new Roman Martyrology. A priest named Mariano da Firenze was the first to put the idea forward in 1523, and others simply accepted it as fact. Some Venetians brought his body back to Europe, and he is buried in the church of the Frari in Venice. His cult was approved by Pope Pius VI (1775-99) in 1795.

See L. Wadding, *Annales*; B. Mazzara, *Leggendario Francescano*, pt. 2 (1680), 1, pp. 409-11; M. da Civezza, *Missions franciscaines*, 3, p. 650; Léon, *Auréole* (Eng. trans.), 3, pp. 109-

12; C. Ortolani, *Il Martirio del Beato Gentile da Matelica* (1924); A. Sanvidotto, *Beato Gentile da Matelica, martire francescano* (1942); *Bibl.SS.*, 6, 165-7.

Bd William Brown, *Martyr* (1605)

Very little is known about William Brown, a layman from Northamptonshire. He was arrested with Bd Thomas Welbourn (1 Aug.) and John Fulthering for "being zealous Catholics, and industrious in exhorting some of their neighbours to embrace the Catholic faith [and were] upon that account arraigned and condemned to suffer as in cases of high treason."

All three were hanged, drawn, and quartered, the first two at York on 1 August 1605 and William Brown at Ripon on 5 September.

M.M.P., p. 280.

6

St Donatian and Others, *Bishops and Martyrs* (*c*. 484)

From the available sources it is difficult to identify the specific names, which were first mentioned in a martyrology by Florus of Lyons sometime in the ninth century. However, there seems to be no doubt about the authenticity of the martyrdom.

According to one account the Arian king of the Vandals, Huneric, decreed in 484 that all Catholic churches in Africa were to be closed and the goods of the clergy taken and distributed to the Arian clergy. The bishops, who had assembled to listen to the king's decree, were banished from the city. Outside the gates, Huneric met a group of them who appealed against its injustice. Huneric's only response was to call out "Ride them down!" to his mounted entourage. Another account says that Huneric arranged for the Catholic bishops to dispute the question of consubstantiality with the Arian bishops. In either case his aim was to get rid of the Catholic bishops, beginning with the most intelligent and able. Donatian and four other bishops, all of the province of Byzacene, were beaten and then driven into the desert, where they died of hunger, thirst, and exposure. Laetus, bishop of Leptis Minor, whom the earlier Roman Martyrology describes as "a zealous and very learned man" (but whose name has been dropped from the heading in the new), had, by his opposition to Arianism, particularly infuriated Huneric. To make an example of him, he had him thrown into a foul cell, from which he emerged only to be burned alive. The feast of these martyrs is kept by the Canons Regular of the Lateran.

AA.SS., Sept., 2, pp. 667-82, mentions Victor of Vita's *Historia persecutionis provinciae Africanae* (*P.L.*, 58, 215, 217) as the source of this account. See also *Bibl.SS.*, 4, 801-2.

St Magnus of Füssen (*c*. 772)

The Life of this popular Bavarian saint is studded with miracles and improbable juxtapositions. He is identified, for example, with Magnoald, a disciple of St Gall (16 Oct.), and is said to have travelled from Ireland to the Continent in the company of Gall himself and St Columbanus (23 Nov.). This scenario, which is set out in the first part of the Life, is clearly impossible, unless Magnus was over 150 years old when he died in about 772. The second part of the Life—barring mention of the Columbanus-Gall connection and tales involving dragons and other monsters—is more reliable. From this it emerges that Magnus was a monk of the monastery at Saint Gall (Sankt-Gallen). At the request, or at least with the support, of Wichpert, bishop of Augsburg, he

41

undertook to preach the gospel to the people of the Allgäu region of Bavaria. According to the Life he set out with two companions: a monk named Theodore, who came as far as Kempten, where he stayed to preach for a while before returning to Saint Gall; and a priest named Tozzo, who stayed with him until they reached a place between Kempten and Füssen where they founded a church. Tozzo is said to have remained here until 771, when he succeeded Wichpert as bishop of Augsburg.

Magnus, meanwhile, moved on to Füssen. He established a cell there in about 746, and it eventually became the centre of his missionary activity. Some young clerics sent by Wichpert as assistants formed the nucleus of a monastic community. The monastery itself—later known as Sankt-Mang—was built on land donated, at Wichpert's request, by the Frankish king, Pepin the Short, in about 752. With the king's support Magnus did not simply preach Christianity to the people of the area. He was concerned about the conditions in which they lived and full of practical ideas as to how they could remedy them. Having shown them how best to clear the land for cultivation and settlement, he set about tapping into the mineral wealth of a nearby mountain. His hope was that income from the mining would alleviate their poverty.

After twenty-six years of constant missionary activity, Magnus died at Füssen. The date given by the Life is 6 September 772. He subsequently enjoyed enormous popularity, especially in Bavaria, although by the thirteenth century the cult had spread throughout Germany and beyond. Sometime between 843 and 848 a church was built over his tomb at Füssen. After 847, when a synod held in Mainz decreed that his relics should be exposed, his name began to appear in monastic and other calendars. From the fifteenth century on he was often named among the Holy Helpers (*Nothelfer*), presumably on account of his alleged powers against storms, insects, dragons, and other natural phenomena. There are numerous church dedications, especially in Bavaria and Switzerland, and a Benedictine priory at Colbitz in Saxony was named after him as early as 1010. His feast is celebrated on 6 September in the dioceses of Augsburg, Bressanone, Chur, Freising, and Munich.

Regarding the Life itself, there is some disagreement about how and when it was written. One long-held theory was that the first account was produced by Magnus' companion, Theodore, and filled out by Ermenricus of Ellwangen (874); that later, in about 890, when the relics were translated to Sankt-Gallen, an anonymous writer revised it, adding new material; and that it finally received its definitive form from Otloh of Saint-Emmeran in the second half of the eleventh century. However, in the 1960s this theory was challenged by the Bollandist Maurice Coens. He took the view that one thing only is certain: that the entire text existed as we know it in the tenth century. He also believed that the idea of writing Magnus' Life came from Füssen but that it was actually written in Augsburg. Conceding that we do not really know how it was put together, he insists that Otloh's contributions were purely stylistic.

For M. Coens's edited version of the Life see *Anal.Boll.* 81 (1962), pp. 159-227, 321-32. See also *AA.SS.*, Sept., 2, pp. 735-58; *Festschrift zum 1200-jährigen Jubiläum des heiligen Magnus* (1950); R. Bauerreis, *Kirchengeschichte Bayerns*, 1 (1958); *Bibl.SS.*, 8, 542-6 (with additional bibliography).

In art Magnus is usually shown dressed as a monk and carrying the staff with which he was said to have killed serpents and other harmful animals. Symbolic of the paganism against which he fought as a missionary, these usually appeared under his feet. A good example of this is a fifteenth-century wooden statue in the Bayerisches National Museum in Munich. The earliest representation, in a codex of Sankt-Gallen, dates from the tenth century. For the iconography see Künstle, 2, pp. 420; H. Roeder, *Saints and Their Attributes* (1955), p. 57.

Bd Eskil of Lund, *Bishop* (*c.* 1100-81)

Lund was established as a suffragan diocese to that of Hamburg-Bremen in the middle of the tenth century, and that is what it remained for about 150 years. Then, in 1104, it became an independent archiepiscopal see with Eskil's uncle, Asker, as archbishop and head of the newly-created Nordic province. Throughout this period the southern part of Sweden (Skåne), in which it is situated, belonged to Denmark. So Eskil, who was born into a noble family in about 1100, is officially regarded as Danish. We know little about his early life. As a young man he spent a good deal of time abroad, notably at Hildesheim in Germany and at the Cistercian abbey at Clairvaux in France, where he formed a close friendship with St Bernard (20 Aug.). It is not clear when or where he became a priest, but when he returned home he was appointed provost of the cathedral in Lund and then, in 1132, bishop of Roskilde in Denmark. Finally, in 1137, he succeeded his uncle as archbishop of Lund.

Eskil presided over the church in this region during a period of consolidation. The magnificent Romanesque cathedral in Lund was completed and in 1147 was consecrated in the presence of all the Nordic bishops. Several religious houses were founded, both in Skåne and in Sjælland, and through his friendship with Bernard, Eskil was almost certainly responsible for the coming of the Cistercians to what is now Sweden in 1143. The first monastery they established—*Monasterium beatae Mariae de Alvastro*—was at Alvastra in Östergötland. Then they founded one at Nydala, further north in Småland, and this was followed by others.

The monks made a most important contribution to the development of Christianity in Sweden. One of their preferred vehicles for passing on the Faith seems to have been Gregorian chant, and a large body of liturgical hymns written during this period survives, bearing witness to its popularity. But with the support of successive kings, they also made a significant cultural contribution to the country, passing on the techniques they had mastered in such skills as building, agriculture, and gardening, as well as in more intellectual pursuits.

It was while Eskil was archbishop of Lund that Sweden and Norway were visited for the first time by a papal legate. In 1152 Nicholas Breakspear, the

English cardinal who two years later would become pope as Hadrian IV (1154-9), came to implement a plan whereby Sweden and Norway would be ecclesiastically independent. It was adopted immediately for Norway, and various ecclesiastical areas including parts of the archdiocese of Lund were united to form the diocese of Nidaros (Trondheim). But Sweden, where the church was subject to the authority of the king, who did not acknowledge that of the pope, had to wait another decade or so for complete ecclesiastical independence. However, Eskil did manage to fight off a final attempt by the archbishop of Hamburg-Bremen to recovery authority over the Nordic Church. To enlist the support of the pope in this matter he travelled, via Clairvaux, to Rome, where he arrived in 1156, having been imprisoned for a while by the German emperor on his way.

Back in Sweden, he was the pope's representative at the inauguration of a new archiepiscopal see at Uppsala in 1164. But shortly after this he was forced by the political situation between Sweden and Denmark to spend a good deal of time away from his diocese. He went abroad and for a while made Clairvaux his base. He eventually returned to Lund in 1170 and carried out his episcopal duties for another seven years. Then, in 1177, the pope allowed him to resign in favour of his chosen successor, Axilon, and he was able to do what he had wanted to do all along: become a monk at Clairvaux. He died there in 1181.

See *AA.SS.*, Apr., 1, p. 856; *Bibl.SS.*, 5, 91-2; *O.D.C.C.*, pp. 1562-3; I. Andersson, *A History of Sweden* (trans. C. Hannay, 1955).

Bd Bertrand of Garrigues (1230)

One of the original members of the Order of Preachers, Bertrand was born at Garrigues, near Alès, in the diocese of Nîmes, in the second half of the twelfth century. At the time France was a divided country, in which a disproportionate influence was exerted by the Albigensians, or Cathars. According to this dualist sect the material world is evil and redemption can be achieved only by the liberation of the soul from the flesh. This was offered to the few *perfecti*, who were expected to live a life of virtuous austerity, leaving the majority, the *credentes*, or believers, to do more or less as they pleased because it did not matter anyway. Eventually the Catholics were sufficiently roused to challenge the heretics. This challenge was taken up, and in 1200 the Albigensian Count Raymund VI of Toulouse marched through Languedoc harrying the orthodox monasteries—one is said to have been saved from destruction by the prompt action of a beekeeper, who opened his hives in the faces of the soldiers. The Cistercians, as official preachers against the heretics, became the main targets of this offensive. Bertrand was not himself a Cistercian, but he was already a priest and now joined the Cistercian mission as a preacher. Matters came to a head in 1208, when the papal legate, Peter of Castelnau (15 Jan.), was murdered in Count Raymund's territory. Pope Innocent III (1198-1216) responded

44

by making a decision he would later come to regret. He gave approval for a crusade against the Albigensians, and this set off, led by Simon de Montfort. It was probably some time after this that Bertrand first met St Dominic (8 Aug.). The latter was attempting, through prayer and preaching, to limit the damage done by the crusade, in particular by Simon's brutal methods, and to bring about reconciliation with the Albigensians. Bertrand recognized a kindred spirit and began working with Dominic. By 1215 they had been joined by a further five preachers, and by the following year their number had increased to sixteen. Under Dominic's leadership the group met at Prouille, where he had already established a community of nuns, to lay the foundations of the Order of Preachers. For a year they lived in community in Toulouse. Then, early in 1216, when Dominic took the bold step of dispersing the friars, Bertrand was sent with six others to Paris. Here they founded a house near the university, but Bertrand did not stay in the city for long. Dominic called him to Rome, and from there he went with John of Navarre to found a house of the Order in Bologna. The early Dominican writers speak of Bertrand as a loved and trusted companion of Dominic, who shared not only his journeys but, most importantly, his vision and his ideals. In 1219, travelling from Toulouse via the sanctuary at Rocamadour, they went together on the only visit Dominic made to Paris. Here Dominic was pleasurably and humbly surprised to find about thirty young men who had joined the Order and owed him obedience without knowing him.

At the second general chapter of the Order, which took place in 1221, the year of Dominic's death, Bertrand was appointed prior provincial in Provence. For the remaining nine years of his life he preached energetically in the south of France, where he founded the priory of Marseilles and generally extended the activities of the Order. One of the friars said of him that "he succeeded in making himself so like his beloved Father that one might have said of him as he passed by: 'The disciple is indeed like the master; there goes the very image of the blessed Dominic.'" Bertrand died at the abbey of Bouchet, near Orange, in about 1230. The exact date is not known, although he was still alive in 1229, for in that year he and his brothers gave some of their land to extend that of the friary of Saint-Romain in Toulouse. His cult began in a small way at Bouchet, and when that monastery declined during the Western Schism (1309-78) it too declined. Initially, his relics were preserved by the friars at Orange, but in 1561, during the Wars of Religion, they were burned. The cult was nevertheless approved by the bishop of Valence in 1870, and Bertrand was beatified in 1881.

For a full account see *AA.SS.*, Oct., 13, pp. 136-45, 919-21. See also Gerard de Fracheto, *Vitae fratrum, and other Dominican chronicles*; J. Procter, *Short Lives of the Dominican Saints* (1902), pp. 253-6; I. Taurisano, *Catalogus hagiographicus O.P.*, p. 9; Jordan of Saxony (ed. S. Tugwell), *On the beginnings of the Order of Preachers* (1982); S. Tugwell, *St Dominic* (1995).

Bd Peregrine of Falerone (1240)

There is only one real source of information about this early Franciscan, and that is the *Actus beati Francisci et sociorum ejus*, compiled largely by Ugolino da Montegiorgio, who lived near Falerone. For the rest we have to rely on the *Fioretti di San Francesco*, which says almost nothing, apart from the fact that Francis' companion Bernardo described Peregrine (Pellegrino) as "one of the most perfect friars in the world."

Peregrine was born at Falerone, north of Ascoli Piceno, toward the end of the twelfth century. He was the son of the lord of Falerone, of whom little is known, and was related to various noble families in the area. Besides being well connected he was intellectually gifted, and he was successfully pursuing a university course in Bologna when St Francis of Assisi (4 Oct.) came to preach there, probably in 1222. He and a fellow-student, Bd Rizzerio della Muccia (7 Feb.), were so impressed by what they heard that they applied immediately to join the Friars Minor. Francis accepted them both but told Peregrine that in spite of his considerable learning it was God's will that he join as a lay brother. Peregrine accepted this and persevered humbly as such all his life. There is no strong evidence for the assertion that he went to Palestine. Miracles were attributed to him both before and after his death, which occurred in 1240. His cult was confirmed on 28 July 1821, and his relics are in the church of the Madonna dei Lumi, which is now run by the Cistercians. The Friars Minor celebrate Bd Peregrine, together with St Liberatus (below) and Bd Santes of Monte Fabri, who, having killed a man in self-defence, became a lay brother in the Order and died in 1390 after a most holy life.

For Peregrine's story see *Speculum Vitae*; P. Sabatier (ed.), *Actus beati Francisci et sociorum ejus* (1902), ch. 36; S. Hughes (ed.), *The Little Flowers of St Francis* (1964); E. M. Blaiklock (ed.), *The Little Flowers of St Francis: the acts of St Francis and his companions* (1985); I. C. Gentili, *Saggio sopra l'ordine serafico*, p. 27ff.; Léon, *Auréole*, 1, pp. 527-9; *Bibl.SS.*, 10, 463-4. On Bd Santes see L. Wadding, *Annales Ordinis Minorum*, 9, pp. 94-6.

St Liberatus of Loro (c. 1260)

Liberatus is one of the more obscure Franciscan saints, and the details of his life remain uncertain. According to tradition he was born at Loro Piceno, thirty miles south of Macerata, and had connections with the noble Brunforte family. At a relatively young age he joined the Friars Minor at Soffiano, where the remains of the convent can still be seen. As a Franciscan he led a contemplative, eremitical life and was supposedly associated with Bd Humilis and Bd Pacificus in a project that aimed to maintain strict observance in the Order. Again according to tradition, after his death in about 1260 his brethren, taking his relics and those of the other deceased friars with them, left Soffiano for a more congenial location. The new convent was later named after Liberatus. There is no doubt that the friars at what became San Liberato were Spirituals, members of the group that insisted on adherence to the letter of the Rule and eventually separated from the Order, and that it eventually became the centre of the movement in the Marches.

Attempts have been made to identify Liberatus with an unnamed friar of Soffiano, mentioned in the *Fioretti*, who had a vision of Our Lady, but this raises serious problems, as does the theory that he and Peter of Macerata are one and the same person. Peter, who was the leader of the Spiritual movement in the Marches, took the name Liberatus when his group separated from the Friars Minor. Liberatus of Loro was the object of a cult almost from the time of his death, but nearly five centuries passed before it was made official in 1747. Pope Pius IX (1846-78) finally approved it in 1868.

See *Bibl.SS.*, 8, 13-15. Also Salvi, *Cenni storici sul b. Liberato da Loro* (1896); Léon, *Auréole*, 3, pp.431-2; P. Sabatier, *Actus beati Francisci et sociorum ejus* (1902), pp. 195, 215n; L. Damiani, "San Liberato da Loro Piceno e gli 'Actus Fioretti' di San Francesco," in *Collectanea Franciscana* 32 (1962), pp. 35-45. On the unnamed friar see *Fioretti*, cc. 46-7 (Eng. trans., E. M. Blaiklock and A. C. Keys, 1985).

7

St Regina, *Martyr* (date unknown)

The *passio* of St Regina (or Reine) is not in any way reliable. Its author claims to have been an eyewitness to the events it records, but his account is just a little too similar to the legend of St Margaret of Antioch (20 July). However, there is strong evidence—including the discovery in 1923, at Alise-Sainte-Reine in Burgundy, of the foundations of a basilica dedicated in her honour and the fact that her name appears in the *Hieronymianum*—to suggest that her cult began early. She was venerated at Alise (Alesia) before 628, and by about 750 a cathedral had been built to house her relics, with a monastery nearby. According to one account they were moved from here to Flavigny in 854; but ninth-century liturgical books suggest that the body remained at the site of the martyrdom until there was a church in which to place it and that once such a church had been built it became a place of pilgrimage. In the seventeenth century there was a dispute between some who said the remains were at Flavigny and others who insisted they were at Osnabrück. This was resolved in 1693 by the bishop of Autun, who imposed silence on both parties and ordered them to display the relics they had.

The Roman Martyrology tells us nothing except that Regina died for her faith in the region of Autun. According to her legend, however, she was the daughter of a man named Olybrius, a pagan citizen of Alise, north-west of Dijon. Her mother died giving birth, so she was placed in the care of a woman who brought her up as a Christian. When Olybrius heard of this he would not have her in the house, so she went back to live with her nurse, earning her living as a shepherdess. She attracted the attention of the local prefect, who told her father he wished to marry her. Olybrius, seeing this as a good match for his daughter, was now prepared to acknowledge her, but Regina refused to listen to either of them. She was imprisoned in an attempt to break her spirit, and when this failed the prefect vented his rage and disappointment by having her tortured. That night she was consoled by a vision of the cross and a voice telling her that her suffering would soon be over. Next day, allegedly 7 September, the prefect had her tortured again and then beheaded. Many onlookers were converted by the sight of a shining dove hovering over her as she died.

See *AA.SS.*, Sept., 3, pp. 24-43; *Bibl.SS*, 11, 71-2. On the remains of the basilica see J. Toutain in *Bulletin archéologique du Comité des Travaux historiques* (1914), pp. 365-87. For the legend see F. Grignard, *La Vie de Ste Reine d'Alise* (1881); Quillot, *Ste Reine d'Alise* (1881).

48

St Sozon, *Martyr* (date unknown)

The alleged Acts of this martyr are preserved in two Greek texts, the second of which is a reworking by St Simeon Metaphrastes (28 Nov.). These are so unspecific, however, that it is difficult to say who exactly Sozon was or when he died. According to the legend, which seems to have been associated with a fountain that was regarded as miraculous, he was a shepherd in Cilicia, or perhaps Licaonia. Originally named Pharasius or Tarasius, he took the name Sozon when he was baptized. One day, as he lay sleeping under a tree, he had a vision of Christ, who told him to leave his sheep and follow him to death. Sozon went immediately to nearby Pompeiopolis, where a pagan festival was being celebrated. Walking straight into the temple of the god, he shattered the golden image with a blow of his crook. He then broke the hand into smaller pieces and distributed them to the poor. When he realized that several people had been arrested on his account he went and gave himself up. After a long interrogation by the magistrate he was told that he could go free if he would worship the god, but he merely mocked the idea of worshipping a god that could be broken by a shepherd's crook. After he had been made to walk round the arena with nails in his sandals, the magistrate said he could go free if he would play a tune on his pipe. Sozon refused. He had often piped for his sheep, he said, but now he would make music only for God. He was sentenced to be burned, and later that night local Christians came to collect and bury his charred remains.

St Sozon appears in the Byzantine synaxaries on this day. He was introduced into the West by Baronius.

One of the Greek texts is printed in *AA.SS*, Sept., 3, pp. 14-19, the other in *P.G.*, 115. See also *Bibl.SS*, 11, 1336-7.

St John of Nicomedia, *Martyr* (303)

The real name of this martyr is not known, although his martyrdom is mentioned both by Eusebius and by Lactantius. He was given the name John in the so-called *Parvum Romanum*, an ancient martyrology sent from Rome to a bishop of Aquileia, and it is as John that he is venerated. According to the Roman Martyrology, which based its account on those of Ado, Usuard, Bede, and others, he was in Nicomedia when copies of the edict of Diocletian (284-305) were posted in the forum. "Fired with zeal for the faith," he tore these posters down and destroyed them. On hearing about this, the emperor Diocletian and the future eastern emperor Maximian (306-10), who both happened to be in Nicomedia at the time, sent orders that he should be tortured. John endured everything patiently and was finally burned alive in 303. He is sometimes identified (most improbably) with St George (23 Apr.). The Syrians know him as Euhtis (Euetios).

Eusebius, *Ecclesiastical History*, 7, ch. 5. Eusebius and Lactantius are mentioned in *AA.SS.*, Sept., 3, pp. 12-4. On the name see H. Quentin, *Martyrologes historiques*, p. 439. See also *Bibl.SS.*, 6, 856; R. Aigrain, *L'Hagiographie* (1953).

St Clodoald (*c.* 560)

During his childhood and youth Clodoald (or Cloud) was a victim of the brutality of Merovingian politics. When his grandfather, the Frankish king Clovis, died in 511, the kingdom was divided between his four sons, Theodoric, Clodomir, Childebert I, and Clotaire I. Clodomir, who had already murdered the Burgundian king, St Sigismund (1 May), himself died fighting his cousin, the new Burgundian king, Gondomar. He left three sons, of whom Clodoald was the youngest, to inherit his domains. The three boys were brought up in Paris with great care and affection by their grandmother, Clovis' wife, St Clotilde (3 June), while their kingdom was administered by their uncle Childebert. When Clodoald was eight, Childebert and his brother Clotaire began plotting to get rid of the boys and divide their territories among themselves. One of Childebert's henchmen was sent to ask Clotilde to choose whether the boys should be killed or forcibly tonsured and shut up in a monastery. He so distorted her reply that she was made to appear to choose their death, and Clotaire immediately stabbed Teodoald, the oldest, himself. The second brother, Gunther, fled in terror to Childebert, who, sickened by Teodoald's murder, tried to protect him. But Clotaire, despising such softheartedness, took the boy and killed him. Clodoald managed somehow to escape, and was taken by friends to safety.

Having seen enough of the world of power and politics, he showed no inclination, when he came of age, to reclaim his kingdom. Gregory of Tours says that instead he entered Holy Orders, possibly reaching the priesthood. Another version has it that he went to a hermitage near Paris and lived there under the guidance of another hermit, also a St Severinus; it is unlikely that Severinus lived in Provence—as a later Life suggests. Eventually he moved to another hermitage near Nogent-sur-Seine, to the south-west of Paris. There he spent his time passing on the Faith to the local people. He died, probably in 560, when he was about thirty-six. Thanks to a pun on the French version of his name, he is venerated as the patron saint of nail-makers.

Gregory of Tours, *Historia Francorum*, 3, 18. The *Vita S. Clodoaldi* is in *AA.SS.*, Sept., 3, pp. 91-8. There is also a ninth-century Life, edited by B. Krusch, in *M.G.H., Scriptores merov.*, 2, pp. 350-7. J. Legrand, *St Cloud: prince, moine, prêtre* (1922), is an uncritical booklet. See also *Bibl.SS*, 4, 63-4; G. Kurth, *Ste Clotilde* (1897), pp. 100-8.

St Stephen of Châtillon, *Bishop* (*c.* 1150-*c.* 1208)

Little is known for certain about this Carthusian saint. A thirteenth-century Life consisting of eighty lines of indifferent Latin verse is too short to provide much detailed information, and its even shorter appendix, *Miracula*, has no historical value. There is a slightly later prose Life, accompanied by its own *Miracula*, but this is no more than a compilation of material taken from the Lives of other saints, notably St Anthelmus (26 June), abbot of La Grande Chartreuse. The bare facts seem to be that Stephen (Etienne) was born at Châtillon-les-Dombes, north-west of Lyon, in 1149 or 1150. In about 1175 he joined the Carthusians at Portes-en-Bugey and later on served for a while as prior. Then, sometime after 1207, he agreed, with many misgivings, to become bishop of Die—he only did so, in fact, when ordered to by Pope Innocent III (1198-1216). He died on 6 or 7 September (the latter preferred by the new Roman Martyrology), but the year is uncertain. It has been given as late as 1213. But unless he resigned as bishop of Die and then lived on for another few years, this is not possible, since his successor was already installed by 1209. The most commonly accepted date is 1208.

Miracles were attributed to him while he was still alive, but it was those reported after his death that in 1231 prompted the archbishop of Vienne and his suffragans to press for his canonization. Although nothing definite seems to have come of this, people continued to venerate his relics, and during a recognition in 1557 his body was found to be intact. Three years later his remains were destroyed by the Huguenots. Finally Pope Pius IX (1846-78) approved the cult of St Stephen for the diocese of Die, and then, in 1857, extended it to the Carthusian Order.

AA.SS., Sept., 3, pp. 175-201; *N.C.E.*, 13, p. 698; *Bibl.SS.*, 11, 1396-8; *D.H.G.E.*, 15, 1220-2; D. Le Vasseur, *Ephemerides ordinis Cartusiensis*, 3 (1891), p. 150; J. de Font Réaulx, "La chronologie des évêques de Die dans la première moitié du XIIIᵉ siècle," in *Bulletin de la Société d'archéologie et de statistique de la Drôme* 65 (1935-6), pp. 267-73.

SS Mark, Stephen, and Melchior, *Martyrs* (1619)

The martyrdom of Mark Körösi, Stephen Pongrácz, and Melchior Grodecz was significant in the history of the Catholic Reformation in Hungary. Stephen was born in the castle of Alvinc in Transylvania, probably in 1583. He entered the Society of Jesus at Brno in Moravia on 11 July 1602 but pursued his studies in a number of places, including Prague, Klagenfurt, and Graz. When he was ordained he went to the Jesuit college at Humenné. Melchior, who was a year younger, came from Cieszyn in Silesia, where he was born, also in his family castle, in 1584. He was educated at the Jesuit college in Vienna and joined the Society in 1603. It was in the novitiate at Brno that he and Stephen first met. After his ordination he taught for a while at the Institute of St Vincent in Prague. Mark was born into a distinguished Croat family at Crisium, in the diocese of Zagreb, in 1589. He was educated by the Jesuits and knew Stephen and Melchior. He nevertheless chose to become a diocesan priest and did his studies first in Graz and then at the German-Hungarian College in Rome. In 1615 he returned to Hungary, where the Catholic primate, Archbishop Pazmany, entrusted him with important duties in the archdiocese of Esztergom.

In 1619 all three men were involved in pastoral and educational work near Kassa (now Kosice, Slovakia). Stephen and Melchior had been invited by the king's lieutenant, Andras Dóczy, to encourage the few Catholics in this pre-dominantly Calvinist area, who from 1604 had been deprived of their churches. Their mission went well, but its very success provoked a reaction, and they became caught up in the power politics of the region. The local Calvinist prince, Bethlen Gabor, who was attempting to take land from the Catholic king, sent an army, led by General Gyorgi Rákóczi, to march on Kosice. Stephen and Melchior hurried to the scene, as did Mark, and the three men met up in the city. It was taken by General Rákóczi on 5 September 1619.

With prompting from Bethlen Gabor, the general had the three men apprehended, and along with the king's lieutenant they were placed under house arrest. At dawn on 7 September soldiers arrived with orders from the general to persuade them to renounce their Catholicism. When all three refused, they took them one by one and subjected them to a series of brutal and degrading tortures. Mark was the first to die, then Melchior. When they had finished with Stephen, the soldiers threw all three bodies into a ditch. But Stephen was not yet dead, and it was only after a further twenty-four hours of terrible suffering that he finally died, on 8 September. At first no one was allowed to bury them, but eventually Bethlen Gabor gave a local noblewoman permission to take the bodies. For a while the burial place was a local chapel, but in 1636 the remains were taken to the monastery of the Poor Clares in Trnava. Mark, Stephen, and Melchior were beatified together in 1905 and canonized by Pope John Paul II on 2 July 1995. At the ceremony the pope expressed respect for the Protestant martyrs of the Thirty Years War.

See Schmidl, *Historia Provinciae Bohemicae S.J.*, 3, p. 193ff.; *Etudes* 104 (1905), pp. 5-27; N. Angelini, *I beati Marco Stefano Crisino. . . .* (1904); J. N. Tylenda, *Jesuit Saints and Martyrs* (1985); H. Leclercq, *Les Martyrs*, 8, pp. 338-52.

Bd Thomas Tsuji, *Martyr* (*c.* 1571-1627)

Thomas was born at Sonogi, near Omura, on the southern Japanese island of Kyushu, in about 1517. His family belonged to the Japanese nobility, but they must have been, if not Christian, at least sympathetic to Christianity, because he was educated by the Jesuits in Arima, near Osaka. In 1589 he entered the Society and was eventually ordained in Nagasaki. He soon made a name for himself in the area as a preacher but was moved to Hakata when his penetrating comments about their behaviour antagonized some Christian Japanese in

52

Nagasaki. Then came the edict which banished Catholic priests from the country and opened a period of persecution. Along with eighty other Jesuits, Thomas obeyed the order and went to Macao, where he remained for four years. In 1618 he decided to resume his apostolic work and returned to Japan disguised as a merchant. In this way he had one great advantage over the European missionaries: he was Japanese, and provided he went in disguise he could move about freely during the day. He would vary the disguise, sometimes appearing as an artisan, sometimes as a member of the prosperous and educated classes, or else as a wood seller, which was a particularly convenient and unremarkable way of gaining access to a Christian household.

But it was not easy. Enormous demands were made on him, physically and emotionally, and the fact that so many of his fellow Jesuits were being put to death for their faith left him discouraged and depressed. Fearing that if it came to the point he would not be able to stand firm, he applied for release from his vows. By the time the permission arrived, however, he had changed his mind and asked to be readmitted immediately. This was not possible, but his superiors were sympathetic to his case and placed him on probation. During the six years in which he remained on probation he recovered from his depression and worked bravely and tirelessly. When he was finally readmitted to the Society in 1626, he was sent to Nagasaki, and it was there that he was captured on 22 July of the same year. He had gone that day, the feast of St Mary Magdalene, to celebrate Mass in the home of Louis Maki and his son John. Soldiers raided the house unexpectedly, and the three men were arrested. Arraigned before the local governor, Thomas admitted that he was a Jesuit and was sent to prison in Omura. Louis and John were also imprisoned for inviting a priest into their home.

While he was in prison, members of Thomas' family visited him continually, begging him to give up his religion and stop bringing shame on them. But Thomas stood firm, insisting that nothing they offered him would make him change his mind. Finally, on 7 September, after thirteen months in prison, Thomas was taken, with Louis and John Maki, to a hill outside the city, and tied to a stake. As the fire was prepared, Thomas encouraged the others, and as the flames rose round them he blessed them before falling silent in prayer. According to a number of witnesses, his breast burst open as he died, and from it a huge flame rose upward and out of sight.

Thomas was beatified by Pope Pius IX (1846-78) on 7 July 1867. He shares the feast, on 6 February, with others who died during this and other periods of persecution.

Bibl.SS., 12, 728-30; D. Bartoli, *Dell'historia della Compagnia di Gesú, 4, il Giappone* (1650); G. Boero, *Relazione della gloriosa morte di ducento e cinque beati martiri nel Giappone* (1867), pp. 139-40; J. N. Tylenda, *Jesuits Saints and Martyrs* (1985). For a general account of the martyrs of Japan in the present work see 6 February.

BB John Duckett and Ralph Corby, *Martyrs* (1644)

John Duckett came from the same family as Bd James Duckett (19 Apr.), a London bookseller, who was hanged at Tyburn in 1602. His father was another James, and John was born at Underwinder, near Sedbergh in the West Riding of Yorkshire, in 1613. He went to study at the English College in Douai and was there ordained to the priesthood in 1639. After three years of further study in Paris, where people commented on his prayerfulness and reputed gifts of contemplation, he spent a fortnight with the Carthusians at Nieuport in Flanders preparing for the English mission under the direction of "his kinsman" Fr Duckett (son of Bd James). For almost a year he carried out his ministry in Co. Durham. Then, on 2 July 1644 he was arrested, along with two laymen, while on his way to baptize some children. At first he refused to admit to the parliamentary committee of sequestrators that examined him in Sunderland that he was a priest. They had in fact found evidence on him in the form of his holy oils and *rituale*, but because they wanted a personal admission from him they threatened to torture him. When he realized that the two laymen were being questioned on his account and that inquiries were being made among his friends and family, John decided to admit that he was a priest. He was sent immediately to London, together with a Jesuit, Ralph Corby, who had been seized near Newcastle.

The Corby (or Corbington) family came from Durham, but Ralph himself was born at Maynooth, outside Dublin. When he was five his family returned to England. After some years of persecution every member of the family, in what must be some sort of record, went into religion. John's father, Gerard, became a temporal coadjutor with the Jesuits; his mother, Isabel, died a Benedictine in Ghent; his two surviving sisters joined the same Order in Brussels; and his older and younger brothers became Jesuits. He himself joined the Society of Jesus at Watten in Flanders, returning to work on the English mission in 1632. His ministry among the widely scattered Catholics of Co. Durham lasted for twelve years, until he was arrested at Hamsterley Hall, near Newcastle, while he was celebrating Mass.

When the two priests arrived in London they were sent to Newgate prison to await trial. The English Jesuits abroad attempted to get Ralph exchanged for a Scots colonel then being held prisoner in Germany. When it looked as though this might be successful, he offered the reprieve to John on the ground that the younger man was better qualified for the mission than himself. John was reluctant to accept, but in the end the decision was taken out of their hands. They were both sent to trial and the death sentence was pronounced. Ralph "appeared to be in an agony of sadness and fear" as he celebrated his last Mass in their Newgate lodgings, but this passed. When they were taken to Tyburn in the morning of 7 September 1644, it was "with their heads shaved, in their cassocks, and with a smiling look." John hardly spoke at all, except to bless those who asked and to tell a Protestant minister who tried to speak to him,

"Sir, I come not hither to be taught my faith but to die for the profession of it." Ralph, on the other hand, made a short speech. The two men then embraced each other, and the cart was drawn away. The sheriff would not allow them to be cut down and disembowelled until they were both dead, and he took extraordinary precautions to prevent any part of them from escaping the flames. However, one of John's hands and some parts of their cassocks were saved. In the archives of the Westminster archdiocese there is a letter written by John on the evening before he died to Dr Richard Smith, titular bishop of Chalcedon and vicar apostolic of England, who was then living in Paris. "I fear not death," he wrote, "nor I contemn not life. If life were my lot, I would endure it patiently; but if death, I shall receive it joyfully, for that Christ is my life and death is my gain."

Bd Ralph Corby features in his brother's *Certamen Triplex*. See also *M.M.P.*, pp. 457-66; Records of the English Province of the Society of Jesus, 3, pp. 68-96; J. Brodrick, *A Procession of Saints* (1949), pp. 111-30. For John Duckett see also Anstruther, 2, p. 90.

Bd John Baptist Mazzucconi (1826-55)

John (Giovanni) was born at Rancio di Lecco in the province of Milan on 1 March 1826. He came from a wealthy and charitable family, and one brother also became a priest, while two sisters became nuns. After a normal childhood he entered the Istituto delle Missioni Estere di Milano as one of its first students. He was ordained to the priesthood in 1850; about two years later, in March 1852, he set off by sea for the South Pacific. The next three years he spent bringing the Christian faith to the people of Rooke Island (now Kampalap Siassu) off what is today Papua New Guinea. He then fell seriously ill with malaria and because of the lack of medical facilities was sent for treatment to Sydney, where he was nursed by the Marist Brothers and recovered. On the way back to Rooke his ship was driven off course in a storm and made a forced landing on Woodlark Island, about four hundred miles to the south-east. At the same time three other missionaries were abandoning the island on account of the savage treatment they had received at the hands of the inhabitants. John was promptly killed by the inhabitants, as were the rest of the crew of the boat, who were suspected of numbering more missionaries among them. News of his martyrdom took a year to reach the outside world. It is known that he kept a notebook in which he was entering interesting facts about the islands of the archipelago, but this was lost at the time of his death, the precise date of which is not known.

John was fully conscious of the danger he was going into. Just before embarking he wrote two letters to his family (included in the documentation for the the process of his beatification), in one of which he said, "I don't know what the Lord is preparing for me on this new journey beginning tomorrow: I just know one thing, that he is good and that he loves me greatly; everything else, calm and storm, danger and safety, life and death are but passing and changeable expressions of his fervent, unchanging, eternal love." John was beatified by Pope John Paul II on 19 January 1984.

G. B. Tragella, *Le Missioni Estere di Milano* (1950); G. Scurati, *Cenni del Sacerdote Giovanni Mazzucconi, missionario apostolico nella Malesia morto per la fede il settembre 1855* (1957); T. Lelièvre, *100 nouveaux saints et bienheureux de 1963 à 1984* (1985), pp. 229-30; F. Holböck, *Die neuen Heiligen der katholische Kirche*, 2 (1992), pp. 15-16.

THE BIRTHDAY OF OUR LADY (over page)
Lilies, symbol of purity
(from a wood engraving by Frank Martin)

8

THE BIRTHDAY OF OUR LADY

Like some other feasts of Our Lady, this one originated in the East. Its model was probably that of the Birthday of St John the Baptist (24 June), which was known at least from the beginning of the sixth century. In some parts of the West it was certainly commemorated before the middle of the seventh century—the calendar of St Willibrord (*c.* 704) has an entry for it, as does the Auxerre *Hieronymianum* (*c.* 600). But it finally reached Rome during the reign of Pope St Sergius I (687-701; 8 Sept.). This pope ordered that four feasts of Our Lady—the Nativity, the Annunciation, the *Hypapante* or Purification, and the Assumption—should be celebrated in Rome and marked by a procession. It is not clear why this particular day, which in any case was not adopted universally, was chosen for the Nativity.

Of the circumstances of Mary's birth we know nothing. Her parents, traditionally known as Joachim and Anne (26 July), are not mentioned in the Bible. Like Abraham's wife, Sarah; Hannah, the mother of Samuel; Zachary and Elizabeth; and others in the Bible who eventually produced a remarkable child, they are said to have been childless. According to the apocryphal gospels Joachim withdrew into the desert to lament his lot—the place is identified by some as Wadi Yabis, east of the Jordan, where the ancient monastery of St George, dedicated to Mary, still stands, now much restored. While there, he learned in a dream or vision that he and Anne would have a daughter. Mary's birthplace is equally obscure. An ancient tradition, accepted in the West, names Nazareth, but another tradition favours Jerusalem, even going so far as to specify the neighbourhood of the pool of Bethsaida, where a crypt under the church of St Anne is venerated as the actual spot. In support of this, there is evidence that a small oratory existed there from the early third century and perhaps the end of the second. A basilica dedicated to Mary was built over this oratory in the fifth century, possibly by the empress Eudoxia (348-460). This was destroyed by the Persians in the seventh century but was quickly rebuilt, and the seventh/eighth-century Georgian calendar of Jerusalem mentions two important feasts of Our Lady, the Annunciation on 25 March and the Nativity on 8 September. In its present form the church dates from the time of the Crusades, when the name was changed from St Mary's to St Anne's.

In the end, of course, such details, however interesting, are not what the feast is about. Mary's position in the history of salvation is unique. In the *Magnificat*, through which St Luke has her express her own awareness of this uniqueness, she sees herself at a turning point in human history: "My soul magnifies the Lord, and my spirit rejoices in God, my saviour, for he has regarded the low estate of his handmaiden. For behold, henceforth all generations will call me blessed; for he who is mighty has done great things for me.... He has helped his servant Israel, in remembrance of his mercy, as he spoke to our fathers, to Abraham and his posterity for ever." On this day each year Christians have an opportunity to consider Mary as a sign of God's fidelity to promises made under the old covenant and to look forward in hope to the fulfillment of the new.

See G. Morin, *Revue bénédictine* 5 (1888), pp. 257-64; 7 (1890), pp. 260-70; 19 (1912), pp. 469-70. L. Duchesne, *Christian Worship* (1919), pp. 269-72; H. Graef, *Mary: A History of Doctrine and Devotion* (1963). On the birthplace see *Anal.Boll.* 62 (1943), pp. 272-3; E. Hoade, *Guide to the Holy Land* (1973); M. Walsh, *A Dictionary of Devotions* (1993).

SS Eusebius, Nestabus, Zeno, and Nestor, *Martyrs* (*c.* 362)

The only source for the story of these martyrs is the church historian Sozomen, according to whom they lived during the reign of Julian the Apostate (361-3). Having taken part in the destruction of a pagan temple in Gaza, Eusebius, Nestabus, and Zeno, who were brothers, were imprisoned and scourged. Not satisfied with what they regarded as too light a sentence, some of the local people forced their way into the prison and dragged the brothers out into the street. Here they threw them to the ground and began to strike them with anything that came to hand, while others came out of their houses and poured scalding water on them or pierced them with the spits they used for cooking. When the three men finally died, their mangled bodies were dragged to a place outside the city where dead animals were thrown. There they were mingled with the carcasses of animals and burned. A Christian woman managed to salvage some of their bones, which she had taken to a relative of theirs, also named Zeno. He kept them hidden until the reign of Theodosius (379-95) when, as a bishop, he built a church in their honour and buried them there. Nestor was a young man, possibly their cousin, who was arrested with Eusebius, Nestabus, and Zeno and like them suffered imprisonment and scourging. Allegedly because of his good looks, the crowd spared him the worst of the treatment meted out to the brothers and left him lying by the city gate. He nevertheless died of his wounds in the house of the other Zeno, who eventually buried his remains with those of the others. When he included them in the Roman Martyrology, Cardinal Baronius arbitrarily chose 8 September for their commemoration. The Greek synaxaries and menologies commemorate them on 20, 21, or 22 September.

Sozomen, 5, 9; *AA.SS.*, Sept., 3, pp. 256-9; *Bibl.SS.*, 5, 275; *D.H.G.E.*, 15, 1431.

St Isaac I the Great, *Katholikos of the Armenians* (*c.* 348-438)

Isaac (or Sahak) was born in Caesarea in Cappadocia in about 350, and when he was about three his mother died. Although marriage was not a bar, even to the episcopate, in the Armenian Church at this time—indeed, there were families in which the episcopate passed, if not directly, from father to son, and Isaac himself was the great-great-great-grandson of St Gregory the Enlightener (30 Sept.)—it is likely that his father, St Nerses I (19 Nov.), was already a widower when he was ordained and eventually became *katholikos*, or bishop. Little is known of Isaac's early life, but he went to study in Constantinople, where he became well versed in rhetoric and philosophy. While he was there he married and had one child, but it was not long before his wife died, perhaps in childbirth. After her death the evidence suggests that he became a monk and devoted most of his time to further study.

In 387 Armenia became divided politically between the Byzantine and Persian empires, and the two parts were ruled by princes answerable to their respective capitals. At the same time, the immediate successor to Nerses I severed his Church's dependence on Caesarea, of which St Basil (2 Jan.) was then metropolitan, effectively taking it into schism. Isaac realized the potential danger of this and in about 390, with the support of Kosroes, the Persian prince in Armenia, had himself recognized as *katholikos*. This far-sighted move, which was made over the heads of a small pro-Caesarean group in Armenia and looked at the time like disregard for ecclesiastical authority, would eventually have positive results. Initially the anti-Christian Persian king objected, and Kosroes was deposed, while Isaac was forced to resign. However, with the arrival of a new king the persecution stopped, Isaac was able to take up his post, and Kosroes was reinstated. All of which coincided with the beginning of the golden age of Armenian letters and ushered in a period of reform and progress within the Church.

This process of reform had started under Nerses I, whose aim was to bring the Church more into line with Byzantine law and practice. Isaac completed the process. Despite the protests of those who resented the tightening of church discipline, monasticism began to flourish again, church-run schools and hospitals were established, and churches destroyed by the Persians were rebuilt. One notable effect of Isaac's enforcement of Byzantine canon law was that married priests could no longer become bishops—he was himself the last descendant of Gregory the Enlightener to rule the Armenian Church.

Isaac received support from the emperor Theodosius II (408-50), who was happy to encourage the spread of Christianity throughout Armenia in order to promote the Greek influence. But there were parts of Armenia where Greek language and culture were absolutely banned, so Isaac was forced to devise ways of avoiding division. He managed successfully to do this by taking elements from both cultures, Byzantine and Syrian, and recasting them in a specifically Armenian mode. For the liturgy he went to that of Caesarea (now the Byzantine liturgy of St Basil) and adapted it for Armenian use. He also gave St Mesrop (19 Feb.) the task of devising an Armenian alphabet, which led to a flurry of significant literary activity. The first book to be translated was the Bible, and this was followed by other books. Some of the translations are particularly important, since the originals are now lost. By the time Isaac died Armenians were able to read the works of many of the Greek and Syrian Christian writers in their own language, and the first original works were being written.

In 428 the Armenian tributary prince was driven out by the Persians. Isaac, who was known to favour Christian Byzantium, was forced to retire to the western corner of the country. It was once thought that the city of Theodosiopolis (Karin, Erzerum) was built at this time by order of Theodosius to harbour Isaac, but this is impossible: the city is much older in origin and had been renamed in honour of the emperor thirteen years earlier. Isaac was eventually invited to return to his see, but he preferred not to, appointing a vicar in his place. When the latter died, Isaac did return, but he was by now old and so frail that he could not attend the Council of Ephesus in 431. He did send people to get copies of the proceedings, however, and made sure that these were translated and then circulated in Armenia. He died at Bagrerand on 8 September 438. In 439, when his feast was celebrated, his remans were taken to Ashtitat, the first Armenian ecclesiastical centre. He is mentioned by name in the intercession of the Armenian Mass and is frequently given the title "the Great."

For the principal sources see V. Langlois (ed.), *Collection des historiens de l'Arménie*, 2 (1867). Modern works include S. Weber, *Die katholische Kirche in Armenien* (1903); F. C. Conybeare, "The Armenian Canons of St Sahak," in *American Journal of Theology* (1898), pp. 828-48; P. Gulleserian (trans. V. T. Poladian), *Armenian Church* (1939; rp. 1970); V. Zahirsky, *The Conversion of Armenia* (1985). See also K. Sarkissian, *A Brief Introduction to Armenian Christian Literature* (1960); *O.D.C.C.*, p. 106); *Bibl.SS.*, 7, 916-8.

St Kieran of Clonmacnois, *Abbot (c. 512-c. 545)*

This Kieran (Cíarán, Quérán) is sometimes called "the Younger" to distinguish him from St Kieran of Saigir (5 Mar.). He was one of the seven children of Beóit, a cartwright—and carpenter according to the legend, though this could be one of the several ways in which the legend seems to create parallels between Kieran's life and that of Christ—and his wife, Darerca. Kieran was born between 510 and 520 in Connaught, where the family had fled from oppression by its chieftain in Antrim. The facts of his life are that after some preparatory education he went, aged fifteen, to study under St Finnian (12 Dec.) at Clonard, taking with him, the legend has it, a cow to provide him with milk. Finnian thought very highly of him and when the time came for him to leave Clonard would have resigned as abbot in his favour. Kieran refused, saying that Finnian should not leave the monastery for anyone but God, who had favoured him above them all.

From Clonard Kieran went to Inis Mór in the Aran Islands, where he spent seven years as a monk under St Enda (21 Mar.) and was ordained to the priesthood. Then, in about 541, he moved south to Scattery Island, in the mouth of the Shannon, to visit St Senan (8 Mar.), who had founded a monastery there. According to one of the many legends and miraculous episodes associated with Kieran, Senan gave Kieran a new cloak, and Kieran later repaid the kindness by floating another cloak down the Shannon to Senan. After this, Kieran travelled inland. His supposed stopping places were monasteries, first at a place called Isel, which he had to leave when the monks complained of his excessive generosity to the poor, and then on Inis Aingin in Lough Ree. Setting off again, this time with eight companions, he eventually came to a grassy ridge on the west bank of the Shannon. Here, sometime between 544 and 548, he founded and helped to erect the first buildings of the great monastery of Clonmacnois, which would become one of Ireland's great centres of learning. A monastic Rule said to be by him has survived, but although it accurately represents the austere spirit that prevailed in his and other Irish monasteries of the period, it is probably not his.

All the Lives—three Latin, one Irish— agree that Kieran died after only seven months as abbot of Clonmacnois (whether he was really thirty-three or this was another attempt to liken him to Christ is not clear). Refusing physical comfort to the end, he is said to have asked his monks to take him up onto the Little Hill to die. When they asked him what they should do during the persecution he assured them would come, he urged them to preserve his spirit, even if that meant abandoning his relics: "Arise and leave my bones as the bones of a deer are left in the sun. For it is better for you to live with me in heaven than to stay here with my relics." In fact, although over time it was raided by the Vikings and plundered by Irish and Anglo-Norman armies, the monastery of Clonmacnois survived as his living monument until 1552. Kieran's shrine, too, was plundered on several occasions during the Middle Ages, but the so-called Clonmacnois Crozier in the National Museum in Dublin is thought to have come from it.

Kieran is one of the so-called Twelve Apostles of Ireland, all of whom were supposed to have been trained at Clonard by St Finnian. In fact some lived before Finnian, and certainly not all were trained at Clonard. The other eleven are Brendan of Birr (29 Nov.), Brendan the Navigator (16 May), Canice (11 Oct.), Kieran of Saigir, Columba (9 June), Colum of Tir da Glas (13 Dec.), Laserian (18 Apr.), Mobi of Glasnevin (12 Oct.), Ninnaid of Inismacsaint (16 Jan.), Ruadhan of Lothra (15 Apr.), and Sinell of Cleenish (12 Nov.).

For the Lives see *AA.SS.*, Sept., 3, pp. 370-83; *V.S.H.*, 1, 200-16; R. A. S. MacAlister, *The Latin and Irish Lives of Cíarán* (1921). See also *Bibl.SS.*, 3, 1247-8; *O.D.S.*, pp. 99-100; P. Grosjean, "Notes d'Hagiographie Celtique," in *Anal.Boll.* 69 (1941), pp. 102-6; R. I.

Best, "The Graves of the Kings of Clonmacnois," in *Eriv* 2 (1905), pp. 163-71; J. Ryan, "The Abbatial Succession at Clonmacnois," in *Feil-Sgribbin Eoin Mic Neill* (1940), pp. 490-507; J. McNawse, "The Chronology of the life of St Cíarán of Clonmacnois," in *Journal of Ardagh and Clonmacnois Antiquarian Society* (1945), pp. 2-16.

St Sergius I, *Pope* (701)

Born, probably in Antioch, of Syrian parents, Sergius was educated in Palermo, where the family eventually settled. Sometime during the pontificate of Adeodatus II (672-6) he went to Rome. There he studied at the *schola cantorum*, or choir school, was ordained, and in 683 became titular priest of the church of Santa Susanna on the Quirinal. The five immediate successors of Adeodatus reigned on average for about two years, and by the time Pope Conon (686-7), an elderly compromise candidate, was elected, Rome was buzzing with factions. When Conon died, the vote was split between the archdeacon, Paschal (who, thanks to a massive bribe, had the support of the Byzantine exarch, John Platyn), and the archpriest, Theodore, who was backed by the Roman militia. As neither side would budge, the majority of the Roman clergy, together with high-ranking civil and military officials, met at the Palatine palace to vote again.

This time Sergius emerged as a strong candidate and was elected unanimously. When he arrived to take possession of the Lateran Palace, it was still occupied by Paschal, Theodore, and their various supporters. Theodore immediately deferred to Sergius, but Paschal was less amenable and secretly persuaded John Platyn to come to Rome with a view to overturning the election. John did come, but he quickly realized the extent of the support for Sergius and decided to approve his consecration—not, however, without first demanding from him the substantial quantity of gold that he had been promised by Paschal. This was pure extortion, so although Sergius, who had been freely and legitimately elected, handed the gold over, he did so under strong protest.

Despite this unpropitious start, Sergius turned out to be a determined and capable pope, concerned in particular, like so many popes in this early period, to consolidate the position of the Roman See. There is no written record of what his character was like, although Alcuin described him as a holy and worthy successor of St Peter. The details of his pontificate that have survived suggest an approachable, conciliatory man with wide sympathies and a natural authority. It was, for example, while he was pope that, for the first time since the sixteen-year period from 666 when the emperor Constans (641-68) declared the see of Ravenna independent of Rome, a bishop of Ravenna came to Rome to be consecrated. And in 700, after a council that had been convened in Pavia by the Lombard king, Cunibert, he welcomed Aquileia, which had been in schism since the condemnation of the Three Chapters in 553, back into communion with Rome.

He seems to have taken a particularly active interest in the English Church. On Holy Saturday 689 he baptized Caedwalla (20 Apr.), the young king of the

West Saxons, who, having "quitted his crown for the sake of the Lord and his everlasting kingdom," had come to Rome only to die there ten days after his baptism. Then in 693 he gave the *pallium* to Beorhtweald of Canterbury. In the same year he sanctioned the mission of the Northumbrian St Willibrord (7 Nov.) to Frisia and three years later consecrated him bishop of the Frisians, granting him the *pallium*. During an audience granted to a deputation of monks sent by St Ceolfrith (25 Sept.) from the abbey of Wearmouth and Jarrow, he confirmed the privileges of the abbey. Later, in 701, he wrote to Ceolfrith asking him to send "that religious servant of God, Bede, priest of your monastery," because he needed to consult learned men. Although Sergius promised that he would return to England as soon as the business was completed, it seems fairly clear that Bede never went.

Toward the beginning of his pontificate he was drawn into the proceedings of the *Concilium Quinisextum*, or Trullan Synod. This had been convened in Constantinople in 692 by the emperor Justinian II (685-95), whose ambition it was to preside over a council as his great namesake Justinian I (527-65) had done. It took place in the domed room (*trullus*) of the emperor's palace, and its declared purpose was to complete the work of the fifth and sixth general councils of the Church (hence *quinisextum*), held at Constantinople in 553 and 680 respectively. Although it claimed to legislate for the whole Church, all except one of the two hundred bishops who attended came from the East, and some of its 102 canons were inspired, if not by hostility, at least by a certain defiance toward the West. It ignored Western canon law, for example, and prohibited various practices that were accepted in the West. Significantly, it also renewed the famous twenty-eighth canon of Chalcedon (granting Constantinople patriarchal status equal with that of Rome), which Pope St Leo the Great (10 Nov.) had refused to endorse. Having forced the papal *apocrisiarii* in Constantinople to sign the acts of the council, Justinian sent copies to Rome to be signed by the pope.

Sergius resolutely refused to sign, and Justinian resorted to bullying tactics. He deported Sergius' chief advisers and then instructed Zacharias, the commander of his bodyguard, to go to Rome and force a signature out of the pope or, failing that, bring the pope himself back to Constantinople. Sergius learned of this plan, and there followed what must be one of the more absurd episodes in papal history. Setting aside their allegiance to the emperor, who was presumably unaware of the extent to which his authority in Italy had been eroded, imperial troops from Ravenna and elsewhere rallied behind the pope. Encouraged by the people of Rome, they made a strong show of force against Zacharias, who fled in terror to the pope for protection and hid under his bed. The soldiers pursued him there and would have killed him without the intervention of Sergius, who managed to restore calm by having him escorted from the city. The whole episode would have been deeply humiliating for Justinian, who no doubt longed for revenge. He was deposed in 695, however, and the matter ended there.

In Rome itself, Sergius took a personal interest in church buildings as well as in the liturgy and its music. He restored or enhanced a number of churches, among them St Peter's, St Paul's, and Santa Susanna, and saw to it that the remains of St Leo the Great (10 Nov.) were moved from the porch of St Peter's to a prominent place within the basilica. As a graduate of the *schola cantorum* he would have enjoyed singing himself, and according to the *Liber pontificalis* he directed that the Agnus Dei be sung by both clergy and people "at the breaking of the Lord's body." This last may have been more than a purely devotional and aesthetic gesture. Among the practices prohibited by the Trullan Council was the representation of Christ as the Lamb of God, and such a pointed change would not have been lost on the emperor. One of Sergius' most important acts from the point of view of the liturgy was to extend to the Roman Church four feasts of Our Lady already celebrated in the East—the Nativity, the Annunciation, the Purification, and the Dormition/Assumption—ordaining that each be marked by a procession.

Sergius died on 8 or 9 September 701 and was buried in St Peter's. The fact that he is mentioned (on 7 Sept.) in the earliest calendar of St Willibrord suggests that his cult began soon after his death.

Liber Pontificalis, 1, pp. 371-82, is an important source. See also E. Caspar, *Geschichte des Papstums*, 2 (1933), pp. 620-36; *O.D.P.*, pp. 82-3; *D.C.B.*, 4, pp. 618-20; *N.C.E.*, 13, p. 112; *Bibl.SS*, 11, 873-5; *O.D.C.C.*, pp. 1486, 1644; H. K. Mann, *The Lives of the Popes in the Early Middle Ages* (1902-32), 1, pt. 2, pp. 76-104; J. Richards, *The Popes and the Papacy in the Early Middle Ages* (1979), pp. 208-11, 266, 274, 278, 280; E. Duffy, *Saints and Sinners: A History of the Popes* (1997), pp. 62, 66.

St Corbinian, *Bishop* (725)

Information about this early apostle of Bavaria is relatively full, thanks to a Life by Aribo, a near contemporary and one of his successors in the see of Freising. According to Aribo, who is generally reliable, especially on the bishop's relations with the dukes of Bavaria, Corbinian was born at Châtres, north-west of Troyes, in France. Another source describes him as *"Britannorum genere ortus,"* but this is less reliable, despite the fact that his work should be seen within the framework of that of the Irish missionaries on the Continent during this period. He was baptized Waldegiso after his father but was subsequently known as Corbinian, supposedly because his mother changed his name to this, after herself. For fourteen years he lived as a recluse in a cell he built near a chapel in Châtres. Here he offered sound advice to any who came to consult him on spiritual matters, and miracles were soon being attributed to his intercession. Word of his holiness began to spread, and it was not long before a religious community was formed under his leadership. Eventually he found guiding a community too much of a distraction, and thinking in terms of finding a new retreat where he could live in obscurity, he set off for Rome.

It is not clear whether or not he was already a priest, let alone a bishop, at this stage. According to one account Pope St Gregory II (715-31; 11 Feb.) appointed him bishop of Freising. But his name does not appear in any list before 784, and more significantly, the see was not established until about 739. What is more likely is that the pope sent him as a missionary bishop to preach in Bavaria. Once there, he was supposed to be under the protection of Duke Grimoald. However, because the latter had married his brother's widow, Biltrudis, he refused to have anything to do with him until the two agreed to separate. The months that followed were tense and uncertain. Biltrudis vilified Corbinian as much as she could and even conspired to have him murdered, while his own shortness of temper, specifically mentioned by Aribo, probably did not make matters easier. He went into semi-exile in Meran, remaining there until Grimoald was killed in battle and Biltrudis abducted by the Franks. Recalled by Grimoald's successor, he organized missionary work throughout Bavaria. When he died in 725 he was buried at a monastery he had founded at Obermais, near Meran, but Aribo, his successor but one, had his remains moved to Freising in 765. He is patron of Munich-Freising, but there is also a chapel dedicated to him at Hotting, near Innsbruck, and some of his relics are in Arpajon, nearer his presumed birthplace in France.

For the genuine text of the Life see *M.G.H., Scriptores*, 4, 6; scholar's edition edited by B. Krusch (1920). See also *AA.SS.*, Sept., 3, pp. 261-96; *Bibl.SS*, 4, 169-71; *H.S.S.C.*, 4, p. 270; Jöckle, pp. 115-6; R. Aigrain, *Hagiographie* (1953), pp. 275, 307.

In art he is generally represented as a priest or bishop, with a book, as for example in the seal of the cathedral chapter in Freising. The legendary incident which gave him his emblem of a bear is supposed to have taken place during his journey to Rome. He was crossing the Brenner, the story goes, when a bear attacked and killed his pack-horse. Thinking quickly, he told his servant to put the leading rein and the pack on the bear, and they continued their journey. On the way, a nobleman in Trento stole one of his horses, and a nobleman in Pavia stole the other (both, the legend has it, were victims of divine retribution: the first died, and the other lost forty-two of his horses to elephantiasis). Eventually Corbinian's party arrived in Rome, accompanied by the now tamed bear. He is shown loading his luggage onto the bear in a painting by J. Polack (1483) in the Alte Pinakothek, Munich.

St Peter of Chavanon (*c.* 1005-80)

A relatively detailed account of Peter of Chavanon has survived in the form of a biography that was written about forty years after his death by a monk of Pébrac. Peter was born into a noble family at Langeac in the Auvergne sometime between 1003 and 1007. He received a good education and fairly early on felt he had a vocation to the priesthood. After his ordination he was sent back to Langeac. Here, in addition to his pastoral duties, which he carried out with great fidelity and commitment while leading a very austere personal life, he was chaplain to the convent at Saint-Pierre-les-Chases. His biographer links his decision to leave pastoral work and join a community directly to an incident involving one of the nuns, who seems to have made advances to him. Exactly what happened is not clear. The biographer describes the nun as "*sanctimonialis femina quae potius daemonialis dicenda est*—a consecrated woman who would better be described as diabolical." According to his version she approached Peter while he was sleeping in a hayloft, having ridden out with the abbess and some of the nuns to oversee the threshing of the grain. This account, which ends with Peter resigning both as chaplain and as parish priest is probably exaggerated in the interest of effect. It is more likely that, inspired by the work of the reforming Lateran Synod of 1059, Peter, who had for some time felt called to live by a Rule, allowed the incident to precipitate a decision.

Having freed himself from his commitments, in about 1060 he founded and built a monastery for canons regular on some land he had been given at Pébrac. He and his companions lived according to the Rule of St Augustine, accepting the common life and individual poverty prescribed for canons regular by the recent synod. Peter died on 8 September sometime between 1080 and 1085. He was buried at Pébrac, and his cult was quickly approved. People would come to his tomb in particular to be cured of any kind of fever.

The Life is in *AA.SS.*, Sept., 3, pp. 460-79. See also *Bibl.SS.*, 10, 682-3.

Bd Seraphina Sforza (1434-*c.*1478)

Seraphina, whose baptismal name was Sueva, was born in Urbino in 1434. She was the youngest child of Guidantonio da Montefeltro and his second wife, Caterina Colonna, who died when her daughter was only four. Five years later, Sueva's father also died, and for the next three years she was in the care first of her brother, Oddantonio, and then, when he died in tragic circumstances, of her stepbrother, Federico. In 1446 she was sent to Rome to be brought up in the household of her uncle, Cardinal Prospero Colonna. When she was about fourteen, the cardinal agreed to an arranged marriage between Sueva and Alessandro Sforza, lord of Pesaro, a widower with two sons. They were married by proxy on 9 January 1448, but Sueva did not join her husband until September of that year.

The couple seem to have lived together happily enough until Alessandro was called away to fight for his brother, the duke of Milan. There followed a period of prolonged absences, during which Sueva was left to bring up her stepsons, Battista and Costanzo, in the company of her aunt, Vittoria Colonna, and her cousin, Elisabetta Malatesta Verano. When Alessandro returned, it was obvious that the separation had done nothing for his relationship with his wife, and he started an affair with a woman named Pacifica, the wife of a local doctor. Unfortunately, the accounts of what happened next look at it exclusively from Sueva's point of view. Alessandro clearly behaved badly, but it may not have been easy to live in an arranged marriage with someone who was so much younger and less experienced than himself and almost certainly insecure.

Sueva, for her part, seems to have done everything she could to win him back, but this only provoked him to physical cruelty. Some of his charges against her reflect the political rivalry of their two families. Having accused her of adultery and of trying to poison him, he claimed that she was conspiring against him with the connivance of Vittoria Colonna and, more significantly, at the instigation of Sigismondo Pandolfo Malatesta, who was attempting to recover the lordship of Pesaro. Whether or not she really did try to poison him, she eventually gave up any thought of reconciliation and took refuge in prayer. This irritated Alessandro even more. In the end he threw her out of the house, telling her to find a home in some convent.

She was taken in as a guest by the Poor Clares, but soon she was sharing their life and was eventually clothed, taking the name Seraphina (Serafina). Having got what he wanted, Alessandro began to take Pacifica round Pesaro as though she were his wife—she even visited the convent wearing Sueva's jewels. Seraphina meanwhile lived the letter and spirit of the Rule she had chosen. She prayed continually for her husband's conversion, and it seems that her prayers were answered: before he died in 1473 he came to the convent and asked her forgiveness. She herself was elected abbess in 1475 and died three years later, on 8 September 1478.

Research carried out in this century has shown that Sueva may not have been quite the innocent victim she was assumed to be. There is a suggestion, for example, that she was party to a plot against her husband. What is certain is that she entered the convent when she was twenty-five and that, whatever she had to repent of, she grew holy by living from day to day a most austere religious rule. Her local cult was approved by Pope Benedict XIV (1740-58) in 1754.

G. B. Alegiani, *Vita della Beata Sveva Feltria Sforza* (1754); *AA.SS.*, Sept., 3, pp. 312-25; *Bibl.SS.*, 11, 1010-2; *Anal.Boll* 24 (1905), pp. 311-3; G. Franceschini, "Di Sveva Montefeltro Sforza, Signora di Pesaro (la beata Serafina)," in *Studia Picena* 25 (1957), pp. 133-57. B. Feliciangeli introduces the new research in *Sulla monacazione di Sveva Montefeltro-Sforza, Ricerche* (1903). Two poems by Seraphina in honour of Our Lady were published in Pesaro in 1871.

St Thomas of Villanova, *Bishop* (1486-1555)

Thomas (in Spanish, Tomás) takes his surname from the town of Villanueva de los Infantes, where he was brought up. His father, Tomás García, who was a miller, came from Villanueva, as did his mother, Lucía Martínez de Castellanos, but they moved to nearby Fuenllana, and that is where Thomas was born. When he was sixteen he went to the famous Complutensian University at Alcalá de Henares, which was being established as an instrument of intellectual reform in the Church by Cardinal Francisco Ximénez de Cisneros. When the university was formally recognized by papal Bull in 1508, Thomas was chosen to join the staff of the Colegio San Ildefonso. Four years later, when he was only twenty-six, he was made professor of philosophy. He did not remain long in this post, however. On 21 November 1516 he left the university and joined the Augustinian friars in Salamanca.

For years before this he had led a fervent spiritual life, and this was not lost on his superiors. In 1518, after less than two years, he was ordained and immediately started preaching as well as giving a theology course in his own convent. In daily life he tended to be absent-minded and had a poor memory. However, once he started developing an argument he was exceptionally clear-headed, and his sound judgment was much valued by his students. He based his lectures on the works of Peter Lombard and St Thomas Aquinas (28 June), and it was not long before students from the university were asking if they could attend. In 1519 he was elected prior, a position he held in a number of houses—including those in Burgos, Salamanca, and Valladolid—in the course of the next twenty-five years. As prior he was personally concerned for each friar, especially those who were sick. Over the years he also held a number of regional positions, including that of vicar general. In governing he showed wisdom and strength combined with a rare willingness to admit that his own plans did not always turn out for the best.

Sometime before 1534 he was appointed provincial of Castile and in that capacity sent the first group of Augustinians as missionaries to Mexico. Then, sometime in the same decade, he was nominated archbishop of Granada by the emperor, Charles V (1519-56), an honour he had no wish to accept. On this occasion he succeeded in declining it, but he was less successful in 1544, when Don George of Austria resigned as archbishop of Valencia. According to the traditional account of what happened the emperor wanted to appoint Thomas to the see. However, having decided to respect the latter's wish not to become a bishop, he told his secretary to draw up a letter of nomination for another religious. When the secretary produced the letter for the emperor's signature, Charles saw that it was addressed to Thomas of Villanova. Asked to explain, the secretary said that that was the name he had heard. Charles took this to be the will of God and signed the letter. Thomas was consecrated in Valladolid on 7 December 1544.

Dressed in his old monastic habit, with a hat he had worn since his profession, and accompanied by one religious and two servants, he travelled on foot to Valencia. His mother, who had turned her house into a hospital for the use of the poor, suggested that he take in Villanueva on the way, but Thomas said no. He believed that his primary duty lay with his new flock, beyond any other consideration—though later he did spend a month's holiday with his mother at Liria. When he arrived in Valencia he went straight to the Augustinian priory and spent several days in prayer and penance preparing himself for his consecration, which took place on 1 January 1545. Seeing his poverty, the cathedral canons made him a gift of 400 crowns to furnish his house. It was a kind and well-intentioned gesture, and Thomas accepted the money graciously. But he passed it on immediately to the hospital, explaining to the canons: "Our Lord will be better served and glorified if your money is spent on the poor in the hospital, who need it so much, rather than on me. What does a poor friar like myself want with furniture?"

Thomas' outward appearance clearly became a source of some embarrassment to his canons as well as to his own household. They did not understand that becoming archbishop of Valencia had done nothing to alter the way he saw himself or his relationship with people with whom he came in contact. He continued to wear a habit—for some years the one, much mended by himself, that he had brought from his monastery. They, meanwhile, would have preferred to see him in clothes better suited, as they saw it, to his episcopal dignity. "Gentlemen," he told them, "I am much obliged for the care you take of my person, but I really do not see how my dress as a religious interferes with my dignity as archbishop. You know perfectly well that my position and duties are quite independent of my clothes, and consist in taking care of the souls committed to me." When the canons finally persuaded him to replace his old cloth hat with a silk one, he would point to it with wry amusement: "Behold, my episcopal dignity."

Thomas' real interest and concern was his diocese, which had been without a resident bishop since 1527. He took the trouble to visit all its churches in order to get an idea first-hand of how each was faring. This visitation had an immediate and powerful effect on the people, many of whom were inspired by his preaching to change their lives. But at the same time it brought to his attention various abuses among the clergy. To remedy these he convened a provincial synod in 1548 at which he discussed them with his fellow-bishops and drew up guidelines aimed at abolishing them. The guidelines read like a preview of the Council of Trent.

Not for nothing was Thomas known as "the almsgiver." Every day several hundred people would come to his door, where they could be given a meal, with wine, and a piece of money. He showed particular concern for poor young brides and for orphans and foundlings (to encourage his porters to keep an eye out for foundlings, he used to give them a crown for every one they brought to him). And in 1550, when pirates ransacked a coastal town near Valencia, he sent fabric for clothing together with money to buy other necessities and to ransom the captives. People occasionally complained that some of those he helped were taking advantage of him. To this he replied: "If there are vagabonds and workshy people here, it is for the governor and prefect of police to deal with them—that is their duty. Mine is to assist and relieve those who come to my door." His generosity was matched by the efforts he made to encourage wealthy people to give too.

As a pastor Thomas was always reluctant to use his authority to pressure or shame people into doing something. Realizing that what he called "inconsiderate use of authority" almost never has the effect desired, he preferred to appeal and persuade. When a theologian and canon lawyer objected to what he regarded as unnecessary delay in dealing with concubinage among the clergy, Thomas said of him: "He is without doubt a good man, but one of those fervent ones mentioned by St Paul [29 June] as having zeal without knowledge.

Is the good man aware of the care I have taken and the pains I have suffered to correct those against whom he fulminates?" On one occasion a priest whom he was rebuking for his behaviour turned on Thomas, delivered himself of some abusive remarks and left in a rage. The chaplains made to go after him, but Thomas stopped them: "It was my fault," he said, "my remonstrances were a little too rough."

Thomas took the same attitude to the *nuevos cristianos*, or *Moriscos*. These were Moors who had converted to Christianity but whose conversion either did not last or was not genuine in the first place. Many of them were harshly treated by the Spanish Inquisition. Thomas was unable to do a great deal for them, but he managed to persuade the emperor to provide financial support for priests who had been designated to work with them, and he founded a college for the children of the newly converted.

Many instances were recorded of Thomas' supernatural gifts, including miracles worked at his intercession both before and after his death. But even more striking than these was his deep spirituality, which expressed itself in constant recourse to prayer. So impressed were his servants that they were reluctant to disturb him while he was praying. He had to order them not to make his visitors wait but to call him as soon as they arrived.

It is not entirely clear why Thomas, like many other bishops, did not attend the Council of Trent, though the most likely reason is that his diocese needed him even more. He was represented by the bishop of Huesca, and the Castilian bishops consulted him before they left. He took the view, which he urged them to put forward, that the Church needed to legislate for internal reform quite as much as it needed to deal with the teachings of Luther. He also made two interesting suggestions, neither of which was acted on though both were typical of his thinking. One was that a benefice involving pastoral work should be filled whenever possible by someone local; the other, that an ancient canon forbidding the movement of bishops from one see to another should be re-enacted. He himself felt a particularly close, almost nuptial, bond with his diocese and a deep anxiety about the way in which he discharged his duties—he even asked leave to resign on several occasions, but this was always refused.

In August 1555 he developed angina. Realizing that he probably did not have much time left, he distributed his money to the poor and all his possessions, apart from his bed, to the rector of his college. The bed he gave to the local prison, but borrowed it back for as long as he should need it. On 8 September Mass was celebrated in his room at his request. He died quietly just after the priest's Communion and was buried, as he had wished, in the church of the Augustinian friars in Valencia. During his lifetime he had been called "the model of bishops," "the almsgiver," "the father of the poor," and a cult grew up soon after his death. An Augustinian friar, Angelo Le Proust, founded the Sisters of St Thomas to continue the work he did for the poor. Thomas was beatified in 1618 and canonized on 1 November 1658 by Pope Alexander VII

(1655-67), who dedicated the parish at Castelgandolfo to him. His relics are now in the cathedral in Valencia.

Spanish spiritual literature was influenced as much by his sermons as by his writings, in both of which he maintained a consistently high standard. He was essentially a pastoral theologian: his writings related to his preaching, which in turn was the fruit of his pastoral work and his prayer. His teaching on Our Lady and on the love of God earned him the title "the Spanish Bernard." Universities have been named after him in Australia, Cuba, and the United States.

AA.SS., Sept., 3, p. 206; 5, pp. 799-992—the material here includes a translation of a Spanish Life by a contemporary, Miguel Salón, who published a first version in 1588 and a second, which uses materials from the canonization process, in 1620. For St Thomas' works see *Opera Omnia* (6 vols., 1881-97); *Sermones de la Vírgen y obras castellanos* (1952). Also P. Jobet, *Evêque des pauvres* (1961); *N.C.E.*, 14, pp. 123-4; *Bibl.SS.*, 12, 591-5; *O.D.S.*, pp. 464-5; *O.D.C.C.*, p. 1771.

In art Thomas is usually shown engaged in some form of practical charity. The earliest painting is by Juan de Juanes, who knew him. Others, of which there are quite a few, include one by José Vergara that hangs in the chapel dedicated to St Thomas in Valencia Cathedral, one by Ribalta, and two by Murillo (one of which is in the Alte Pinacothek, Munich). Yet another belongs to the Stirling Collection in Keir, Scotland.

Bd Frederick Ozanam (1813-53)

By the beginning of the nineteenth century the Ozanam family had long been Christian. They were proud, however, to trace their origins to a Jew, Samuel Hosannam, who had been converted to Christianity by St Didier (Deodatus of Nevers; 19 June) during the seventh century. Anthony Frederick (Antoine-Frédéric) was born in Milan on 23 April 1813, one of the four to survive infancy among the fourteen children of Jean-Antoine Ozanam and his wife, Marie Nantas. Jean-Antoine, who for some time served as an officer in the army of Napoleon, had settled in Milan when he left the army and trained to become a doctor. In 1816, after the fall of the empire, the family moved to Lyons. Here, Frederick, spiritually and intellectually precocious but also, according to his own assessment, moody and headstrong, was educated at the Collège Royal. When he was only fifteen his philosophical studies provoked a serious crisis of faith. The sensitive and intelligent way in which he was guided through this by his professor and mentor, Abbé J.-M. Noirot, left him with strengthened faith and the firm conviction that his life's project must be to dedicate himself to "the service of the truth."

When the Revolution of 1830 broke out, Frederick was studying law, to the satisfaction of his father, who hoped that he would someday become a judge. In the following year he went to Paris, where two crucial things happened. First, he realized that his true interest was not the law but literature and, more specifically, the history of literature. Second, he formed a number of connections that were significantly to affect the course of his life. He had become actively involved in the debates generated by the Revolution, and when he was still only eighteen he published a long article, "Réflexions sur la doctrine de Saint-Simon," in which he denounced the form of liberalism then in vogue, with its belief in limitless human progress and its tendency toward pantheism. This caught the attention of a number of liberal Catholic thinkers that included Félicité de Lamennais, leader of the group, the Dominican Henri-Dominique Lacordaire, and the historian Charles de Montalembert. Other significant friendships made at this time were with the historian François René de Chateaubriand, the poet Alphonse de Lamartine, and perhaps most significant of all, Emanuel Bailly.

Contact with the group that centred round Lamennais enabled Frederick to sharpen his ideas about the nature of freedom—the only true freedom, he came to believe, is that of "a Christian conscience enlightened by a sound philosophy and by revelation"—and about the importance of a historical perspective. In this connection he later lost his intellectual respect for Lamennais. As he saw it, the latter, in contrast to conservative thinkers who failed to recognize the rights of the future, had abandoned the historical perspective and with it the faith of the past. He admired Chateaubriand precisely for the wisdom with which he managed in his thinking to hold past, present, and future in balance. Frederick kept up his contact with all the members of this circle, and he was instrumental in bringing Lacordaire to the pulpit of Notre-Dame so that his Lenten sermons could reach a wider audience.

Contact with Emanuel Bailly brought Frederick's thinking down to earth and gave it a practical focus. He joined the small group of young men that Bailly had been directing since 1819, hoping that they would spearhead a religious renaissance in France, and he was soon avidly discussing the defence of the Christian religion in the context of history, literature, and society. From these discussions he came to understand that Christian commitment is both/ and rather than either/or—that apostolic activity must be informed by sound thinking and sound thinking must lead to action. He is usually thought of as the founder of what came to be known as the Society of St Vincent de Paul, but it is more accurate to describe him as co-founder. He was Bailly's right-hand man and the moving spirit behind the new project, but it involved four other young men besides himself. Although the Society was not formally established, with rules drawn up by François Lallier, until 1835, the first *"conférence de charité"*—so-called in contrast to the *conférences* on political economy and the philosophy of history that Frederick had been helping to organize since 1832—took place on 23 April 1833. Bailly himself remained president for the next eleven years, with Frederick as his vice-president. The society used the method of home visits pioneered by St Vincent de Paul (27 Sept.), and in the early stages members were instructed and supported by a Daughter of Charity, Sr Rosalie Rendu. Sr Rosalie, who was known in Paris as "the mother of the poor," had been working among the poor of the city for thirty years when Frederick met her and probably knew more about their circumstances than he and his companions would ever know. Her role in the foundation of the S.V.P. deserves to be better known.

In 1836, when Frederick had just gained his doctorate in law, his father died. This provoked a crisis for him. Jean-Antoine had been set on his son's pursuing a legal career; the intellectual battles of the age were being fought in the fields of literature in the broad sense, history, and philosophy. It did not take Frederick long to make up his mind: he saw himself as "a missionary of the faith to science and society," and he followed his inclination. He began to study for a doctorate in literature and in 1839 defended his thesis, *Essai sur la philosophie de Dante*. After this he returned to Lyons, where for a year he was professor of commercial law at the university. As an exposition of Catholic social teaching the twenty-fourth lecture of his course looked forward to the encyclical *Rerum novarum* (1891)—and, indeed, to the *Communist Manifesto* (1848). Throughout this period he had flirted with the idea of becoming a priest, but in 1840 he was offered the post of assistant professor of foreign (that is, non-French European) literature at the Sorbonne. Seeing this as a call from God, he moved definitively to Paris. In June 1841 he married Marie-Joséphine (Amalie) Soulacroix, daughter of the rector of Lyons University, with whom he had one daughter, Marie, born in 1845. It was an extraordinarily happy marriage, and although curiously little emerges about Amalie from the standard sources for Frederick's life, her love and loyalty undoubtedly helped to make his work possible. In addition to his university commitments (he succeeded to the chair of foreign literature in 1844), to the lectures he gave at the Cercle Catholique, and to his regular visits to the poor, Frederick maintained at home an open-door policy for his students. This would have been difficult, to say the least, without the unstinting support of his wife. He was much loved by the students, who were inspired as much by his enthusiasm as by his intellectual and moral integrity. A moderate and wise man, he was well aware of the difficulties involved in living the Christian life, and he admitted that he himself had to struggle against arrogance, impatience, and constraining perfectionist tendencies.

Alongside his active work, there was his writing. Frederick was familiar with the classical languages as well as with Hebrew and Sanskrit, and of the modern languages he was proficient in German, English, Spanish, and Italian, especially Italian. This opened up to him a huge world of literature, which he linked, as always, to the history of Christianity. In 1846, he told a friend that his plan was to write "a literary history of the Middle Ages from the fifth century to Dante." But, he added, "in studying literature I shall be studying above all the work of Christianity." His early death meant that the project was not completed, but what he did finish is wide-ranging enough. There are two volumes on the civilzation of the fifth century and a volume each on pre-

Christian Germany and the Christian civilization of the Franks. Apart from two miscellaneous volumes, the remainder are devoted to poetry and philosophy: one on the Franciscan poets of thirteenth-century Italy (Amalie translated the *Fioretti* for this volume), one on Dante and Catholic philosophy, and finally one on Dante's *Purgatorio*, in which Frederick was responsible for the translation as well as the editing. Among his smaller works is *Les Deux Chanceliers d'Angleterre* (1835), a double study of St Thomas Becket (29 Dec.) and Francis Bacon.

In 1848, believing that Catholics should play an active part in the creation of a democratic state, he stood for the Partie Populaire against Louis Philippe. He did not win, but Lacordaire successfully contested one of the Marseilles seats. Together they founded *L'Ere Nouvelle* as a conduit for their Christian Socialist ideas—only to become disillusioned when Napoleon III seized power in 1851.

Like many people whose health is not robust but whose physical and especially intellectual energy is considerable, Frederick pushed himself to the limit. By 1850 he knew his condition was incurable, and it was partly for health reasons that he went to Italy in 1853. It was partly, also, to accept membership of the prestigious Accademia della Crusca, which wished to recognize his contribution to Franciscan and Dante studies. While he was there he became a member of the Third Order of St Francis. But on the way back to Paris he collapsed in Marseilles, and it was there that he died on 8 September 1853, surrounded by his family and members of the Marseilles branch of the St Vincent de Paul Society. His body was taken to Paris, where it was buried in the crypt of the Carmelite church near the Institut Catholique.

Frederick Ozanam was beatified by Pope John Paul II in the Cathedral of Notre-Dame in Paris on 22 August 1997. The pope proposed him as a model for laypeople in the Church. "We are struck with admiration," he said, "for all that this student, professor and family man, burning with faith and inventive in charity, was able to accomplish for the Church, for society, and for the poor in the course of a life that ended too soon." Frederick's life was, indeed, tragically short. And yet by the time he died the S.V.P. had spread throughout France and was beginning to take hold abroad, Ireland being one of the first countries (in 1844) to establish a conference. Today the Society has nearly a million members in 132 countries, and women are accepted as members by some conferences.

There are several editions of the *Oeuvres Complètes*; Bd Frederick's letters are in volumes 10 and 11 of the 8th edition (1912-). Studies of his life and work include those by his brother, C. A. Ozanam (1879); K. O'Meara (1876); L. Baunard (1913, Eng. trans., 1925); M. Murphy (1981); A. Fagan (*c.* 1989); J. P. Derum (1995); M. Casey (1997)—this concentrates on the development of the S.V.P. in Ireland. See also *F. Ozanam: le livre du centenaire* (1913); E. Galopin, *Essai de bibliographie chronologique sur Antoine-Frédéric Ozanam* (1933); E. Renner, *The Historical Thought of Frédéric Ozanam* (1959); A. Romero Carranza, *Ozanam et ses contemporains* (1953); A. Foucault, *La Société de Saint Vincent de Paul: Histoire de cent ans* (1933); *Bibl.SS.*, 9, 1329-34; *Dict.Sp*, 11, 1078-84; *N.C.E.*, 10, pp. 847-8; *O.D.C.C.*, p. 1206; A. Latham-Koenig, "Gentle servant of the poor," in *The Tablet*, 23 Aug. 1997.

A black slave in sixteenth-century Spain.
See St Peter Claver, facing page.

9

ST PETER CLAVER (1580-1654)

Peter (in Spanish, Pedro) Claver was born, probably on 25 June 1580, into a profoundly Christian working-class family at Verdú in Catalonia. Having graduated with distinction from the Jesuit-run university of Barcelona, he received minor orders. But in 1601 he decided that what he really wanted to be was a Jesuit and in that year was accepted into the novitiate at Tarragona, making his first vows on 7 August 1602. From Tarragona he was sent in 1605 to the college of Montesión at Palma in Majorca, where the person who had the greatest lasting influence on him was the college porter, St Alphonsus Rodriguez (30 Oct.). It was Alphonsus who, apart from serving as a model of holiness for the young scholastic, inspired him with the idea of going as a missionary to serve in the colonies of the New World.

When Peter first offered to go, he was told by the provincial that his future would be decided in due course by his superiors. Then, in 1610 when he had finished his theological studies in Barcelona, he was chosen to represent the province of Aragon on a mission of Spanish Jesuits that was going to New Granada. In April 1610 Peter left Spain—forever as it turned out—and after a difficult journey landed with his companions at Cartagena in what is now Colombia. From there he went first to the Jesuit house at Santa Fé de Bogotá to complete his theological studies and work as sacristan, porter, infirmarian, and cook; and then on to the house at Tunja, where he did his tertianship. In 1615 he returned to Cartagena, where he was ordained to the priesthood on 19 March 1616. It was then that he embarked on the work among the slaves that was to become his life's mission.

By this stage the slave trade was already well established. Monarchs such as the emperor Charles V (1516-56), who saw a profit in it, encouraged it, and despite opposition not a few moralists condoned it. In the Americas it received a new impetus when people realized that Africans were physically better fitted than the local Indians for work in the gold and silver mines. The traders would buy them in West Africa for four crowns a head and then transport them across the Atlantic in indescribably foul and inhuman conditions. Although a third of all the slaves on any given ship used to die during the six- or seven-week voyage, some ten thousand living slaves would arrive each year, Cartagena and Vera Cruz being the most important ports of entry. And they continued to arrive, even though authorities from Pope Paul III (1534-49) onward had condemned the trade as a great crime. All most slave-owners did in response to this was to have their slaves baptized, after which they carried on as before. Since the slaves received no instruction and no priest ministered to them, while their conditions remained as cruel and comfortless as before, Baptism became identified in their minds with oppression. The clergy were more or less powerless. They could protest and they could minister to the odd individual, but they had no money at their disposal and tended to find themselves dismissed by the owners and ignored by the slaves.

When Peter first went to work among the slaves he did so under the guidance of Alfonso de Sandoval. This great Jesuit missionary, who had himself already been involved in this apostolate for forty years, in 1627 published *Naturaleza, policía sagrada i profana, costumbres i ritos, disciplina i catecismo evangélico de todos Etiopes* as a distillation of his experience. He was a great source of inspiration for Peter, who, after working alongside him for a while described himself as "Petrus Claver, *Aethiopum servus*"—slave of the Africans. So total was his dedication that when the time came for his final profession in 1622 he wanted to add an extra vow to this effect.

Although he was shy and somewhat lacking in self-confidence, Peter threw himself heart and soul into the work, which he approached with method and organization. Paying with money, goods, or services, he built up teams of assistants and was there, ready and waiting, whenever a slave ship entered the port.

The scene that followed the disembarkation of the slaves was truly horrible—so horrible, in fact, that even someone as experienced as Alfonso de Sandoval never got used to it. Hundreds of human beings, most of them ill, some of them dying, who had for the last several weeks been shut up in unspeakable conditions in the ship, were now herded together in a confined space and ogled by the crowds (Alfonso de Sandoval described the latter as "idle gazers drawn thither by curiosity and careful not to come too close"). It was into these crowded yards or sheds that Peter went, taking with him comfort in the form of medicines, food, brandy, lemons, and tobacco. Although many of the slaves were too frightened or too ill to accept what he offered, Peter felt that this was the right approach. "We must speak to them with our hands," he would say, "before we try to speak to them with our lips."

Many of the clergy decided that their own ignorance of the African languages exempted them from the task of introducing the slaves to the gospel and offering them instruction in the truths of the Faith. Not so Peter. He made attempts to learn Angolan, since so many of the slaves came from there, and for the rest went in with teams of interpreters (one of whom was fluent in four African languages). He would immediately baptize any who were dying, as well as any babies born during the voyage, and then turn to the physical and spiritual needs of the rest.

Because of the language difficulty he made much use of pictures to put across the Christian message and above all to restore the slaves' self-respect by giving them some idea of themselves as individuals with dignity and worth. Some of these pictures were his own, but he also used the 161 illustrations in Bartolomeo Ricci's *Vita Domini Nostri Jesus Christi*, which had been published in Rome in Italian and Latin in 1607. It cannot have been easy to instill a sense of contrition and repentance in people so abused. Peter nevertheless set out to convince them, individually and collectively, that they were loved even more than they were abused, and that the God of love should not be offended by cruel or licentious behaviour. It was an uphill struggle from every point of view—apparently they did not even find the concept of names easy, and Peter took to baptizing them in groups of ten and giving them all the same name so that they could remember it. But he was endlessly patient, and within the difficult framework he not only baptized them but taught them how to use the sacrament of Penance. He is said to have heard the Confessions of more than five thousand slaves in a single year, and in the course of forty years to have instructed and baptized more than 300,000.

Once the slaves had been sold they were taken off to the mines or the plantations, and that was generally the last Peter saw of most of them. He trusted that God would take care of them, but at the same time he refused, naïvely in the eyes of some, to accept that their owners were irredeemable monsters of wickedness. He believed that they too had souls to save. Appealing to their better nature, he would urge them, for their own sake as well as for that of the slaves, to deal justly with them within the unjust framework. Had he known the reality of what went on once the slaves were out of his sight he would probably have been disappointed, though only the worst of the Spanish owners compared for cruelty with their later English counterparts in the Caribbean.

One significant difference between the two systems was that Spanish law allowed slaves to marry and forbade the splitting up of families. Peter did everything in his power to make sure that the law was obeyed. Every spring, after Easter, he would visit plantations within striking distance of Cartagena in order to see how his Africans were getting on. During these missions he would avoid as far as possible the hospitality of the owners, preferring to share the accommodation of the slaves. Not unexpectedly, he sometimes met with hostility. The owners complained that he wasted the slaves' time; their wives complained that they could not enter the church after the slaves had been to Mass; everyone blamed him if the slaves misbehaved. He would sometimes ask himself what sort of person he could be when his attempts to do a little good caused such confusion. But he persevered, even when the church authorities seemed to take the side of the owners against him.

Many accounts of Peter's heroism relate to his care of the sick, some though by no means all of them slaves, in circumstances that almost no one else, black or white, could stomach. There were two hospitals in Cartagena. St Sebastian's, served by the Brothers of St John of God, was for general cases. That of

St Lazarus was specifically for lepers and sufferers from St Anthony's Fire (erysipelas). Peter visited both every week, ministering to the physical as well as the spiritual needs of the patients. In the spirit of the times he was particularly concerned for the spiritual welfare of the Protestant traders, sailors, and others he came across in the course of his hospital work. He made a number of converts to Catholicism among them, including, it seems, an archdeacon of London. His efforts with the Muslims were less successful, but he did make some converts among them, including one man who held out for thirty years until he was convinced by a vision of Our Lady. Peter was also in demand in the prisons, where he would spend time both with criminals who were awaiting execution and with ordinary prisoners, listening to their stories, reproving them, consoling them, and absolving them.

His work with Protestant sailors and traders in the hospitals led eventually to a regular autumn mission directed at all the traders and seamen who landed at Cartagena in great numbers at that time of year. He would stand for hours in the great square of the city preaching to any who would listen to him, in this way becoming the apostle of Cartagena as well as of the slaves. Few have carried on their work in such repellent circumstances, but he made light of his tolerance. That he was willing to overlook the foulest manifestations of wretchedness and disease in order to help their human victims he put down to lack of sensibility. "If being a saint consists in having no taste and a strong stomach," he once said, "I admit I may be one."

In 1650 Peter, who was by now about seventy, went to preach that year's jubilee among the Africans along the coast. He had not been there long when he fell ill and was recalled to Cartagena. In his weakened state he was the first of the Jesuits there to succumb to a virulent epidemic of the plague which spread rapidly through the city, and it seemed as though he was going to die. After receiving the Last Sacraments he did recover, but physically he was broken. For the remainder of his life he was in constant pain, and an uncontrollable tremor made it impossible for him to celebrate Mass. He lived in a state of enforced inactivity, largely neglected by his dwindling community. It is true that they were more than fully occupied in the plague-ridden city, but their indifference is somewhat surprising all the same. Every now and then Peter was strong enough to hear a few confessions—one of his regular penitents was Doña Isabela de Urbina, who through the years had provided generous financial support for his work—or to visit a sick person in prison or hospital. Otherwise he stayed in his cell, where Doña Isabela, her sister, and probably Br Nicholas González visited him when they could. He was looked after by a young Negro who tended to be impatient and rough and frequently ignored him for days on end. The only time the authorities woke up to his existence was when someone reported that he was in the habit of rebaptizing Africans. This was untrue, but he was nevertheless forbidden to baptize in the future. Uncomplaining as ever, he compared himself to the ass: "When he is evilly spoken of he is dumb. When he is starved he is dumb. When he is overloaded he is dumb. When he is despised and neglected he is still dumb. He never complains in any circumstances for he is only an ass. So also must God's servant be."

In 1654 Fr Diego Ramírez Farina arrived from Spain with a commission from the king to work among the slaves. Peter, overjoyed to know that someone else was to carry on his work, dragged himself out to greet his successor. Shortly after this he heard Doña Isabela's confession and told her that would be the last time he would do so. Then on 6 September, after he had been to Mass and received Communion, he warned Br Nicholas Gonzales that he would soon die. That evening he was taken seriously ill and lapsed into a coma. Once word of this spread round the city, people flocked to his cell to kiss his hands and obtain something, however small, in the way of a relic—the cell was soon stripped of everything that might pass as such. Peter never fully regained consciousness and died two days later, on 8 September. The authorities, civil and religious, had regarded his work among the slaves as misplaced enthusiasm and a waste of energy, but now, as so often happens, they competed with one another in honouring his memory. The vicar general of the diocese officiated at the funeral, and Peter was buried with great ceremony at public expense. The Africans and Indians organized a splendid Mass of their own, to which they invited the Spanish authorities.

Word of Peter's life and work spread throughout the world. In 1888, together with his friend and mentor, St Alphonsus Rodriguez, he was canonized by Pope Leo XIII (1878-1903), who named him patron of all missionary activity among Negroes.

There is no fully satisfactory biography, but much valuable material can be found in the depositions obtained during the beatification process, and in A. Astraín, *Historia de la Compañía de Jesús en la Asistencia de España,* 5 (1916), pp. 479-95. The best biography is J. M. Sola, *Vida de San Pedro Claver* (1888). See others by M. D. Petre (1896); J. Charuau (Fr., 1914); A. Lunn (1935); G. Porras Troconis (1954); A. Valtierra (1954); A. Roos (1965). See also: C. C. Martindale *Captains of Christ,* pt. 3; *Bibl.SS.,* 10, 818-21.

St Gorgonius, *Martyr* (date unknown)

According to the Roman Martyrology Gorgonius was an official of the emperor Diocletian in Nicomedia. He and a colleague named Dorotheus were put to death for protesting against the torture of a Christian named Peter. Gorgonius' body was eventually taken to Rome and buried on the via Lavicana (the Martyrology says Latina, but this is a mistake) "between the two laurels." In fact this account, for which the martyrologist St Ado (16 Dec.), followed by Usuard and Baronius, was almost certainly responsible, confuses two different martyrs. The Gorgonius whose body was taken to Rome and who is commemorated on this day was venerated as a martyr from a relatively early date, but that is all we know about him. The earliest document to mention him at all is the *Depositio*

Martyrum, which speaks of *"Gorgoni in Lavicana"* but provides no further information. All the later references agree that he was buried "in Rome, on the via Lavicana, between the two laurels." He was certainly venerated at least until the end of the fourth century, because Pope St Damasus (366-84; 11 Dec.) wrote some verses in his honour.

The confusion—and it is easy to see how it arose—is with another martyr known as Gorgonius of Nicomedia. The latter suffered with several others, including probably Dorotheus and Peter, and he appears in a number of calendars, both Eastern and Western, on 12 March.

The confusion is dealt with in H. Quentin, *Martyrologes historiques*, pp. 613-5. See also *C.M.H.*, pp. 497-8; B. Kirsch in *Ehrengabe Deutscher Wissenschaft für J.G. von Sachsen* (1920), pp. 58-84.

St Audomarus, *Bishop* (*c.* 670)

Several Lives of St Audomarus (more commonly, Omer) have survived. The least unsatisfactory dates from the ninth century and forms a unit with Lives of St Bertinus (5 Sept.) and St Winnoc (6 Nov.). Audomarus was born at Guldindal or at Orval, not far from Coutances, at the beginning of the seventh century. He was possibly an only child, since we are told that his parents devoted all their energies to his upbringing and education. When his mother died he was still in his teens, so he accompanied his father to the monastery of Luxeuil. They received a warm welcome from St Eustace (29 Mar.), who had succeeded St Columba (9 June) as abbot, and were eventually professed together. Twenty or so years later, in about 637, the Frankish king, Dagobert I (629-39), was looking for someone to evangelize the mostly pagan Morini, who lived in the district of Thérouanne. One of their rulers had converted to Christianity in the fourth century, and sees, including Thérouanne and Boulogne, had been created. However, all this had been swept away during the barbarian invasions of the fifth century, and although St Walaricus (1 Apr.), as well as monks from Ireland, had begun to reverse the process, a new missionary thrust was needed. The bishop of Noyon and Tournai, St Achaire, suggested Audomarus, who was immediately approached by the king.

It was not what Audomarus had envisaged for himself—"how great," he wrote, "is the difference between the secure harbour in which I now enjoy calm, and that tempestuous ocean into which I am pushed, against my will and destitute of experience." But he obeyed and, as bishop of Thérouanne, threw himself into his new work. His method seems to have been to revive the faith of the few who had already been baptized and only then to attempt to make new converts. He was evidently successful on both counts, since by the time he left it the diocese was equal to the most thriving in France. His secret appears to have been a combination of eloquent preaching and the example he gave of unstinting service of others—not to mention the help he received from the monks, notably St Bertinus and St Mommolinus (16 Oct.), who were sent out from Luxeuil. Using land on the river Aa given him by a wealthy convert named Adroald, Audomarus enabled them to found the monastery of Sithiu (later Saint-Omer), which became one of the great centres of Christian scholarship in France. He is said to have lost his sight toward the end of his life, but this did nothing to diminish his pastoral concern for his people. Various miracles, none of them very convincing, were attributed to him both before and after his death—for example, that he briefly recovered his sight during the translation of the relics of St Vedast (6 Feb.) to a monastery built in that saint's honour. Most were connected with particular sites.

Audomarus died at Sithiu, where he was buried. His cult spread rapidly, and as so often happened, there was a battle over the relics. The cathedral built in the seventh century on the plain where Audomarus founded Sithiu was the origin of present-day Saint-Omer. As well as Saint-Omer, Pont-Audemer, between Rouen and Caen, is named after him, and the cathedral at Lilliers is dedicated to him.

AA.SS., Sept., 3, pp. 384-417; *Bibl.SS.*, 2, 586-7; *H.S.S.C.*, 4, 217-22. See also N. Huyghebaert, "Du nouveau sur la vie de Saint Omer," in *Bulletin de la Société des antiquaires de Morinie* 18; *Illuminations: Vie de Saint Omer*, Ms.fr. 698, in Bibliothèque Nationale.

St Wulfhilda, *Abbess* (940-*c.* 1000)

Wulfhilda (Wulphida, Wilfrida), who was born in 940, is thought to have been the daughter of a West Saxon nobleman named Wulfhelm. As a young child she was sent to be brought up and educated by Benedictine nuns, and when she was old enough she joined the community. In about 970 Edgar the Peaceful (959-75) appointed her as abbess of the monastery at Barking, which had been founded in the late seventh century by Erkenwald, bishop of London. Under her leadership it flourished and before long had as many as five dependent houses, notably Horton, Shaftesbury, and Wareham. Wulfhilda died in London sometime between 1000 and 1003 and was buried at Barking. She has been confused, principally by Goscelin in his *Vita Wulphidae*, with Wulftruda of Wilton. This is partly because both had a connection with King Edgar, partly because of the similarity of their names.

AA.SS., Sept., 3, pp. 454-60; *Bibl.SS.*, 12, 1360-1; *N.C.E.*, 14, p. 1048; M. Esposito, "La vie de Ste Vulfhilde par Goscelin de Cantorbéry," in *Anal.Boll.* 32 (1913), pp. 10-26; J. L. Tolhurst, *The ordinal and customary of Barking Abbey*, 1 (1927), pp. 297, 308.

Bd María de la Cabeza (? Twelfth Century)

María de la Cabeza is the name that was given to the wife of St Isidore the Farmer (15 May), who lived outside Madrid during the twelfth century. The Life of Isidore written by Juan Egidio de Zamora in the second half of the thirteenth century mentions that he had a wife and a son but tells nothing about either.

The earliest written documentation about María dates from the time at the end of the sixteenth century when her body was discovered outside a hermitage dedicated to Our Lady, on the Jarama River, and the process of beatification began. But the cult, which is much older, dates back to the moment when her skull came to light and was venerated as the relic of a saint at the same hermitage. The name given to her referred to Our Lady and to the fact that her head (*cabeza*) was the venerated relic. There is nothing to tell us for certain what her name was, although according to a popular tradition that survived at least to the end of the sixteenth century it was Toribia. Popular tradition is similarly the only—largely unreliable—source of information about her life and virtues. During the beatification process, which opened in 1615, she was described as a perfect counterpart to her husband. In the same year her remains were moved to Torrelaguna.

AA.SS., May, 3, pp. 550-7; *Bibl.SS.*, 8, 970-2; Baudot et Chausson, 9, p. 189; J. Bleda, *Vida y milagros del glorioso San Isidoro, el Labrador* (1622).

There is also pictorial evidence that María was venerated for herself and not just as Isidore's wife: paintings at Caraquiz, Torrelaguna, Madrid, Uceda, Salamanca, Buitrago, and Canillejas, all of which claimed to be her birthplace.

Bd George Douglas, *Martyr* (1587)

George Douglas was born in Edinburgh and educated in Paris. It is thought that he was also ordained there in about 1560. Challoner clearly doubted that he was a secular priest but was unable to suggest what the alternative might be. "Molanus," he said, "calls him a priest of Doway College; but this circumstance is not found in any other catalogue, nor have I met with his name in the journals of the college." The explanation could be, as others have suggested, that George was a Franciscan. He was hanged, drawn, and quartered in York on 9 September 1587 for persuading the queen's subjects to accept the Catholic faith. He is one of the Eighty-Five Martyrs of England, Scotland, and Wales who are celebrated collectively on 22 November.

M.M.P., p. 125.

Bd Jacques Laval (1803-64)

In 1803, France was still reeling from the effects of the Revolution. It was only ten years since huge numbers of Catholics, especially priests, had been massacred. A concordat had been signed with the Vatican in 1802, but the Church felt uneasy. There was an atheistic, free-thinking spirit in the air, especially in the urban centres, and even the rural areas, where traditionally Catholicism was deeply entrenched, were affected. On 18 September 1803 twin sons, Jacques and Michel, were born at Croth, in the diocese of Evreux in Normandy, to

Jacques Laval, the local mayor, and his wife, Suzanne Délerablée. The Lavals, who already had three daughters, expressed their delight at having a male heir by giving Jacques the second name of Désiré. They had two more children, and then, when Jacques was only eight, Suzanne died, leaving her husband with six children—Michel had died when he was only ten days old. M. Laval married again, and although details of this early part of Jacques's life are hard to come by, it seems that despite his loss and his introspective nature, the next six years were happy ones for him. When he was fourteen he was sent to Tourville-la-Campagne, where his priest uncle, Nicholas Laval, gave him the basis of an education. From there he went on to the minor seminary at Evreux, which was also a secondary school. This was not a success, and he returned home, but he was soon back at his studies again, this time at the Collège Stanislas in Paris. On the advice of his uncle, to whom he had confided his intention to become either a priest or a doctor, he went on from there to the university of Paris to study medicine. He qualified in 1830, but the revolution of that year put an end to his idea of continuing his studies, and before he could return home he had to do his duty as a citizen by helping to man the barricades.

He finally got back to Normandy that September and began to practise, first at Saint-André-de-l'Eure and then, after he had become the victim of a smear campaign, at Ivry-la-Bataille. He is described at this time as tall and slim with one shoulder higher than the other, a birth defect he disguised by careful, elegant dressing; he loved riding, enjoyed a varied social life, and gradually became less observant in the practice of religion. As a doctor he was much appreciated by his patients for his gentleness and thoroughness.

A bad fall from his horse, which he felt should have killed him but which left him with no more than bruises on his legs, led him to reassess his life. On 15 June 1835, after a period of soul-searching, he entered the seminary of Saint-Sulpice in Paris and was ordained three and a half years later, on 2 December 1838. It was while he was at Saint-Sulpice that he first met Francis Libermann, a man of his own age and a Jewish convert to Catholicism who dreamed of founding a new missionary organization. The presence at Saint-Sulpice of two French Creole students, one from La Réunion and one from Haiti, who described the miserable predicament of the slaves on the sugar plantations, gave a shape to Francis' dream and fired Jacques with the desire to become a missionary himself. But he was already thirty-six, and his superior suggested that, rather than go to the Far East, which would have meant learning a new and difficult language, he should wait for an opening in one of the French-speaking colonies.

So in December 1838 the newly-ordained Fr Laval was sent to the country parish of Pinterville, where, as a result of years of neglect, apathy prevailed. For the next two years, less by preaching than by prayer and example, he strove to bring the people back to the practice of their religion. He opened a

84

school, which won him the support of many of the parents; his house was always open, which led the poor to trust him; and he started evening classes, which gave many of the young factory workers a chance to learn to read and write as well as to receive some religious instruction. By the time he learned, in 1840, that Francis Libermann had gone to Rome to present his proposals for a new missionary organization to the pope, Pinterville had a living, active parish community.

Jacques' sense that his moment had come was confirmed in January 1841 when Bishop William Collier, an English Benedictine who was vicar general for Mauritius, came to France looking for French-speaking priests who could come to the island as missionaries. It was eventually decided that Jacques should go to Mauritius as the first missionary of Francis' new Congregation of the Holy Heart of Mary.

With Bishop Collier and four other priests he set sail for Mauritius on 4 June 1841. The originally uninhabited island was explored first, in 1510, by the Portuguese and then, in 1598, by the Dutch. But there was no permanent settlement until the French came in 1721, bringing with them East African slaves to work the sugar plantations they intended to establish. The British, who took the island from the French in 1810, put their Indian servants to work in the plantations. But when Jacques landed at Port-Louis on 14 September 1841, the eighty thousand blacks on the island had only recently obtained their freedom—in 1839, to be precise. He saw the degrading effect on them of the years of slavery, and the difficulties they were experiencing in adjusting to their newfound freedom. Starting with the reality he found in front of him, he would devote himself exclusively to their spiritual welfare for the remaining twenty-three years of his life.

Weathering the governor's prejudice against him as a Frenchman, the total lack of any support from the generally lax priests already on the island, and the resentment of the minority white population at his attempts to nurture the blacks, Jacques looked for ways to enable the latter to believe in their own dignity. He began by setting himself up not in the presbytery but in a small, two-room hut behind the cathedral, the door of which he always left open. As fast as he was able he learned the local patois so that he could instruct them in their own language. He kept all his sermons and the church services as simple as possible. He wrote a simple catechism for them and was soon training catechists to help him with his work. And as at Pinterville, he taught above all by prayer and example. Gradually enthusiasm among the blacks for what he was doing began to spread outside Port-Louis, and not a small number of whites saw his worth and came to his support. Eventually he was able to establish centres for prayer and catechetical instruction throughout the island. It has been estimated that in the end he made about sixty thousand black converts.

Although some of the whites never forgave him for, as they saw it, under-

mining the social structure, the authorities did come to appreciate him. For-
getting their prejudice against the French, they appointed him chaplain to the
prison and the hospital in Port-Louis and were grateful when, during the
cholera epidemics of 1854, 1857, and 1862, he himself set up and organized
hospitals. The cost of all this in terms of his own well being was, inevitably,
enormous, and it is there to be read in the detail of his face in the only
photograph ever taken of him, three years before his death. First of all, there
was the sheer loneliness of it all. He confided in his superiors about this, but he
had been in Mauritius for five or six years before more missionaries arrived.
Then there was the loss of Francis Libermann, who died in 1852, four years
after his Congregation had merged with the Congregation of the Holy Ghost.
And there were the demands he placed on his own body. After 1856 he had a
series of strokes, which permanently weakened him. He was forced to move
into the presbytery and to curtail some of his activities, although the door was
still open to anyone who wanted to see him. Prematurely worn out by his
unremitting hard work, he died on 9 September 1864 at the age of sixty-one.
After the funeral on 11 September, which was attended by forty thousand
people, he was buried in a temporary vault at the church of Sainte-Croix. That
church was destroyed by a cyclone in 1960, but when it was rebuilt Jacques's
remains were placed in a new vault in the grounds, and this is visited by
literally hundreds of people every day. Jacques Laval was beatified during the
first ceremony of its kind presided over by Pope John Paul II, on 29 April
1979.

The most important biography, on which most others are based, is by J. Delaplace (1877;
rev. ed., 1933). Others include T. Bonnefoy (1873); E. Beaupin (1931); L. Lagesse (1955);
P. Christian (1970); J. Fitzsimmons (1973); J. Michel (1976). Pamphlets by E. Cowper(1984);
M. Campion (n.d.). See also Mamet, *Annales du diocèse de Port-Louis, 1926-36*; *Dictionary
of Mauritian Biography*, 8 (1943), pp. 249-50; *Bibl.SS*, 7, 1130.

Bd Francis Gárate (1857-1929)

Francis (Francisco), the second of seven sons, was born on 3 February 1857 at
Azpeitia, in the hills behind San Sebastián in the Basque region of Spain. His
parents were poor, and when he was fourteen he went to work for the Jesuits at
their college in Oduña. Three years later he decided to enter the Society
himself. In normal circumstances the novitiate would have been in Azpeitia
itself. However, because the Jesuits were expelled from Spain in 1868 at the
beginning of a new period of unrest, it had been moved, and he had to travel to
the village of Poyanne, over the border in France. After he had made his
profession as a lay brother on 2 February 1876, he returned to Spain and spent
ten years caring for the sick of the three colleges, one Jesuit-owned, two Jesuit-
run, at La Guardia, on the Galician coast south of Vigo. He gave himself so
unstintingly to his work that in the end his own health began to show the
strain. In 1888, therefore, he was sent to the Jesuit university of Deusto, out-

side Bilbao, where he worked as door keeper for the remaining forty-one years of his life.

Like his patron, that other great Jesuit door keeper, St Alphonsus Rodríguez (30 Oct.), he was constantly attending to other people's needs. Yet, like Alphonsus, he was consistently cheerful, welcoming, and patient. A visiting cardinal asked him how he managed to remain calm when he had so much to attend to. "I do what I can," he replied, "and the Lord, who can do all things, sees to the rest." Francis died on 9 September 1929. The cause for his beatification was introduced in 1950 and he was beatified by Pope John Paul II on 6 October 1985.

A.A.S. 42 (1950), p. 557; J. M. Pérez Arregui, *El Hermano Francisco Gárate* (1935); C. Testori, *Un portinaio santo* (1941); T. Toni, *El Siervo de Dios, Francisco Gárate* (1942). See also J. N. Tylenda, *Jesuit Saints and Martyrs* (1985).

10

St Nemesian and Companions, *Martyrs* (257)

There is some confusion about the identity of this group of martyrs. Earlier editions of the Roman Martyrology mention Nemesian, Felix, and Companions on this day. However, they should perhaps have referred instead to a martyr named Nemesius and his companions who suffered in Alexandria. They are mentioned in the *Hieronymianum* on this day, and Nemesius is probably identical with a martyr who appears as Menmais in the Syriac *breviarium* on 10 September. He and his companions suffered in 257, the first year of the eighth general persecution, ordered by the emperor Valerian (253-60). During this persecution some Christians were tortured and killed immediately, while others were sent to endure hard labour in the quarries first. To comfort and encourage this second group the bishop of Carthage, St Cyprian (16 Sept.), wrote a letter from Curubis, where he had been banished by the proconsul of Africa. Their leader, Nemesian, wrote on behalf of them all to thank Cyprian. His letter, they said, had made it easier for them to bear the terrible conditions in which they were living and the physical torture they had to endure. What is more, his own courage in confessing his faith before the proconsul and accepting banishment had inspired them to persevere. Finally, they asked for his prayers, adding, "Let us assist one another by our prayers, that God and Christ and the whole choir of angels may send us help when we shall most want it." Nine of today's martyrs, all of them bishops, are mentioned by name, but according to Cyprian many priests and deacons and laypeople of all ages and states of life suffered with them.

The text of St Cyprian's letter is in *AA.SS.*, Sept., 3, pp. 483-7. See also *Bibl.SS.*, 9, 798-800; H. Quentin, *Martyrologes historiques*, p. 289.

St Finnian of Moville, *Bishop* (*c.* 580)

Said to have been the son of Cairbre of the royal clan of Dal Fiatach and his wife, Lassara, Finnian (Finnén, Fennin, Vinnin, Wynnin), patron of Ulster, was born in the region of Strangford Lough. His parents may or may not have been Christian, but he was educated first at Dromore by St Colman (7 June), then at Nendrum (on what is now Mahee Island in Strangford Lough), and later at the *magnum monasterium* founded by St Ninian (16 Sept.) at Whithorn in Scotland. He seems to have become involved in some sort of scandal at this double monastery. In order to make a clean break he travelled to Rome, where he was ordained to the priesthood, and then returned to Ulster, bringing with him relics and, possibly, a copy of the Pentateuch and the Gospels in the version of St Jerome (30 Sept.). There is evidence that he preached in several places on his way back, including Anglesey—the church at Llanfinnan is thought to be his foundation. Back in Ireland he founded two monasteries, one at Moville (Maghbile) in Co. Down, the other at Dromin in Co. Louth, at both of which the Celtic monastic tradition was followed.

It is difficult to say anything very detailed or definite about Finnian of Moville. He was referred to as a bishop, for example, but there is no evidence that he was ever consecrated. Nor is it easy to confirm dedications apparently made to him, because he has been confused both with St Frigidian or Frediano (18 Mar.), an Irishman who became bishop of Lucca (some scholars in fact claim that the two are the same person), and with St Finnian of Clonard (12 Dec.). The Penitential of Vinnian is sometimes attributed to him, sometimes to Finnian of Clonard.

The miracle stories likewise appear to add to the confusion. One tells how he altered the course of a river so that it could reach a mill that the monks had built near the monastery. Exactly the same story is told of St Frigidian, which is used in support of their case by those who claim the two men are one and the same. It could equally well be a coincidence, however, since the story is told of several saints and is part of the Scottish hagiographical tradition. According to the *Aberdeen Breviary* Finnian went to Scotland, where he founded a monastery at Holywood (Dumfries) and dedicated a cross to St Brigid (1 Feb.).

Finnian of Moville died in 579 according to the *Annals of Ulster* and the *Chronicon Scotorum*, in 580 according to the *Annals of Innisfallen*. The *Félire* of Oengus adds a further, poetic twist in his entry for this day: "A kingpost of red gold and purity, over the swelling sea he came with law, a sage for whom Ireland is sad, Findbarr of Mag Bile."

See D. P. Pochin Mould, *The Irish Saints* (1964), pp. 169-71; L. Gougaud, *Christianity in Celtic Lands* (rev. M. Joynt, 1992); J. Ryan, *Irish Monasticism* (1931); *Bibl.SS.*, 5, 833-6; *O.D.S.*, p. 180; *K.S.S.*, p. 465.

St Salvius of Albi, *Bishop* (584)

Nearly all we know of St Salvius (Salvy) can be found, with telling detail, in the *Historia Francorum* of his friend St Gregory of Tours (17 Nov.). He was born in Albi, where he trained initially as a lawyer and served for a while as a magistrate. He never married and throughout this time lived with his mother. Soon, however, he abandoned his legal career and joined a monastery on the outskirts of Albi. Temperamentally he was something of a recluse, and on his own admission he carried his austerities to excess. His brethren eventually elected him as their abbot, although he seems to have chosen to spend most of his time in a solitary cell some distance from the rest. This was in part a form of protest against the worldliness of other abbots; his door was always open to his monks and to any layperson who wanted his help or advice. It was at this stage that he fell ill with a violent fever and had what today would be called an out-of-body experience—everyone, himself included, was convinced he had died and been restored to life.

In 574 he was brought from his retreat to become bishop of Albi, but he continued to live as austerely as ever, immediately distributing to the poor anything that was given to him. He travelled frequently within the diocese in order to acquaint himself at first hand with what was going on. His two main challenges were Arianism and paganism. Gregory of Tours relates several incidents from this period, including one in which he and Salvius combined forces to bring King Chilperic of Soissons (561-84), who fancied himself as a theologian, back to orthodoxy—Chilperic had written a treatise in which he adopted the Arian version of the doctrine of the Trinity. When Gregory was accused of calumniating the queen, Fredegond, Salvius intervened successfully on his behalf at a council that was held at Braisne to settle the matter. In 584 an unspecified but serious epidemic, probably the plague, raged through Albi. Ignoring the well-intentioned efforts of his friends to persuade him to look after his own health, Salvius went about the city tending the sick, helping them where necessary to prepare for death, and comforting their families. When, inevitably, he fell ill himself, he ordered his coffin, changed his clothes, and was ready for death when it came on 10 September 584.

He was buried not at Albi but at a monastery that subsequently acquired his name. The fact that more than twenty-five churches in the region were dedicated to him is evidence of a once-thriving cult, as is the existence of such villages as Saint-Salvy de Carcaves (Tarn), Saint-Salvy (Lot-et-Garonne), and Saint-Sanvy (Gers). The iconography is rather uncertain because this Salvius is sometimes confused with St Salvy of Amiens (11 Jan.).

Gregory of Tours, *Historia Francorum*, 5, 44-50, and 7, 1; *AA.SS.*, Sept., 3, pp. 574-9; *Bibl.SS*, 11, 605-7; *F.E.*, 2, p. 43.

St Theodard of Maastricht, *Bishop* (? 670)

What little we know of Theodard is contained in an eighth-century Life, probably by Anselm, a canon of Liège, most of which has to do with his death. This is mentioned for the first time in the mid-tenth-century *Gesta Episcopum Leodiensum*. There is also a second Life by Anselm of Liège and another by Sigebert of Gembloux, but neither adds a great deal to the original. Theodard seems to have come to the region of Maastricht from Gaul sometime during the reign of Clotaire II (613-22). He was probably a disciple of St Remaclus (3 Sept.) and may have spent some time in the monastery at Stavelot while Remaclus was abbot there. Exactly when he became bishop of Tongres-Maastricht is uncertain. It has been suggested that Remaclus was his immediate predecessor, but that is unlikely because Remaclus was a missionary—that is, peripatetic—bishop. Theodard's biographers describe him as a cheerful and sympathetic person who fulfilled his role as bishop with great energy and pastoral concern.

The precise date of his death is not certain. He is mentioned in a document dated 6 September 669 or 670 in which Chilperic II asks him and one of the palace officials to go and measure the property of the double abbey at Stavelot-Malmédy. In any case, it was probably in 670 that a group of local nobles seized some land that belonged to the Church. Theodard decided to go personally to Childeric II of Austrasia (656-75) so that the matter could be settled justly. As he was travelling through the forest of Bienwald, near Speyer, he was attacked by robbers and killed. According to his biographer he made a long speech to his attackers, to which they replied with a quotation from Horace. As he was on his way to defend the rights of the Church, he was venerated as a martyr, and his former pupil and successor, St Lambert (17 Sept.), had his body moved to the church in Liège. His remains, along with those of St Magdelbata, who was eventually buried alongside him, were exhumed on 7 September 1489. A magnificent reliquary in which they were placed is now missing.

For the Life see *AA.SS.*, Sept., 3, pp. 588-99. See also J. Chapeauville (ed.), *Gesta Episcopum Leodiensum* (1612), pp. 101-5; G. Kurth, *Etude critique sur St Lambert* (1876), p. 67ff.; L. Van der Essen, *Etude critique et littéraire sur les Vitae des saints mérovingiens de l'ancienne Belgique* (1907), pp. 135-43; J. Demarteau, "Saint Théodard et Saint Lambert (Vies anciennes)," in *Société des Bibliophiles Liégeois*, 30 (1886-90); *Bibl.SS.*, 12, 209-11.

St Aubert of Avranches, *Bishop* (? *c.* 725)

Two things are known for certain about St Aubert: that he was elected bishop of Avranches by popular acclaim and that he founded the famous church of Mont-St-Michel. According to his legend he had a vision of St Michael the Archangel, who told him to build a church on Le Rocher de la Tombe, just round the coast from Avranches. In trying to carry out this command he met with every sort of unexpected obstacle, and it was not until he had received two further visitations from St Michael and a divine rebuke for his lack of determination that the project was completed. The church was finally dedicated in 709 in honour of St Michael for those in peril from the sea. Two things remain unclear: when the church was built, as opposed to dedicated, and when Aubert became bishop of Avranches. The evidence is contradictory. In the list of bishops of Avranches he appears before Rahentrannus, who lived in the middle of the seventh century. On the other hand, his vision of St Michael is said to have taken place during the reign of one of the Childeberts. If that is true, he could have been active in the sixth century under Childebert II, who died in 595, or in the seventh and eighth centuries under Childebert III (695-711). The church itself was originally placed in the care of a chapter of canons, but they were replaced in the ninth century by monks, who built the abbey. On 16 October, the traditional anniversary of the dedication of the church, a feast of St Michael in Monte Tumba is celebrated in the diocese of Coutances and in St Michael's Abbey, Farnborough.

See *AA.SS.*, June, 3, pp. 603-4. Also Motet in *Mém. Soc. archéol. d'Avranches* (1847), p. 28ff.; C. Claireaux, *Les reliques de S. Aubert* (1909).

St Nicholas of Tolentino (1245-1305)

With Nicholas of Tolentino, as with not a few saints of this period, it is not easy to get behind the wonder-worker presented by the available sources to the flesh-and-blood individual. There is a contemporary Life by Pietro di Monte Rubiano, and further information comes from the beatification process, during which people went out of their way to give examples of his holiness and charity. Unfortunately none of this contemporary or more or less contemporary material has been treated very critically by later writers.

Nicholas (in Italian, Nicola) was born to Compagnone dei Guarutti and Amata dei Guidiani (or Gaidani) at Castel Sant'Angelo, near Fermo, in the March of Ancona, in 1245. His parents, and particularly his mother, regarded him as an answer to prayer. They had been happily married for many years but still had no children when they made a pilgrimage to the shrine of St Nicholas (6 Dec.) at Bari. While she was there, his mother begged God for a son who would serve him faithfully. She duly conceived, and she and her husband seem to have imbued the child, who was named Nicholas after his patron, with a strong religious sense. It is even said that as a child he would go to pray in a small cave outside the town in imitation of the hermits then common in the Apennines, though this is probably a hagiographical gloss. He was certainly still a boy when he became an oblate with the Augustinian friars in Castel Sant'Angelo. As soon as he was old enough he joined the community, and he was professed in 1263 just before his eighteenth birthday.

He studied grammar and logic in Tolentino and in Cíngoli before going on to do his theological studies at the friary in San Ginésio. Here his main non-academic task was to distribute food to the poor who gathered each day at the gate. His liberal interpretation of this assignment maddened the procurator, who decided he was being far too generous with the resources of the monastery and reported him to the prior. But it was also during this period that miracles were first attributed to him—a sick child was cured when Nicholas placed his hands on its head and said, "The good God will heal you."

Nicholas was ordained at Cíngoli in 1269 by the bishop of Osimo, St Benvenuto (22 Mar.). Here again he acquired a reputation as a healer after an incident similar to the one with the sick child, only this time a blind woman was healed. But he did not stay long. For the next four years he moved from one friary to another, including that of Sant'Elpidio, where for a short time he was novice-master. Then in about 1275 he visited a relative who was prior of a monastery near Fermo. This monastery was more affluent and distinctly more comfortable that the friaries with which he was familiar, and when the prior invited him to extend his stay, Nicholas, attracted by the idea, seems to have experienced a crisis of conscience. This was resolved while he was praying in the monastery chapel by an inner voice which seemed to be saying, "To Tolentino, to Tolentino. Persevere there." Shortly after this he was indeed sent to Tolentino, where he would remain for the rest of his life.

Tolentino had been a victim of the civil unrest provoked by the rivalry between the pro-papal Guelphs and the Ghibellines, who supported the emperor. The situation called for firm measures, and Nicholas was instructed to start a campaign of street preaching. With the majority of citizens he was an immediate success. The effect of his preaching was later described by St Antoninus (10 May), a fifteenth-century bishop of Florence: "When his superiors ordered him to take up the public ministry of the gospel, he did not try to display his knowledge or show off his ability, but simply to glorify God. Looking at his audience you could see the tears and hear the sighs of people . . . repenting their past lives." Inevitably there were some who remained unmoved by what he had to say and actively opposed him. One man who led a particularly reprobate life consistently tried to shout him down and break up his audiences. But Nicholas refused to be intimidated. Eventually his patient perseverance began to make an impression on the man, who one day, after fencing with his friends in an attempt to distract the crowds, eventually stopped to listen. When Nicholas finished preaching, the man went up to him and apologized and from then on began to change his ways.

This conversion created a great stir in the town, and soon Nicholas found he was having to spend almost the entire day in the confessional. But he also found time to visit the slum areas of Tolentino, where he comforted the sick (whom he sometimes cured) and the dying, counselled married couples, befriended children, and reconciled people who had fallen out with one another. He had a profound understanding of social problems and was constantly reminding the rich of the social function of wealth. With the permission of his superiors he set up a special fund to assist the poor. He would visit the rich only if he was actually invited to do so and then simply in order not to be rude. The poor he was always ready to visit, and he would frequently drop in on them uninvited.

Many people in Tolentino bore witness to the miracles that took place as a result of Nicholas' intercession—his own comment was always: "Say nothing of this. Give thanks to God, not to me. I am only an earthen vessel, a poor sinner." The miracle described by the earlier Bollandists as the most extraordinary attributed to him was recorded by an Augustinian friar, Jordan of Saxony, who wrote a Life of Nicholas in about 1380. Jordan tells how a man was waylaid by his enemies in the hills near Padua. Ignoring his pleas for mercy, or at least for a priest to hear his confession, they killed him and threw his body in a lake. A week later a man wearing the Augustinian habit recovered the body and led the man back, alive and seemingly well, to his family. But as soon as he had spoken to a priest, who gave him the Last Sacraments, he died again, this time receiving Christian burial.

Several of the other miracle stories relate to the Augustinian custom of blessing and distributing bread on Nicholas' feast-day. In his later years, when he was already weakened by chronic illness, his superior encouraged him to take meat and other body-building foods. Nicholas was caught between genuine desire to obey and reluctance to give in to his body. One night Our Lady seemed to be present to him. She told him he would recover if he asked for a small piece of bread, dipped it in water and ate it. After that he used to do the same for the sick he visited. Not all his alleged miracles were mentioned during the process of beatification, but in the end the tribunal accepted about thirty as authentic. All were done to relieve some manifestation of human misery, and all, according to witness, were accompanied by prayer.

But Nicholas' claim to holiness is not based solely on his miracles. His spirituality was based on the Augustinian virtues of obedience, humility, and poverty, which he practised simply, constantly, and self-effacingly. The qualities that the people of Tolentino observed and loved in him were his kindness, his joyfulness, and his unfailing good humour.

Nicholas' last illness lasted nearly a year, but he managed to hide it from the people. Toward the end, however, he was unable to get up at all, except once. On that occasion he went to hear the confession of a man who had committed a serious sin, which, Nicholas realized, he would not confess to anyone but himself. He died peacefully on 10 September 1305. A commission was immediately set up to gather evidence about his heroic virtue and the miracles attributed to him, but its work was interrupted by the transfer of the papacy to Avignon in 1309. Nicholas of Tolentino was eventually canonized in 1446, and from the sixteenth century on his cult spread throughout Europe.

Pietro di Monte Rubiano's Life, together with other material, is in *AA.SS.*, Sept., 3, pp. 636-743. More recent biographies include P. Giorgi, *Vita del taumaturgo S. Niccolo da Tolentino* (1856-9); two in French by A. Tonna-Barthet (1896) and "H. P." (1899); a short English one by E. A. Foran (1920); an Italian one by N. Concetti (1932); D. Gentili, *Un asceta e un apostolo, San Nicola da Tolentino* (1978); P. Trape, *San Nicola da Tolentino, un contemplativo e un apostolo* (1985). A sort of periodical entitled *Sesto centenario di San Nicola da Tolentino* (1899-1905) throws light on the cult of the saint. See also N. Occhioni (ed.), *Il processo per la canonizzazione di San Nicola da Tolentino* (1980); *Bibl.SS.*, 9, 953-68; *H.S.S.C.*, 7, pp. 190-6.

In art he is shown, frequently in the company of other saints, with a star on his breast and with a lily, a rule book, and a cross or crucifix. There are no less than five representations of him in the National Gallery in London, all dating from the sixteenth century, when his cult began to expand; those elsewhere include one in the Museo Poldi Pezzoli in Milan by Piero della Francesca (*c.* 1420-95). In the basilica of St Nicholas in Tolentino there is a cycle of scenes from his life by the Master of Tolentino. On the iconography see A. Anselmi, *Iconografia classica di San Nicola da Tolentino* (1906); G. Kaftal, *Iconography of the Saints in Central and South Italian Paintings* (1965); Jöckle, pp. 337-8.

St Ambrose Barlow, *Martyr* (1585-1641)

Edward Barlow was born at Barlow Hall near Manchester in 1585, the fourth of the fourteen children of Sir Alexander Barlow and his wife. He seems to have conformed briefly to the Church of England, but in 1607 he returned to the Roman Catholic Church and went to study at the English College in Douai. Returning to England, he spent a year in prison, though for what reason we do not know. On his release he returned to France and applied to enter the English Benedictine abbey of St Gregory in Douai, where his brother Dom Rudesind was prior. He received the habit, taking the name Ambrose, and in 1617 was ordained to the priesthood. After his ordination he joined the English mission, going to work in his native Lancashire.

For the next twenty-four years Ambrose worked in the vicinity of Manchester and Liverpool, his base being Morleys Hall in the parish of Leigh. He worked hard and discreetly to bring the Mass and the sacraments to the Catholics of the area, many of whom left in writing their impressions of him. One notes "his great zeal in the conversion of souls and the exemplary piety of his life and conversation." Another mentions in particular his simple way of life: "Although God had put into his hands (as I think) enough wherewithal to have played the housekeeper [he had a stipend of £8 a year], he chose rather to subject himself, and become a sojourner with a poor man and his wife, to avoid thereby . . . distracting solitude and dangerous dominion, and to expose sensuality to be curbed with the simple provision of poor folks." A third paints the portrait of an attractive personality: "He was so mild, witty and cheerful in his conversation that of all men that ever I knew he seemed to me the most likely to represent the spirit of Sir Thomas More [22 June]."

In 1628 Ambrose took the Last Sacraments to St Edmund Arrowsmith (28 Aug.), who was in prison awaiting execution. According to Challoner, after his death Edmund appeared to Ambrose in a dream and told him: "I have suffered and now you will be made to suffer. Say little, for they will endeavour to take hold of you by your words." For thirteen years Ambrose lived in constant anticipation of that moment. He was taken and imprisoned on four occasions, but each time they let him go. Then in March 1641 Charles I (1625-49), under extreme pressure from Parliament, signed a bill which decreed that any Roman Catholic priest who did not leave the country would be arrested and treated as a traitor. At about the same time Ambrose suffered a stroke, which left him partially paralyzed.

Six weeks after Charles signed the bill, the vicar of Leigh celebrated Easter by arming his congregation and leading them to Morleys Hall. Ambrose had just finishing celebrating Mass and was preaching to his congregation. They seized him, set him on a horse with a man behind him to prevent his falling off, and took him with an escort of sixty to a justice of the peace. The latter had him imprisoned in Lancaster Castle, where he remained without trial for four months. Finally he was brought before a magistrate, to whom he acknowledged that he was a priest. When he was asked why he had not complied with the new law, he pointed out that it specified Jesuits and seminary priests, whereas he was neither, and that in any case he had recently had a stroke and was not able to travel. The magistrate then asked him his opinion of the penal laws, to which Ambrose replied that he thought them both unjust and barbaric. The magistrate, surprised by his outspokenness but nevertheless impressed, offered to free him if he would undertake "not to seduce the people any more." "I am no seducer," Ambrose told him, "but a reducer of the people to the true and ancient religion. . . . I am in the resolution to continue until death to render this good office to these strayed souls."

On 3 September the English Benedictine Congregation chose him to succeed his brother Rudesind as titular cathedral prior of Coventry, but on the 8th he was condemned to death. On Friday 10 September he was taken from the castle on a hurdle to the place of execution, where he was hanged, drawn, and quartered. His skull is preserved at Wardley Hall in Lancashire, now the episcopal residence of the diocese of Salford; his left hand is at Stanbrook Abbey, near Worcester. St Ambrose Barlow is one of the Forty Martyrs of England and Wales, who are commemorated collectively on 25 October.

M.M.P., pp. 392-400; B. Camm, *Nine Martyr Monks* (1931), pp. 258-92; *The Apostolical Life of Ambrose Barlow* (ed. W. E. Rhodes, Chetham Miscellanies, 2; 1909, Chetham Society, 83); J. Stonor, *Ambrose Barlow* (pamphlet, 1961); *N.C.E.*, 2, p. 101; *O.D.S.*, p. 38; G. Scott, O.S.B., "Three Seventeenth-Century Benedictine Martyrs," in D. H. Farmer (ed.), *Benedict's Disciples* (1995), pp. 266-82.

11

SS Protus and Hyacinth, *Martyrs* (date unkown)

Although we do not know for certain when they died, these martyrs are mentioned in the fourth-century *Depositio martyrum* as well as in early sacramentaries, including the Gelasian Sacramentary, and in the Naples calendar of stone. The fact of their martyrdom is indisputable, and their ancient cult was definitively confirmed in 1845. In that year Giuseppe Marchi, S.J., found the undisturbed burial place of Hyacinth in the cemetery of Basilla on the Old Salarian Way. The slab that closed the niche bore the inscription: *DP III Idus Septebr/ Yacinthus/Martyr* (Hyacinth Martyr, buried 11 September). The niche itself contained charred bones, which suggests that he was burned to death. Close by was another inscription: *Sepulcrum Proti M* (the tomb of Proteus M[artyr]) but no remains. Pope St Damasus (366-84; 11 Dec.) in an epitaph for the two men referred to them as brothers, a conclusion to which he may have jumped simply because they were buried close to each other. St Jerome (30 Sept.) simply describes them as "teachers of the Christian law." It is thought that Pope St Leo IV (847-55; 17 July) brought the remains of Proteus, which are now in the church of San Giovanni dei Fiorentini, into Rome in the middle of the ninth century; those of Hyacinth were translated to the church of the Urban College in Rome in 1849 and are now in the college of Propaganda Fide.

In sharp contrast to the simplicity of the inscriptions and the events to which they refer are the *acta* of St Eugenia (25 Dec.). Following a tradition that has eunuchs in the service of women—see also SS Calogero and Partenio (19 May) and SS John and Paul (formerly 26 June)—this elaborate fiction makes the eunuch brothers Protus and Hyacinth Eugenia's slaves and parties to her bizarre adventures. This apart, there is evidence that from an early date Protus and Hyacinth enjoyed a widespread cult: they are mentioned in the Old English martyrology as well as in the martyrology of Bede, and in the Sarum calendar. It is also likely that St Pratt's church in Blisland, Cornwall, is dedicated to St Protus.

See *AA.SS.*, Sept., 2, pp. 746-62; *C.M.H.*, pp. 501-2; G. Marchi, *Monumenta delle arti cristiane primitive* (1844); *Bibl.SS*, 10, 1221-3; *O.D.S.*, p. 408. The question of the dedication of St Pratt's church is discussed in *Anal.Boll.* 69 (1951), p. 443.

SS Protus and Hyacinth are among those whose deaths are depicted in the menology of St Basil in the Vatican Library; they appear full length in the mosaics in the basilica of Sant'Apollinare Nuovo in Ravenna; and in the mosaic medallions in the Capella Palatina in Palermo Protus is shown with a beard, Hyacinth clean-shaven.

97

St Paphnutius, *Bishop* (*c.* 350?)

At least one calendar mentions more than one St Paphnutius on this day, and it is generally agreed that they are different people. The principal sources for details regarding this one are the *Historia Ecclesiastica* of Rufinus and Eusebius' *Martyrs of Palestine*. He is said to have been an Egyptian who spent some years in the desert under the direction of St Antony (17 Jan.) before being made bishop of the Upper Thebaid. During the persecution of Maximinus (308-13) he, like many other Christians, was blinded in one eye and made lame in one leg and then sent off to work in the mines. When the persecution was over, he returned to his diocese bearing the marks of his sufferings. He was distinguished for his personal holiness and for his tireless defence of the orthodox faith against the Arians, and as someone who had continued to profess his faith in the face of persecution he was one of the outstanding figures at the Council of Nicaea in 325.

There are scholars who question its authenticity, but it is widely accepted that his main contribution at the council was to the debate on clerical celibacy. Many of the bishops wanted to introduce a general ruling that would have meant that bishops, priests, deacons, and subdeacons would have had to separate from wives they had married before their ordination. Paphnutius strongly opposed the motion, saying that the ancient ruling that forbade clerics to marry after ordination was enough. He reminded the council fathers that marriage is its own form of chastity and begged them not to impose the burden of separation on clerics and their wives. In the end he carried the council with him, and to this day in the Orthodox Churches married men may be admitted to all orders below the episcopate, and they may continue to live with their wives.

Paphnutius always remained in close contact with other orthodox bishops, especially St Athanasius, the great bishop of Alexandria (2 May), whom he, along with other Egyptian bishops, accompanied to the Council of Tyre in 335. When they arrived they quickly realized that most of the participants were professed Arians. Paphnutius was particularly concerned to see Maximus, bishop of Jerusalem, who had suffered as he had himself in the recent persecution, taking his seat among them. Gently, he took Maximus aside and told him that to see a man who still bore the marks of his suffering in defence of the Faith being led by men who denied one of the central tenets of that faith was more than he could bear. Maximus was so moved by this appeal that he took his seat among the supporters of Athanasius, to whom he remained loyal.

No one knows exactly when Paphnutius died, although it is likely to have been in about 350. There is no evidence of a cult, either in the East or in the West, until Baronius introduced him into the Roman Martyrology in the sixteenth century.

Rufinus of Aquileia, *Historia Ecclesiastica* (ed. F. Schwartz and T. H. Mommsen), 2 (1908), p. 963; Eusebius, *The Martyrs of Palestine*. See also *AA.SS.*, Sept., 3, pp. 778-87, which brings together material from a number of sources; *Bibl.SS.*, 10, 35-7; *D.C.B.*, 4, p. 185. On the authenticity of St Paphnutius' pronouncement on celibacy see *D.T.C.*, 2, 2078.

SS Felix and Regula, *Martyrs* (? Fourth Century)

The facts round which the legend of these saints was woven are few and disputed. Sometime before the beginning of the ninth century a double monastery was built over their tomb in Zurich, and there are records to show that this was generously endowed by Louis the German (843-76) in 853. Their relics were identified in the ninth century, and their cult flourished in Switzerland and elsewhere until the Reformation. Early in the twentieth century a number of scholars suggested that Felix and Regula were North African saints, whose cult in Zurich was the result of a translation of relics. This argument was effectively disposed of on the ground that there is no documentary evidence to support it.

According to the legend which grew up around them Felix and Regula were a brother and sister who followed the Theban Legion (22 Sept.) into the Valais. They managed to survive the massacre by fleeing into the mountains and making their way first to Glaruns and then on to Zurich. There they were beheaded for their faith sometime during the persecution of Decius (248-51). From the thirteenth century a third figure, their servant Exuperantius, begins to feature in the legend.

AA.SS., Sept., 3, pp. 772-3; L. Burgener, *Helvetia Sancta*, 1 (1860), p. 180ff. The best survey of all the problems is E. Egloff, *Wer hat das Christentum nach Zürich gebracht?* (1948). See also *Bibl.SS.*, 5, 594-6; H. Roeder, *Saints and Their Attributes* (1955), p. 74.

The iconography is interesting. The first known representation is a twelfth-century bas-relief on the Grossmünster in Zurich. Felix and Regula are shown together, with palm branches as a symbol of their martyrdom. Later, when Exuperantius has joined them, the symbolism is more graphic. They are shown as *cefalophori*, carrying their heads as a sign that they were beheaded. The seal of the city of Zurich (1225), now in the Landesmuseum there, is a fine example of this, as is a sixteenth-century painting, also in the Landesmuseum, by Hans Leu the Elder.

St Patiens of Lyons, *Bishop* (*c.* 480)

There is no ancient Life of St Patiens, but information is provided by Sidonius Apollinaris (21 Aug.), Gregory of Tours (17 Nov.), and others. He was born into one of the more influential families in Lyons and sometime before 450 succeeded Eucherius as bishop there. Sidonius, a personal friend with whom he exchanged letters, described him as "a holy, active, ascetic and compassionate man" with a particularly balanced attitude to life and a great love for the poor. Besides making sure that the latter had enough to eat, he seemed always to have enough money to build and repair churches—according to one source it was he who completed the great church of St Etienne in Lyons.

During the thirty years Patiens spent as bishop of Lyons, from about 450 to about 480, Gaul was under attack from the Goths, and the times were violent, confused, and difficult. When their incursions led to a serious famine between 472 and 475, Patiens is said to have fed thousands of needy people at his own expense. He also had great scope for his pastoral zeal. The Arian heresy had made serious inroads in the region around Lyons—even some bishops had been seduced by it—so he worked tirelessly through his preaching and his practical charity to bring people back to the orthodox faith. His influence went beyond his own diocese. He took part in various councils, for example, including that of Arles in 474, and when the bishop of Chalons-sur-Saône died, the bishop of Autun called him in to mediate in the dispute that arose over the succession. He is also known to have found time to write, and his surviving works include a book on church dogmatics and a number of sermons. The Life of St Germanus of Auxerre (3 Aug.) by Constantius, one of the priests of the Lyons diocese, was written at Patiens' request and is dedicated to him. The exact date of his death is not known, but it was certainly before 494 and probably much earlier. He was buried in the church of Saint-Juste.

The *Epistolae* of Sidonius Apollinaris are in *P. L.*, 58, 486,532, 560-4. *AA.SS.*, Sept., 3, pp. 791-7. For Gregory of Tours, see *Historia Francorum*, 2, 24 and 71, 221. See also S. L. Tatu, *St Patient, évêque de Lyon* (1878); *F.E.*, 2, p. 163; *Bibl.SS.*, 10, 426-7.

St Deiniol, *Bishop* (*c.* 584)

Relatively little detail has survived about this once popular saint, who was known in Wales as Deiniol Wyn (Blessed Daniel). The principal source is the *Legenda novem lectionum de S. Daniele, episcopo Bangorensi*, copied from an ancient manuscript by Sir Thomas Williams of Trefriw in 1602. Deiniol was believed to be a descendant of Coel Godeborg, a Celtic chieftain from northern Britain, but most of his activity seems to have been in Wales. It was he who established the monastery of Bangor Fawr on the Menai Strait, which formed the nucleus of the medieval diocese of Bangor. Bede described it as the most famous monastery in the British church, and in its heyday it had more than two thousand monks. Before that Deiniol, together with his brothers, is said to have been a disciple of St Cadoc (23 Sept.) at Llancarfan. Cadoc sent them to found the monastery of Bangor Iscoed on the river Dee in Clwyd. Daniel was later regarded as first bishop of Bangor (Gwynedd)—thus earning for himself the sobriquet "Daniel of the Bangors." Sources differ on the matter of who consecrated him bishop, the three candidates being St Dyfrig (14 Nov.), St Teilo (9 Feb.), and St David (1 Mar.). The latter is supposed to have sent him into Gaul to counter a resurgence of Pelagianism, and Pelagianism may have reared its head again in connection with the synod at Llandewi Brefi, though it is more likely that this concentrated on penitential discipline. According to Rhygyfarch, David at first refused to attend the synod, but Deiniol and Dyfrig successfully persuaded him to change his mind, and once he got there "his eloquence swept all before him."

Many of the miracle stories told about Deiniol share the vengeful element characteristic of much Celtic hagiography. When he died in about 584 he was buried on Ynys Ynlli (Bardsey Island). Although his feast is kept on this day in the diocese of Menevia he is mentioned on several dates, and churches dedi-cated to him can be found throughout Wales: in Marchwiail and Worthenbury (Clwyd), for example; at Llanuwchllyn and Llanfor, near Bala; and at a few places in south Wales, including one at Itton, which used to be called Llandeiniol. One of these no doubt inspired the dedication of W. E. Gladstone's library at Hawarden. The cult of St Deiniol was popular in Brittany as well as in Wales.

See R. Rees, *An Essay on Welsh Saints* (1836), p. 258ff.; E. G. Bowen, *The Settlements of Celtic Saints* (1956); *L.B.S.*, 2, pp. 325-31; T. F. Tout in *D.N.B.*, *s.v.* "Daniel"; *Bibl.SS.*, 4, 467-8; *O.D.S.*, p. 130.

St Bodo, *Bishop* (*c.* 670)

Bodo (or Leudovinus) was one of two brother of St Sadalberga (22 Sept.), and less is recorded of him than of her. When she founded a monastery at Laon, he and his wife, St Odile (13 Dec.), are said to have donated a substantial sum of money, which made possible the building of the men's monastery, and then joined the community themselves. This immediately presents certain prob-lems: Odile's legend, which has little value as history, claims that she never married; it also shows a number of close similarities with that of Sadalberga. Whether or not he was married, let alone married to Odile, Bodo did join the community. He later became bishop of Toul and founded three monasteries himself. In the version that says he was married his own daughter, Tietburga, was the first abbess of the one at Bonmoutier (Bodonis Monasterium), near Cirey (Meurthe-et-Moselle). In about 670, when he had been bishop for only about two years, he died. He was buried first in Toul, but later his remains were moved to a place alongside his sister in the abbey church at Laon.

AA.SS., Sept., 3, pp. 521-9. See also *Bibl.SS*, 7, 1350, and 11, 571-3.

Bd Louis of Thuringia (1200-27)

Although his cult has never been officially confirmed, veneration for Louis (in German, Ludwig) was as spontaneous among his people as it was for his more famous wife, St Elizabeth of Hungary (17 Nov.). He was born on 28 October 1200, the eldest son of Herman I, landgrave of Hesse, and his wife, Sophia of Bavaria. When he was eleven he was betrothed to Elizabeth, the four-year-old daughter of the Hungarian king, Andrew I. The two grew up together at the Thuringian court, and in 1221, when Louis succeeded his father, the marriage was ratified. Although it had been arranged for purely political reasons, it was an extraordinarily happy one—they seem in every sense to have grown up together and their devotion was mutual. They had three children, a son,

Herman, and two daughters, Sophia and Gertrude. Gertrude, who was born eighteen days after her father's death, became abbess of Altenberg and was eventually beatified (13 Aug.).

Much of what we know about Louis reaches us through the double prism of his wife and hagiographical exaggeration. He nevertheless had great qualities and comes across as a good, warm-hearted, and generous man with a nice sense of humour and a readiness to adapt and change. On the famous occasion when Elizabeth laid a leper in their bed, his first reaction was anger, but in the next instant he recognized the suffering Christ in the man, and instead of complaining paid for a leper hospital to be built at the foot of the Wartburg hill. While he consistently encouraged Elizabeth's religious devotion and her works of charity, his good-humoured practicality was a necessary foil to her sometimes impractical exuberance. She once suggested that they might serve God better if, instead of a castle and a great estate, they had enough land for one plough and a couple of hundred sheep. To which he laughingly replied that they would hardly be poor with that much land, and many would say they were too well off.

Louis was a strong and committed ruler who personally championed the rights of his people. In 1225 some Thuringian merchants were robbed and beaten up on the Polish side of the border. Louis demanded reparation, and when none was forthcoming rode into Poland and used force to extract it from the citizens of Lubitz. On another occasion a Thuringian trader was robbed of his stock in the prince-bishopric of Würzburg, so Louis marched in to recover it. Occasionally this fierce determination to see justice done worked against him. He was twice excommunicated, once in 1218 as the result of a territorial dispute with the bishop of Mainz and again in 1221 during an inheritance dispute with his stepsister. He seems to have emerged victorious from both disputes, and in either case the excommunication was temporary.

His loyalty was particularly valued by the emperor, Frederick II (1220-50), who used his advice at the Diet of Cremona and in 1226 asked him for military assistance. On this occasion he was away for a long, hard winter and spring, and when he returned he characteristically asked Elizabeth how the people had fared during the terrible frost. "I gave to God what was his," she replied, "and God has kept for us what was ours." "Let her do good and give to God whatever she will," he said to his complaining treasurer, "as long as she leaves me Wartburg and Neuenburg."

In the following year, 1227, he volunteered to follow Frederick on the Sixth Crusade, realizing a commitment that had probably been made as early as 1221. To stir up enthusiasm for the Crusade he had a passion play presented in the streets of Eisenach, and he went personally to monasteries throughout his territories to ask for prayers. One of the less fortunate by-products of this activity was his introduction into Elizabeth's life of one of the most enthusiastic preachers of the Crusade, the austere and humourless Conrad of Marburg.

As her confessor Conrad had a repressive influence on Elizabeth—we can only speculate as to how Louis would have handled the situation had he lived.

When the central German forces finally gathered that summer at Schmalkalden, Louis was in command. It was there that he took leave of Elizabeth on 24 June, feast of the birthday of St John the Baptist, and set off for the Holy Sepulchre. He met the emperor at Tróia, and in September the army embarked. But three days later, when the fleet put into Otranto, Louis was forced to take to his bed. He had contracted malaria and, realizing he was dying, asked for the Last Sacraments. When news of his death finally reached Elizabeth sometime in October she was overwhelmed by her grief. Louis' body was brought back to Thuringia and buried in the Benedictine abbey of Rheinhardsbrunn, where is he known as St Louis to this day. The miracles recorded at his tomb may or may not be historically certain, but they do bear witness to the veneration in which he was held from an early date.

The Latin Life by Bertoldus, a monk of Rheinhardsbrunn who was Louis' chaplain, survives only in a fourteenth-century German translation. See also *Bibl.SS.*, 8, pp. 312-4; C. Wenck in *Allgemeine Deutsche Biographie*, 19, pp. 594-7; German biography by G. Simon (1854); Michael, *Geschichte des deutschen Volkes seit dem 13 Jarh.*, 1, p. 221, 2, p. 207ff.; Lives of St Elizabeth of Hungary.

Bd Bonaventure of Barcelona (1620-84)

Miguel Bautista Gran was born at Riudoms in the province of Tarragona on 24 November 1620. Because of straitened family circumstances, he had to abandon his hopes of study and instead started life as a shepherd in the countryside near Barcelona. He married when he was eighteen—a marriage that, according to his biographers, he did not want, though that may be contemporary hagiographical convention. In any case, within two years his wife was dead, and on 14 July 1640 he entered the Franciscan Order at Escornalbou as a lay brother, taking the name Bonaventure. Always a deeply spiritual man, he began to experience ecstasies and other unusual phenomena. Possibly because these attracted so much attention locally, or perhaps for some other reason, for the first seventeen years of his religious life he seems to have moved around a good deal, serving variously as cook, porter, infirmarian, and questor in several houses in Catalonia. Then in 1658 he felt called to ask his superiors' permission to go to Rome. This was granted, and he travelled there via Assisi and Loreto.

He spent the first two months at the generalate, after which he moved to the friary of San Isidoro as porter. It was here that he attracted the attention of two cardinals, Francesco Barberini and Cesare Facchinetti, thanks to whose support he was able to pursue what he regarded as his real vocation—the establishment of retreat houses for members of the Roman province of the Reformed Franciscans. With only grudging support from his superiors, who were not entirely in favour of the project, the first of these was set up at Ponticelli in

1662. Then, despite the obstacles, which Bonaventure met with characteristic calm and good humour, several more were founded, the best known being the one on the Palatine in Rome. In 1845 two houses in Florence and one in Prato, initially part of the Roman province of the Reformed Franciscans, became autonomous to form the Riformella. This state of affairs continued until 1900, when all united again to form the Order of Friars Minor.

Although he was guardian of the house at Ponticelli more than once, Bonaventure never became a priest—he did not want to. His gifts of contemplation went hand in hand with an intuitive understanding of others and a very practical spirituality, which expressed itself in the poverty and simplicity of his own life and in his dedication to the poor. He died in Rome 1684 and was beatified in 1906.

See F. Galluzzi, *Vita di Fra Bonaventura da Barcelona* (1723); *Acta Ordinis Fratrum Minorum*, 29 (1910); L da Pofi, *Il beato Bonaventura* (1906; Eng. trans., 1910); *Bibl.SS*, 3, 283-5.

St John Gabriel Perboyre, *Martyr* (1802-40)

John (Jean) Gabriel Perboyre was born on 6 June 1802, the eldest child of Pierre Perboyre and Marie Rigal. When he was fifteen he felt inspired by a sermon he heard to become a missionary. In the following year he went with his brother Louis to join the Congregation of the Mission (Lazarists, Vincentians) and was ordained in 1826. At first his desire to serve in the mission field had to be postponed. He did so brilliantly in his theological studies that as soon as he was ordained he was sent as lecturer to the seminary of Saint-Flour. Two years later he became rector of the minor seminary there, and then, because it had become apparent that he had personal and spiritual qualities to match his intellect, he was sent to Paris as assistant novice-master. So, although he asked at intervals to be sent to China it was not until 1835 that he finally received permission to go.

As soon as he reached Macao, on 29 August 1835, he set about learning Chinese, and after four months was ready to go on the Hunan mission. He described himself in a letter to his community in Paris as "a very curious sight: my head shaved, a long pig-tail, stammering my new languages, eating with chop-sticks." He immediately became involved in the Lazarists' work of rescuing abandoned children, of whom there were many, and educating them as Christians. He proved to be a talented teacher, and after two years he was moved on to Hupeh. Then, suddenly, in September 1839, the missionaries were forced into hiding by an unexplained renewal of persecution. Unfortunately John was betrayed, for thirty tael (a trivial but symbolic amount), by a recent convert. He was taken in chains from bureaucrat to bureaucrat, as each questioned him and passed him on to the next. Finally he was brought before the governor and mandarins of Wuchangfu, who ordered him to reveal where his fellow missionaries were and trample on the cross. When he refused he was tortured, and this performance was repeated twenty times, each time with a new, more sophisticated form of torture. At one stage he was branded on the face with four characters that meant "teacher of a false religion." A Chinese priest who managed to bribe his way into the prison described him as a mass of open wounds.

On 11 September 1840, almost a year after he was captured, John was strangled to death along with five common criminals. He was buried beside another Lazarist martyr, Bd Francis Regis Clet, who had died twenty years earlier (and is mentioned with the other Chinese martyrs on 17 February). John was beatified in 1889, and in China his feast is celebrated on 7 November, the nearest convenient date to that of his beatification. One happy result of his death was that two years later, when it was negotiating the treaty of Nanking, the British government insisted on the inclusion of a clause providing that any missionary who was arrested in future should not be dealt with by the Chinese authorities but handed over to the nearest consul of his nation.

He was canonized on 2 June 1996. This angered the Chinese authorities, who had understood that no foreign missionaries to China would be canonized before a Chinese candidate. The government described him as a "bandit" who had been justly put to death under the law and forbade any public Mass to commemorate him. It would appear that someone in the Vatican had forgotten the agreement.

Biographies include J.-B. Etienne, *Notice sur la vie et la mort de M. Jean Gabriel Perboyre* (1842); F. Vauris, *Le disciple de Jésus* (1853); G. de Montgesty, *Témoin du Christ: le bienheureux Jean Gabriel Perboyre* (1905; Eng. trans., F. Gilmore, 1925); L Castagnola, *Missionario martire* (1940); A Châtelet, *Jean-Gabriel Perboyre, martyr* (1943). See also *Bibl.SS.*, 10, 484; *O.D.C.C.*, pp. 330-1; P. M. D'Elia, *The Catholic Missions in China* (1934); C. Cary-Elwes, *China and the Cross* (1957); works by A. Launay on the Chinese missions. There is a general entry on the martyrs of China in the present work under 17 February.

12

St Ailbe, *Bishop* (? *c.* 526)

Although St Ailbe (Ailbhe) is commemorated throughout Ireland on this day, and the diocese of Imlech (Emly) in Co. Tipperary celebrates him as its patron, the surviving information about him is contradictory and confusing. And much of it is the stuff of legend, with obvious borrowings, rather than history. One version of his origins, for example, is strongly reminiscent of the story of Romulus and Remus. Accounts of his introduction to Christianity differ too: one says he was instructed and baptized by a British priest who overheard him wondering about the beauty of the natural world and the possibility of a creator; another says he was brought up and baptized by members of a British colony in Ireland. He is supposed to have been consecrated bishop while on a visit to Rome, although there is some doubt even about this. What does seem certain is that he preached throughout Ireland and with such authority that many were not only converted to Christianity but inspired by his example to live as Christians too. And he is reputed to have written a monastic Rule and founded the see of Imlech.

According to his legend Ailbe asked Oengus, king of Munster, to hand the Aran Islands over to St Enda (21 Mar.). Oengus had never heard of them, but when he saw them in a dream he was happy to do so. Whatever the truth in this, the monastery founded at Killeany (Cell Énda—church of St Enda) on Inis Mor later earned the islands the title "Aran of the saints." There seems to be little authority for the suggestion that Ailbe preached in Ireland before St Patrick (17 Mar.). This idea and others like it were almost certainly introduced to indicate that Ailbe was equal to, if not greater than, Patrick. It is probable that he died sometime in the sixth century.

For details regarding the Life see R. Sharpe, *Medieval Irish Saints' Lives* (1991). The Rule reputed to be Ailbe's has been edited by J. O'Neill in *Ériu* 3 (1907). pp. 92-115. On St Patrick and the Life of St Ailbe see R. Sharpe in *Sages, Saints and Storytellers. Studies in honour of James Carney* (1989). See also J. F. Kenney, *Sources of the Early History of Ireland* (1929); *Bibl.SS.*, 1, 636-8.

St Guy of Anderlecht (*c.* 1012)

The accounts we have of St Guy (in French, Guidon; in Flemish, Gewijde, Wyden) come from late, not very reliable sources, embellished with supposedly edifying but nevertheless incredible details. It is clear, however, that he deserves his place in the category of saints that includes John Calybites (15

Jan.), Isidore the Farmer (15 May), and Benedict Joseph Labre (16 Apr.). He was born in the countryside outside Brussels, probably sometime in the second half of the tenth century. His parents were so poor that they could not afford to send him to school, although, with their strong Christian faith, they made sure that he was fully instructed in the truths and practices of religion. Guy was very receptive and took particularly seriously an observation of St Augustine (28 Aug.) that it is as dangerous to grieve over the loss of one's comforts as it is to receive them all here on earth. He prayed constantly for the grace to love the poverty in which he found himself and was always generous with what little he did have. When he grew up he lived a wandering existence for a while until he came to the church of Our Lady at Laeken, near Brussels. The parish priest, struck by the simple but willing and devout young man, took him on as a sacristan.

The job was entirely suited to Guy's temperament and capabilities, and things would no doubt have remained like this had he not met a merchant from Brussels who invited him to invest his small savings in a business venture. In his simplicity Guy agreed, thinking it would give him more money to help the poor. He left his job to go into partnership with the man, but when the ship carrying their goods sank on its way out of the harbour he was left with no employment and no money. To make reparation for what he regarded as his mistake in giving up humble but good employment to involve himself in the affairs of the world he made a pilgrimage, on foot, first to Rome and then to Jerusalem. He was away for seven years. When he returned to Belgium he went to Anderlecht, where he died from illness and exhaustion. He was buried in the cemetery of the canons of Anderlecht, who translated his remains to a shrine once miracles were reported at his grave. He has always been popular with sacristans as well as with those who work with horses or in the fields.

A Life can be found in *AA.SS.*, Sept., 4, pp. 36-48. On the folklore elements in the cult see E. H. van Heurck, *Les Drapelets de pèlerinage en Belgique* (1922); F. Mortier in *Folklore brabançon* 10 (1930), pp. 46-55; J. Lavalleye in *Annales de la Société d'Archéologie de Bruxelles* 37 (1934), pp. 221-48. See also *Bibl.SS.*, 7, 496-501; J. Leclercq, *Les Saints de Belgique* (1953).

In art Guy is represented either as a pilgrim, as in a fourteenth-century fresco in the collegiate church at Anderlecht, or as a peasant with a horse and ox, as, for example, on the coat of arms of the city of Anderlecht.

Six Martyrs of Omura (1622)

By the early sixteenth century, despite sporadic persecution under the military regent Hideyoshi, who had died in 1598, the number of Christians in Japan had grown to some 300,000. Tokugawa Ieyasu emerged as the victor from the outbreak of local wars that followed Hideyoshi's death; he at first appeared favourable to Christianity, but changed his approach in around 1612 and renewed persecution of Christians. He issued an edict banning Christianity in

1603, followed in 1614 by a decree banishing all foreign missionaries, with the threat that any Japanese who had any dealings with such were to be burned alive.

Some thirty-five missionaries defied the edict and remained in the country, and eighteen of these died in a mass martyrdom in 1617. While few Japanese priest were ordained priests, many served as catechists and many of these were martyred with foreign missionaries. In 1622 twenty-two missionaries and Japanese converts were burned over a slow fire in Nagasaki on 10 September, while thirty more Japanese were beheaded. On 12 September the six commemorated today were burned to death at Omura, a few miles to the north of Nagasaki. They were all Japanese converts: Mancio Shibata, Dominic Mogoshichi, and four companions. They were among the 205 martys beatified by Pope Pius IX in 1867.

See the bibliography under the general entry on The Martyrs of Japan, 6 February

ST JOHN CHRYSOSTOM (over page)
Above: beehive denoting eloquence—"golden tongue"
Below: chalice and book of the Gospels:
gold chalice and book, bordered silver with red bookmark, on gold field

13

ST JOHN CHRYSOSTOM, *Bishop* (*c.* 350-407)

John Chrysostom was an idealist, always in search of perfection for himself and for the world in which he lived. He was constantly being let down and, lacking the steel of a St Athanasius (2 May) or of contemporaries such as St Basil (2 Jan.) and St Ambrose (7 Dec.), generally emerged less successfully from his conflicts with the temporal authorities. His great attraction is that he never allowed himself to become cynical or disillusioned, always finding a way to hold on to his vision. He was born in about 350 in Antioch, where his aristocratic father, Secundus, was probably an officer in the army. Because Secundus died while his son was still very young, the boy was brought up almost entirely by his mother, Anthusa, whose courage and enthusiasm gave him an enduring respect for women. She also made sure that he received the best possible education.

It was an exciting time to be studying, and he emerged not just thoroughly grounded in oratory and in the law but with a sound doctrinal formation and an exceptional knowledge of the Bible. He had been baptized when he was eighteen and would have liked to join a monastery immediately. However, at this stage his mother needed him, and it was not until about 373 that he joined a group of hermits who were following the Rule of Pachomius in the mountains outside Antioch. He was there for about seven years, during which his austerities and the dampness of his cave seriously damaged his health. In 381, exhausted, sick, and disappointed by his experience, he returned to Antioch. His low mood did not last long, however. He had learned that there is a limit to the value of individual asceticism and that for most the way to salvation is with and through others. Soon he was fully involved in training for the priesthood, to which he was finally ordained in 386.

Fourth-century Antioch still reverberated with the clash of views as the Church hammered out its understanding of its Faith, and for this and many other reasons it was in no way a restful place to be. But instead of seeking out a pseudo-monastic environment to replace the one he had left, John threw himself into the action. Recognizing his quality, the bishop appointed him his special assistant, particularly in the spiritual and temporal care of the poor of the city. This kept him busy, but he always found time to preach, for which he had a great gift. He was undoubtedly one of the greatest preachers of the early Church, not to say of all time, and eventually—at least a hundred years after his death—was given the title *chrysostomos*, "golden tongue."

He used his preaching gift most famously in 387 to help restore peace and understanding in the incident of "the Statues." During a riot against the emperor's taxes, statues representing Theodosius (379-95) himself, his father, his sons, and his dead wife had been broken. Serious reprisals were expected. However, in the end an amnesty was obtained, thanks to the efforts of Flavian, the elderly bishop of Antioch, and, not least, to twenty-one sermons preached by John with a view to taking the heat out of the situation. These sermons are particularly interesting as a record of what happened and for the sense they convey of the fear-laden atmosphere of the time. His exposition of the orthodox teaching of the Church was clear, almost terse, as for example against the Anomoeans, one of the many contemporary sects, whose position was similar to that of the Arians:

> That the Son is God and, while still remaining the Son, is God on the same level as the Father becomes clear from the very addition of the word "Father." If this name of God belonged only to the Father and if it could not designate for us another personal reality but only that first and unbegotten personal reality, inasmuch as the name "God" can belong to and designate only that personal reality, the addition of the name "Father" would serve no purpose ("On the Incomprehensible Nature of God," 5, 10).

He made a name for himself as a commentator on the Gospels of Matthew and John and the Epistles of Paul. In the Antiochene tradition he favoured the literal interpretation of scripture and its practical application to contemporary problems. And he was ever concerned to remind individual Christians of the support they could expect from the Church in the journey of faith:

> If the prayer of a single person is so powerful, much more so is the prayer that is offered along with many other people. The sinewy strength of such a prayer and the confidence that God will hear it is far greater than you can have for the prayer you offer privately at home (*ibid.*, 3, 36).

When the archbishop of Constantinople died in 397, Theodosius' son and successor, Arcadius (395-408), was determined that John should take his place. Fearing popular resistance in Antioch, he sent an envoy to bring the bishop out secretly. After a hair-raising eight-hundred-mile journey John was consecrated on 26 February 398 by Theophilus, archbishop of Alexandria, uncle of St Cyril of Alexandria (27 June), who had hoped to be appointed to Constantinople himself. The problems facing John were considerable, and with his particular blend of integrity and blunt honesty he did not make life easy for himself. To counter the effects of years of wastage and corruption, he launched a vigorous programme of reform that left no group untouched. Beginning with his own household, he radically reduced spending in the diocese. With the money that was saved he helped to set up hospitals for the sick poor and strangers in the capital. Each was properly staffed, not only with medical personnel but with cooks and chaplains. Enlisting the cooperation of deaconesses in the city—

notably St Olympias (17 Dec.), with whom he had a strong friendship based on shared spiritual ideals—he maintained a service for widows and their families. The disciplinary measures he directed at the clergy were so strict that they received, and deserved, criticism—as did his attacks on the Jews. As for the court, it came in for wide-ranging rebuke. He denounced, among many other things, the clothes and the make-up of the women, Christians who went to the races on Good Friday, and games in the stadium on Holy Saturday. Arcadius' wife, Eudoxia, who took the individual criticisms as well as the entire reform programme as a personal slight, decided to get her own back. A silver statue of her was erected outside the cathedral church of Santa Sophia and the dedication ceremony was followed by public games, which provided an opportunity for all manner of unrestrained behaviour.

Matters came to a head in 402 when John gave shelter to some monks who had been excommunicated as Origenists by Theophilus of Alexandria. He appealed on their behalf to the emperor, who convened a synod, which Theophilus was summoned to attend. He himself was to preside. But Theophilus, who had accepted the leadership of a group of bishops in support of the empress, turned the tables on him. Instead of settling the ecclesiastical position of the monks, the synod, which came to be known as the Synod of the Oak (or Oak Tree Synod) after the Constantinople suburb in which it was held, was to judge him. The assembled bishops condemned John, who refused to defend himself, on a series of trumped up charges. In particular, they said he had committed treason by calling Eudoxia "Jezebel" and demanded that he be banished.

John was duly sent into exile, but when Constantinople was hit by an earthquake shortly afterwards, the terrified Eudoxia called him back. John made no attempt to conceal or moderate his views, and Eudoxia was infuriated once again. Seeing this, Theophilus appealed to an Arian council in Antioch and John was banished for returning to work in a see from which he had been "lawfully deposed." Despite the efforts of his own people, in 404 he was exiled first to Cucusus in Armenia and then to the fortress at Arabissos. From here he wrote a vast number of letters, especially to bishops in the West alerting them to his predicament. Pope St Innocent I (401-17; 28 July) did send him letters of support and encouragement, and he refused to recognize the man who had been appointed in his place. But by and large it is clear that John felt let down by them all, and when the desired help did not come he turned to various patrician ladies in Rome. This sort of publicity was not what his captors wanted, and they decided to move him to Pontus. He died on 14 September 407 as a direct result of being forced to travel there on foot in bad weather, despite constant pleas of exhaustion.

In 414 he was rehabilitated by order of the pope, still Innocent I. His feast was celebrated from 438, and in 448 his body was taken back to Constantinople, where it was reburied in the church of the Apostles. He was recognized as a Father of the Church at the Council of Chalcedon in 451, and in 1568 Pope St Pius V (1566-72; 30 May) proclaimed him a Doctor of the Church. Many of his writings survive, including some letters and many homilies. These show him to be a pastor rather than a theologian or moralist. Starting at the point where his listeners found themselves, he held out a vision of life based on the Gospels and aiming at perfection. The basis for this is revealed in a letter written at the end of his life, when he was already in prison, to his friend Olympias.

> Please listen to what I have to say. I am going to try to make you a little less depressed and get rid of the dark clouds in your mind. Why are you so worried, sad and agitated? Because the storm that has attacked the churches is harsh and menacing, and because it has wrapped everything in unrelieved darkness? Because it is reaching crisis point? Because it brings dreadful shipwrecks every day, while the whole world collapses about us?
>
> We see the ocean whirling up from its uttermost depths and sailors' bodies floating on it. We see others overcome by the force of the waves. . . . It is all so hopeless they can only scream, groan, cry and weep. . . . Everywhere monsters of the deep rise up and threaten travellers. But no mere words can express the unutterable. No terminology I can think of can adequately convey the terror of these times.
>
> Though I am aware of all these miseries, I never cease to hope. I always remember the universal Pilot. He does not rely on steersmanship to suffer the storm and come through it. He merely nods to calm the roaring oceans, and if he takes his time in doing so, well that is the Pilot's way. He does not stop dangers straightaway, but banishes them only when they get close to their most ghastly point, and almost everyone has abandoned hope. Only then does he show us marvels and miracles. Only then does he reveal the power which he alone possesses, and teach the suffering how to be patient.

Of the rest, his exegetical works and his treatise on priesthood, *De sacerdotio*, are the best known. He was certainly not responsible for the adoption of the so-called Liturgy of St John Chrysostom, which happened after his time.

According to a curious legend that circulated in the countries of the Reform, John had a child by a princess. It is not explained when this lapse is supposed to have occurred, but as a penance he had to go around for a while naked and on all fours.

St John Chrysostom is invoked in the West as one of the Four Greek Doctors—the others are St Athanasius (2 May), St Basil (2 Jan.) and St Gregory Nazianzen (2 Jan.)—and in the East, again with St Basil and St Gregory Nazianzen, as one of the Three Holy Hierarchs.

AA.SS., Sept., 4, pp. 401-709; Life by Palladius in critical edition by P. R. Coleman-Norton (1928). The most significant of the modern Lives is J. N. D. Kelly, *Golden Mouth* (1995). Others include A. Moulard (1941); P. C. Baur (1929-30; Eng. trans., 1959-60); R. Van de Weyer (1996). For the works see *P.G.*, 47-64, in S.C. (1966-); Eng. trans. in Nicene and Post-Nicene Christian Fathers (1887-1900), first series, 9-14, and in Ancient Christian Writers series (1946-67). See also B. H. Vandenberghe, *Saint Jean Chrysostome et la parole de Dieu* (1961); S. Neill (ed.), *Chrysostom and His Message* (1962); F. Halkin, *Douze récits byzantins sur S. Jean Chrysostome* (1977); E. A. Clark, *Jerome, Chrysostom and Friends* (1982); R. A. Krupp, *Shepherding the Flock of God* (1991); *H.S.S.C.*, 3, 192-9; *Bibl.SS.*, 6, 669-701; *O.D.C.C.*, pp. 342-3 (good bibliography); Wuescher-Becchi, *Saggi d'iconografia di San Giovanni Crisostomo* (1908); Jöckle, pp. 246-7. The letter to Olympias is in J. Cumming (ed.), *Letters from Saints to Sinners* (1996), pp. 81-2.

The iconography in general is huge, mostly following the Eastern stereotype. John is almost invariably shown as a bishop, tall, bearded, and wearing the vestments of the Greek rite. Two of the finest representations are the twelfth-century mosaic in the cathedral at Cefalù, east of Palermo on the northern coast of Sicily, and another in the basilica of San Marco in Venice. Also in Venice, in the church dedicated to him, there is a painting by Sebastiano del Piombo. And he appears in the frescoes created by Fra Angelico on the chapel of Nicholas V at the Vatican. Dürer and Cranach, among others, used the subject of his penance in their paintings.

St Marcellinus of Carthage, *Martyr* (413)

Marcellinus Flavius, who was probably born in Toledo in Spain, became a tribune and *notarius* in the service of the emperor Honorius (395-423). Described as "a cultured, generous aristocrat, interested in theology," he was a friend of St Augustine (28 Aug.), who dedicated three of his works, including part of *The City of God*, to him. Some of the correspondence between the two men has survived, and Marcellinus also exchanged letters with St Jerome (30 Sept.).

In 411 he became involved in the Donatist controversy, which had begun in north Africa shortly after 311 and was still simmering a century later. A hardline and ultimately schismatic group within the Church, the Donatists took the view that Christians who sinned mortally after Baptism, and in particular those who denied their faith during persecution, should never be readmitted to communion. Attempts were made over the years, sometimes involving the civil authorities, to resolve the matter, but the schism was never really healed and in fact continued in north Africa for another two or three centuries. In 409 Honorius had granted the Donatists permission to worship publicly. Then, two years later, Marcellinus was sent in to preside over a conference that brought together orthodox north African bishops and Donatist bishops. The aim had been to heal the breach between the two parties, but in the end no agreement could be reached. Marcellinus, having listened to the arguments, decided against the Donatists, ordering them to give up their separate status and join in communion with their opponents. He was then responsible, with his brother Apringius, pro-consul of Africa, for enforcing that order. The two carried out their duty with a severity that caused Augustine himself to remonstrate with them. The Donatists meanwhile attempted to avert persecution by having the brothers charged with corruption and with taking part in an insurrection against the emperor. Ignoring Augustine's efforts to save them, the general charged with putting down the insurrection had them executed without trial. The imperial court later acknowledged that they had been put to death unjustly.

Both Augustine and Jerome wrote panegyrics about the two brothers. There is no evidence that a cult developed, but Cardinal Baronius added Marcellinus' name to the Roman Martyrology in the sixteenth century on the grounds that he died in the defence of orthodox Catholic teaching.

AA.SS., Apr., pp. 539-42, brings together the relevant passages from St Augustine and St Jerome. See also *Bibl.SS.*, 8, 650; *Encyclopedia of the Early Church* (1992), 1, pp. 521-2; Baudot et Chaussin, 4, pp. 140-3. On Donatism see *O.D.C.C.*, pp. 599-600.

St Maurilius of Angers, *Bishop* (453)

What is now known to be the only authentic Life of St Maurilius was written in about 620 by Magnobodus (Maimbodo), one of his successors. It relates that Maurilius was born in Milan but moved up into Touraine, where he became a disciple of St Martin of Tours (11 Nov.). After his ordination he is said to have established himself at Châtillon-sur-Loire. There he worked hard and tirelessly as a missionary, seizing every opportunity that came his way to get his message over. To illustrate this Magnobodus tells how, when a pagan temple was struck by lightning, he told the people this was a sign of God's anger and immediately set about building a church in its place. He was eventually made bishop of Angers in 423, governing wisely and firmly for thirty years. He died on 13 September 453 and was buried in the church of Our Lady, later of St Maurilius, in Angers.

Other, unreliable, accounts include one rewritten in 905 by a deacon named Archanaldus, who passed it off as the work of Venantius Fortunatus (14 Dec.), corrected by Gregory of Tours (17 Nov.)—the deception was not uncovered until 1649. These later versions contain many fabrications, including one, not without its own charm, which borrows elements from the legends of other saints, particularly St Renatus. Maurilius, it relates, failed to go to the bedside of a dying boy until it was too late. Overcome with remorse, he made his way to the Breton coast, wrote on a rock the words "I, Maurilius of Angers, passed this way," and sailed to Britain, accidentally dropping the key of his cathedral into the sea on the way. When the distressed people of Angers eventually discovered his whereabouts, some of them set out to bring him back. While they were crossing the channel, a fish jumped into the boat and was found to have the lost key in its belly. When they found Maurilius, who was working as a gardener, they begged him to return to Angers, but he said he couldn't without the key to his cathedral. When the key was produced he gladly accompanied them. Once in Angers, he went immediately to the grave of the boy who had died without the sacraments and called him by name. The boy rose from the grave, received the new name Renatus, and lived to succeed Maurilius as bishop of Angers, where he is venerated as a saint, as he is in Sorrento in Italy.

There is a tradition in Angers that Maurilius introduced the feast of the Birthday of Our Lady into the diocese after someone had a vision of singing angels on the night of 8 September, but this is no more reliable than any of the other stories told about him. His relics were solemnly transferred to a new urn on 16 August 1239. In 1791 they were partially dispersed when the church was sacked during the Revolution; the remains are in Angers Cathedral. St Maurilius is the patron of Angers, and he is invoked by fishermen and gardeners.

For Magnobodus' Life see *M.G.H., Auctores Antiquissimi*, 4, pt. 2, pp. 84-101. See also *Bibl.SS.*, 10, 184-7; *Anal.Boll.* 18 (1899), pp. 417-21; J. Levron, *Les saints du pays angevin* (1943), pp. 53-64.

In art Maurilius is represented as a bishop, his attributes being a fish with a key or a garden spade. He appears in one of the windows of Angers Cathedral, and his story is told in fifteenth- and sixteenth-century tapestries in Angers. See L. de Farey, *Les Tapisseries de l'Eglise d'Angers* (1901).

St Eulogius of Alexandria, *Patriarch* (*c.* 607)

Eulogius was a Syrian by birth. When he was still young he became a monk at the monastery of the Mother of God in Antioch, where he was eventually elected abbot. He also found time to write, and some important works date from this period, including a letter denouncing the Monophysite teachings of Eutyches. The relative tranquillity of his life was not to last for long, however. The Monophysite heresy had been condemned at the Council of Chalcedon in 451, but it nevertheless took hold in three particular churches, one of which was the Coptic Church. As a result confusion reigned in Alexandria, and when the patriarch, John, died in 579, Eulogius was appointed in his place as someone able and prudent enough to handle the situation.

Three years later, while he was in Constantinople on church business, he met and struck up a friendship with St Gregory the Great (3 Sept.), who was then *apocrisiarius* (papal ambassador) at the Byzantine court. The surviving letters from Gregory's side of the correspondence are interesting for the light they throw on the preoccupations and problems of the time and in particular for their recurrent reference to the three sees of Rome, Alexandria, and Antioch and the relationship between them. In one letter, Gregory, now pope, is trying to encourage Eulogius in his efforts to counter Monophysitism and bring its adherents back to orthodoxy. He tells him about the success the Roman monk Augustine (27 May) has been having among the pagan Angli, ten thousand of whom had been baptized on the previous Christmas Eve. Elsewhere he reproves Eulogius for addressing him as "Ecumenical Pope"—he was already signing himself "Servant of the Servants of God" as a rebuke to the patriarch of Constantinople, who had assumed the title "Ecumenical Patriarch." We also get a glimpse of Eulogius' other activities as bishop, as, for example, when

Gregory mentions some beams he is sending as a gift, possibly as trusses for the roof of the basilica Eulogius is building in honour of St Julian of Antinoe— they are too large, Gregory tells him, for the ships that have been sent from Alexandria.

Of Eulogius' own writings, most of which were occasioned by his fight against heresy, only a sermon and a few fragments remain. Yet he is known to have written five books against the Novationists; a two-volume work in defence of the *Epistle to Flavianus* of Pope St Leo the Great (461; 10 Nov.), whom he greatly respected and admired; and at least eleven theological treatises on various subjects. The one treatise he submitted to Gregory for approval came back with the message: "I find nothing in your writings but what is admirable." Eulogius died in Alexandria in 607. (The new draft Roman Martyrology assigns his date of death to 13 June, which will be followed in future editions of the present work.)

See *AA.SS.*, Sept., 4, pp. 83-94; O. Bardenhewer, *Patrology* (1894; Eng. trans., 1908), pp. 575-6; *D.C.B.*, 2, p. 283. Also *Bibl.SS.*, 5, 214-7; *Theologische Quartalschrift* 78, pp. 353-401. For Eulogius' writings see *P.G.*, 86. St Gregory's letter about St Augustine is in his *Epistolae*, 8, 1, no. 30.

St Amatus, *Abbot* (*c.* 630)

Two saints named Amatus (or Amé) are commemorated on this day. The Latin Life of the earlier of the two was originally accepted as the work of a monk of Remiremont, a near contemporary of the saint. However, many scholars now believe that it was written at least fifty years and perhaps as much as two centuries after Amatus' death and that it is completely untrustworthy. That said, the account it gives of Amatus is as follows. He was born in Grenoble of a Gallo-Roman family, probably between 565 and 570, and was sent as a child to the abbey of Agaunum. Here he spent over thirty years of his life, first as a schoolboy, then as member of the community, and later as a hermit in a cell behind the monastery. While he was living alone he cultivated a small garden to support himself. In 614 he attracted the attention of St Eustace (29 Mar.), who persuaded him to return with him to the monastery founded by St Columbanus (23 Nov.) at Luxeuil.

The story most frequently told of Amatus concerns a Merovingian nobleman named Romaric. He was dining with Romaric when the latter asked, "What should I do to possess eternal life?" Pointing to a silver dish, Amatus repeated Jesus' answer to the rich young man, "Sell what you have and give the money to the poor . . . then come and follow me." Taking the words literally, Romaric freed his serfs, gave away his goods, apart from his estate at Habendum on the Moselle, to the poor and the Church, and then joined the monastery at Luxeuil. Later, in about 620, he used the estate to found a double monastery, which took its name, Remiremont (Romarici Mons), from him. It followed the Rule of St Columbanus, and Amatus was its first abbot.

During the early years of the monastery, Amatus and Romaric became embroiled in an unfortunate quarrel with Eustace, which involved another monk of Luxeuil named Agrestius. After the death of Agrestius (he was allegedly murdered by a jealous husband) peace was restored between them. In his last years, Amatus reverted to the solitary existence he preferred. He lived apart in a small cell, cultivating his garden and looking after the nuns' bees, and only came to choir on Sundays and major feasts. When Amatus died in about 630, Romaric took over as director of the two communities, and like Amatus was eventually venerated as a saint (8 Dec.).

For a critical edition of the Life see B. Krusch in *M.G.H., Scriptores merov.*, 4, pp. 215-21. M. Besson gives an alternative view in *Zeitschrift für Schweitzerische Kirchengeschichte* 1 (1907), pp. 20-51. See also *AA.SS.*, Sept., 4, pp. 95-107; *Bibl.SS.*, 1, 938-9; *Anal.Boll.* 26 (1907), pp. 342-3.

St Amatus, *Bishop* (*c.* 690)

Both the extant Latin Lives of this Amatus (Amé), are thought to date from the eleventh century. They tell us nothing about the date and place of his birth or about his education, but they do record that he became bishop of Sion (Sitten) in what is now Switzerland in about 660. After another gap of about sixteen years, they take up again at the point when, for reasons unknown, Thierry III, king of Austrasia (675-91), banished Amatus to the monastery at Péronne. The abbot at the time was St Ultan of Fosse (2 May), brother of the founder, St Fursey (16 Jan.). When Ultan died, Amatus was placed in the care of St Mauruntius (5 May), who had recently founded an abbey at Breuil, in Flanders. Mauruntius, who recognized Amatus' holiness, found the situation embarrassing, but it seems not to have worried Amatus. He lived in a cell near the monastery church, where he spent most of his time praying and was a great source of inspiration for the monks. He died at Breuil in about 690, and his remains were later taken to a church dedicated to him in Douai. The twelfth-century martyrology of Sion confuses him with Amatus of Remiremont (above). The Roman Martyrology has added to the confusion by listing him as bishop of Sens. However, while some scholars disregard this as the result of a confusion between Senonensis and Sedunensis, others argue that accepting Sion as his see presents difficulties of its own and that Sens should not be ruled out.

One Latin Life is in *AA.SS.*, Sept., 4, pp. 120-3, the other in the *Catalogue of Historical Manuscripts of Brussels*, 2, pp. 44-55. For the Sion-Sens discussion see H. Bouvier, *Histoire de l'Eglise de Sens*, 1 (1906), pp. 457-60; M. Besson, *Monasterium Agaunense* (1913), p. 171; *F.E.* 1, p. 246, 2, p. 239. See also *Bibl.SS.*, 1, 939-40.

Bd Mary of Jesus (1560-1640)

Mary (María) Lopez de Rivas was born at Tartanedo, in the Spanish province of Guadalajara, on 18 August 1560. While she was still very young her father died, and she was sent to Molina de Aragón to be brought up by her paternal grandparents. Her spiritual education was entrusted to a Jesuit named de Castro. When she was seventeen, she applied to enter the recently-founded Discalced Carmelite Order. St Teresa of Avila (15 Oct.), who accepted her for the monastery in Toledo, must have thought highly of her, because she wrote to the prioress: "I am sending her with a dowry of 5000 scudi, but I must say that I would willingly give quite as much as that myself to have her. She shouldn't be regarded as being on a par with the rest—God willing, my hope is that she has it in her to become something extraordinary."

Mary received the habit on 12 August 1577. But her physical health was giving serious cause for alarm, and a year later there was talk of not allowing her to make her profession. Again Teresa intervened: "Let them think carefully about what they are doing, because if they don't allow Sr Mary of Jesus to make her profession I will bring her to Avila, and the house that has her will be the most fortunate of all. Left to myself, whichever monastery I was living in I'd always like to have her with me, even if she had to spend her entire life in bed." This swayed the balance decisively in Mary's favour, and she was professed on 8 September 1578. Far from spending her time in bed, she went on, despite continuing bad health and many personal difficulties, to lead a long and active life as a Carmelite. In 1583, when she was only twenty-three, she was made mistress of novices, a post she held on a number of occasions in her own monastery and, once, in Cuenca. She also held the offices of prioress and subprioress more than once between 1587 and 1627. During her last term as prioress false accusations were made against her, and she was forced to step down. Undeterred by the attitude of some members of the Order, including the provincial and the general (Teresa had died in 1582), she managed to keep things in perspective and always showed great respect for authority. Meanwhile, the more perceptive sisters in her own house ignored the accusations and reinstalled her as novice-mistress.

Teresa of Avila had recognized Mary's inner strength from the start, and it was undoubtedly this that kept her going. She lived constantly in the presence of God (so much so that Teresa would speak good-naturedly of the need to "distract" her with work in the sacristy or the infirmary), and she had a particular devotion to the Sacred Heart of Jesus. She acquired a reputation as a saint while she was alive, and soon after her death on 13 September 1640 the nuns were being asked for sworn testimony regarding her holiness. For some reason there was then a delay of three centuries, but Mary's cause was finally introduced in 1926 and she was beatified in 1976.

F. de Acosta, *Vida prodigiosa y heroicas virtudes de la ven. M. María de Jesús* (1643)— important because he knew her; *Artículos para la causa de la Sierva de Dios, María de Jesús*

(1914). See studies by Joaquín de la Sagrada Familia (1919); Serafino de Santa Teresa (1919); Evaristo de la Vírgen del Carmen (1926); "A Carmelite," in *Etudes Carmélitaines*, 12 (1927), pp. 8-48. Also *Positio super virtutibus ex officio concinnata* (1867).

14

St Maternus, *Bishop* (Fourth Century)

The extravagant legend connected with St Maternus was concocted in ninth-century Trier by a monk named Eberhard as part of an attempt to find apostolic origins for the sees of Cologne and Trier, both of which claimed links with St Peter (29 June). The matter, which in any case is fraught with difficulties, is further complicated by the fact that Cologne mentions two bishops named Maternus, one in the first and one in the fourth century, and bishops of that name appear in the lists of Trier and Liège.

According to the apocryphal story, which attempts to identify all of these as one person, Maternus was the resurrected son of the widow of Nain (Luke 7:11-16) and one of the seventy-two disciples. With St Eucharius and St Valerius, he was sent by St Peter to preach Christianity to the Gauls. When they reached Ehl, in Alsace, Maternus died. His companions returned to Rome, where St Peter gave them his staff, with instructions to lay it on the dead man. Maternus thus rose from the dead a second time, and lived to take the gospel to "the peoples of Tongres, Cologne, and Trier and other neighbouring parts." The story is told of other missionaries to Gaul, and is, of course, historically worthless.

The facts, such as they are, seem to be that Maternus was the first bishop of Cologne of whom there is certain knowledge and possibly the founder of the diocese. He was one of the three bishops—the others being Reticius of Autun and Marinus of Arles—who were summoned to Rome in 313 by Constantine the Great (306-37). The emperor wished them to arbitrate in the controversy between Caecilian, the orthodox bishop of Carthage, and Donatus, the schismatic bishop, and his followers. When the synod gave judgment against the Donatists on 2 October, they asked for a fresh hearing. The emperor ruled that another synod should be held to deal with the matter. That synod took place in Arles in 315, and Maternus was one of the signatories to its decrees. He seems to have died, probably before 343, in Trier. There is very little evidence of a cult in Cologne.

The text of the legend is in *AA.SS.*, Jan., 2, pp. 918-22. See also *D.C.B.*, 3, p. 862; A. Hauck, *Kirchengeschichte Deutschlands*, 1, pp. 46-7; W. Neuss, *Die Anfange des Christentums im Rheinlande* (1923), pp. 13-20; *F.E.*, 3, pp. 34, 178; *Bibl.SS.*, 9, 85-9, with good bibliography.

In art Maternus is always represented as bishop, fully vested, and sometimes with three churches or a church with a tower.

St Albert of Jerusalem, *Bishop and Martyr* (*c.* 1150-1214)

On 15 July 1099 after a five-week siege the Crusaders, under Godfrey de Bouillon, stormed and captured Jerusalem. Among the steps they took to establish their presence was to drive out the Greek incumbents of the principal sees and replace them with bishops from the West. In the course of the next century the Latin patriarchate of Jerusalem was occupied by men whose character was as equivocal as the position in which they found themselves. By the time Patriarch Michael died in 1203, the Canons Regular of the Holy Sepulchre were thoroughly dissatisfied with this state of affairs. With the support of the king of Jerusalem, Amaury II de Lusignan (1197-1205), they asked the pope to send someone whose abilities and holiness had been tested and who was known even in Palestine. Although reluctant to spare him, the pope chose Albert, who at the time was bishop of Vercelli.

Albert came from a distinguished Parma family. Little is known about his early life, but he was born at Castel Gualtieri in the middle of the twelfth century. After he had completed (brilliantly) his theological and legal studies, he became a canon in the abbey of the Holy Cross at Mortara, near Pavia, in Lombardy. In 1134, when he was about thirty-five, he was made bishop of Bobbio, but he had no time to put down roots there because he was moved almost at once to Vercelli. For more than fifteen years, besides carrying out his duties as bishop, he made himself invaluable as a mediator and diplomat in the wider sphere of papal politics. He was chosen to mediate between Pope Clement III (1187-91) and Frederick I Barbarossa (1152-90) in the process of reconciliation between Church and Empire that had begun under Clement's predecessor, Gregory III (1187). Later on, as legate of Pope Innocent III (1198-1216), he brokered peace between Parma and Piacenza in 1199. Innocent did not want to let him go, but he appreciated the wisdom of the choice. In 1205 Albert set off as patriarch of Jerusalem and papal legate in Palestine.

By this time the Third Crusade was over, and the sultan, Saladin, had retaken much of Palestine, including Jerusalem. The court of the Frankish king had moved to Akka (Ptolemais), as had the see of the Latin patriarch. From his base at Akka, Albert set about gaining the confidence of the Muslims as well as of the Christians—something his predecessors had signally failed to do. Over the next nine years he exercised his talent for diplomacy and reconciliation to the full, trying to keep the peace between the Frankish leaders and their followers within the different Western factions, and between the Muslim natives of the country and their Christian invaders.

Albert is mainly remembered, however, for something entirely different. Between 1205 and 1210 St Brocard (2 Sept.), the prior of the hermits who lived on Mount Carmel, asked him to translate their way of life into a Rule. Albert agreed, and the result was a document with sixteen short, clearly defined chapters. These provided, among other things, for complete obedience to an elected superior; separate accommodation for each hermit; a shared oratory;

manual work for all; long fasts and total abstinence from meat; silence from Vespers until after Terce; constant prayer. This Rule, which made Albert the first legislator if not the founder of the Carmelite Order, was confirmed by Honorius III (1216-27) and modified later by Innocent IV (1243-54).

In 1213 Innocent III asked Albert to be ready to attend the Fourth Lateran Council, which was due to open in November 1215. With this in mind, Albert spent the next twelve months doing what he could to further the pope's efforts to regain Jerusalem. But he never made it to the council. He was taking part in a procession in Akka on the feast of the Exaltation of the Holy Cross (14 Sept.), when a man whom he had dismissed a short while before from his post as master of the Holy Spirit hospital in the city stepped out of the crowd and stabbed him to death. Albert's feast was introduced by the Carmelites in 1411—ironically, it was not celebrated by his own Order, the Canons Regular of the Lateran, until much later.

For a short early Life see *AA.SS.*, Apr., 1, pp. 769-802. See also *Bibl.SS.*, 1, 686-90; *Analecta Ordinis Carmelitarum Discalceatorum* 3 (1926), p. 212ff.; *D.T.C.*, 1, 662-3; B. Zimmerman, *Monumenta historica Carmelitarum* (1907), pp. 277-81 (this also includes an edited version of Albert's Rule); F. de Ste-Marie, *La Règle de Carmel et son esprit* (1949).

St Albert's iconographical symbols are the crucifix and a knife. Dosso Dossi shows him with both in a painting that now hangs in the Carmel in Modena. In a painting by Luigi Morgari in the cathedral at Bobbio he is sitting at his desk.

St Notburga (*c.* 1264-*c.* 1313)

No contemporary documents relating to Notburga have survived, and scholars do not even agree as to when she lived—some put her as early as the tenth century. The oldest text of her legend, which is in German, is on a wooden panel that was used to decorate her tomb. This disappeared in 1862, but fortunately the text had been copied. That text, which places her in the thirteenth century, contains various miraculous details that can be found in the Lives of other saints and should be treated with caution.

According to the legend Notburga was born into a peasant family at Rattenberg in the Austrian Tirol, north-east of Innsbruck, in about 1264. When she was eighteen she entered the service of Count Henry of Rattenberg and his wife, Ottilia, who put her to work in the kitchens. As there was always a good deal of food left over, Notburga would distribute it to the poor who gathered at one of the side doors. She would also go short herself so that the poor could have more. As long as Henry's mother was alive no one interfered with what Notburga was doing, but when she died Ottilia gave orders that all leftovers were to go straight to the pigs. For a while Notburga obeyed, giving to the poor only what she saved from her own food and drink, but it was not long before she was slipping them the leftovers as well. When Ottilia found out, she was immediately dismissed.

Notburga's next employment was with a farmer at Eben. She was working in his fields one Saturday when the incident for which she is best known is supposed to have occurred. The bell rang for Vespers, indicating that Sunday had begun. Notburga stopped work and prepared to go to church. The farmer told her to go on working, but she refused, pointing out that good Christians do not reap on Sundays in fine weather. When he argued that the weather might change she said, "Let this decide," and threw her sickle in the air. There it hung like the first quarter of the harvest moon, a sign of good weather. Meanwhile, Count Henry, who had remarried, needed someone to manage his household. Convinced that his many problems were due to the meanness of his first wife and her dismissal of Notburga, he re-employed the latter, this time as his housekeeper. During this happy period of her life she certainly would not have forgotten the poor, and one of her dying wishes to Henry was that he should not forget them either. Her other wish was that her body should be laid on a wagon and buried wherever the oxen came to a halt. This turned out to be outside the chapel of St Rupert in Eben, so she was buried there. There is plenty of subsequent evidence about the chapel of St Rupert as a place of pilgrimage during the Middle Ages. The local cult of St Notburga as patroness of peasants and domestic servants was approved by Pope Pius IX (1846-78) in 1862.

The main source is the Life by H. Guarinoni (1646), though from Rader's *Bavaria Sancta* it is clear that earlier sources existed. *AA.SS.*, Sept., 4, p. 710, prints a Latin translation of Guarinoni's narrative, together with some "curious engravings" relating to the cult of St Notburga. See also *Bibl.SS.*, 9, 1070-3; N. von Pfaundler, *Sankt Notburga* (1962); H. Bachmann, "Die historischen Grundlagen der Notburga-Legende," in *Tiroler Heimat*, 24 (1960), pp. 5-49; Jöckle, p. 341.

Representations of her in art, the earliest of which date from the sixteenth century, normally show her in Tirolese costume with her sickle.

St Peter of Tarentaise, *Bishop* (*c.* 1102-74)

There are, confusingly, two *beati* and one canonized saint who, at one time or another, were known as Peter of Tarentaise. There is the Peter born in about 1240 near Tarentaise who in 1276 became pope (the first Dominican to do so) as Innocent V and died later that year after a five-month pontificate. And there is Peter a monk of Cîteaux who became archbishop of Tarentaise and died in 1140.

The Peter (Pierre) of Tarentaise who is commemorated on this day was born in about 1102 at St-Maurice-de-l'Exil, in the diocese of Vienne. There are two principal sources of information about him: a contemporary Life by Geoffrey, abbot of Hautecombe, commissioned by Pope Lucius III (1181-5) and published no later than 1185; and Walter Map's *De nugis curialum*, which is particularly useful for the light it throws on his personality. He was one of the six children—five sons and one daughter—of devout parents who were particularly hospitable to travelling monks who happened to pass by their home. It was as a result of this hospitality that Peter came to know Cistercians from

Cîteaux and from the recently-founded abbey at Bonnevaux. When he was twenty-one, he followed his eldest brother, Lambert, to Bonnevaux—where they were subsequently joined by their father and youngest brother; their mother and sister joined the Cistercian nuns at St-Paul-d'Izeaux.

Bonnevaux already had two daughter houses when, at the request of the archbishop of Tarentaise (the second Peter mentioned above), the abbey of Tamié was founded from it in 1132. Today's Peter was appointed abbot, which he remained for the next eight years, becoming known for his holiness and for his practical care of those in need. During this period, with the help of Amédée III, count of Savoy, he built a guest house and hospital for travellers.

In 1140 the archbishop of Tarentaise (the mountainous region around Moûtiers in what is now the *département* of Savoie) died. He was succeeded by Amédée III's chaplain, Isdraël, but the latter proved so unsuitable for the job that the pope was compelled to remove him. Peter, who was asked to take his place, at first refused, but eventually, at the insistence of St Bernard (20 Aug.) and other Cistercian abbots, he agreed to accept the appointment. For the next fifteen years he worked hard to push through and consolidate a programme of reform in the archdiocese. As a matter of priority he appointed a new cathedral chapter—Augustinian Canons, with whom he lived in community while continuing, like his Cistercian predecessor and namesake, to wear his religious habit and to follow the Rule of the Order. Having appointed dedicated and exemplary priests to the parishes, he supported them by frequent visitations, and he encouraged the foundation of schools and hospitals. He also gained a reputation as a mediator, and several popes, including Bd Eugenius III (1145-53; 8 July) and Hadrian IV (1154-9), came to rely on his skills, as did the count of Savoy.

Miracles said to have been worked through his intercession while he was sorting out a dispute on behalf of Hadrian IV gained him a reputation for holiness that horrified him. Hoping to recover the solitude he had lost, he left the archdiocese in secret sometime in 1155 and journeyed into Switzerland. Once there he joined the Cistercian abbey at Lucelle, in the diocese of Basel, as a lay brother. When his whereabouts were discovered a year later and he was forced to return to his archdiocese, he threw himself into his work with characteristic dedication. He turned the archbishop's palace into an open house for the poor, with whom he shared his meals, and he founded various charitable institutions to cater for their needs. Best known among these was the *Pain de mai*, which is said to have continued until the time of the Revolution: at his own expense soup and bread were distributed to any who came in need to the door of the archbishop's palace during the period immediately prior to the harvest. Ever concerned for pilgrims and travellers, he also rebuilt and expanded the guest house near the Little St Bernard Pass.

In 1159 Peter was drawn into the murky world of papal and imperial politics. Hadrian IV, who had made the mistake of alienating Frederick I Barbarossa (1152-90), whom he himself had crowned as emperor on 18 June 1155, died on

1 September. His death was followed by a disputed election. A majority of the electors voted for Orlando Bandinelli, who became pope as Alexander III (1159-81), but a group of pro-imperial electors voted for Cardinal Ottaviano of Monticelli, whom they installed as Victor IV, thus inaugurating a schism that was to last for eighteen years. A staunch defender of the unity of the Church, Peter was one of the few bishops who stood up effectively to the emperor and the antipope. He travelled tirelessly throughout the Tarentaise, as well as through Burgundy, Alsace, and Lorraine, preaching union and loyalty to Alexander III. Several times during the years that followed he tried to persuade Frederick to be less intransigent by appealing directly to his better nature. However, each attempt was unsuccessful—despite the fact that he had the support of a number of Cistercian abbots, among them Lambert of Cîteaux and Aelred of Rievaulx (12 Jan.).

In 1173, at the pope's request, Peter was in Limoges at the court of the English king, Henry II (1154-89), helping to bring about a rapprochement between the latter and Louis VII of France (1137-79). While he was there he was looked after by Walter Map, then in attendance on Henry, who described him as "a cheerful man and of a merry countenance in all circumstances, clean, modest, humble, every way perfect, as I and many others thought." Map added that he "saw one miracle wrought by the Lord by his hands and heard of many." Peter was, according to Map, "a man of such virtue and distinguished by so many miracles that he might very properly be proclaimed equal in merit to the old fathers whom we reverence in the Church, by whose hand the Lord ... cured sick and drove out devils, nor did he ever attempt what he did not perform."

On Ash Wednesday 1174 Peter was at the Cistercian abbey of Mortemer, where he blessed the ashes and celebrated Mass for the English king and his retinue. He had not long returned to the Tarentaise when he was requested by the pope to go to the abbey of Bellevaux in the Franche Comté and sort out differences that had arisen between the monks. On the way he was taken ill with a fever, and although he did manage to reach the monastery, he died on 14 September. He was buried in the monstery church at Bellevaux in front of the altar of Our Lady. Within the next ten years Geoffrey of Auxerre, then abbot of Hautecombe, who had been in frequent contact with Peter, wrote a Life, with a view to his canonization. He was indeed canonized less than twenty years later, on 10 May 1191, by Pope Celestine III (1191-8). The most important relics are held by the abbeys of Tamié and St Georges de Vesoul.

The Life by Geoffrey of Hautecombe is in *AA.SS.*, May, 2, p. 321ff. In the Oxford Medieval Texts series see Walter Map, *De Nugus curialum* (1983), pp. 134-41, and D. L. Douie and D. H. Farmer (eds.), *Magna Vitae Hugonis, The Life of Hugh of Lincoln* (1961), pp. 38-40. Modern biographers include J. M. Chevray (1841), H. Brultey (1874), and A. Dimier (1935). See also L. F. Barmann, "Peter of Tarentaise. A Biographical Study of the 12th Century," in *Revue de l'Université d'Ottawa* 31 (1961), pp. 96*-125*; *Bibl.SS.*, 10, 781-7; *O.D.S.*, pp. 401-2; *O.D.C.C.*, p. 1268.

Bd Gabriel Taurin Dufresse, *Martyr* (1750-1815)

One of the most indefatigable of the French missionaries to China in the eighteenth and early nineteenth centuries, Gabriel was born at Lezoux, east of Clermont-Ferrand, on 8 December 1750. He studied for the priesthood at the seminary of Saint-Sulpice in Paris, and when he was still a deacon signed up with the Société des Missions Etrangères de Paris. It was there that he was ordained in December 1774. Almost exactly a year later, on 4 December 1775, he set sail for China. When he arrived he was made responsible for the northern part of the Szechwan district, where he found the scattered Christians hungry for his ministry.

Things began well; for the next eight or so years he did not spare himself, and his efforts bore fruit. But in 1784 a wave of persecution started up and a spy reported Gabriel to the mandarins. The first time he was arrested and imprisoned he managed to escape and was taken in by a Christian family. But by harbouring a priest, families like this were putting themselves at risk, so when the coadjutor to the vicar apostolic was arrested in the following year, he told the priests in his area to give themselves up. Gabriel did so, and for the first six months he was held in relatively decent conditions. Then the Lazarists in Beijing pleaded with the authorities on his behalf and that of other French missionaries. As a result they were all released on condition that they remain in Beijing or Macao. Gabriel chose Macao, believing that from there it would be easier to return to his mission. This he did on 14 July 1789 and was given the district of Chongking. He was immediately hard at work again, building a church, visiting his scattered parishioners, and administering the sacraments— in 1790 he baptized 140 adults, 532 children, and 310 catechumens, and in the following years the numbers increased. In 1793 he was appointed pro-vicar apostolic, and in 1800 he became a coadjutor bishop.

Despite the constant difficulties and the size of his workload, in 1803 Gabriel found time to convene a diocesan synod. This produced a series of constitutions that the Sacred Congregation Propaganda Fide in Rome recommended to all missionaries as a rule of conduct. Things were apparently going well, but in 1805 persecution reared its head again. From then until 1814, when he was again betrayed to the mandarins, Gabriel was forced to move constantly from place to place. He managed to continue this nomadic existence for another six months, but on 18 May 1815 he was finally arrested, taken to Chengtu, and condemned to death. After enduring imprisonment for four months he was beheaded on 14 September. He was beatified on 27 May 1900.

Annales de la Propagation de la Foi 1 (1822), IV pp. 48-81, VI pp. 25-6, XXI pp. 9-10; A. Launay, *Les cinquante-deux serviteurs de Dieu . . . mis à mort pour la foi en Extrême Orient de 1815 à 1856*, 2 (1893), pp. 203-30; *idem.*, *Les bienheureux martyrs de la Société des Missions Etrangères* (1929), *passim*; T. Saint-Roch, *Un enfant de Lezoux: le bienheureux Taurin Dufresse* (1932); *Bibl.SS.*, 4, 851-2.

15

St Nicomedes, *Martyr* (date unknown)

There is reliable documentary evidence for the existence of Nicomedes and for his martyrdom, but few details have survived. The most ancient account of his death, which dates from the fifth or sixth century, occurs in the legendary *passio* of SS Nereus and Achilleus (12 May). The Roman Martyrology, quoting from this, describes him as a priest who was arrested and put to death for burying the body of St Felicula (13 June). This is pure speculation. All that can safely be said is that he was a martyr of the Roman Church and that he was buried in a catacomb on the via Nomentana, just outside the Porta Pia. It is likely that this happened during the reign of Domitian (81-96), although there is a seventh-century *passio* that puts it on 1 June during that of Maximian (286-305, 306-10).

Nicomedes is not mentioned in the *Depositio martyrum* of 354, but the itineraries and sacramentaries show that he was venerated in Rome from a fairly early date. During the seventh century pilgrims were venerating his tomb, over which Pope Boniface V (619-25) had built a basilica. The burial place was discovered in 1864. The Gelasian and Gregorian sacramentaries mention Nicomedes both on 1 June and on 15 September, as do the *Hieronymianum* and the later martyrologies. Baronius accepted 15 September as the *dies natalis* and omitted the 1 June commemoration from the Roman Martyrolgy.

For a discussion of the evidence see *C.M.H.*, pp. 291, 510. See also *AA.SS.*, May, 3, pp. 10-11, and Sept., 5, pp. 5-12; *Bibl.SS.*, 9, 981-2; Baudot et Chaussin, 9, p. 294.

St Valerian, *Martyr* (178)

Valerian was a companion of St Pothinus, the bishop of Lyons and leader of the group venerated as the Martyrs of Lyons and Vienne (2 June). The account of their martyrdom is preserved in Eusebius' *Ecclesiastical History* and provides the earliest evidence of an organized Christian community in Gaul. Fantastic accusations were levelled against the martyrs, and they were put to death with appalling violence that included being mauled by wild animals in the ampitheatre (which still survives as a substantial ruin). Valerian suffered a year later than the group described in the letter reproduced by Eusebius.

H.E., 5, 1, and see bibliography under 2 June.

St Nicetas the Goth, *Martyr* (375)

St Nicetas, along with St Sabas (12 Apr.), is one of the best known of the Christian Visigoths who suffered for his faith in the early centuries of Christianity. The information comes from two Passions, the older of which dates from the fifth century. St Simeon Metaphrastes (28 Nov.) used details from these to compile another *passio*, but this is less valuable.

According to these sources Nicetas was born near the banks of the Danube in Dacia (modern Romania). Most of the Goths in this area were still pagan, but there were two Christian groups, one Arian and the other Catholic. While he was still young, Nicetas became a Catholic and was subsequently ordained by a great missionary named Ulfilas, who among other things translated the Bible into the local language. Nicetas was carrying out his priestly ministry in 369 when the Visigothic chieftain, Athanaric, raised a persecution against the Christians that lasted until 372. Angered by the Roman authorities' ill treatment of a number of Visigoths who had taken refuge from the Huns in Moldavia, Athanaric decreed that a chariot carrying the image of one of the local gods should drive through every village known or thought to have Christian inhabitants. Any Christian who refused to worship it would be put to death—the normal method was to burn such people in their homes or their churches. Nicetas died in this way, probably in his church. The day of his death is not known, so the feast is on the day of the translation of his relics. These were taken to Mopsuestia in Cilicia, where a shrine was built for them. He is venerated as a martyr throughout the Greek and Syrian Churches, which place him in the category of the "great martyrs."

For the Greek text of the *passio*, as presented by St Simeon Metaphrastes (28 Nov.), see *AA.SS.*, Sept., 5, pp. 40-43. *Anal.Boll.* 31 (1912), has an edited version of the original of this account (pp. 209-15), plus a commentary (pp. 281-7). See also *Bibl.SS.*, 9, 888-90.

There is a miniature showing his martyrdom in the *Menology of St Basil* in the Vatican Library.

St Aichardus, *Abbot* (*c.* 624–*c.* 687)

None of the three known Lives of St Aichardus (or Achard) is completely trustworthy, but between them they give the basic facts. He was educated in the monastery school at Poitiers, where he remained until his father, Anchaire, decided it was time for him to be introduced to life at court and in the army. His mother, Ermena, who is said to have had only one ambition for her son, that he should become a saint, opposed this idea. Whether or not their considerable disagreement was resolved, as the biographers say, by his disarming his father and gaining his consent, Aichardus went straightaway to join the monastery of Saint-Jouin at Ansion in Poitou. After he had been at Saint-Jouin for thirty-nine years, he was involved, with St Philibert, abbot of Jumièges (20 Aug.), and Bishop Ansoald in the foundation or possibly reformation of the priory of St Benedict at Quinçay. The sequence of events at this point is not entirely clear, but Aichardus went to Quinçay, which is thought to have been built on land owned by his family, as prior. The community, which started with fifteen monks, flourished under his rule.

Later, when Philibert retired as abbot of Jumièges, he nominated Aichardus as his successor. This did not please every member of the large community and was only accepted, according to one tradition, because a monk was told in a vision that it should be. Aichardus' task was a daunting one: the community was huge, and not all the monks responded to his habit of preaching by example. However, a dream, in which he saw the approaching death and judgment of 442 of them, is said to have done much to improve observance. When he realized he was going to die, Aichardus had himself laid on ashes and covered with sackcloth. His parting message to his community stressed the love they should bear toward one another: "You have borne the yoke of penance and are grown old in the exercise of religious duties in vain, if you do not sincerely love one another. Without this, martyrdom itself cannot make you acceptable to God." He was buried at Jumièges, but during the Norman invasion his remains were sent for safety to Haspres. They were returned later to Jumièges.

St Aichardus should not be confused with a Cistercian, Bd Aichardus, who is also commemorated on this day: he was for a while novice-master at Clairvaux and died in about 1170.

There is a full account in *AA.SS.*, Sept., 5, pp. 80-102. See also *Bibl.SS.*, 1, 147-8; *H.S.S.C.*, 4, p. 250; R. Poupardin, *Monuments de l'histoire des abbayes de S. Philibert* (1905).

St Mirin (? Seventh Century)

St Mirin (or Meadhran) was an Irish missionary to Scotland whose shrine at Paisley became a place of pilgrimage. Few details of his life have survived. According to the Aberdeen Breviary he was a disciple of St Comgall (11 May) and was for a while abbot of Bangor. He is known also to have been co-titular of the medieval abbey at Paisley, and several other churches in Scotland bore his name. Some of the more fanciful stories told about him have a vindictive element not uncommon in Celtic hagiography of the period—for example, that he laid the pains of childbirth on a king who opposed him. His feast is kept in the diocese of Paisley, where the cathedral is dedicated to him. St Mirin should not be confused with a Cornish saint named Merryn who has not been certainly identified but was probably a woman.

See: *AA.SS.*, Sept., 5, pp. 2-3; *K.S.S.*, pp. 397, 406. Also M. Barrett, *A Calendar of Scottish Saints* (1904), p. 184; J. O'Hanlon, *Lives of the Irish Saints* (1923), 9, p. 377.

Bd Roland de' Medici (c. 1330-86)

The original Life of Bd Roland was written in 1386, the year of his death, by a Carmelite named Domenico de Domenicis. This survives in the form of a copy made in the mid-fifteenth century, which is now in the Biblioteca Laurenziana in Florence. It was eventually translated into Italian by Silvano Razzi, a Camaldolese monk, in 1601. Roland seems to have aroused a good deal of interest, and both versions, the Latin and the Italian, were used as sources.

Roland was born into the Milan branch of the powerful Medici family in about 1330. Nothing is known about his childhood and youth, which is tantalizing in view of the almost complete isolation in which he chose to live the second half of his life. The first thing recounted of him is that in 1360, when he was about thirty, he withdrew into the forest between Tabiano and Salsomaggiore, near Bargone in the province of Parma. Here, in his desire to become holy, he subjected himself for the remaining twenty-six years of his life to the most extreme forms of penance. According to the Life he observed total silence, communicating with others only when he absolutely had to and then by signs. He wore the habit he had on when he went into the forest until it was in shreds, and when he could no longer patch it with leaves he exchanged it for a goat's skin. Living out in the open all year round, he subsisted on what grasses, berries, and other fruits he was able to forage for himself. Clearly he was not far from human habitation, since we are told that many who came across him regarded him as deranged and would throw things at him or strike him. He, meanwhile, strove to remain in a state of constant prayer.

Eventually, however, his extreme austerity caught up with him. He was found one day lying on a footpath near the castle of Niccolò Pallavicino, lord of Bargone, by servants of the latter's wife, Antonia Casati, who was out hunting with falcons. He made signs that he did not want help, but on Antonia's orders he was taken to a church near the castle. Here he accepted visits from Antonia's confessor, the Carmelite Domenico de Domenicis, who would become his biographer. At last he broke his silence, gave an account of his life and received the sacraments of which he had deprived himself for so long. Thanks to these attentions he lived for another few weeks before he died on 15 September 1386.

In death he was given the recognition he had shunned in life. His body was taken by a great company of priests and laypeople to Busseto and buried behind the main altar in an oratory next to the parish church of St Bartholomew. At the time this oratory was dedicated to St Nicholas (6 Dec.), but for a while it was dedicated to Roland himself, before finally being dedicated to the Holy Trinity. Numerous miracles were reported at his tomb, and a cult developed immediately. In 1749 Pope Benedict XIV (1740-58) mentioned the fact that his predecessor Pius IV (1559-65) had initiated a canonization process in 1563, at the request of the Medici family, but that this had been interrupted when Pius died. Nothing further was done, however, until the nineteenth century, when the process was reopened. There was a hitch in 1839, when Gregory XVI (1831-46) decided to withhold confirmation in view of Roland's long absence from the sacraments. The matter was eventually resolved when it was pointed out that not a few people already canonized had been in the same position. On

23 September 1853 Roland was beatified by Pius IX (1846-78). His feast is celebrated in the diocese of Fidenza, although his cult has waned in recent years.

The manuscript *De vita, poenitentia et miraculis B. Rolandis de Medicis* is in the Biblioteca Laurenziana in Florence; on this see A. M. Bandini, *Catalogus codicum latinorum Bibliotecae Laurenzianae*, 1 (1774), 620. See also S. Razzi, *Delle Vite dei Santi e Beati della città di Parma e suo territorio: del Ven. Orlando de' Medici* (1642), pp. 661-87; G. M. Brocchi, *Vita del B. Orlando de' Medici* (1737); *AA.SS.*, Sept, 5, pp. 117-22; *Bibl.SS.*, 11, 300-2.

St Catherine of Genoa (1447-1510)

Catherine (Caterina) Fieschi was born in Genoa in 1447, the fifth and last child of Giacomo Fieschi, who according to some sources died before the birth, and his wife, Francesca di Negro. The Fieschi were one of the great Guelph families of Liguria, prominent in Church and State from the thirteenth century onward. Sinibaldo Fieschi reigned vigorously if not always edifyingly from 1243 to 1254 as Pope Innocent IV, and twenty years later his nephew Ottobono reigned for a month as Hadrian V (1276). The family reached the height of its power in the fifteenth century, when one member, Roberto dei Fieschi, was a cardinal and Catherine's father, who was descended from a brother of Innocent IV, was viceroy of Naples for René of Anjou.

Many of the details Catherine's early biographers give of her childhood can probably be dismissed as conventional after-the-event attempts to enhance her image. Along with her three brothers and her sister, she received an education based on religion and the humanities that would have been typical for someone of her class. It does nevertheless seem clear that from the age of about thirteen she had a strong desire to enter the religious life. Her sister, Limbania, was already a Canoness Regular of the Lateran, and since the convent chaplain was her own confessor, she tried to persuade him to let her enter as well. Having consulted the nuns, he told her she was too young and should wait. Then circumstances intervened to turn her life in a different direction. In the absence of her father, who had certainly died by this time, the other male members of her family took it upon themselves to organize her future, and on 13 January 1463, when she was not yet sixteen, she was married to Giuliano Adorno. There was nothing personal about the marriage, which was a purely political arrangement. The Ghibelline Adorno family, seeing its fortunes decline, thought it could salvage something for the future through an alliance with the powerful Fieschi. The Fieschi were willing and Catherine became their victim. Not all saints who are said to have married out of obedience when what they really wished to do was to enter a monastery were actually coerced into marriage. Catherine undoubtedly was.

In the past hagiographers have had a tendency to denigrate the spouses of their subjects in order to highlight the virtues of the latter. But even allowing for that, at the personal level the marriage between Catherine and Giuliano cannot be said to have been anything but a mismatch. She was physically beautiful, highly intelligent, sensitive, and profoundly religious; she also displayed what her most sympathetic biographer, Friedrich von Hügel, described as a "wearying vehemence"—in other words, she was extremely intense—and she lacked a sense of humour. Giuliano should not be held entirely responsible for his failure to understand and appreciate her. For one thing, people who lack humour are not the easiest to live with. What is more, the marriage was as much a political arrangement for him as it was for her, and as later events showed, he had his worthwhile side. But his failure to elicit more from her at first than the dutiful obedience expected of a wife at that time was due to his own behaviour. Undisciplined, hot-tempered, and inordinately pleasure-loving, he was on his own admission frequently unfaithful to her and for the first five years was hardly ever at home. Left to herself, Catherine understandably became depressed, though for the second five years she followed the advice of relatives and friends and tried to distract herself by taking more part in social and recreational activities. Thanks to her beauty, her culture, and her intelligent conversation she shone in company, although this was evidently something she later felt guilty about. Anyone hearing her speak then would have concluded that her earlier behaviour must have been appalling, but by that stage even the slightest venial sin seemed terrible to her.

In any case, none of her efforts did much to relieve her sadness. She seems nevertheless to have continued throughout this ten-year period to practise her religion. On 20 March 1473 she was praying in a church near the coast outside Genoa. It was dedicated to St Benedict (21 Mar. at the time, now 11 July), whom she begged to "pray to God that he make me stay three months sick in bed." This cry for relief was answered, though not in the way she was expecting. Two days later, as she knelt before the chaplain at her sister's convent for a blessing, she was overcome by a sense of God's love and her own unworthiness; on the feast of the Annunciation (25 Mar.), having made a full and heartfelt general confession, she received Holy Communion with fervour for the first time in years. The change was complete. Shortly after this she became a daily communicant and was to remain one to the end of her life. At the time this was rare enough in laypeople to invite comment, and she envied priests for this reason.

It was at about this time, ten years into their marriage, that Giuliano's profligate behaviour brought him to the verge of financial and personal ruin. This, combined with Catherine's prayers, prompted him to take stock and to reform his life, even to the extent of becoming a Franciscan tertiary. He and Catherine moved from their *palazzo* to a small house in an even poorer district of Genoa than was really necessary. Here they lived together as brother and sister, devoting their energies to the care of the sick in the hospital of Pammatone. Also working at the hospital was Tommasina Fieschi, one of Catherine's cousins, a humorous and talented woman, who became a canoness and then a Dominican after her husband died. Outwardly, little changed for the next six years. Then in 1479 the couple went to live in the hospital itself, and eleven years later Catherine was appointed matron. She proved to be as capable an administrator as she was a devoted nurse, especially in 1493 when four-fifths of those who stayed in the city died of the plague. Catherine herself nearly died from a severe viral infection that she caught from a dying woman she had kissed in order to comfort her. It was almost certainly during this epidemic that she met Ettore Vernazza for the first time. This Genoese lawyer and philanthropist was only twenty-three at the time, but the two had a common outlook on life and shared the same ideals. Ettore, who unlike Catherine was very happily married, became one of her devoted admirers and preserved many details of her life and conversation.

In 1496 Catherine's health broke down. She was forced to resign as administrator of the hospital, though she and Giuliano continued to live in the building. Then in the following year Giuliano died of a painful illness. "Messer Giuliano has died," Catherine told a friend. "As you are well aware, he had a rather wayward nature, and I suffered interiorly a great deal. But even before he died, my tender Love assured me of his salvation." Toward Giuliano's illegitimate daughter Tobia she showed an extraordinarily generous tenderness and constantly made sure that the girl and her unmarried mother, both of whom were provided for in his will, never went without anything they needed.

Unlike Tommasina, Catherine made no attempt to join a Third Order when Giuliano died or, indeed, at any time in the years that followed. In fact, she seems to have had no formal spiritual direction at all between 1479, the year of Giuliano's conversion, and 1499, when she met a secular priest, Don Cattaneo Marabotto. He had just been made rector of the hospital, and in him she seems at last to have found a priest capable of understanding her.

Yet from the time of her own conversion in 1473 she led an intense spiritual life that found expression in tireless work for the sick and the sad, both in hospital and throughout Genoa, all of whom she held in warm affection. She practised great austerities but never made a fetish of them, always being prepared to moderate them at a word from someone in authority, be it ecclesiastical, medical, or social. She exhibits a fascinating mixture of complete otherworldliness and, as von Hügel would have put it, "all-thereness"—she was so concerned, for example, that her property be appropriately disposed of that she made four wills with several codicils. Her mystical side was responsible for two important works, a treatise on purgatory and a *Dialogue* between the soul and the body. The Holy Office pronounced that these two on their own were enough to prove her sanctity, and they are indeed among the best mystical literature, though Alban Butler described them tersely as "not for the common." In fact, it is unlikely that Catherine wrote a single word of either. Von Hügel concludes that Ettore Vernazza's daughter, the Venerable Battista, wrote the *Dialogue* and was the final redactor for the treatise on purgatory, with its emphasis on God as pure and exacting Love. But he demonstrates at the same time that the teaching is authentically Catherine's.

From 1493 onward Catherine's health was poor, and in 1507 it gave way completely. For the last few months of her life she was in severe pain, though none of the doctors who attended her, including Giovanni Battista Boerio, principal physician of Henry VII of England, could diagnose what was wrong. In the end, because she had no symptoms they could recognize, they decided it must be "a supernatural and divine thing." On 13 September 1510 her temperature rose dangerously and she became delirious. At dawn on the 15th she died. She was buried in the church of the Annunciation at the hospital, and her cult was recognized by Clement X (1670-6) in 1675. She was beatified in 1737, and Benedict XIV (1740-58) added her name to the Roman Martyrology with the title of saint.

The title was hard won. And von Hügel, whose dense two-volume work studies her life, her teaching, and her spiritual significance within the context of his wider discussion of the three "elements" of religion, is concerned to show just how hard. In his interesting section on her spiritual significance, he makes plain his intention to "try to note everywhere what she was not as definitely as what she was." Only thus, he says, will we gain "some adequate apprehension of the 'beggarly elements' she found, and of the spiritual organism and centre of far-reaching influence which she left." Catherine's mind was "without humour or wit," and her temperament "of so excessive a mentality, as to amount to something more or less abnormal." What is more, she was "greatly lacking that quite innocent and normal sensuousness, which appears to form a necessary element of the complete human personality." Hers was, in short, "a highly nervous, delicately poised, immensely sensitive and impressionable psycho-physical organism and temperament." In the absence of "a mind and will at least its equals" and without the support of "a definite, rich, and supernaturally powerful, historical, and institutional religion," this temperament "would have spelt, if not moral ruin, at least lifelong ineffectualness." Fortunately for her she had both:

> In her case, all this unusually turbulent raw material was in unusually close contiguity to powers of mind and of will of a rare breadth and strength. And this very closeness of apposition and width of contrast, and this great strength of mind and will, made all that disordered multiplicity, distraction and dispersion of her clamorous, many-headed, many-hearted nature impossible and unnecessary to bear. And yet to achieve the actual escape from such a tyranny, the mastering of such a rabble, and the harmonization of such a chaos, meant a constant and immense effort, a practically unbroken grace-getting and self-giving, an ever-growing heroism and indeed sanctity, and, with and through all these things, a corresponding expansion and virile joy. It can thus be said, in all simple truth, that she became a saint because she had to; that she became it to prevent herself going to pieces: she literally had to save, and actually did

save, the fruitful life of reason and of love, by ceaselessly fighting her immensely sensitive, absolute, and claimful self.

The most perceptive study is F. von Hügel, *The Mystical Element of Religion as studied in St Catherine of Genoa and her Friends* (1908/1961), from which the above paragraph is quoted (pp. 222-3). See also *AA.SS.*, Sept., 5, pp. 123-95. For an English translation of the written works see H. D. Irvine and C. Balfour (trans.), *Treatise on Purgatory and the Dialogue* (1946). See also Umile Bonzo di Genona, *S. Caterina Fieschi Adorno* (1961-2); *idem*, in *Dict. Sp.*, 2, pp. 290-325; L. de Lapérouse, *La Vie de Ste Catherine de Gènes* (1948); *Bibl.SS.*, 3, 983-90; *O.D.S.*, p. 89.

Bd Anton Schwartz, *Founder* (1852-1929)

Anton Schwartz was born on 28 February 1852 in Baden, near Vienna, the fourth of thirteen children. His father was a minor civil servant and theatre musician. After primary school Anton became a choirboy at the famous Cistercian abbey of Heiligenkreuz (Holy Cross) near Vienna and later continued his education at the Schottengymnasium, a well-known Benedictine grammar school for boys in Vienna. His father died while he was still at school, and the family fell upon hard times.

In 1869 he joined the Piarist Order in Krems, in lower Austria. The Piarists had been founded in 1597 by St Joseph Calasanz (25 Aug.), who cared for the street children of Rome and established the first free primary school in Europe. Anton admired the founder from this time on, but he soon left the Piarists on the advice of his superiors, who viewed the Order's future pessimistically, fearing it would be dissolved in the wake of Bismark's *Kulturkampf* (struggle between Church and State), and enrolled in the diocesan seminary in Vienna.

His health was precarious, and he was often confined to bed. A serious lung infection shortly before his ordination led to his being told to have the customary memorial picture taken, as he was not expected to live much beyond his ordination. When this took place on 25 July 1875 he was so poor that he had to borrow the liturgical vestments and a chalice for the ceremony, during which he added the name Maria to his baptismal name. Contrary to expectations his health improved, and he worked as a curate in Marchegg, east of Vienna on the borders with Slovakia and Hungary. His strictness and commitment to social work earned him the nickname "Pope of Marchegg."

In September 1879 he was appointed chaplain to the hospital run by the Sisters of Mercy at Sechshaus, in the 15th District of Vienna. Here he witnessed the hardships endured by apprentices and young workers forced to work long hours in factories for pitiful wages and under appalling conditions. The Church deplored the "moral quagmire" and "religious destitution" of the working classes, but when Anton asked the archbishop of Vienna, Cardinal Cölestin Ganglbauer, if he could be relieved of his chaplaincy duties to devote himself full time to ministering to poor apprentices, his request was refused.

Eventually the mother superior of the Sisters of Mercy persuaded a group of wealthy aristocrats not only to pay off the considerable debts Fr Anton had incurred in his work for the apprentices but to fund his work in the future. He openly denounced the exploitation of factory workers and urged them to found associations for their own protection and further education; this was several years before Pope Leo XIII issued his famous social encyclical *Rerum novarum*, in 1891.

Anton saw that rectifying social injustice was "one the most significant and hardest problems of our time." In 1886 he founded a Catholic Apprentices' Association: apprentices were invited to a good and wholesome meal on Sunday afternoons and then encouraged to act in plays and to learn musical instruments, after which Anton prayed with them until they went home. In 1886 he followed this with an Apprentices' Refuge, where those who came from outside Vienna could be supervised and cared for.

Three years later, in 1889, he and five religious Brothers founded the *Congregatione Operarii Christianes*, or "Congregation for the Devout Workers of St Joseph Calasanz," of which he was to remain father superior until his death thirty years later. He built the church of Our Lady Help of Christians in Vienna's 15th District, and the street in which it stands is today called "Father Anton Schwartz Street." The Brothers placed their apprentices with Catholic master-craftsmen, founded savings assiciations for workers, promoted unemployment insurance, and established a home for the apprentices who migrated to Vienna from all parts of the Austro-Hungarian Empire. Fr Anton and his Calasantine Brothers literally combed the streets of Vienna for homeless apprentices and provided them with food and shelter. He joined striking workers demanding fairer wages and regular working hours, supporting a strike of tramway workers in 1889 and later, in 1905, of carpenters and waiters, as well as siding with impoverished tailors and cobblers against their employers. He dreamed of winning workers and craftsmen back into the Church and of re-evangelizing Austria. This was no mean task: the greater his involvement in political controversies, the sharper attacks on him and his Order became.

In 1908 he withdrew from public life and concentrated solely on helping young workers. The Order faced opposition from within the Church for a long time, but in 1913 the archbishop of Vienna, Cardinal Friedrich Piffl, recognized his merits and became a close friend and supporter. Anton died on 15 September 1929 and was buried in the church he had built. The process for his beatification was begun twenty years later, and he was finally beatified by Pope John Paul II in Vienna on 21 June 1998.

There is nothing written about him in English apart from brief newspaper reports of his canonization. In German there are only pamphlets and the material prepared by his Order for the diocesan process.

16

ST CORNELIUS, *Pope and Martyr* (253)

When Pope St Fabian (20 Jan.) died in January 250, the Decian persecution, in which he suffered, had become particularly violent. For this reason and because the man most favoured to succeed him, a priest named Moses, was in prison, the clergy of Rome decided to defer the election of a new pope. For the next fourteen months they governed the Church together as a college, their chief spokesman being a priest named Novatian. By March 251, when there was a lull in the persecution and it was feasible to hold an election, Moses had died. So the electors were forced to think again. Much to the dismay of Novatian, who saw himself as the natural candidate, they chose a Roman priest named Cornelius. Novatian had a point: Cornelius, a patrician who may well have belonged to one of the great Roman families, the *gens Cornelia*, was undoubtedly the less qualified of the two. He had, however, two great advantages: he took the soft-line majority view in the dispute about lapsed Christians that had originated in Africa and also involved Novatian; and he enjoyed the support of the powerful bishop of Carthage, St Cyprian (16 Sept.). Having made an unsuccessful attempt to challenge the legality of the election, Novatian gathered his supporters together and had himself consecrated bishop, thus moving into schism. This, together with the question of the lapsed, was to absorb most of Cornelius' energy during his brief pontificate.

The dispute, which had arisen while the Roman see was vacant, was about how the Church should treat Christians who, having denied their faith under pressure of persecution, had repented and wished to return to communion. Up until the moment when he failed to win the election, Novatian appears to have taken a relatively moderate position. Afterwards, supported by a small but effective group of clergy and laity in Rome, he took the hard-line view and opposed the readmission of the lapsed. The more compassionate—and more pragmatic—Cornelius felt they should be readmitted after they had done some appropriate penance. Novatian did not let the matter drop, but eventually Cornelius obtained the support of two heavyweights among the African bishops, St Dionysius of Alexandria (17 Nov.) and Cyprian. Cyprian irritated Cornelius by insisting on making certain inquiries before he pronounced in favour of either side, but once he backed Cornelius the latter felt he had enough support to act. In the autumn of 251 he convened a synod in Rome, which was attended by sixty bishops. Novatian and his followers were excommunicated (they formed a sect that was to survive into the fifth century), and the more lenient approach to lapsed Christians who repented was adopted as the Church's teaching.

Cornelius' moderate attitude to life clearly included a willingness to listen to another's point of view, even when the view in question had been condemned. In 252 he annoyed Cyprian, as their exchange of letters shows, by receiving the emissaries of an African bishop, Fortunatus, who shared Novatian's views. A number of his letters survive, including an important one to Fabius, bishop of Antioch, in which he asks Fabius to reconcile himself to the fact that the consensus in the Church was in favour of compassion and leniency and to abandon his support for Novatian. This letter contains an unattractive portrayal of Novatian, which does not reflect particularly well on Cornelius, but it is important from the historical point of view because of the detailed statistical picture it gives of the Roman clergy at the time.

In 252 the city was attacked by the plague. People began to blame the Christians for provoking the anger of the gods, and early in 253 the persecution flared up again. Reluctant at first because of his high profile and loyal following to condemn Cornelius to death, the authorities banished him to Centumcellae (Civitavecchia). While he was being held there he received a warm and encouraging letter from Cyprian, who congratulated him on the opportunity he had been given to suffer for Christ and on the steadfastness of the Roman Church as a whole. The letter ends with a call for prayer: "Whichever of us shall be first taken hence, let our charity persevere in never-ceasing prayer to the Father for our brothers and sisters." Cornelius was the first to die, in June 253. In the years that followed Cyprian frequently referred to him as a martyr, and there is indeed a legend in the *Liber Pontificalis* according to which, having been imprisoned for taking possession of the remains of SS Peter and Paul (29 June) and fraternizing with a foreign agent (Cyprian), he was tried and beheaded. There is, however, no evidence for this, and it is more likely that he died of the hardships of life at Civitavecchia. His body was eventually taken back to Rome, where it was buried "*in chripta juxta cymiterium Callisti.*" This is the crypt of Lucina, where the tomb bearing the inscription "Cornelius Martyr" can still be seen. Cornelius is mentioned with Cyprian in the First Eucharistic Prayer of the Roman Mass, and they have traditionally been celebrated together on this day. (The joint celebration is continued by the 1969 Calendar reform, but their lives are sufficiently independent for them to be give separate entries here.)

AA.SS., Sept., 4, pp. 143-91; *Bibl.SS.*, 4, 183-9; *H.S.S.C.*, 2, pp. 269-70; *O.D.P.*, pp. 17-8; *O.D.S.*, pp. 112-3; E. Duffy, *Saints and Sinners: A History of the Popes* (1997), pp. 14, 15. For Cornelius' letters see collected letters of Cyprian, 49-50. See also J. Chapman, *Studies in the Early Papacy* (1928); A. Wilpert, *La cripta dei Papi e la cappella di santa Cecilia* (1910)—cf. *Anal.Boll.* 29 (1910), pp. 185-6.

The iconography is relatively extensive. The fresco on the crypt wall dates from the eighth century. Cornelius also figures in the sixth-century procession of martyrs in mosaic on the walls of Sant'Apollinare Nuovo in Ravenna, and again on the walls of Santa Maria in Trastevere in Rome, where he is anachronistically shown wearing the *pallium* (Duffy, p. 15). This mosaic dates from the twelfth century, after which Cornelius' cult seems to have declined in Italy. The existence of relics in Compiègne in the thirteenth century suggests that interest began to grow in the north as it waned in Italy. There is even a screen painting of Cornelius, dressed in papal vestments and carrying a triple cross and a horn, in the church in the village of Portlemouth, Devon.

ST CYPRIAN OF CARTHAGE, *Bishop and Martyr* (258)

Thascius Caecilianus Cyprianus—or Cyprian, as he is now more familiarly known to English speakers—played an important part in the history of the Western Church and the development of Christian thought throughout the third century. Little is known about his background, but he was born in Carthage in about 200. At the time the city, caught between the claims of rival emperors on the one hand and barbarian invasions on the other, was on the verge of decline, but the Church had begun to flourish. Cyprian eventually became an orator and a teacher of rhetoric as well as an advocate in the courts. A large-hearted, energetic, all-or-nothing man, he participated to the full in the life of the city, public and social. When he was about forty-five the example of an old priest named Caecilian caused him radically to rethink his life, for which he remained grateful to the end. The respect, moreover, seems to have been mutual: on his deathbed, Caecilian recommended his wife and children to Cyprian's care and protection.

Cyprian's conversion was complete. Before his Baptism he made a vow of chastity, which seems to have astonished those who knew him in Carthage. Then, which must have been a great sacrifice, he gave up the pagan authors with whom he was so familiar—there is not a single quotation from them in his Christian writings. This was in order to concentrate his mind on the scriptures and the Christian writers, among whom his fellow-countryman, Tertullian, became his favourite. He was ordained to the priesthood shortly after his Baptism and in 248 was named bishop of Carthage. Reluctant to accept, he tried to leave the city, but once persuaded that he was the choice of the vast majority of the people and all but a handful of the clergy he was duly consecrated and took up his duties.

The closest approach to an authentic description of Cyprian at this time is in the brief biographical sketch by his deacon, St Pontus (8 Mar.), not all of which is universally accepted as historically useful. But if Pontus is to be believed, Cyprian's appearance and manner were impressive, earning him the love and respect of those who came in contact with him, and he administered his diocese with a combination of charity and firmness.

Cyprian had been bishop for less than a year when a period of relative freedom from persecution came to an end with the accession of the emperor Decius (249-51). When the edict ordering all inhabitants to offer sacrifice to the gods reached Carthage, many Christians were too frightened to stand out against it. Instead they queued up to register their apostasy with the magistrate and receive a *libellus*, or certificate, to that effect. Meanwhile, there were cries for Cyprian's blood. However, by the time he had been proscribed and his goods declared forfeit he had gone into hiding. He was criticized for this in Rome, where Pope St Fabian (20 Jan.) had just been killed, as well as in Africa and was sufficiently put on the defensive to feel the need to justify himself in writing to his clergy. But in fact he was able, through frequent letters, to govern well from his hiding place, providing a much-needed focus of encouragement for his people. "Let each of us," he wrote, "pray to God not for himself only but for all the brethren, according to the pattern which Our Lord gave us, wherein we are taught to pray as a common brotherhood, for all, and not as individuals, for ourselves alone. When the Lord shall see us humble, peaceable, in unity among ourselves, and made better by our present sufferings, he will deliver us from the hands of our persecutors." He was particularly careful to encourage Christians who were standing firm in prison, and made sure that priests took turns to visit them and bring them the sacraments.

There was one development that may have made Cyprian regret his absence from the city. He himself took a humane but firm line with those who had apostasized (*lapsi*), readmitting them to communion after a suitable period of penance. In his absence the leader of the small minority of clergy who had opposed his election as bishop, a man named Novatus, had taken to receiving them back without any canonical penance at all. When a number of priests and some of the laity gave Novatus their support, he took them into schism. Cyprian denounced him, and at a council held in Carthage once the persecution had let up read an uncompromising treatise on the unity of the Church. "There is," he said, "one God, one Christ, and but one episcopal chair, originally founded on Peter, by the Lord's authority. There cannot therefore be set up another altar or another priesthood. Whatever any man in his rage or rashness shall appoint, in defiance of the divine institution, must be a spurious, profane, and sacrilegious ordinance." When they were excommunicated, Novatus and the other schismatics took themselves off to stir things up in Rome. Here a Roman priest, confusingly named Novatian, had set himself up as antipope to the lawfully elected Pope St Cornelius (251-3; 16 Sept., above). Novatian's views on the *lapsi* were the extreme opposite of those of Novatus. He believed that there could be no forgiveness for them at all and was eventually excommunicated as a heretic. Cyprian, who had recognized Cornelius' election as pope and actively supported him during the ensuing schism, continued to take a moderate line in the matter of the *lapsi*. It was his view, compassionate but firm, that in the end prevailed.

From 252 to 254 there was a terrible epidemic of the plague in Carthage. Cyprian wrote a treatise, *De mortalitate*, to comfort his people and give them courage. At the practical level he organized the Christians of the city, reminding them that they had a duty to care not only for each other but for anyone, even their enemies and persecutors, who had fallen victim to the plague. Tasks were efficiently distributed. The wealthy contributed money; the poor gave their time and labour. As bishop, Cyprian always showed great concern for the poor, mentioning them frequently in the letters he wrote from hiding. "Do not," he would say, "let anything sleep in your coffers which could be profitable to the poor. It is well for you to distribute voluntarily that which you must of necessity part with some time or other, so that God may recompense you in eternity."

Having supported Cornelius in the Novatian affair, toward the end of his life Cyprian opposed Pope St Stephen I (254-7; 2 Aug.) in the debate about the validity of baptisms administered by heretics, schismatics, and apostates. He, along with a number of other African bishops, insisted they were invalid. Although he wrote a treatise on patience at about this time, he showed little himself during this debate, and the same can be said for Stephen. That apart, the situation should be seen in the context of a period in which the Roman Church was still trying to establish its primacy among other powerful Churches, of which that in north Africa was one. Neither Stephen nor Cyprian lived to see the resolution of this dispute, which came with the general acceptance of the Roman view.

In August 257 the emperor Valerian (253-60) published his first edict against Christians. This specifically ordered bishops, priests, and deacons to participate in official pagan worship. Cyprian refused, appeared before the consul, and was exiled with Pontus and others to Curubis, a small town on the sea fifty miles from Carthage. In August 258 he was brought back to Carthage, where he seems to have been kept under some sort of house arrest. On 14 September he was tried again, and when he refused to change his attitude he was condemned to death by the sword. He was buried, according to one of the accounts of his trials and death that have survived, in "the graveyard of Macrobius Candidianus the procurator, which is on the road to Mappalia, near the reservoirs."

The cult of St Cyprian was most active in North Africa, where his relics were distributed, and there are dedications from the fourth and fifth centuries. But there is evidence that it also flourished from the beginning of the fourth century in Rome, where his feast was celebrated, his works were read, and eulogies were written about him. Some interest and enthusiasm continued well into the Middle Ages, though unfortunately he became confused, especially but not exclusively in the East, with an imaginary magician named Cyprian of Antioch.

Cyprian's greatest legacy is his writings, which had the honour, rare at the time, of being translated into Greek. Interestingly, they included very little in the way of theological speculation. In fact, Cyprian is the first Latin Father of the Church whose substantial writings fall into the category of pastoral theology rather than that of dogmatics. Many of his letters survive, as do a few sermons, thirteen treatises on a variety of subjects, and some biblical commentary. From these it is possible to form a good idea of his concerns: the unity of the Church; the place of the bishop, as servant of that unity, in the local Church; the role of the sacraments, especially those of Penance and the Eucharist, in the Christian life. So much of what he said remained valid over the centuries, and he was still being quoted in the documents of Vatican II.

AA.SS., Sept., 4, pp. 191-348; A. Musurillo, *Acts of the Christian Martyrs* (1972). On the *passio* see H. Delehaye, *Les passions des martyrs et les genres littéraires* (1921), pp. 82-104. Biographies by E. W. Benson (1897); P. Monceaux (1914); J. Fichter (1942); M. M. Sage (1975). On Cyprian's teaching see A. d'Alès, *La Théologie de S. Cyprien* (1922); H. Koch, *Cyprian und der römischer Primat* (1910). For his works see W. Hartel (ed.) in *C.S.E.L.* (1868-71); R. E. Wallis (Eng. trans.) in *A.N.C.L.* (1868-71); T. A. Lacey (ed.), *Select Epistles of St Cyprian* (1922). See also M. Bévenot (ed.), *St Cyprian: the Lapsed, the Unity of the Catholic Church* (1957); G. S. M. Walker, *The Churchmanship of St Cyprian* (Ecumenical Studies in History 9, 1968); P. Hinchcliff, *Cyprian of Carthage* (1974); P. Monceaux, *Histoire de l'Afrique Chrétienne* (1902); *H.S.S.C.*, 2, pp. 121-30; *Bibl.SS.*, 3, 1260-78; *O.D.S.*, pp. 119-20.

Surprisingly, given his enormous popularity, the cult of St Cyprian was never widespread. It flourished in North Africa, however, and there is evidence that his relics were distributed during the fourth and fifth centuries. The iconography is small, with nothing really early.

St Euphemia, *Martyr* (? *c.* 303)

The only certain facts here are that a young woman died a martyr's death in Chalcedon and that for a while her cult was extremely popular and widespread. According to her *passio*, which was compiled after the Council of Chalcedon (451) and is thought by modern scholars to be of dubious value, Euphemia was arrested when she refused to attend a festival in honour of the god Ares. Having overcome miraculously a succession of brutal tortures—they are summarized in the Roman Martyrology—she was finally killed by a wild beast while other beasts sat meekly at her feet. According to St Asterius of Amasea (30 Oct.), who mentioned them in his panegyric of the saint sometime between 380 and 410, there was a series of frescoes depicting her torments on the walls of the great church erected in her honour in Chalcedon. The historian Evagrius describes the church in detail and bears witness to the popularity of her cult. Civil and ecclesiastical leaders as well as ordinary people, he says, came to Chalcedon to benefit from the blessings granted through her intercession, as well as from the many miracles that were reported there.

The fact that the Council of Chalcedon, which condemned Monophysitism, took place in her church in 451 was probably responsible in part for the extraordinary prestige Euphemia once enjoyed. On the other hand, there is absolutely no truth in the legend that, to reach a conclusion, the council fathers placed two books, one outlining the Monophysite position and the other the orthodox position, in her shrine, prayed for three days, and then opened the shrine to find the Monophysite book at her feet and the orthodox in her right hand.

Place names on the east coast of Italy suggest that the cult arrived there from Asia Minor and then spread throughout Italy, especially to the Milan area, and even to France, where it is mentioned by St Victricius of Rouen (7 Aug.). That Pope St Sergius (687-701; 8 Sept.) restored the ruins of a church dedicated to Euphemia in Rome implies that although intense the cult may not have been very long-lived, at least in the West. On the other hand, she was still sufficiently well known for Andrea Mantegna to paint her (with lion, lily, palm and sword) in the fifteenth century. And Pope Pius XII (1939-58) mentioned her in the encyclical *Sempiternus Christus Rex*, written to commemorate the fifteenhundredth anniversary of the Council of Chalcedon in 1951. She is also mentioned in the canon of the Ambrosian rite and at the preparation in the Russian Byzantine rite. In the East she is often referred to as St Euphemia the Far-Renowned.

See *AA.SS.*, Sept., 5, pp. 252-86; *C.M.H.*, pp. 187, 515; *Bibl.SS.*, 5, 154-62; *H.S.S.C.*, 2, p. 272; H. Roeder, *Saints and Their Attributes* (1955).

St Abundius and Companions, *Martyrs* (? *c*. 304)

The Lateran museum in Rome possesses part of an epitaph that was found at Rignano, about twenty-six miles from the city. It reads: "*Abundio presbytero martyri sancto. dep. VII idus dec.*" Archaeologists are divided as to its authenticity, but some believe that it refers to a St Abundius who is mentioned in the Roman Martyrology on this day: "At Rome, on the Flaminian Way, the holy martyrs Abundius the priest and Abundantius the deacon, whom, together with the distinguished man Marcian and his son John, who had been raised from the dead by Abundius, the Emperor Diocletian ordered to be slain by the sword by the tenth milestone from the city." The December date could be a problem, but G. B. Rossi suggested that it might be that of the handing over of the bodies to Theodora.

The unreliable *acta* of these martyrs add that Abundius and his deacon were ordered to sacrifice to Hercules and, when they refused, were thrown into the Mamertine prison. A month later they were brought out, tortured, and condemned to death. On their way to the place of execution they met Marcian, who was mourning the death of his son. Abundius prayed over the boy's body, to which life returned, at which point Marcian and John bore witness to Christ and were beheaded along with the priest and his deacon. All four were buried in the cemetery of a woman named Theodora, near Rignano on the Flaminian Way.

In 1001 under the emperor Otto III (996-1002) their relics were brought to Rome, along with those of Theodora (whom the Roman Martyrology mentions on 17 Sept.). They were placed first in the church of San Bartolomeo ad Isola and then in that of SS Cosmas and Damian. Finally, in 1583, the relics of SS Abundius and Abundantius were taken to the Gesù, the Jesuit church. Two years later St Aloysius Gonzaga (21 June) attended Mass at their shrine before he entered the Society of Jesus.

AA.SS., Sept., 5, pp. 293–310, discusses the relics. On the inscription see G. B. Rossi, "I monumenti antichi cristiani e la loro distribuzione geografica nel territorio dei Capenati," in *Bullettino di Archeologia Cristiana* 11 (1883), pp. 115–59; H. Delehaye, *Origines du culte des martyrs*, p. 322.

St Ninian, *Bishop* (? 432)

There are three relatively late sources of information about St Ninian (Ninias): a Life by St Aelred of Rievaulx (12 Jan.) and two late eighth-century poems, all of which are probably based on a Latin Life, now lost, and Bede's *Historia Ecclesiastica*. The most reliable is the latter. Bede (25 May), who probably got his information from Abbot Pecthelm of Candida Casa (now Whithorn in Galloway), writes:

> The southern Picts who dwell on this side of those mountains had, it is re-ported, long before forsaken the errors of paganism and embraced the truth by the preaching of Ninias, a most reverend bishop and holy man of the British nation, who had been regularly instructed at Rome in the faith and mysteries of the truth. His episcopal see, named after St Martin the Bishop and famous for a church dedicated in his honour (where Ninias himself and many other saints rest in the body), is now in the possession of the English nation. The place belongs to the province of the Bernicians and is commonly called the White House, because he there built a church of stone, which was not usual amongst the Britons.

Not all scholars are fully convinced of Bede's accuracy. In the context of the period, for example, his remark that Ninian was "regularly instructed at Rome in the faith and mysteries of the truth" may be no more than a way of saying that Ninian was a supporter of the "Roman" rather than the "Celtic" position and that the see had an "orthodox" foundation. There is evidence, neverthe-less, to suggest that he is right about the place. Archaeological research at Whithorn has brought to light the remains of an early church. Nearby were discovered stones with Christian inscriptions on them, indicating the existence of a monastery. And Ninian's tomb, which became a place of pilgrimage in the Middle Ages, was found there "with those of many other saints." More contro-versial is the dedication to St Martin of Tours (11 Nov.). That Ninian actually visited Tours, as Aelred claims he did, remains open to question. It is perfectly possible, however, that his form of monasticism was inspired by that of Martin and that he brought a relic of Martin to Whithorn.

There has also been a great deal of discussion about who the "southern Picts" were and where exactly they were living. It is hard to say how far Ninian travelled from his base at Whithorn. If place names and dedications are anything to go by, there is a St Ninian's near Stirling, and there are dedications elsewhere in Scotland as well as three in northern England. But they are difficult to date. The truth is that we do not know how far Ninian's apostolate extended, and if St Patrick (17 Mar.) is to be believed, his success among the Picts was short-lived. There also seems to be no truth in the story that he died during a visit to Ireland. On the other hand, he was undoubtedly influential round Whithorn, which became a centre of study for Irish and Welsh monks, and he paved the way for St Kentigern (14 Jan.). By the time his cult began to decline in the sixteenth century it had spread as far afield as Kent and Denmark.

Bede, *H.E.*, 3, 4; W. Levison, "An Eighth-Century Poem on St Ninian" in *Antiquity* 14 (1940), pp. 280-91; Aelred's Life in A. P. Forbes, *The Historians of Scotland* (1874) and A. O. Anderson, *Early Sources of Scottish History* (1922); J. and W. McQueen *et al* (eds.), *Scotichronicon* (1987). See also *Bibl.SS.*, 9, 1012-4; *O.D.S.*, pp. 357-8; W. D. Simpson, *Saint Ninian and the Origins of the Christian Church in Scotland* (1940); E. A. Thompson, "The origin of Christianity in Scotland," in *Scottish Historical Review* 35 (1958), pp. 17-22; M. Anderson, *St Ninian, light of the Celtic North* (1964); A. Boyle, "St Ninian: some outstanding problems," in *Innes Review* 19 (1968), pp. 57-70; D. Brooke, *Wild Men and Holy Places: St Ninian, Whithorn and the Medieval Realm of Galloway* (1994); F. T. Wainwright, *The Problem of the Picts* (1955); R. P. C. Hanson, *St Patrick* (1968); G. Hay, "A Scottish Altarpiece in Copenhagen," in *Innes Review* 7 (1956), pp. 5-10.

At Whithorn, the remains of a twelfth-century priory ruin, said to have been built on the site of St Ninian's fifth-century church, can still be seen. The priory developed into the cathedral church of Galloway. The "Latinus stone," now in the abbey museum, is the oldest Christian memorial in Scotland.

St Ludmila (*c.* 860-921)

Ludmila came from the region north of Prague where the Elbe (Labe) and the Vltava converge. She was the daughter of a Slav prince and like many women in her position found herself caught up in the power struggles of the time. Born in about 860, she was married when she was barely into her teens to Borivoy, duke of Bohemia and head of the Premyslid dynasty, with whom she had three sons and three daughters. In 874 Borivoy was baptized by St Methodius (14 Feb.), and Ludmila followed him into the Church. There seems to have been an element of political calculation in Borivoy's conversion, since as a pagan he could not sit at table with the Christian nobles of Moravia. On the other hand, the fact that most of the leading families in Bohemia were opposed to Christianity made life difficult for the couple at home. However, although Borivoy did not make matters any easier by trying—as did many rulers of the period—to force his religion on his people, he did manage to overcome the opposition. Together he and Ludmila built the first Christian church in Bohemia, at Levy Hradec. This they dedicated to St Clement (23 Nov.), patron of the mission of SS Cyril and Methodius.

When Borivoy died in 894, he was succeeded by his two sons. The younger, Ratislav, was married to a Slav princess of the Stodorané tribe, with whom he had four daughters and three sons. The eldest son, Wenceslas (28 Sept.), would eventually rule Bohemia and die as a martyr. Because Ratislav's wife, Drahomíra, was only nominally Christian, Ludmila, with Ratislav's blessing, assumed responsibility for Wenceslas' upbringing and education. A kind, gentle, and also learned woman, she took this responsibility seriously, and Wenceslas received a solid grounding in the Faith as well as in Latin and church Slavonic. Things changed radically, however, when Ratislav died prematurely in 916. Having almost certainly felt enormous resentment at Ludmila's influence over her son, Drahomíra, who was acting as regent, now removed the boy completely from his grandmother's charge. In this she had the full support of the anti-Christian party in the country.

Ludmila, who had given most of her possessions to the poor when Borivoy died, now withdrew to the castle at Tetín, south-west of Prague, in order to avoid conflict with Drahomíra. She seems to have felt that if Wenceslas could take over the reins of power as soon as he was able to do so instead of when he came of age, the people would rally and Christianity in Bohemia would be saved. The anti-Christians realized this and were prepared to go to great lengths to keep grandmother and grandson apart. In the end, some went to extreme lengths: whether at the instigation of Drahomíra, as some have suggested, or without her knowledge, two men came to Tetín on 16 September 921 and strangled Ludmila with her own veil. She was buried at Tetín, where Drahomíra later had the church of St Michael built over her tomb. Her body was eventually taken to St George's church in Prague, probably by Wenceslas himself in what would have been the first independent political act of his reign. The legend portrays her death in purely religious terms—she died a martyr, killed by pagans on account of her beliefs—but the matter is not so straightforward. In reality she was caught up in a power struggle in which religion was just one of the elements. Be that as it may, she was immediately acclaimed a martyr, and the cult, which originally focused on her tomb, began to spread during the thirteenth century.

The *passio* of St Ludmila exists in more than one form. These are printed, along with a more detailed account by Christian de Scala, in *AA.SS.*, Sept., 5. For a discussion of the materials and their authenticity, see J. Pekar, *Die Wenzels und Ludmila Legenden und die Echtheit Christians* (1906); *Anal.Boll.* 25 (1906), pp. 512-3, 43, pp. 218-21. See also *H.S.S.C.*, 5, pp. 248-55; *Bibl.SS.*, 8, 293-6; F. Dvornik, *St Wenceslas of Bohemia* (Eng. trans., 1929).

St Edith of Wilton (961-84)

Alban Butler skirts over the question of Edith's origins by saying that she was "the daughter of King Edgar [959-75; 8 July] and Wulfrida (also sometimes called Saint) in circumstances that are obscure and, according to some reports, exceedingly scandalous." The truth appears to be that Edith (Eadgyth, Eadida, Edyva) was the daughter not of one of Edgar's wives (he had two), but of Edgar and a young woman named Wulfthryth (Wulfrida), of whom he was particularly fond and who may at the time have been a novice at Wilton Abbey—Wilton was the Saxon capital of Wessex. The most important source of information, both for the legend and for the cult of Edith, is the Life written in 1080 by Goscelin of Canterbury, whom William of Malmesbury described as "second to none after Bede" as a biographer of English saints. There are anomalies, but he was clearly familiar with life at Wilton Abbey and with its traditions. He also describes Wulfthryth as the "hidden treasure and light" of Wilton.

Wulfthryth gave birth to Edith at Kemsing in Kent in 961. She went (or, if she was already a novice, returned) afterwards to Wilton, where Edith was brought up. Edith's scholastic education was entrusted to two of the chaplains, Radbod of Saint-Rémi and Bernon of Trèves, and she would also have become proficient in lettering, illumination, sewing, and embroidery—she is known to have had exceptional artistic gifts. Edgar made at least two unsuccessful attempts to tempt her back to the world. On the day of her religious profession, for example, when she was not quite fifteen, he is said to have arrived at the abbey with a profusion of gold and silver ornaments and jewels. These he laid out on a red carpet in front of the altar, while her mother, now abbess of Wilton, stood by with a veil and a Psalter. Since Edith chose the cloister, Edgar's next ploy was to offer her the abbacy of three separate houses at Winchester, Barking, and Amesbury. According to tradition, Edith realized that she was far too young and inexperienced to undertake the government of even one house, so she appointed a superior for each of the three and herself remained at Wilton. This may be true; on the other hand, it may be an invention or at least an exaggeration designed to show how detached she was.

Very soon after this Edgar died and was succeeded by his son Edward (the Martyr, 975-9; 18 Mar.). When Edward was murdered in 979, those members of the nobility who had supported him turned to his half-sister Edith in the hope that she would leave Wilton and accept the crown. Once again Edith is said to have preferred the obscurity of the abbey, but if this paints a rather serious picture of her, her more lively side emerges from an exchange she had with Aethelwold, bishop of Winchester. He reproached her for wearing colourful habits, to which she replied that her heart was no less pure underneath them. She built a chapel at Wilton in honour of the French martyr St Denis (9 Oct.), the walls of which were decorated by Bernon with scenes from the passion of Christ and the martyrdom of St Denis. The dedication ceremony was attended by the archbishop of Canterbury, St Dunstan (19 May), who is said to have wept at the knowledge, which came to him in prayer, that Edith would soon die. Just over a month later, on 16 September 984, Edith did die. She was only twenty-three. Miracles were soon being reported at her tomb, and her feast, which was celebrated in many monasteries, appeared in the Sarum calendar. At least three churches in England are known to have been dedicated to her. Her relics were translated in 997 and placed alongside those of St Iwi (8 Oct.).

Apart from Goscelin, the main sources of information about St Edith are William of Malmesbury, Simeon of Durham, and Capgrave. See also *O.D.S.*, pp. 146-7; *H.S.S.C.*, 5, p. 270; A. Wilmart, "La légende de Ste Edith en prose et vers par Goscelin," in *Anal.Boll.* 56 (1937), pp. 5-101, 265-307; C. Horstmann, *S. Editha sive Chronicum Vilodunense* (1883); S. Ridyard, *The Royal Saints of Anglo-Saxon England* (1988).

Wilton House, rebuilt by Inigo Jones after a fire in the seventeenth century, now stands on the site of Wilton Abbey.

Bd Victor III, *Pope* (*c.* 1027-87)

When Pope St Gregory VII (1073-85; 25 May) died in exile in Salerno in 1085, those who supported the reforms he had been trying to push through found themselves in a state of some turmoil. Particularly galling was the presence in Rome of Guibert of Ravenna, who as Clement III was in the middle of the second of his three spells as antipope. Not only did he have the support of at least thirteen cardinals and a significant number of the laity, he had effectively been "elected" "pope" by the Holy Roman emperor, Henry IV (1056-1106), Gregory's powerful adversary in the investiture controversy. The election of a new pope was postponed, but almost exactly a year later, under pressure from Jordan of Capua, one of the Norman princes, the cardinals elected Desiderius, abbot of Monte Cassino. He, it was thought, might have influence with the Normans and bring about some sort of reconciliation with Henry. At first Desiderius refused, believing himself to be unsuitable, but when the cardinals met again on 24 May 1086 and again elected him, he accepted. He took the name Victor III, a tactful choice in that one of his predecessors, Victor II (1055-7), had been Henry's guardian while he was still a minor.

Born in about 1027 and named Daufer (Daufari), he came from a Lombard family and was related to the dukes of Benevento. He was an only son, and his father was anxious for him to marry. He himself felt a strong calling to be a monk, and when his father was killed in battle in 1047 he took the opportunity to slip away from his family and start living as a hermit. His whereabouts were discovered by relatives, who stripped him of his habit and brought him back by force to Benevento. They had reckoned, however, without his determination. A year later he managed to escape, despite the close watch put on him, and to enter the monastery of La Cava. At this point his relatives accepted the inevitable, merely asking that he be transferred to the monastery of Santa Sofia in Benevento. This was arranged in 1048 or 1049, and Daufer's new abbot gave him the name Desiderius, by which he is better known.

If Desiderius was looking for stability, he does not seem to have found it, at least in his early years as a monk. In a series of moves, he left Benevento for a monastery on an island in the Adriatic; he went to Salerno to study medicine; and for a while he became a hermit in the Abruzzi. Then, having attracted the attention of Pope St Leo IX (1049-54; 19 Apr.), he went to Rome and spent a while at the court of Victor II. It was here that he met some monks from Monte Cassino. With their encouragement he went to the monastery on pilgrimage and once there joined the community. In 1057 the abbot of Monte Cassino, who had been elected pope and taken the name Stephen IX (1057-8), called Desiderius to Rome with a view to sending him as his legate to Constantinople. At the same time he instructed the monks at Monte Cassino to elect a new abbot. Desiderius was at Bari, on his way east, when the news reached him that the pope had died and that he himself had been elected abbot.

He turned out to be one of the great abbots of Monte Cassino. As far as externals were concerned, he was responsible for one of the most extensive rebuilding projects in its history. His aim was to establish some sort of coherence between the various buildings by replacing some and renovating others. Particular attention was paid to his projected basilica-style church. For this, which took five years to build, he obtained fine materials and employed workmen from Lombardy and Amalfi and as far afield as Constantinople. The resulting combination of Lombard and Byzantine influences had a lasting effect on artistic endeavour within the monastery, which Desiderius did much to encourage, and, through the activity of the monks, on the wider world. Desiderius' abbey was destroyed in an earthquake on 9 September 1349, but thanks to the *Chronica monasterii cassinensis* of Leo of Ostia, a description of it survives.

Desiderius also encouraged literature, learning, and the arts. During his time as abbot a Cassinese school of writers, poets, historians, and painters began to flourish, and the great library was considerably expanded. He himself wrote three books of dialogues, inspired by those of Pope St Gregory the Great (590-604; 3 Sept.), on the miracles of St Benedict (11 July). But these were not the only areas in which he aimed for the best. He insisted on strict observance of the Rule and was such an inspiring leader that the number of monks increased to two hundred during his régime. One of those who joined the community was Constantinus Africanus, the best-known physician of the early Salerno school and a personal friend of Desiderius—they had presumably met during the latter's brief sojourn in Salerno.

At this time it had become customary to appoint monks from Monte Cassino to a variety of church offices. Desiderius was no exception and had other duties besides those that fell to him as abbot. After a disputed election, the man whom he supported was chosen to succeed Stephen IX and as Nicholas II (1058-61) made him a cardinal. He was also appointed papal vicar for Campania, Calabria, Capua, and Puglia, in which capacity he had power to make appointments to vacant sees and abbacies. By nature a reconciler and a lover of peace, he also did what he could to improve relations between the papacy and the secular powers. In June 1080, for example, he successfully reconciled Pope Gregory VII with the Norman duke of Puglia, Robert Guiscard. On the other hand, his attempt to bring Gregory and Henry IV closer together merely incurred the wrath of the pope, who felt he had conceded too much to Henry.

The breach between them did not last, however, and when Gregory was forced to leave Rome in 1085, Desiderius took him in at Monte Cassino and was with him when he died in Salerno on 25 May 1085.

Desiderius remained absent from Rome after Gregory died but was forced to return in May 1086 when he was elected pope himself. As Victor III, he was certainly one of the more reluctant holders of the papal office. Already weakened by ill health and aware that his election was far from acceptable to the more extreme Gregorians, not to mention the anti-Gregorians, he used a riot which occurred four days after his election as an excuse to return to Monte Cassino. Once there he removed the papal insignia and resumed his duties as abbot. In March 1087 Jordan of Capua persuaded him, not as pope but as papal vicar in southern Italy, to convene a synod at Capua. Here, despite the opposition of a minority led by the bishop of Lyon, he finally agreed actively to accept the papal office, and on 9 May he was at last consecrated in St Peter's basilica.

Rome was occupied at the time by the troops of the antipope Clement III, and Victor was unable to establish his authority there, even with the help of such powerful supporters as Jordan of Capua and Matilda of Tuscany (1055-1115). After a week he gave up and returned to Monte Cassino. But in early June, in spite of persistent ill health, he responded to Matilda's pleas and went back to Rome, this time by sea. By the end of the month, thanks to military help from Matilda, he had wrested control of the city from the antipope. He was back in Monte Cassino by the middle of July, having heard that Henry IV was about to arrive in Italy, but he nevertheless managed to fit a fair amount of papal business into the last few weeks of his life.

Perhaps his most important act was to convene a synod in late August at Benevento, where a number of significant decisions were made. Not least of these, though not unexpected from a man who saw himself as the custodian of Gregory VII's legacy, was the decision to republish Gregory's condemnation of lay investiture. When the synod was over this wise and peace-loving pope was too ill to do anything but allow himself to be taken back to his monastery. Lying on a couch in the chapter house he gave his last instructions to his monks and recommended that Eudes (Odo), bishop of Ostia, be elected to the apostolic see. He died on 16 September 1087. He was buried in Rome, but in 1692 his remains were taken to a chapel that had been dedicated to him at Monte Cassino. This was destroyed in the 1944 bombing raids, and with it paintings depicting episodes from Victor's life by Luca Giordano. His remains were taken safely to Rome, however, and were returned to a chapel in the new basilica at Monte Cassino in 1963.

The cult, which began immediately, had a twofold source, in the admiration felt by the monks of Monte Cassino for their abbot and in that felt by the Roman church for its bishop. Benedict XIII (1724-30) approved it for the abbey, but Prospero Lambertini, later Benedict XIV (1740-58), did not regard this as canonization *equipollentis*. So although the cult was confirmed by Pope

Leo XIII (1878-1903) in 1887, Victor has the title blessed, except at Monte Cassino, where he has been given that of saint.

There is a detailed account of Bd Victor's life in *Chronica Monasterii Cassinensis*, 3. It is printed also in *M.G.H.*, *Scriptores*, 7, pp. 698-754. See also H. K. Mann, *Lives of the Popes*, 7, pp. 218-44; *Bibl.SS.*, 12, 1286-9; *O.D.P.*, pp. 157-8; H. E. J. Cowdrey, *The Age of Abbot Desiderius* (1983); *D.T.C.*, 14, 2866-72; *N.C.E.*, 14, 667; F. Hirsch, "Desiderius von Monte Cassino als Papst Victor III," in *Forschungen zur deutschen Geschichte*, 7 (1867), pp. 1-112; F. X. Seppelt, *Geschichte der Papste*, 3 (1954-9), pp. 95-100, 115-8.

Bd Vitalis of Savigny, *Abbot* (1122)

The main source of information about St Vitalis is a biography written by Stephen de Fougères, a chaplain to King Henry II who subsequently became bishop of Rennes. This is rather fulsome, but as Stephen died in 1178 it has the advantage of being more or less contemporary. It records that, having completed the regular course of studies, Vitalis went to serve for a while as chaplain to William the Conqueror's half-brother, Robert de Mortain. Then in 1095 he went off to live as a hermit at Dompierre, in a place he had already been using as a retreat. When disciples began to gather round his hermitage he founded the abbey of Savigny, where as abbot he introduced a number of reforms and made sure that the Rule of St Benedict was faithfully observed. He seems to have travelled a great deal and to have gained a reputation as one of the great preachers of the age. It was said that on one of the several occasions on which he visited England he was understood by every member of a crowded congregation, despite the fact that he spoke no English and they by and large understood no French.

But he was not content simply to preach. His dealings with those with whom he came in contact were practical as well: he built an orphanage and a hostel for pilgrims, and he showed particular concern for the welfare of prostitutes, doing what he could to help them to marry. He had a reputation for speaking his mind and was no respecter of persons. Hearing him make an intervention at the Synod of Reims in 1119, Pope Callistus II (1119-24) observed that he had never heard anyone speak the truth with greater force and less flattery. Vitalis died, according to his biographer, on 16 September 1122 while reciting the Office of the Blessed Virgin in choir. His body was taken to Savigny, and miracles were recorded at his tomb. On 1 May 1243, with the permission of the abbot of Cîteaux (Savigny had joined up with Cîteaux in 1147), his remains were placed in the abbey church. The coffin was desecrated in 1793 during the Revolution, but the remains were gathered together into a wooden casket. The Savigny "reform" proved popular and was introduced by other abbeys, including Buckfast in Devon.

For the Life by Stephen de Fougères see *Anal.Boll.* 1 (1882), pp. 355-90. See also L. Delisle, *Rouleaux des Morts* (1886), p. 282-344; *AA.SS.*, Jan., 1, pp. 389-90; *Bibl.SS.*, 12, 1222-4; D. Knowles, *The Monastic Orders in England* (1949), pp. 202, 227.

Bd Louis Allemand, *Bishop* (*c.* 1390-1450)

Had he been judged by his external actions alone, Louis Allemand (or Aleman) would have been an unlikely candidate for canonization. He was born at Arbert Castle in the diocese of Beiley, east of Lyon, in about 1390. When he was still young he went to Avignon, where he eventually read law at the university. Once he had taken his first degree—he went on to obtain a doctorate in 1414— his uncle, Cardinal François de Condié, who was a chamberlain at the papal court, managed to obtain for him a number of ecclesiastical benefices. In 1409 Louis accompanied this uncle to the Synod of Pisa, where he was introduced to the complex and frequently disedifying world of ecclesiastical politics.

The synod had been called in the hope that, by deposing both Gregory XII (1406-15) and the antipope Benedict XIII (1394-1417) and then electing a new pope acceptable to all parties, the so-called Great Schism of the West could be brought to an end. Far from resolving anything, the synod made matters worse, and for a while three men—Gregory XII and the two antipopes Benedict XIII and Alexander V (1409-10)—were claiming the papal office. Attempts to re-solve the matter continued, and Louis was present in 1414 at the meeting that eventually became the Council of Constance. This had been called by the German king, Sigismund (1411-37), and the antipope John XXIII (1410-15), who had been elected to succeed Alexander V. Once the two antipopes had been deposed and Gregory XII had been prevailed upon to abdicate, it became possible at last to hold a conclave to elect a new pope. Louis was placed in charge of it as vice chamberlain, a position he retained until he became a cardinal.

Once the election was over, Louis became attached to the court of the new pope, Martin V (1417-31), who made him bishop of Maguelonne and en-trusted him with a number of responsible missions. On 3 December 1423 he was promoted to the archbishopric of Arles and on 24 May 1424 appointed governor of Bologna, Ravenna, and Romagna. A year later he was made a cardinal. Soon after this, however, things began to go less well for him. In Bologna, the powerful Canetoli family turned against him. His soldiers were overcome by theirs and he was taken captive. He was liberated within a few days, but because he was unable to retake the city, on 23 August 1428 he was forced to retire, politically humiliated, to Rome.

Martin, of whom Louis and at least some of the other cardinals seem to have been in awe, died on 20 February 1431. Despite his personal aversion to gen-eral councils and to the idea, then much in the air, that popes were subject to them, one of his last acts had been to call such a council at Basle. The council opened on 19 July 1431 but soon degenerated into a conventicle, and one of the first acts of Martin's successor, Eugenius IV (1431-47), who shared his views but not his scruples, was to issue a Bull dissolving it. Louis, who had suc-ceeded Eugenius (then Gabriele Condulmaro) in Bologna, was a known sup-porter of the so-called "conciliar" position. He was therefore forbidden to leave

Rome for Basle, where some of the bishops had made it clear that they intended to ignore Eugenius and carry on with the council. In a rather dramatic sequence of events he managed to escape in disguise, board a Genoese ship then moored in the Tiber, and make his way to Arles. He spent only a couple of years there at this point, however, because in 1434 the pope withdrew his decree of dissolution. Louis went immediately to Basle, where he assumed the leadership of the extreme pro-conciliar majority who opposed the pope's representative, Cardinal Giuliano Cesarini.

In 1437, with the anti-papal party still in the ascendancy, the pope himself was summoned to attend to account for his alleged disobedience in discussing reunion with the Greeks. He refused and ordered the council to reconvene in Ferrara. Cardinal Cesarini and his supporters obeyed, as did Cardinal Nicholas of Cusa, leaving the now illegal assembly at Basle under the direction of none other than Louis. In 1439 Louis and thirty-two other electors nominated by a commission went so far as to depose Eugenius because of his opposition to the council. In his place they elected Amadeus VIII, duke of Savoy, who as Felix V (1439-49) became the last of the antipopes. He was consecrated and crowned by Louis, who was excommunicated in the following year and deprived of his position as cardinal. He remained in Basle, disregarding the decree of excommunication and actively supporting the antipope, Felix. In vain, as it turned out: no sovereign was willing to recognize Felix's election as valid, not even the German emperor, who had supported the conciliar position. Meanwhile, Louis had not forgotten entirely his pastoral role as a bishop. When plague broke out in the city he was one of the foremost in organizing relief.

It has to be said that many of the "conciliar" party at the Council of Basle were genuinely animated by concern for the Church and for the restoration of unity. What is more, Louis was by no means the only good man who went about achieving this end in a way that, with hindsight, can be said to have been mistaken. For a long time he was supported by the holy and learned Nicholas of Cusa, and also by Aeneas Silvius Piccolomini, then a layman, who subsequently became secretary to Felix V and then pope as Pius II (1458-64). Interestingly too, the assembly at Basle discussed the doctrine of the Immaculate Conception of the Virgin Mary. With Louis's encouragement they declared it consonant with Catholic faith and worship, right reason, and holy scripture.

When Eugenius died in 1447 the council was dissolved, and Felix agreed to resign in favour of Eugenius' duly elected successor, Nicholas V (1447-55). The schism was at last over. In one magnificent conciliatory gesture, Nicholas revoked all the suspensions, excommunications, and other penalties incurred by the antipope, the council members, and their supporters. Louis, who was restored to his position as cardinal, deeply regretted for the rest of his life the part he had played in the schism. He returned to Arles, where he continued the prayer and penance that had always been the strongest feature of his personal life. When he died at the Franciscan friary at Salon (Bouches-du-Rhône) in 1450 he was buried in the church of Saint-Trophime in Arles, and miracles were reported at his tomb. The cult that began then was approved by Pope Clement VII (1523-34) in 1527. Bd Louis's feast is observed in several dioceses in southern France.

AA.SS., Sept., 5, pp. 436-62. See also G. Pérouse, *Le Cardinal Louis Aleman* (1904); N. Valois, *Le Pape et le Concile* (1909); J. Gill, *Personalities of the Church of Florence and other Essays* (1964); *Bibl.SS.*, 1, 757-60; *O.D.S.*, pp. 227-45.

St John Macías (1585-1645)

John (Juan) Macías was born at Ribera del Fresno in Spanish Estremadura on 2 March 1585. According to the lessons of his Office his parents came from noble families but had been deprived of their wealth and status by "the various misfortunes of an unreliable world." Both died while John was still young, and he was left in the care of an uncle who made him earn his living as a shepherd. Sitting out in the fields all day he would say the rosary and meditate on the Christian mysteries. Sometimes he sensed that the protagonists, especially Mary and John the Evangelist, were visibly present with him. It was to an instruction from the latter that he attributed his sudden decision, at the age of thirty-five, to follow the many of his fellow-countrymen who had gone to Peru. Once there he worked for two years on a cattle ranch to make some money. Then, having decided to become a religious, he made his way to Lima. On 3 January 1622 he was accepted as a lay brother by the Dominicans and gave away what remained of his savings.

Not one to do things by halves, he practised personal austerities extreme enough to endanger his health, and his prior was constantly having to insist on moderation. But if he was hard on himself he had enormous compassion for the poor. Once he took over the office of porter the lodge became a meeting place for all the poor, sick, and needy of the city. Like his friend Martin de Porres (3 Nov.), he would beg for the money he needed to buy them food and medicines, and because he did not always have time to beg himself he trained the priory donkey to go round alone, and people would put food and clothing for the poor in its panniers. Many miracles were attributed to him, both before and after his death. When he died in 1645 he was mourned by the entire city, and his cult was approved with that of St Martin de Porres (3 Nov.) in 1837. He became known in Peru as "the father of the poor," and his cult also flourished in the region round Badajoz in Spain, where he grew up. He was canonized by Pope John Paul II on 28 September 1975.

There is an Italian Life published by the Dominicans in Rome at the time of Bd John's beatification. See also *Bibl.SS.*, 9, 12; J. Procter, *Short Lives of the Dominican Saints* (1901), pp. 263-74. For a fuller bibliography see I. Taurisano, *Catalogus Historicus O.P.* The text of Pope John Paul II's address at his canonization is in T. Lelièvre, *100 nouveaux saints et bienheureux de 1963 à 1984* (1985), pp. 54-6.

17

ST ROBERT BELLARMINE, *Bishop and Doctor* (1542-1621)

Robert Bellarmine, described by a contemporary, Cardinal Valfiero, as "the greatest little man on earth," had one of the best minds and most engaging personalities of the Catholic Reformation period. Born Roberto Francesco Romolo Bellarmino at Montepulciano in Tuscany on 4 October 1542, he was one of five sons of Vincenzo Bellarmino, the chief magistrate of the town, and Cinzia Cervini, sister of Marcello Cervini, who reigned for a year as Pope Marcellus II (1555). The couple made sure that there was nothing narrow about their children's education, with the result that by the time he was eighteen Robert had mastered, in addition to the usual subjects and skills, the violin, the art of debating, and the writing of Latin verse. Vincenzo had hopes that his son might take up medicine, but he was to be disappointed. Having spent three years at the school opened by the Jesuits in Montepulciano, the young man was determined to enter the recently-founded Society of Jesus. His father took some persuading, but on 16 September 1560 Robert finally set out for Rome with one of his cousins. Five days later, in spite of his frail constitution, he was accepted by the superior general, Diego Laínez, and began his training. From 1563 to 1567 he taught classics, first in Florence and then in Mondovì. He began his theological studies in Padua in 1568 but finished them in Louvain, and it was there that he was ordained to the priesthood on 25 March 1570.

His first major academic appointment was at the university of Louvain, where he spent seven crucial years, from 1569 to 1576. Even at this relatively early stage he was known for the rigour of his method and the maturity of his thought. When he was not lecturing on the *Summa theologica* of St Thomas Aquinas (28 Jan.) or carrying out his duties as prefect of studies and spiritual director, he devoted as much time as possible to reading and absorbing the teaching of the Reformers. In this way he laid the basis for what was to become his personal speciality: "controversial theology," which focused on the theological controversies that were dividing the Church at the time. But he still found time for other activities. He countered the opinions of Michael Baius on grace and free will. He learned Hebrew in order to refute the anti-Roman *Historia Ecclesiae Christi*, a history of the Church from the beginning to 1400, otherwise known as the Centuries of Magdeburg, and as an offshoot of this he wrote a Hebrew grammar. And he took over from the celebrated Francesco Strada as preacher of the Sunday sermon in Latin—more than filling the two-thousand-seat church, as Strada had done. He was and remained firmly convinced of the mutual importance of preaching and the study of theology. The former, he felt, was a powerful means for promoting Christian teaching and spirituality, but only if underpinned by the latter.

In 1576 Robert returned to Rome to take up the chair of "controversial theology" at the Collegium Romanum, or Gregorianum. This chair had been established by St Ignatius Loyola (31 July) when he founded the college in 1551. The lectures Robert gave there were to form the basis of his famous *Disputationes de Controversiis Christianae Fidei adversus hujus temporis Haereticis* (Disputations on the Controversies of the Christian Faith against the Heretics of this Age). In 1584 he stopped teaching for a while in order to prepare these for publication. In spite of his own misgivings about the project, three volumes were published over a seven-year period, between 1586 and 1593. The result was a work of such wide and deep scholarship that people simply assumed that it had been compiled by a team of scholars. It became essential reading and eventually went into more than twenty editions. Even in England people managed somehow to lay hands on it despite its having been banned by the government.

Although he had given up teaching, Robert continued to act as spiritual director for the students at the Gregorianum and also at the English College, where he offered encouragement to men who later would die for the Faith. One of the best known of the students at the Gregorianum was St Aloysius Gonzaga (21 June). Under Robert's largehearted and enlightened direction the younger man flourished. A strong bond formed between the two, and this was to last until Aloysius died, aged only twenty-three, on 21 June 1591. Robert was unable to be at Aloysius' bedside before he died, but he arrived in time to help place his body in the coffin. He returned to the Gregorianum in 1592, this time as rector, and was at the same time involved in the revision of the Society's *Ratio studiorum*.

During these years Robert also collaborated in the production of a new edition of the Vulgate, the revision by St Jerome (30 Sept.) of certain Old Latin versions of the Old and New Testaments. He was a member of the commission that had been set up to revise the Calendar. And as if that were not enough, he contributed to the production of the Catechism of Christian Doctrine, which remained in use for over three hundred years. Toward the end of this period of his life he was used by Pope Sixtus V (1585-90) for a number of delicate tasks. Notably, he served as theologian and legal expert on the commission that arbitrated in the conflict between the Catholic League and the Huguenot Henry of Navarre over the latter's accession to the throne of France (1562/89-1610).

On 24 November 1594 he was appointed provincial of the Naples province of the Society of Jesus. For his first sermon there he chose a text from the book of Ecclesiasticus: "They have chosen you as leader? Be among them as one"— which turned out to be an accurate description of his style of governing. For just over two years he was fully committed to the members of the Society in his care, and it was typical of him that he visited each house twice in that time. However, in February 1597 the pope's theologian, Cardinal Francesco Toledo, also a Jesuit, died. Pope Clement VIII (1592-1605) summoned Robert to Rome as his successor. Almost immediately he was asked to examine the position of either side in the venomous debate between the Jesuit Luis de Molina and the Dominican Domingo Báñez on the manner in which grace operates. Robert proposed a middle way between the two, but although he urged the pope to bring to an end this dispute, which was damaging relations between the two Orders, it rumbled on for several more years. Meanwhile, in 1599, the pope, to Robert's dismay, made him a cardinal. Outwardly he went along with some of the paraphernalia of office—he wore the red robes, for example, accepted the servants, and travelled in a carriage. But he was determined in his personal life to continue as a Jesuit, which is what he always remained at heart. He lived extremely simply, giving any surplus funds to the poor, and refused to be tempted when the Spanish ambassador offered him a pension in the name of Philip III (1598-1621).

Three years later he was made archbishop of Capua. In one way this came as a surprise because the pope seemed to rely on him for so much. On the other hand, not everyone appreciated his integrity, and even the pope had reservations about the freedom he had given him to speak his mind. By the end of April 1602 he had been consecrated as a bishop and had taken possession of his see. In some respects this was a difficult time for him, and the humid climate affected his never very robust health. He nevertheless approached his new task with characteristic commitment and proved to be an effective and much-loved pastor. He regarded the religious instruction of adults as particularly important and would himself preach in the cathedral on every Sunday and feast-day. But he was equally concerned to reform and educate the clergy, and he played a major part in this too. And his strong ideas about the pastoral aspects of his role led him to become personally involved in the welfare work of the diocese.

In 1605 he was back in Rome to take part in the election of a successor to Clement VIII, who died at the end of March. When the new pope, Leo XI, died a month later, Robert narrowly escaped being elected himself. Cardinal Camillo Borghese, the compromise candidate, who reigned as Paul V (1605-21), immediately appointed him prefect of the Vatican Library and asked him in addition to serve on a number of Roman congregations. Realizing that this was incompatible with the work of diocesan bishop, Robert resigned his see and returned to Rome, where he would remain for the rest of his life. He now became, in James Brodrick's phrase, the "factotum of the Holy See," always acting with his own personal blend of integrity and moderation. This can be seen in the case of the Servite friar Paolo Sarpi during Paul V's dispute with the republic of Venice. And it was in the background in 1606, when he had to remind George Blackwell, superior of the secular missionaries in England, of the significance of the Oath of Allegiance. James I (1603-25) was a personal friend, and he would have preferred a less confrontational approach.

A different sort of case was that of Galileo, who for some time had been championing Copernicus' belief that the earth travels round the sun, against the Ptolemaic idea that the earth is the centre of the universe. Robert was Galileo's friend and admirer, and his mind was large enough to accept the possibility that what he was trying to say might be true. During the first stage of the process against Galileo, some of whose arguments were not convincing even though his theory was valid as such, he managed to prevent his being condemned. But he nevertheless advised Galileo not to damage his own position by failing to distinguish hypothesis from proven fact. And in the end he was himself unable to break free from the rigid and over-literal interpretation of scripture on which the anti-Galileo position was based.

In his old age Bellarmine stopped writing on controversy and turned to producing devotional books, including *De Ascensione mentis in Deum* and *De arte bene moriendi*. Although in his personal life he remained austere to the end, he was anything but severe. His entire life was permeated by the joy of the gospel and the spirit of the Exercises of St Ignatius. Despite his small physique he had great presence, and his combination of sharp intelligence and enormous human warmth attracted people to him. Not only did he receive numerous visitors, but he kept up a huge correspondence. One of his most valuable traits, which no doubt explained the number and diversity of his friendships, was his ability to separate individuals from their opinions. When he opposed the latter the attack never became personal, and he prayed daily for his theological opponents.

In August 1621 he managed to persuade the pope, now Gregory XV (1621-3), to allow him to retire to the Jesuit novitiate on the Quirinal. He arrived there on 25 August but was taken ill only three days later. For the next three weeks there was a stream of visitors, each one anxious to see him one last time. He died on 17 September 1621 and was buried in the Lady Chapel of the Gesù. In 1923, the year in which he was beatified, his remains were taken from the Gesù to the church of St Ignatius. He was canonized in 1930 by Pope Pius XI (1922-39), who in the following year proclaimed him a Doctor of the Church.

Robert Bellarmine's works have been published in Cologne (1617-21) and Rome (1942-50). There are two seventeenth-century Lives: J. Fuligatti (1624); D. Bartoli (1678). For a modern treatment see especially J. Brodrick, S.J., *The Life and Works of Blessed Robert Cardinal Bellarmine* (1928, rev. ed., 1966); *idem, Robert Bellarmine, Saint and Scholar* (1961). See also X. M. Le Bachelet, *Bellarmin avant son cardinalat* (1911); E. A. Ryan, *The Historical Scholarship of St Bellarmine* (1936); A. Bernier, *Un cardinal humaniste* (1939); R. J. Blackwell, *Galileo, Bellarmine and the Bible* (1991); *Bibl.SS.*, 11, 248-59; *H.S.S.C.*, 8, pp. 245-50; *Dict.Sp.*, 13, 713-20.

St Satyrus (*c.* 330-*c.* 379)

Uranius Satyrus was born into a rich, aristocratic family of the *gens Aurelia* soon after 330. He was the elder brother of St Marcellina (17 July) and St Ambrose (7 Dec.). When their father, who was prefect of the *praetorium* of the Gauls, died in 354, the family moved to Rome. Here the two boys were well educated under the watchful eyes of their mother and sister. Satyrus, who chose a career in public service while Ambrose went into the Church, practised for a while as a lawyer and then became governor of one of the provinces of the empire. In 374, when Ambrose became bishop of Milan, he resigned his post and went to administer the temporal affairs of the diocese. He made several journeys to Africa, the purpose of which seems to have been to recover some money that was owing to Ambrose. During the last of these journeys his ship went down off the coast of Sardinia and he nearly lost his life. This prompted him to ask for Baptism at the first opportunity—until then he had been only a catechumen. Ambrose, who is our only source of information about his brother, described Satyrus as an immensely kind man of great integrity. We are also given an impression, rare for this period, of his personal appearance. Like his brother he was small and of delicate build, and each was frequently taken for the other.

Satyrus died suddenly in Milan in about 379 in the arms of his brother and sister. Ambrose preached movingly at his funeral, and Satyrus was buried near the tomb of the martyr St Victor in the Ciel d'Oro annexed to the basilica of St Ambrose. Following his request that they deal with it as they thought best, Marcellina and Ambrose distributed his estate to the poor. In 881 a church with a monastery attached was built in his honour in the centre of Milan.

For St Ambrose's *De excessu fratris*, which contains two funeral orations, see *C.S.E.L.*, 73, 207-51. See also *AA.SS.*, Sept., 5, pp. 485-508; *Bibl.SS.*, 11, 664-6; A. Tamborini, *I Santi Milanesi* (1927); E. Ricci, *Mille santi nell'arte* (1931).

In the surviving few portrayals of him alone, without Marcellina and Ambrose, he is shown as young, with a beard. There is a painting by Tiepolo of the shipwreck episode in the church of St Ambrose in Milan.

St Lambert of Maastricht, *Bishop and Martyr* (*c.* 635-*c.* 705)

Landebehrt, known subsequently as Lambert, was the subject of no less than five Lives, the first of which was written in the eighth century, the last in the twelfth. He was born sometime between 633 and 638 into a noble and wealthy family in Maastricht, soon to be the main town in the diocese of Liège. If, as his earliest biographer says, his parents were Christian, they would have been unusual, since paganism was still very strong in the area at the time. Nevertheless, Lambert was educated at court, according to his biographers, by the bishop of Tongres-Maastricht, St Théodard (10 Sept.), and eventually entered the priesthood himself. The same biographer gives an account of him at this time, probably accurate enough despite its retrospective glow: "a prudent young man of pleasing looks, courteous and well behaved in his speech and manners; well built, strong, a good fighter, clear-headed, affectionate, pure and humble, and fond of reading." When Théodard was murdered in about 670, Lambert was chosen as his successor.

He had scarcely been bishop for five years when he became involved in the political turmoil that followed the death of Childeric II of Neustria and Burgundy (656-75). Ebroïn, the power-hungry former mayor of the palace of Neustria, taking advantage of the situation, returned to revenge himself on all who had supported Childeric, and while this was going on Lambert was expelled from his see. Dagobert II of Austrasia (676-9), with whom he initially took refuge, asked the monks at Stavelot-Malmédy to take him in and keep him under a sort of house arrest for his own safety. Meanwhile, his place was taken in the diocese of Liège by a man named Pharamond.

So it was that for the next seven years Lambert lived as a simple member of the Stavelot-Malmédy community. To illustrate this his biographer tells how one winter night Lambert dropped a shoe rather noisily. The abbot ordered whoever was responsible for the noise to go out and pray by the great cross outside the church door. Without a word, Lambert went out, barefoot with only his shirt on. He had been praying by the cross for three or four hours when the abbot asked the monks, who were warming themselves after Matins, if they were all there. Hearing that the person who had made the noise was still outside, he asked that he be brought in and was astonished to see the by now half-frozen Lambert.

In 680 Ebroïn was assassinated, and Pepin of Herstal took his place as mayor of the palace. Wishing to consolidate his position, Pepin immediately reinstated all banished priests and bishops, among them Lambert. After the years of enforced separation from his flock, the latter returned to Maastricht full of energy and zeal, and the next period of his life was a fruitful one for him. Not only did he take very seriously his duties as bishop within the Tongres-Maastricht area, but he went personally to convert the pagans who still remained in Kempenland and Brabant. And in collaboration with St Landrada (8 July) he founded a monastery for nuns at Munsterblizen.

There are two versions of the circumstances that led to Lambert's death. According to the later one, which dates from the ninth century, Pepin started an affair with Alpais, the sister of his wife, St Plectrudis. When Lambert reproved the guilty couple Alpais complained to her brother, Dodo. Dodo took the matter into his own hands and with a group of followers attacked Lambert while he was praying in the church of SS Cosmas and Damian in Liège and killed him. The version favoured by Lambert's earliest biographers, who were writing in the eighth and ninth centuries, related to the fact that Clovis III (675) had granted a privilege of immunity for the goods of the church of Our Lady in Maastricht. The royal agents, furious that they could not tax the church, eventually managed, through their harassment of the bishop, to provoke a quarrel with two of Lambert's relatives. Incensed, the latter took matters into their own hands and killed the royal agents. Dodo, a powerful administrator in the royal household and a relative of the men who had died, came with members of his private army to exact revenge. Lambert warned his relatives that they would have to expiate their crime, and in the event they were killed on the spot. One of Dodo's men then climbed up to the window of Lambert's locked room and hurled a spear, which killed the bishop as he prayed. The date was 17 September and the year 705 at the latest.

Whichever version best reflects reality, the nature of Lambert's death, coupled with the evident holiness of his life, soon led to his being venerated as a martyr. His body was moved to Maastricht, but when people began to report miracles at the house where he died a church was built there, and his successor, St Hubert (3 Nov.), had his relics translated. The city of Liège grew up around this church, which became the cathedral when Hubert made the new city rather than Maastricht the centre of the see. Lambert is still the patron of this city. There is evidence that the cult became widespread at an early date. By the middle of the century several churches had been dedicated to St Lambert, and today there are about 144 dedications in Belgium alone. By the end of the eighth century the cult had spread to the Rheinland, Bavaria, and Saxony. There is also evidence of it in France and in England, where there are two early churches dedicated to St Lambert, and his name appears in several monastic calendars as well as in the Sarum calendar. In addition to the official cult, there was a strong popular cult. Lambert was invoked against illness in domestic animals as well as against hernia and gall and kidney stones. And because his feast so often coincided with the end of the harvest, traditions grew up around it. In Hainaut, Limburg, and Brabant, for example, apples were picked on this day; in Liège barley was sown. In Berlin, the expression *Lambertus Wetter* (Lambert's weather) is used to describe a brilliantly sunny day, while elsewhere the saying goes, *"Saint Lambert pluvieux, neuf jours dangereux"* ("Rain on St Lambert's day means danger for nine days").

For most of the medieval Lives see *AA.SS.*, Sept., 6, p. 574. The earliest and most important, critically edited by B. Krusch, is in *M.G.H., Scriptores merov.*, 6. On the cause of Lambert's assassination see *Anal.Boll.* 33 (1914), pp. 247-9; G. Kurth, in *Annales de l'Académie archéologique de Belgique* 33 (1876); *ibid.*, "La Vita Sancti Lamberti et M. Krusch," in *Etudes franques* 2 (1919), pp. 319-47. See also *H.S.S.C.*, 4, pp. 182-6; *Bibl.SS.*, 7, 1079-82; *O.D.S.*, p. 287; L. Vaux, *Vie de Saint Lambert* (1930); J. L. Kupper, "Saint Lambert, de l'histoire à la légende," in *Revue d'Histoire Ecclésiastique* (1984), pp. 5-49; Jöckle, pp. 263-4, 273.

In art St Lambert is variously represented as a bishop, in armour, in scenes showing the many miracles attributed to him, and at the moment of his death. The cathedral in Liège houses the superb reliquary bust that was made to contain his head.

St Columba, *Martyr* (853)

The story of this martyr was recorded by St Eulogius of Córdoba (11 Mar.) in *The Memorial of the Saints*, his account of those Christians who suffered in the persecution that began in Spain in 850. Columba was born in Córdoba, the youngest of a family of three. Her sister, Elizabeth, had, with her husband, founded a double monastery at Tábanos, to which they retired with their children. Her brother, Martin, was abbot of the men's side of this same monastery. Inspired by their example, Columba, who even allowing for exaggeration, had a high reputation for holiness, was determined to become a nun herself. Her plans were thwarted for a while at least by her mother, a widow, who wanted her to marry. Then her mother, who had in any case begun to realize that her opposition was fruitless, died unexpectedly, and Columba joined the community at Tábanos. In 852, when the persecution had already been going on for two years, the community was driven out of Tábanos and the nuns took refuge in a house in Córdoba, near the church of St Cyprian (16 Sept.).

Apparently ignoring a ruling of the bishops that Christians should not provoke persecution, Columba left the house one day, presented herself before the Muslim magistrate, and denounced Mohammed and his law. The magistrate condemned her to be beheaded. Her body, which was thrown into the Guadalquivir, was recovered by some of her fellow-Christians and buried in the basilica of St Eulalia (10 Dec.) at Fragellas. Relics are supposed to have been taken later to the abbey of Santa María de Nájera and to its dependent priory, which was dedicated to St Columba.

St Eulogius' account is in *AA.SS.*, Sept., 5, pp. 618-23. See also *Bibl.SS.*, 4, 99-100; Baudot et Chaussin, 9, p. 364ff.

St Unno, *Bishop* (*c.* 880-936)

Unno (Guino, Unni, Wino) was one of the great missionary bishops of the ninth and tenth centuries. The most trustworthy source of information about him is Adam of Bremen, who died in about 1075. Two other sources—the *Liber Gestorum Hammaburgensis Ecclesiae Pontificum* and the *Chronicon Corbeiense*—offer more detail, but they are less reliable. There were two further Lives, one in prose, the other in verse, written shortly after Unno's death by a monk of Korvey named Sigebert, but these have unfortunately been lost. Apart from the fact that he was born in about 880, the first thing known for certain about him is that he became a monk in the monastery at Korvey in Westphalia. He is also known to have served for a while as chaplain to the provost of the cathedral chapter in Bremen until 1 October 916, when he was elected archbishop of Hamburg-Bremen.

This was no sinecure. Politically the area in which the diocese was situated was part of what would very shortly become the German Empire. In reality it faced in two directions: south toward Germany, and north toward Denmark, which came within its confines and which at the beginning of the tenth century was the most significant power in the region. Attempts had been made before the ninth century to introduce Christianity into the country, but the first successful missionary was St Anskar (3 Feb.). He was brought in by a king named Harald in about 825 and after a few false starts managed to lay the groundwork for the establishment of a church. However, despite his achievements and the efforts of his successor, St Rembert (4 Feb.), after his death in 865 the country gradually reverted to paganism. The main reason for this was the anti-Christian stance of Gorm the Old, the first member of a new dynasty, who had expelled or killed any priests who remained when he came to the throne. But the situation changed in 934 when the German king, Henry I the Fowler (919-36), invaded Denmark and Gorm was forced to recognize his sovereignty.

With the spread of German influence, Christianity began to flourish once again, and in this Unno played a major part. This was especially true when Gorm was succeeded by his son, Harald Blåtand (Bluetooth, *c.* 936-86), whose wife, Thyra, became a Christian herself. With Christianity thus officially sanctioned, Unno was able to move forward with his programme for evangelization. Under Harald's protection he travelled about the Danish mainland and the islands preaching the Faith and organizing the religious life of the people. In particular, he brought comfort and strength to Christian prisoners, and it was they who formed the first communities for which he ordained priests. Some time in 936 he crossed the Baltic Sea into Sweden, travelling first to the island of Birka (now Björkö, on lake Mälar), which had not seen a Christian priest since Rembert died in 888. Eventually he went as far as Uppsala, but his dream of taking the Faith even farther north was thwarted by sickness. Tired and ill, he returned to Birka, where he died sometime in September of the same year. He was buried on Birka, but his companions took his head back to St Peter's church in Bremen.

The cult, which developed almost immediately, was not very widespread, and it seems to have become confused with that of Unno's successor Adaldagus. But Unno was given the title saint from the eleventh century onward. Some of his relics were taken to Korvey, where they became the object of veneration, but they were lost during the mid-seventeenth century when the monks went into exile in Austria.

For a general history see O. Klopp, *Geschichte Ostfriedlands*, 1 (1845); G. J. Kamp, *Histoire de l'Eglise catholique au Danemark depuis le IXe siècle jusqu'au milieu du XVIe* (1861); A. Hauck, *Kirchengeschichte Deutschlands*, 3 (1904); H. von Schubert, *Kirchengeschichte von Schleswig-Holstein*, 1 (1907). On the Hamburg-Bremen diocese see G. Dehio, *Geschichte des Erzbistums Hamburg-Bremen*, 1 1877; J. S. Schöffel, *Kirchengeschichte Hamburgs*, 1 (1929). See also *Bibl.SS.*, 12, 831-3 (which lists books in Danish); A. Schütte, *Handbuch der deutschen Heiligen* (1941), p. 332; *O.D.C.C.* (1997), p. 469.

St Hildegard of Bingen, *Abbess* (1098-1179)

Hildegard of Bingen would have been remarkable in any century. In her own century her achievements and her influence, particularly as a woman, were extraordinary. She was born at Bermersheim, on the Nahe near Alzey, in the summer of 1098. Apart from the fact that her father, Hildebert of Bermersheim, was a nobleman and possibly in the service of the bishop of Speyer, little is known of her family background. When she was only eight years old she was sent to be educated by a recluse, Bd Jutta (22 Dec.), who was living at Disibodenberg in an anchorhold (perhaps a cottage) attached to the church of the abbey founded by St Disibod (8 July). Hildegard was a delicate child, but her education, which seems to have included learning to read and sing Latin and acquiring the domestic skills expected of women of all classes at the time, continued uninterrupted. Over the years other girls or young women came to join her, so Jutta, realizing that this was in effect a religious community, gave them the Rule of St Benedict (11 July) and herself assumed the role of abbess. Hildegard received the habit when she was fifteen, and for the next seventeen or so years her external life was uneventful enough.

But her inner life was far from ordinary. From the age of three she experienced visions or revelations that, in the early stages at any rate, caused her pain and embarrassment. "When I was completely absorbed in what I saw," she owns, "I used to say many things that seemed strange to those who heard me. This made me blush and cry, and often enough I would have killed myself had that been possible. I was too frightened to tell anyone what I saw, except the noblewoman to whom I was entrusted [Jutta], and she told a little to a monk whom she knew." The revelations continued into her adult life, and all the time she experienced an uneasy combination of chronic ill health—headaches and other physical symptoms accompanied by spiritual aridity, the absence of what she came to call "greenness"—and vast creative energy demanding an outlet.

In 1136 Jutta died, and Hildegard became abbess in her place. Her revelations and visions were still causing her anxiety. She believed she was being urged to write them down but feared that others would mock her and that in any case her Latin was inadequate. Finally she decided to tell her confessor, a monk named Godfrey, and asked him to speak to his abbot, Conon, about it. Having given the matter some thought, Conon asked Hildegard to write down at least some of the things she believed God had revealed to her. Hildegard obeyed, producing material on the love of Christ, the kingdom of God, the angels, and hell and the devil, which was submitted to the archbishop of Mainz. At the age of forty-two years and seven months—she is precise about it—she was suddenly set free. Her health remained uncertain but she had no more headaches, her pent-up creative energy was released, the heaviness was gone, and she became, as she put it, "a feather on the breath of God."

The archbishop and his theologians concluded that the visions were "from God." At her request, Conon supplied Hildegard with an amanuensis, a young monk named Volmar. Over the next ten years, with his help and that of others when he was unable to keep up, she produced her principal work, *Scivias* (short for *sci vias Domini*, "Know the Ways of the Lord"). In the course of its three volumes she refers to twenty-six separate visions dealing with the relationship between God and human beings through creation, through redemption, and in the Church. There is also a certain amount of apocalyptic prophecy as well as warnings and symbolic utterances that are not always easy to understand—the delphic quality of some of her sayings earned her the title Sibyl of the Rhine. And some of her teaching verges on the pantheistic and might well be described as panentheist. Yet there is a remarkable consistency about her symbolism, which centres on the life-giving power of God. She refers constantly to the *viriditas* or greening power of God, to the "lush greenness" brought by Christ to withered individuals and institutions, and to the Holy Spirit as greening power in motion.

Although she claims that her understanding of the scriptures is purely intuitive, directly revealed by God like everything else she has to say, it is hard to take this literally. She never cites her sources, but they are there and they are wide-ranging: the scriptures, of course, and Christian writers from the Shepherd of Hermas through St Jerome (30 Sept.) and St Augustine (28 Aug.) to St Gregory the Great (3 Sept.), Bede (25 May), and others. Perhaps they were mediated through commentators or compendia. It is also possible that, convinced as she was of the truth and urgency of her message, she found it convenient to claim divine inspiration as a way of bypassing the slow, cautious inspections of those in authority. But her age prized continuity, and she now seems daring in not citing the traditional authors whom most theological and spiritual writers and thinkers relied on as protection against these authorities. She is also as remarkable for her disregard of standard orthodox devotional themes, such as personal redemption from the stain of sin, as for the subjects she does treat. It has been seriously suggested (Dronke) that while she atttacked heresy, she actually "got away with" what amounts to an early form of Manicheism.

In 1147 the archbishop of Mainz passed Hildegard's work to the pope, Bd Eugenius III (1145-53; 8 July), then on a visit to Trier. Adopting a predictably cautious approach, Eugenius first appointed a commission to examine Hildegard and her writings. Only when the commission had submitted a report that was favourable did he read the writings himself and discuss them with some close advisers. Among the latter was St Bernard of Clairvaux (20 Aug.), who was enthusiastic and urged the pope to approve them. Eugenius's letter to Hildegard is a combination of encouragement and caution. He is pleased and full of wonder at the favours she has been granted but warns her against pride. In her long reply Hildegard gives as good as she gets, alluding in parables to the troubles of the time and warning Eugenius to be on guard against ambitious members of his own household.

In his letter, the pope told Hildegard to live with her sisters, faithfully observing the Rule, in the place she had seen in a vision. This was a reference to the nuns' proposed new home on the Rupertsberg, an exposed and barren hill near Bingen. Since the house on the Disibodenberg could no longer accommodate the growing community, the move made sense. But Hildegard, who claimed that God had shown her the new site in a vision, met with fierce opposition from the monks of St Disibod's. Much of the importance of the abbey derived from its proximity to the convent, which had Jutta's relics and Hildegard herself as its two attractions. The abbey also relied on the dowries of the nuns. They were loth to lose any of these, and the abbot accused Hildegard, whose health had given way, of acting from pride. However, when he saw her and realized her illness was genuine his attitude changed and he told her to get up and go to the Rupertsberg. The monks were less easily won over, until their leader was cured of a painful disease in her church.

Hildegard and eighteen other nuns moved to the Rupertsberg sometime between 1147 and 1150. It was an unforgiving spot, but thanks to Hildegard's boundless energy they soon had a house large enough to accommodate a community of fifty, "with water piped to all the offices." And she was creative and inventive as well as practical. She provided the nuns with a large number of hymns and canticles for which she composed both the words and the music; she wrote a morality play-cum-sacred cantata, *Ordo virtutum*, for them to perform; and for reading in the refectory she produced about fifty allegorical homilies—which cannot have been easy listening. Her Lives of St Disibod (8 Sept.) and St Rupert (29 Mar.) were said to be revelations, but since they contain items of local tradition they probably involved more hard work than that implies. When she was able to enjoy some leisure (which surely cannot have been often), she liked to work on her so-called "unknown language." This was a sort of Esperanto based on Latin and German with frequent use of a final Z—about nine hundred words have come down to us.

She also, somehow, found time to research and write on subjects that fascinated her. A book on natural history, clearly based on careful scientific observation, discusses among other things the elements, minerals and metals, trees and other plants, fishes, reptiles, birds, and quadrupeds. Another, on medicine, looks at the human body and the causes, symptoms, and treatment of the ailments that afflict it. This, in particular, shows how far her imagination if not her knowledge was ahead of her time. For example, five centuries before William Harvey she came close to giving an accurate description of how the blood circulates in the body.

Then there was her voluminous correspondence, a substantial part of which has survived. Her writing style is not easy. When she was reproving or warning—and she did a lot of both—she tended to adopt a preaching style full of allegory and allusion. As she saw it, her role in life was to communicate the content of her visions to the people of her generation in order to lead them back to the way of justice. For her, prophesying was a burden and a responsibility rather than a gift, and in this she resembled more an Old Testament prophet than a Christian mystic. Among the individual recipients of her homily-like letters were various popes, bishops, and abbots, including St Bernard, and several monarchs, among them Henry II of England. But she also wrote to groups such as the clergy of Trier and Cologne—fierce, outspoken letters in which she chided them for their shortcomings and warned them what would happen if they did not reform. Sometimes she could be quite sharp. When the archbishop of Mainz told her to send a particular nun as abbess to another convent, she replied: "All the reasons given for the promotion of this young woman are worthless before God. The spirit of this jealous God says: 'Weep and cry out, pastors, for you know not what you do, distributing sacred offices in your own interest and wasting them on perverse and godless men. . . . As for yourself, arise, for your days are numbered.'" Understandably this sort of approach did not make her universally popular. People from all walks of life came to consult her, but at the same time there were others who denounced her as fraudulent, mad, or worse.

Neither this opposition nor her constant ill health deterred Hildegard from pursuing her activities outside her own convent. She believed God was using her as his mouthpiece—"I am a poor earthen vessel, and say these things not of myself but from the serene Light," she wrote to a friend—and her boldness and sincerity were a formidable combination. Between 1152 and 1162 she made numerous journeys in the Rhineland during which she preached publicly, which was almost unheard for a woman at the time. She founded one daughter house at Eibingen, near Rudesheim, but she seems to have assumed the role of abbess-visitor to a number of other monasteries and convents. Since she always came down hard on lax discipline wherever she found it, these visits cannot always have increased her popularity. The same can be said of her meetings with bishops, clergy, and laypeople.

Hildegard continued to the end to stand her ground against what she saw as the wrong use of authority. During the last year of her life a young man, who had at one point been excommunicated, died and was buried in the cemetery at St Rupert's. The vicar general of Mainz said he could not be buried in hallowed ground and called for the removal of the body. Hildegard refused, arguing that the young man had received the Last Sacraments and was therefore no longer to be regarded as excommunicated. When the order was repeated, this time by the bishop, Hildegard sent back the message: "Come, your grace, my lord archbishop, and dig him up yourself." The bishop came, accompanied by members of the cathedral chapter, but Hildegard had removed all signs of the burial, so they had to leave empty-handed. When the bishop then placed her church under an interdict, Hildegard responded with a long letter on the apparently unrelated subject of sacred music, "which helps man build a bridge of holiness between this world and the World of all Beauty and Music." Her meaning became clear at the end: "Those therefore who, without good reason, impose silence on churches in which singing in God's honour can be heard will not deserve to hear the glorious choir of angels that praises the Lord in heaven." The archbishop, to whom she took the precaution of writing at the same time, ignored various admonitions that were personal to himself, but he did lift the interdict.

By this stage, Hildegard, now over eighty, was so frail physically that she had to be carried from place to place. But she continued to write, advise, instruct her nuns, and encourage all who came to her for help, until she died peacefully at St Rupert's on 17 September 1179. Miracles, which had also been recorded during her life, were immediately reported at her tomb, and there is evidence of a cult from the thirteenth century. In 1324 Pope John XXII (1316-34) gave permission for public veneration, and she appears in local martyrologies from the fifteenth century. Her relics, which were taken to Eibingen during the Thirty Years War, were recognized in 1489 and again in 1498. Although she has never been formally canonized, she is named as a saint in the Roman Martyrology, and several German dioceses commemorate her on this day.

Hildegard's visions and revelations are among the best documented of this type of phenomenon. The language in which she describes what she has seen and understood is vivid and colourful and full of symbolism. It is as if she is stretching language to its limits to describe the indescribable. She herself is aware of this: "These visions that I saw I beheld neither in sleep nor dreaming nor in madness nor with my bodily eyes or ears, nor in hidden places. I saw them in full view and according to God's will, when I was wakeful and alert, with the eyes of the spirit and the inward ears. And how this was brought about is indeed hard for human flesh to search out." But she was not content to use words only to describe what she saw. She illustrated the *Scivias* herself, and those illustrations that have survived (even if only in meticulous copies)—vivid, original, and rich with symbolism—come closer in spirit to the work of William Blake than to anything anyone other than she was painting at the time. She was also an accomplished musician; as such she enjoyed an unexpected surge of popularity in the early 1990s when some of her music found a place in the charts. She is the patron of philologists and Esperantists.

The best of the early Lives is in *AA.SS.*, Sept., 5, pp. 629-701; and see M. Klaes (ed.), *Vita Sanctae Hildegardis* (1993). For some of the material from the unfinished canonization process see P. Bruder, "Inquisitio de virtutibus et miraculis S. Hildegardis," in *Anal.Boll.* 2 (1883), pp. 116-29. More recent Lives: P. Franche (1903); J. May (1911); F. M. Steele (1914); J. Christophe (1942). See also R. Pernoud, *Hildegarde de Bingen: conscience inspirée du XIIe siècle* (1994); B. Newman, *Sister of Wisdom: St Hildegard's Theology of the Feminine* (1987); idem., *Vision: the life and music of Hildegard von Bingen* (1995); P. Dronke, *Women Writers of the Middle Ages* (1984); S. Gougenheim, *L'Eschatologie dans la vie et l'oeuvre d'Hildegarde de Bingen* (1990); L. von Acker, *Hildegardis Bingensis epistolarium* (1991); A. P. Brück, *Hildegard von Bingen, 1098-1179: Festschrift zum 800 Todestag der Heiligen* (1979); H. Leibeschutz, *Das allegorisches Weltbild der heiligen Hildegard von Bingen*, Studien der Bibliothek Warburg, 16 (1930); P. Escot, *The Ursula Antiphons* (1994);

Bibl.SS., 7, 761-6; *H.S.S.C.*, 6, pp. 173-8; *O.D.S.*, p. 231. On the *Scivias* illustrations see L. Baillet, "Les Miniatures du 'Scivias' de Sainte Hildegarde conservé à la Bibliothèque de Wiesbaden," in *Monuments et Mémoires publiés par l'Académie des Inscriptions et Belles-Lettres*, 19 (1911), pp. 49-149; and especially M. Fox, *Illuminations of Hildegard of Bingen* (1985), which contains several very fine reproductions, as does H. Schipperges, *Die Welt von Hildegard von Bingen* (1997; Eng. trans. by J. Cumming, *The World of Hildegard of Bingen: Her Life, Times, and Visions*, 1998).

St Peter Arbués, Martyr (*c.* 1440-85)

One of the main problems in medieval Spain was how to balance the interests of the Christian majority with those of the Jewish and Muslim minorities. This inherently delicate matter was complicated by a number of factors. There was the ignorant prejudice of ordinary Christians, not to mention clergy, who had none of the tolerance of the more enlightened of their leaders. Then there was the fact that during the fourteenth century, while most Jews were small traders, artisans, or small farmers, a few families had acquired great influence, both financially and as holders of civil and even ecclesiastical office. This aroused great envy among the Old Christians (those who could trace their Christian ancestry back through a number of generations). Riots against Jews had been sparked off by an anti-Semitic preacher in Seville in 1391, and violence spread rapidly to many cities across Spain. Out of terror, large numbers of Jews converted to Christianity; later these were given the chance to revert to Judaism, but most did not take up the offer, thinking it safer to remain Christian. Not surprisingly, some of the conversions were superficial, and the *conversos* received little or no instruction after Baptism. Further mass conversions followed in the fifteenth century.

As Christians, converted Jews and Muslims could hold civil and even ecclesiastical offices and compete for these with Old Christians, which they did with marked success, thereby increasing resentment against them. In 1449 a major pogrom took place in Toledo, bringing the first (unsubstantiated) accusations that converted Jews were reverting to Judaism on a wide scale. This view was never upheld by the crown, which believed that their special skills in fields such as finance and medicine made them deserving of protection. This in turn provoked popular resentment against the monarchy and led to the establishment of the Inquisition. As an ecclesiastical tribunal whose task was to uncover and prosecute heresy, the Inquisition had existed as a Roman institution since the twelfth century, though by the beginning of the fifteenth century it was in decline. Aragon already had an old-style Inquisition, but in 1478 Ferdinand II of Aragon (1474-1516) brought it under royal control and began to target the *conversos*. Castile, where anti-Semitism was more pronounced, got its own Inquisition when Isabella I (1474-1504) persuaded Pope Sixtus IV (1471-84) to create an independent Spanish tribunal. In 1483, despite his protests, the pope was persuaded by Ferdinand to extend the authority of the inquisitor general for Castile, the Dominican Tomás de Torquemada, to Aragon.

There was massive opposition to this from Old Christians as well as from *conversos*; troops had to be sent in to enable the tribunal to be set up in the city of Teruel, one of the main centres of opposition, the other being Zaragoza.

Not long before this a young man named Peter (Pedro) Arbués was professed as a canon regular at Zaragoza. Born at Epila in the region of Zaragoza in about 1440, he had studied first in Spain and then at the Spanish College in Bologna, where he achieved brilliant results in theology and canon law. In terms of character he was known as an austere man of absolute integrity. Although he would have preferred to live as a simple religious, his zealous concern for orthodoxy and his learning caught the eye of Torquemada, who appointed him provincial inquisitor for the kingdom of Aragon. There is no doubt that in the few months that he filled this role Peter worked hard and methodically, and there is evidence that several Jewish Christians were at least tortured as a result. Not unexpectedly his zeal made him enemies, and it was they who spread abroad the image of a cold, cruel, and narrow man. The idea of assassi-nating an inquisitor gained currency in prominent *converso* circles, supported by some Old Christians.

On the night of 15-16 September 1485 eight conspirators entered the cathe-dral of St Saviour in Zaragoza while Peter was praying. He had been warned about threats against his life and was wearing a coat of mail under his gown and a steel cap on his head. But a knife-thrust to his neck went between the two and was to prove fatal: canons of the cathedral rushed in to find him dying. He died twenty-four hours later and was buried in the cathedral of Zaragoza. His death changed the whole atmosphere: he was immediately hailed as a saint, and mobs roamed the streets in search of *conversos*. The Inquisition came into its own, and over the next seven years his murderers and those thought to be behind them were being rounded up and killed with exteme brutality. *Conversos* should certainly have foreseen that this would be the outcome, and it is en-tirely possible that Peter's murder was the work of an anti-Semitic faction aiming to place the blame on them. He was beatified in 1664 and canonized in 1867.

There is no early Life, but the chronicles of the period supply information. See *AA.SS.*, Sept., 5, pp. 728-54. Also G. Cozza, *Della vita, miracoli e culto del martire S. Pietro de Arbues* (1867); *Bibl.SS.*, 10, 665-6; *O.D.C.C.*, pp. 836-7. On the background see A. Mackay, *Spain in the Middle Ages* (1977), esp. pp. 184-7; H. Kamen, *The Spanish Inquisition, An Historical Revision* (1997), which accepts the main conclusions of Benzion Netanyahu, *The Origins of the Inquisition in Fifteenth-Century Spain* (1995). Netanyahu shows that contemporary Jews regarded the vast mass of victims of the Inquisition not as martyrs for Judaism but as apostates from Judaism and sincere Christians.

A painting by Murillo of Peter Arbués at the moment of his death hangs in the Vatican Gallery.

St Francis Mary of Camporosso (1804-66)

Giovanni Crocse, one of the four children of Anselmo Croese and Maria Antonia Gazzo, was born at Camporosso, a small town on the Ligurian coast, on 1 December 1804. His parents, who had a smallholding on which they farmed and cultivated olives, gave their children a simple, religious upbringing, and all worked on the farm as a matter of course as soon as they were able. When Giovanni was eighteen he met a Conventual Franciscan lay brother who inspired him with the idea of joining the Order. He was accepted as a tertiary at the friary in Sestri Ponente, outside Genoa, and given the name Antonio. But after two years he decided that he was looking for a more austere way of life and applied to the Capuchins. He was sent to the novitiate in Genoa and in 1825 was clothed as a lay brother with the name Francis Mary (in Italian Francesco Maria). After his profession in the following year, he worked for a while in the infirmary. Soon, however, he was given the office of questor, his task being to go from door to door begging food for the community. Francis had never done anything like this before, and he found it so disagreeable that he thought of asking if he could do something else. But when the guardian asked him if he would go and beg in Genoa itself he overcame his distaste and accepted with enthusiasm.

In fact, Genoa was not an easy place to beg in. Not everyone who lived there was sympathetically disposed to religious, and at first Francis had to put up with a certain amount of abuse. Nevertheless, he persevered for ten years, becoming the best-known questor in the city. He was a particularly familiar figure in the dockyards, where, because it was said that he could give correct information about individuals he had never seen, people would come to ask him about friends and relatives who had gone to live abroad. When he returned to the friary in the evening he would invariably find a crowd of needy people waiting for him. "Go to Our Lady [or St Francis, or St Antony, or St Catherine of Genoa]," he would say, "and tell her Francis sent you." Miracles of healing were also attributed to him, and to the majority of citizens he became know as "Padre santo"—despite his protests that he was not a priest but a lay brother.

For two years at the end of his life he suffered from varicose veins which, because he did not mention them, became much worse than they need have done; they were operated on, but this was not really very successful. Then in August 1866 Genoa was devastated by cholera. Francis, like all the religious in the city, went out to help the victims and their families. He was so moved by what he saw that he solemnly offered his own life to God in order that the epidemic might cease. On 15 September he succumbed to the disease, and two days later he died—at which point the epidemic began to abate. He was buried in Staglieno cemetery, and a cult developed immediately; many miracles were reported at his tomb. In 1911 his remains were taken into the church. Francis was beatified in 1929 and canonized in 1962.

The decree of beatification—see *A.A.S.*, 21 (1929), pp. 485-8)—includes a biographical sketch. There are biographies by L. da Porto Maurizio (Italian, 1911; n.e., 1930); C. de Pelissanne (French, 1929); P. Lyons (English, 1930); T. da Voltri (Italian, 1962). See also *Bibl.SS.*, 5, 1205-7.

A statue of Francis stands in the port of Genoa, and there are various idealized prints and other portraits. The closest likeness is a reproduction in marble, made from a photograph three years after Francis' death by C. Rubatto.

ST CORNELIUS (p. 137)
Gold triple cross and brown horn "of unction" on red field

ST CYPRIAN OF CARTHAGE (p. 139)
Silver double-headed battle axe and gold crown on red field
Alternative emblems are burning his books of magic; gridiron and sword.

18

St Ferreolus, *Martyr* (? Third Century)

Although the *passio* of St Ferreolus is more or less worthless there is no doubt that he died a martyr, and his cult, mentioned by Gregory of Tours (17 Nov.) and Venantius Fortunatus (14 Dec.), is very ancient. According to the *passio* he was a tribune who had been baptized but kept his Christianity secret. He lived in Vienne, and St Julian of Brioude (28 Aug.) lodged in his house. When persecution broke out, Julian, who had professed his faith publicly, was put to death, while Ferreolus was taken into custody for failing to arrest Christians. The judge pointed out that he was paid a salary by the State and was therefore expected to obey orders. To this Ferreolus replied that he would happily do without the money provided he could live quietly and serve God, but he would prefer to lose his life rather than to abandon his religion. The judge responded by having him scourged and placed in the foulest cell in the prison. On the third day his chains fell away miraculously and he made a spectacular escape, leaving the city by the Lyons gate and swimming across the Rhone. But he was recaptured at this point and beheaded on the banks of the river. Christians from Vienne recovered his body and buried it, and a church was built over the grave. Some time later the Rhone flooded, making this church unsafe. In about 473 St Mamertus (11 May) built a new one within the city walls in which to house the relics—their transfer is described in detail by Gregory of Tours. The legend that Julian of Brioude's head was found in Ferreolus' grave is discussed by Fr Delehaye, who sets no store by it. This Ferreolus should not be confused with St Ferreolus of Limoges, who died in about 591 and is commemorated on the same day.

The *passio* is in *AA.SS.*, Sept., 5, pp. 764-5. See also *Bibl.SS.*, 5, 651-2; Gregory of Tours, *De virtutibus S. Juliani*, in *M.G.H. Scriptores merov.*, 1, pp. 564-5; *C.M.H.*, pp. 517-8; H. Delehaye, *Les Légendes hagiographiques* (4th ed., 1955), p. 114.

St Richardis (*c.* 840-95)

Since there is no formal Life of St Richardis, what is know about her comes mainly from a handful of Breviary lessons, panegyrics, and so on. A daughter of Duke Erchanger of Alsace, she was born in about 840 and educated by nuns in the monastery of Sainte-Odile. At the age of twenty-two she was married to Charles le Gros, who ruled variously as king of Alemannia (876-82), emperor of the West (881-7), king of Germany (882-7), and king of France (884-7). As a young woman she was a great benefactor of monasteries. Many benefitted from her generosity, including those at Seckingen and Zurzach, and those of SS Felix and Regula in Zurich and St Martin in Pavia. Much later, in 880, using land inherited from her father, she founded a monastery at Andlau on the edge of the Vosges and installed her niece Rotrudis as abbess.

In February 881 Charles, accompanied by Richardis, went to Rome, where he was crowned emperor of the West by Pope John VIII (872-82). By 884, having succeeded his father, Louis II the German (843-76), and his two brothers, Carloman and Louis, he was the ruler of vast territories. Unfortunately he was not up to the task, and it was not long before his incompetence was compounded by illness. One of his nephews led an uprising against him, and in 887 he was deposed.

Up to this point the marriage of Richardis and Charles had been happy and harmonious. However, not long after Charles was deposed Richardis was accused of infidelity, and Liutward, bishop of Vercelli, once her husband's chancellor, was named as her lover. For whatever reason, Charles chose to believe the charges, and Richardis and Liutward, a man widely respected for his integrity and his learning, were called to appear before the imperial assembly. Liutward denied the allegation under oath; Richardis appealed to the judgment of God and chose ordeal by fire. This, it is said, was accepted, and, barefoot and wearing an inflammable smock, she walked unharmed over burning embers. Despite this vindication she separated from Charles, who died at Neidingen a few months later. Richardis went for a while to a convent at Hohenburg and then to the abbey of Andlau. Here she lived peacefully, sharing the life of the community, caring for the poor, and writing verses. And it was here that she was buried when she died on 18 September in about 895. When Pope St Leo IX (1049-54; 19 Apr.) visited Andlau in 1049 on his way back from a council at Mainz he asked that her relics be disinterred and enshrined in the monastery church so that people could venerate them. The cult has continued, especially in the diocese of Strasbourg; St Richardis is invoked in particular against fire.

AA.SS., Sept., 5, pp. 793-8; *Allgemeine Deutsche Biographie*, 28, p. 420ff.; M. Corbet, *Ste Richarde* (1948); *Bibl.SS.*, 11, 157-8; M. Barth, "Die hl. Kaiserin Richardis und ihr Kult," in *Festschrift zurn 900 Jahrfeier der Weihe der Stiftskirche con Andlau* (1949), pp. 11-100.

St Richardis is depicted in the windows of Strasbourg Cathedral, as well as on her tomb at Andlau. Her iconographical symbol is the fire by which she proved her innocence. On the iconography see J. Braun, *Tracht und Attribute der Heiligen in der deutschen Kunst* (1943), pp. 630-1.

St Lambert of Freising, *Bishop* (957)

The history of the cult of this St Lambert is interesting. If there ever was a Life it has not survived, and he is not mentioned by the Bollandists in the *Acta Sanctorum*. The few known facts are that he became bishop of Freising in 955 when the Hungarian campaigns in the West had just come to an end and Otto I the Great (936-73), who was to become the first Holy Roman Emperor in 962, was consolidating his power base; that he died on 19 September 957; and that some documents give him the title "saint" from the eleventh century onward, although others that mention his name on 19 September do not, and there was at that stage no liturgical cult. The legend does what it can to fill in the gaps: it claims, for example, that Lambert fasted even as a baby at his mother's breast and that his prayers saved the cathedral in Freising when the city was attacked by the Huns (*sic*) at the beginning of his two years as bishop. It was also suggested that he was a Benedictine, but there is no evidence for this. When he died, Lambert was buried in the crypt of the cathedral in Freising. A formal cult seems to have developed after 1350, when his relics were translated. It was also at this time that the legend began to develop.

Lambert of Freising should not be confused with his namesake, St Lambert of Maastricht (17 Sept.). The latter was venerated in Freising from the end of the eighth century. Gradually, however, the cult of the local Lambert took over, and by the late sixteenth century it had completely replaced that of Lambert of Maastricht in Freising.

J. A. Fischer, *Der heilige Lantbert, Bischof von Freising (937-57) und seine Zeit* (1957); *idem.*, *Lantbert von Freising. Der Bischof und Heilige* (1959); *Bibl.SS.*, 7, 1077-8.

St Joseph of Copertino (1603-63)

Joseph (Giuseppe) Desa was born at Copertino, south of Brindisi, on 17 June 1603. His parents, Felice Desa and Franceschina Panaca, were poor, and at the time in such straitened circumstances that it is said his mother had to give birth in a shed because his father, a carpenter, had been forced to sell their house to pay his debts. After this unpromising beginning Joseph did not have a happy childhood. His father died while he was still an infant and his desperate mother looked on him as a nuisance and a burden. As a child he suffered from an unspecified illness that kept him out of school for about three years. In spite of a cure regarded as miraculous he remained lethargic and absent-minded, and his response to all reproof would be, "I forgot." But he also had a hot temper, and this, together with his habit of wandering round the village, aimless and open-mouthed—earning the nickname *Boccaperta* (Gaper)—did not help to make him popular. How much this behaviour was a simply a response to his mother's handling of him we do not know, but it is possible that he suffered from a mild form of epilepsy, or what are known as absence seizures. Yet in spite of everything the fidelity with which he performed his religious duties was exemplary.

When the time came for him to earn his own living, he was apprenticed to a shoemaker. But although he worked hard he also tended to become distracted, and the project was not successful. He decided instead to try his vocation to the religious life and applied first to the Conventual Franciscans, who refused him, and then to the Capuchins. On 15 August 1620 the latter accepted him as a lay brother. But after eight months they were compelled to dismiss him because he seemed unable to carry out simple, routine duties on which the community relied. He would drop dishes and piles of plates on the refectory floor, forget to do things he had been asked to do, and fail to build and tend the fire in the refectory. When a rich uncle rejected his appeals for help he returned home in despair. His mother, who was not at all pleased to see him, enlisted the help of her brother, a Conventual Franciscan. Joseph was accepted as a servant by the friars at Grottella, who gave him the habit of a Franciscan tertiary and set him to work in the stables.

Perhaps because he was happier and someone had at last shown confidence in him, Joseph began to change. He carried out his duties more effectively, and the gentler, brighter side of his personality began to emerge. This, with his remarkable spirit of prayer and penance, earned him such respect within the community that in 1625 he was admitted as a novice and at the same time began to train for the priesthood. His only problem was his complete lack of scholastic aptitude, which made the academic side of his training difficult. However, he did manage to learn to read the Missal and the Breviary, and luck was on his side. In the examination for the diaconate he was asked to expound the only text ("Blessed is the womb that bore thee") on which he had anything to say. And when it came to the priesthood the first candidates were so good that the examiners waived the rest, including him, through. In 1628 he was ordained.

Insofar as he was able to control his circumstances, he spent the next thirty-five years serving his community in the ways that he could and devoting himself to prayer and extreme austerities. What he could not control were the unusual and sometimes spectacular supernatural phenomena, including levitation, that he experienced. These seem to have begun on 4 October 1630, and in response he intensified his fasts and penances. He was extraordinarily sensitive to any mention of God or the mysteries of religion, which would immediately put him into a state of ecstasy. It was as if the extreme abstraction he experienced in his childhood now had a focus. Sometimes when he was oblivious to everything going on around him his brethren would attempt to bring him to by hitting or pricking him. Usually, however, it took the voice of his superior to bring him back to himself, after which he would apologize for his "fit of giddiness." Most remarkable of all were his levitations—his being raised from the ground and moved through the air, as far as could be seen by no physical agent. Seventy instances of this were recorded during the seventeen years he spent at Grottella, the majority well attested by independent and reliable observers.

One of the most famous took place in 1645, in Assisi, where Joseph was then living. The Spanish ambassador to the papal court, who was passing through, saw Joseph privately, after which he reported to his wife that he had just met "another St Francis." She expressed a desire to meet the friar herself, so the father guardian told Joseph to go down to the church where he would find her. He obeyed, but as soon as he entered the church his eye was caught by a statue of Our Lady up behind the altar. He was immediately lifted through the air to the foot of the statue. When he had prayed there for a moment, he uttered "his customary shrill cry" and was carried back to the door of the church, at which point he returned to his cell, leaving the ambassador, his wife, and their large retinue "speechless with astonishment."

But that was still in the future. On 21 October 1638 Joseph was brought before the Neapolitan Inquisition, which on 28 November witnessed one of his levitations and accused him of "drawing crowds after him like a new Messiah through prodigies accomplished on the ignorant who are ready to believe anything." The report was sent to the Holy Office, members of which discussed the matter with Pope Urban VIII (1623-44). He cleared Joseph of any attempt to feign holiness or take advantage of popular credulity, but Joseph's superiors, who found the phenomena and the attention they attracted disturbing and inconvenient, decided to do something radical. They had already forbidden him to celebrate Mass in public, attend the divine office or community meals, or take part in processions and other public functions. They now forced him to leave his beloved Grottella, sending him instead to the friary at Assisi, where he could be watched. He stayed there for thirteen years, and they were not happy. People came to him to seek his advice, among them the Infanta Maria of Savoy; a lifelong friend, Johann Friedrich of Saxony, a Lutheran who was inspired by Joseph to become a Catholic; and Prince John Casimir Waza, who was to become king of Poland but wanted to be a Jesuit. But the real or apparent failure of his superiors to understand and their severity, coupled with a spiritual dryness that made him feel that God too had abandoned him, soon reduced him to a state of depression. Fortunately the minister general was made aware of this and called Joseph to Rome, where his sense of God's close presence returned to him.

Then on 19 July 1653 the Inquisition of Perugia started looking into the case and, for reasons that are obscure, decided to remove him from his own order and place him under the Capuchins. For the next three or four years he lived in virtual seclusion, first in an isolated Capuchin friary at Pietrarossa and then at Fossombrone. He was not allowed to celebrate or attend Mass or to communicate with anyone who was not a friar. In 1655 his own friars asked that he be returned to Assisi, but no decision was taken for two years—Pope Alexander VII (1655-7) said one St Francis at Assisi was enough. Finally, on 12 June 1656, he was allowed to leave the Capuchins and go to live in the Conventual friary at Osimo. Even there his association with others, including the friars, was severely restricted.

Although the official reaction was somewhat reserved when he died in Osimo on 18 September 1663, there was an immediate upsurge of public veneration, and miracles were reported at his tomb. When the cause for his canonization was put forward, Prosper Lambertini, later Pope Benedict XIV (1740-58), one of the greatest authorities then or at any time on evidence and procedure in canonization causes, was chosen as *promotor fidei*, or "devil's advocate." Yet in the end Lambertini, who examined the evidence in minute detail and submitted numerous and searching questions, seems to have satisfied himself as to the extraordinary humility, gentleness, and patience that were the basis of Joseph's genuine holiness. For it was he who, as pope, published the decree of beatification on 24 February 1753. In his treatise *De servorum Dei beatificatione* he specifically mentions the case and the "eyewitnesses of unchallengeable integrity" who came forward to give evidence. Joseph was canonized on 16 July 1767.

AA.SS., Sept., 5, pp. 992-1060; A. Pastrovicchi, *Compendio della Vita, Virtù, e Miracoli del B. Giuseppe da Copertino* (1753; Eng. trans. by F. Laing, 1918); G. Parisciani, *San Giuseppe da Copertino alla luce dei nuovi documenti* (1964); H. Thurston in *The Month* (May 1919); *idem, The Physical Phenomena of Mysticism* (1952); G. Parisciani and G. Galleazzi (eds.), *S. Giuseppe da Copertino tra storia ed attualità* (1984); *O.D.S.*, pp. 270-1; *Bibl.SS.*, 6, 1300-3.

ST JANUARIUS
Said to have been thrown to wild beasts, which refused to touch him.
Also shown tied to a tree; with a heated oven by his side; lighting a fire.

19

ST JANUARIUS, *Bishop and Martyr* (? *c.* 305)

Januarius (in Italian, Gennaro) is best known for the liquefaction of his blood, which has allegedly been taking place in Naples since 1389. The records of his martyrdom, which date from the sixth and ninth centuries, are not reliable in any of their details. What is certain, however, is that a bishop named Januarius did die for his faith somewhere near Naples and that he was venerated from an early date. A priest named Uranius, writing in 432, says that in the previous year St Paulinus of Nola (22 June) was comforted on his death-bed by a vision of St Martin of Tours (11 Nov.) and St Januarius, "bishop and martyr and glory of the church of Naples." A wall-painting in the so-called "catacomb of St Januarius" in Naples, which also dates from the fifth century, represents him with a nimbus. And he is mentioned by St Gregory of Tours (17 Nov.), who was writing in the sixth century.

The account of him that has survived gives Naples as his place of birth (though Benevento is an alternative candidate) and states that he was bishop of Benevento when the persecution of Diocletian (284-305) broke out in 303. When he heard that Sossus and Proculus, deacons respectively of Pozzuoli and Miseno, and two laymen, Euticius and Acutius, had been imprisoned, he decided to visit them. Word of this was passed on to the persecutors, and he was arrested. With Festus, his deacon, and Desiderius, a lector in his church, he was questioned by the governor in Nola and then tortured. When the governor went to Pozzuoli, the three men were heavily manacled and made to walk before his chariot. In Pozzuoli they were put in the same prison as Sossus and the others and with them were condemned to be thrown to the wild beasts. As none of the animals would touch them they were beheaded instead and buried near the town.

Sometime in the fifth century Januarius' relics were brought to Naples from the little church of San Gennaro in the volcanic region of the Solfatara, near Pozzuoli. They were moved first to Benevento and subsequently to the abbey of Monte Vergine during the Norman wars in the eleventh century but were returned to Naples, of which he is principal patron, in 1497. St Januarius is mentioned in the fifth-century *Hieronymianum* as well as in the Lindisfarne Gospels in the second half of the seventh century and the calendar of St Willibrord (7 Nov.) at the beginning of the eighth.

The relic of his blood that allegedly liquefies each year on his three feast-days—19 September, 16 December (the day on which he averted a threatened eruption of Vesuvius in 1631), and the Saturday before the first Sunday in May (translation of his relics)—is held in the treasury chapel in Naples Cathedral. It consists of a phial, fixed in a metal reliquary, which is half filled by a dark, solid, opaque mass. Six times on each of the three feast days it is brought out and held by a priest in the presence of a silver reliquary, said to contain the martyr's head, and in full view of all present. Prayers are said by the people, especially by a representative group of women known as the *zie di San Gennaro* ("aunts of St Januarius"), while from time to time the priest turns the relic. After a time—anything from two minutes to an hour—the solid mass is seen to liquefy and increase in volume; it becomes reddish in colour and sometimes bubbles up. The priest announces, "The miracle has happened." Then the *Te Deum* is sung and the relic is venerated.

This is one of the most thoroughly investigated of all alleged miracles. At the very least it can be said that the extraordinary thing that is said to take place does take place. Even sceptics accept that, although they offer natural explanations—for example, that the blood is mixed with wax which melts in the heat. In fact, there seems to be no link between the outside temperature and the rate of liquefaction. Sometimes, when the temperature has been as high as 30°C , two hours have passed before there is any sign of liquefaction; on other occasions it occurs within fifteen minutes, even in temperatures as low as minus 7 or minus 8°C. Other important facts concerning the relic are that the volume of the dark substance in the phial, alleged to be the blood of St Januarius, does not remain constant; that its weight varies as well; and that liquefaction does not always take place in the same way—sometimes the blood almost seems to boil, or else it is sluggish and its colour dull. None of this has any known natural explanation. It has been suggested that it is lamb's blood, but this has been shown scientifically not to be the case.

On the other hand, there are difficulties. There are in the Naples area other blood relics—including those said to be of St John the Baptist (24 June), St Stephen (26 Dec.), and St Ursula—that behave in the same way but are undoubtedly spurious. The relic of St Januarius has been known to liquefy while a jeweller was repairing the reliquary. There have been occasions, particularly on the December feast, when it has failed to liquefy at all. And its authenticity cannot be proven. What is more, and this cannot be ignored, the phenomenon seems to have very little purpose. As one authority has put it, "a conclusive judgment in this matter can hardly be arrived at, but so far no natural explanation has been found."

The blood liquefied unexpectedly during a visit made by the then archbishop of New York, Cardinal Terence Cooke, in 1978. The last time it failed to liquefy is said to have been when Naples elected a communist mayor.

For the *acta* see *AA.SS.*, Sept., 6, pp. 761-894; *C.M.H.*, p. 517. See also H. Thurston in *Catholic Encyclopaedia*, 8, pp. 295-7; *idem*, "The Blood-Miracles of Naples," in *The Month* 149 (1927), pp. 44-55, 123-35, 236-47; *idem*, "The 'Miracle' of St Januarius," in *ibid.* 155

(1930), pp. 119-29; D. Sax, *Relics and Shrines* (1985), pp. 158-60; *H.S.S.C.*, 2, p. 270; *Bibl.SS.*, 6, 135-51; *O.D.S.*, p. 251; Jöckle, pp. 229-30.

In art St Januarius is variously represented in a tunic with a cloak, or else as a bishop, at the moment of his martyrdom—as in the late seventeenth-century painting by Luca Giordano in the National Gallery, London. His accompanying symbols are a palm branch, a crown, and a sword or crozier presented by angels.

St Peleus and Companions, *Martyrs* (310)

Only three of Peleus' companions—Nilus, Elias, and Patermutius—are mentioned by name, and some sources mention no other companions. But there are discrepancies where the numbers are concerned. Other sources suggest there were over one hundred of them, and the *Hieronymianum* says 150. The circumstances suggest that the discrepancies are only apparent. During the last general persecution the Christians who had been condemned to work in the quarries in Palestine formed groups and built little oratories in which they would meet to celebrate Mass and pray. When the emperor Galerius (305-11) was told by the governor of Palestine that this was going on he ordered that those involved should be dispersed to mines in Cyprus, Lebanon, and other places. However, before he carried out the order the officer charged with doing so had four of the obvious ringleaders burned alive. Two, Peleus and Nilus, were Egyptian bishops; Elias was a priest; and Patermutius was a layman, also Egyptian. They are thought to have suffered at Phunion, near Petra, possibly at the same time as St Tyrannio of Gaza and others (formerly 20 Feb.).

The main source of information about these martyrs is Eusebius, *De Martyribus Palaestinae*, 13, 3. See also B. Violet, *Die palästinischen Märtyrer des Eusebius von Cäsarea*, pp. 105-7; H. Delehaye in *Anal.Boll.* 16 (1898), pp. 129-39; *ibid.* 40 (1921), pp. 20, 31, 80; H. J. Lawlor, "The Chronology of Eusebius' Martyrs of Palestine," in *Hermathena* 25 (1908), pp. 117-201; *Bibl.SS.*, 10, 446-9.

St Sequanus, *Abbot (c. 580)*

The anonymous Life of St Sequanus that has survived is not of much value as a historical source. However, he is mentioned by Jonas of Bobbio, who refers to him as Segonus; in the *Hieronymianum*, where he appears as Sigon; and by St Gregory of Tours (17 Nov.) and others, who, like a number of early martyrologies, call him Sequanus. All seem to be referring to the same person, and Baronius opted to call him Sequanus when he included him in the Roman Martyrology. The *Hieronymianum* also names him as the founder of a sixth-century monastery at Saint-Seine-l'Abbaye (then Sicaster or Segestre), about fifteen miles from Dijon. It is supposed to have taken his name sometime in the ninth century. At the beginning of the thirteenth century the church (which still survives) was rebuilt in Burgundian Gothic style, and when it came to be restored during the fifteenth century the legend of St Sequanus was painted on the walls of the transept.

According to the legend Sequanus was born in Mesmont, a small town in Burgundy, and lived for a while as a hermit in a hut he built for himself at Verrey-sous-Drèc. While he was still very young—even as young as sixteen—the bishop of Langres ordained him to the priesthood. This was much resented by the local clergy, who began to victimize him. Having endured this for a while, he went to the monastery of Réome and placed himself under the direction of the abbot. While he was there, in addition to training as a monk, he acquired a deep knowledge of the scriptures. Eventually he went off to build a monastery of his own in the forest of Segestre, near the source of the Seine. The regular discipline he established and his own reputation for miracles attracted disciples, and there was soon a flourishing community. The monks had a very civilizing effect on the people of the neighbourhood, who were said to be cannibals. Scholars disagree about the date of Sequanus' death. Some put it as early as 540, while others prefer about 580. He is assumed to have been buried at his monastery, but of this there is no trace, since the relics were dispersed during the Revolution.

The anonymous Life is in *AA.SS.*, Sept., 6, pp. 33-41. See also *Bibl.SS.*, 11, 848-50; Rossignol-Vallot, "Les peintures de la vie de St Seine," in *Mémoires de la Commission des Antiquités de la Côte d'Or*, 2 (1835), pp. 193-286.

St Goericus of Metz, *Bishop* (647)

The medieval Life of St Goericus (who seems also to have been known as Abbo) is typically unsatisfactory, and the available information raises certain chronological problems. There were two prominent Christian families in Aquitaine in the late sixth and early seventh centuries, the Ansbertina and the Salvia. Goericus was an Ansbertina and numbered several saints among his relatives. The date suggested for his birth is somewhere between 565 and 575, and the official records of the diocese of Metz name him as the thirtieth bishop, from 625 to 642/3. The problems arise with the assertion that he started his career as an officer in the palace of Dagobert I, since Dagobert did not come to the throne until 629, that is, after he, Goericus, had become bishop of Metz. What does seem clear is that Dagobert knew and respected Goericus, because he mentions him in the will he made in 636.

Once the problem of his connection with Dagobert is set aside, Goericus' story, as it has survived, can be summarized as follows. At some time in the course of a distinguished career he lost his sight. He was forced to retire immediately but accepted his new situation patiently. Then, in response to what he felt was a supernatural command, he decided to make a pilgrimage to the church of St Stephen in Metz, where his uncle, St Arnulf (18 July), was bishop. He set off with his daughters, Precia and Victorina, to guide him, and when he reached Metz went straight to the church. There, while he was praying, his sight was restored. In thanksgiving, he decided to become a priest, and in the following year, when Arnulf retired, he became bishop of Metz.

As bishop, Goericus followed very much in the footsteps of Arnulf, whom he visited regularly in his retreat in Remiremont. When Arnulf died, Goericus brought his body to Metz—an occasion said to have been marked by miracles. Goericus also built the church of St Peter in Metz and founded at Epinal a monastery for women, of which his daughter Precia was the first abbess. He kept up a correspondence with Desiderius, bishop of Cahors (15 Nov.), some of which has survived. A church was built in his honour at Metz in the tenth century, and a Breviary published in Paris in 1535 contains prayers peculiar to him for use in the common for an abbot.

For the Life, see *AA.SS.*, Sept., 6, pp. 42-5. St Goericus' correspondence with St Desiderius is in *P.L.*, 86, 318ff. See also *Bibl.SS.*, 1, 38-9; *F.E.*, 3, p. 56; M. Meurice, *Histoire des évêques de Metz* (1634).

St Theodore of Canterbury, Bishop (*c.* 602-690)

A Greek, born (like St Paul) in Tarsus and educated in Athens, Theodore was the last foreign-born of the early archbishops of Canterbury. He was also one of the greatest. When Pope St Vitalian (657-72; 27 Jan.) appointed him to the see he was about sixty-five years old and had already been a monk for many years. His predecessor in the see, St Deusdedit (14 July), died in 664. Oswiu, king of Northumbria (641-70), and Egbert, king of Kent (664-73), sent a priest named Wighard to Rome, the idea being that he should be consecrated and confirmed for the see by the pope. However, Wighard died in Italy, so the pope appointed a monk named Adrian, who was abbot of a monastery near Naples. This man, an African by birth, was well qualified in every way. But his anxiety about the appointment was such that in the end the pope agreed to let him off provided that he could suggest someone else. Adrian's first suggestion was a monk who had to be ruled out because of ill health. His second was Theodore. The pope accepted Theodore on condition that Adrian, who had already travelled through France twice, accompany him to Britain and keep an eye on him (that this was to make sure, as Bede suggests, that Theodore did not introduce any unorthodox teaching seems highly unlikely). Once in England Adrian became abbot of St Augustine's monastery in Canterbury.

Since he was not a priest, Theodore was immediately ordained to the subdiaconate. Then—an interesting detail implying that he may have been an Eastern-rite monk—he waited four months to allow his hair to grow so that he could be tonsured in the Roman style. Eventually the pope ordained him and consecrated him bishop. He was then introduced to St Benedict Biscop (12 Jan.), who happened to be making one of his several visits to Rome. The pope directed Benedict to accompany Adrian and Theodore, acting as guide and interpreter on their journey to Britain. They set out on 27 May 668, reaching Paris in time for Theodore to spend the winter there with St Agilbert (11 Oct.). Agilbert, who had just become archbishop of Paris, had previously been bishop of Wessex. From him Theodore obtained valuable information about the circumstances of the Church in Britain. He also began to learn English. When King Egbert heard that his new archbishop had got as far as Paris, he sent his reeve to meet him. But the journey to Britain had to be delayed because Theodore fell ill at the port of Quentavic (now Saint-Josse-sur-Mer). Eventually he travelled on in the company of Benedict Biscop and took possession of his see on 27 May 669, a year to the day after his departure from Rome.

As metropolitan bishop of all England, Theodore made it his business to visit as many of the churches in the country as possible, taking Adrian with him as interpreter. He was well received and managed to cover a good deal of ground—confirming the Roman practice regarding the date of Easter, introducing into the divine office the Roman chant (plainchant), which until then had been used only in the churches of Kent, and filling a number of vacant sees. In the formation of dioceses and the appointment of bishops it was his policy to unify disparate elements in the Church and when creating new dioceses to make sure they did not straddle two or more different kingdoms. In Northumbria he had to deal with a dispute between St Wilfrid (12 Oct.) and St Chad (2 Mar.), both of whom claimed to be archbishop of York. The situation had arisen because, while Wilfrid was being consecrated in Gaul, Oswiu had appointed Chad, whose background was Irish, to the see. Partly because he believed that Chad had not been properly consecrated and partly to ensure strong support for the pro-Roman policy against Celtic elements in Northumbria, Theodore ruled that Wilfrid was the rightful archbishop. However, he was impressed by Chad's qualities (he was "an extremely meek man," according to Eddius, and "a true servant of God") and appointed him bishop of Lichfield as soon as the see became vacant. He also went as far as Lindisfarne, a stronghold of Celtic influence, and consecrated the church of St Peter there.

Theodore presided over the first synod of the Anglo-Saxon Church, which took place at Hertford in 672. His aim was twofold: to put an end to jurisdictional disputes between bishops and in particular to foster harmony between the "Roman" and "Celtic" groupings within the Church, not to mention the Gaulish elements, in order to form a unified whole; and to ensure stability and some autonomy for the monasteries. The synod's decrees were based on canons, approved at the Council of Chalcedon, which Theodore felt were of special importance for England. These included acceptance of the Roman calculation of the date of Easter (already agreed at the Synod of Whitby), conformity to the diocesan system of the Church, and provision for an annual synod of bishops. The Hertford synod also affirmed the indissolubility of marriage. Seven years later, in 679, Theodore convened a second synod at Hatfield. This was important because it confirmed the orthodox position of the English Church, especially in face of the Monothelite controversy, in which Theodore had taken a prominent part when he was in Rome.

The one instance in which he failed to foster unity was over the question of the diocese of York. In 678 there was friction between Egfrith, king of North-umbria (670-85), and Wilfrid, who as bishop of York had upheld the wish of the king's wife, St Etheldreda (23 June), to enter a convent. The diocese of York was huge, and there had been some criticism of the way in which Wilfrid administered it. Theodore decided that this was the moment to assert his authority in the north. He created three new sees, carving most of them out of the diocese of York (Northumbria) and, in conjunction with Egfrith, appointed bishops to them.

Wilfrid understandably felt that Theodore had gone over his head, so he appealed to Rome. Theodore, meanwhile, ignored him and continued with his appointment of bishops. Pope St Agatho (678-81; 10 Jan.) ruled in favour of Wilfrid, who had gone to Rome to present his case in person, and directed that he be restored to his see with suffragan bishops to help him. Egfrith refused to accept the pope's decision, so Wilfrid went into exile. As far as is known, Theodore did nothing to counter Egfrith's high-handed behaviour, and in 685 he consecrated St Cuthbert (20 Mar.) as bishop of Lindisfarne in York Cathedral. But he atoned later for any injustice he might have done. In the presence of St Erconwald (13 May) he met Wilfrid in London and they came to an agreement that Wilfrid would once again be bishop of York, but in its smaller configuration. He also took the trouble to write to Elfleda, abbess of Whitby; Ethelred, king of Mercia (674-704); and Aldfrith, king of Northumbria (685-704), all of whom had opposed Wilfrid, recommending him to them.

The school Theodore founded in Canterbury was famous for the breadth of the education it offered, and many future English bishops were educated here. Not only were Latin and Greek on the curriculum, but Theodore and Adrian, who still helped him, taught between them the sciences, particularly astronomy and arithmetic, Roman law, biblical exegesis (according to the literal, Antiochian school), the rules of metre and Latin verse composition, and music. Little of what was certainly written by Theodore has survived—the so-called *Penitential of Theodore* is unlikely to be his.

In any case, despite his learning, his gifts were pragmatic and organizational. Arriving in England, he had found a missionary Church riven by dissensions and with nothing to make it cohere. When he died twenty-one years later, on 19 September 690, he left a well-organized Church divided into dioceses with a metropolitan see in Canterbury. He was buried near the first archbishop of Canterbury, St Augustine (27 May), in the abbey church of SS Peter and Paul. Earliest evidence of a cult is in the calendar of St Willibrord (7 Nov.), but Theodore never enjoyed the sort of popularity enjoyed by miracle-working saints. Nevertheless, his effort to unify the Church in England was the most significant single contribution in the period between the arrival of St Augustine and the Norman Conquest. Bede's verdict is as true today as it was then: "The English churches prospered more during the pontificate [of Theodore] than they ever did before."

Butler's Lives of the Saints

AA.SS., Sept., 6, pp. 55-82; Bede, *H.E.*, 4, pp. 1-3, 5-6, 12, 15, 19, and 5, p. 8. For a translation of Eddius' *Vita Wilfridii* and other relevant material see D. H. Farmer, *The Age of Bede* (1998). See also F. M. Stenton, *Anglo-Saxon England* (1943), pp. 130-41; H. Mayr-Harting, *The Coming of Christianity to Anglo-Saxon England* (1972); P. Fournier, *Histoire des Collections Canoniques en Occident* (1931-2); T. M. Neill and H. M. Garner, *Mediaeval Handbooks of Penance* (1938); N. Brooks, *The Early History of the Church of Canterbury* (1984); *O.D.S.*, pp. 451-3; and especially M. Lapidge, *Archbishop Theodore* (1995).

St Mary of Cervellón (1230-90)

The story of Mary of Cervellón, or María de Socos (Mary of Help), as she was and still is known in Spain, became mixed up with the notorious forgeries used to create an imposing record for the beginnings of the Mercedarian Order. A short Latin Life by Juan de Laes and Guillermo Vives is therefore not reliable in its details, particularly where these relate to miracles and wonders. It seems certain, however, that Mary was born in Barcelona on 1 December 1230. Her parents, a Spanish nobleman and his wife who had been childless until then, were said to have attributed her birth to the prayers of the founder of the Mercedarian Order, St Peter Nolasco (25 Dec.). They gave their daughter, who is supposed to have been very beautiful as well as otherwise gifted, a sound religious upbringing. So it is perhaps not surprising that a sermon by the Mercedarian prior in Barcelona, Bernardo de Corbera, inspired her to consecrate her life to God and more specifically to the Christian slaves who were suffering at the hands of the Moors and Saracens.

Mary's father died in 1260, but she remained at home for another five years to keep her mother company. When the latter died in 1265, she joined a community of women who were living under Bernardo's direction and supporting the work of the Mercedarians by their prayers. It was her constant prayerfulness and the generosity with which she spent her time doing good for others that earned her the name Maria *de Socos*. She died in Barcelona in 1290. Miracles were reported at her tomb, and her cult was confirmed in 1692. She is also a patroness of seamen, especially those in danger of shipwreck.

Many of the forged documents were first published in B. de Corbera, *Vida y hechos maravillosos de Doña María de Corveilon* (1639). The Latin Life is in *AA.SS.*, Sept., 7, pp. 166-86. See also *Bibl.SS.*, 8, 1044-5.

Bd Alphonsus de Orozco (1500-91)

Alphonsus (Alonso) de Orozco was born at Oropesa in the diocese of Avila on 17 October 1500. Before going to study law at the university of Salamanca, he was educated in Talavera and Toledo, where he developed the love of music and art that was to stay with him all his life. While he was in Salamanca he attended some sermons preached by the Augustinian St Thomas of Villanova (22 Sept.), then a young friar. These confirmed his conviction, held since he was six, that he had a vocation to the priesthood. So when, aged twenty-two, he had finished his legal studies, he was clothed, along with an older brother, Francisco, in the Augustinian habit. Francisco's death during the novitiate provoked a crisis in Alphonsus from which he did not fully recover until much later. He nevertheless persevered despite bouts of ill health, and apart from a spell as prior of the house in Seville he spent much of the first thirty years of his religious life teaching, preaching, and hearing confessions. In 1547 he did try to go to Mexico as a missionary, but arthritis forced him to turn back when he had got no further than the Canary Islands.

On 13 March 1554, the year in which Philip II (1556-98) married Queen Mary of England, Alphonsus was sent as prior to the Augustinian priory in the royal city of Valladolid. It was a role for which he was particularly well suited, for, despite his own austerity, he was gentle and understanding in his mode of governing. Two years later he was appointed court preacher. As such he had a profound influence on his sophisticated congregation, who were drawn to his sermons by the simple but persuasive quality of his preaching. And the poor benefitted too, because he was very generous with the money he received for his preaching.

In 1561 Philip decided to establish the court in Madrid. Alphonsus went too, but he chose to live at the monastery of San Felice el Real in an austere cell that contrasted sharply with the grandeur of the court. From this cell he conducted an apostolate that took him to convents, hospitals, and prisons as well as to the court. His other activity was writing. While he was prior of the monastery in Seville, he had had a vision of Our Lady, who told him that he should use his talent for writing in the service of God. He fulfilled this injunction faithfully: each year he would produce a new work on Our Lady herself, and these, together with his mystical, devotional, and other works, fill seven large volumes. Toward the end of his life his superiors directed him to write an account of his own mystical experiences, which he did, calling the result "confessions." When he died on 19 September 1591 the entire court turned out in genuine grief to follow his coffin. He was beatified on 15 January 1882.

For Alphonsus' life and writings see T. Camara, *Vida y Escritos* (1882). Also *Bibl.SS.*, 9, 1241; J. A. Farina, *Doctrina de Oración del B. Alfonso* (1927).

St Emily de Rodat, *Foundress* (1787-1852)

Marie Guillemette Emilie de Rodat was born at the handsome manor house of Druelle, near Rodez, on 6 September 1787. When she was not yet two she was taken to live with her maternal grandmother in the *château* of Ginals, near Villefranche-de-Rouergue. It was a remote spot, and she remained there in safety throughout the Revolution. She seems to have been a normally lively child with a strong but not exaggerated religious sensitivity. When she was about sixteen and had been given a glimpse of life in society, her enthusiasm for religion cooled off a bit. She is said to have looked around for another confessor because her own was too strict and to have set aside as little time as possible for her prayers. This, some would say normal, sixteen-year-old behaviour was not lost on her grandmother. Because she rejected the society of "nuns and pious females" in Villefranche, Emily was confined to the austere monotony of life at Ginals, where her parents were by now living. She seems gradually to have settled down and found what she was really looking for. On the feast of Corpus Christi 1804 she had a definitive spiritual experience which gave her a conviction of the abiding presence of God, and she never looked back.

In the spring of the following year Emily, now eighteen, went to help the nuns at the Maison Saint-Cyr in Villefranche, where she had herself been to school. She was made responsible for the children's recreation, prepared them for their First Communion, and taught them geography (even this had an edifying slant, since she was expected to tell them about the saints connected with the place names they put on their maps). She had almost certainly hoped to find a place for herself in the community, but in this she was disappointed. The nuns came from various convents that had been dispersed during the Revolution. The fact that they were now gathered under one roof was not enough to bind them together as a community. What is more, none of them was young, and not all were as welcoming of Emily and her enthusiasms as they might have been. She nevertheless made one important friend, the school chaplain, Abbé Antoine Marty. With his permission she left three times in the eleven years she was there to try her vocation elsewhere—with the Dames de Nevers at Figeac, the Picpus Sisters at Cahors, and the Sisters of Mercy at Moissac. But each time she returned to Villefranche disappointed, restless, and reproaching herself for instability.

Then on a spring day in 1815 she went to visit a sick woman in the parish. There she found a group of neighbours discussing the difficulty they were having, because of their poverty, in getting education for their children. In a flash it came to Emily that she could teach them herself. She put the idea to Abbé Marty, who reacted positively. Within a few weeks she was teaching on her own. The room she started in at the Maison Saint-Cyr was small, but she managed to squeeze forty children into it plus the three young women who helped her with the teaching. So began what was to become the Congregation of the Holy Family (called "of Villefranche" to distinguish it from many other Congregations of that name). The first few months did not go entirely smoothly. The parents of sixteen-year-old Eleanor Dutriac, one of the assistants, threatened legal action to get their daughter back. Some members of the Maison Saint-Cyr community were positively unkind, and Emily and her friends had to endure criticism and mockery from priests as well as laypeople. Emily persevered, however, encouraged by Abbé Marty, and in May 1816 was able to start her free school in rented premises of her own. Shortly after this the community at Maison Saint-Cyr broke up. Emily, who had by now made public vows and had eight companions as well as one hundred pupils, took possession of the property.

In 1819, just as Emily had managed to buy a disused monastery with its own chapel and garden, something occurred that threatened to put an end to the entire project. Starting with Eleanor Dutriac, a number of Sisters died suddenly, and the doctors were at a loss to say why. One view was that it was the influence of the devil. Emily herself decided she was simply not the right person to found a community and thought of amalgamating hers with the Daughters of Mary, recently founded by Adèle de Batz Trenquelléon. However, the Villefranche Sisters would have none of this and things went ahead as planned.

Over the next seven years Emily suffered first from cancerous growths in her nose and then from an unnamed complaint—possibly Menière's disease—which left her with permanent tinnitus. It was while she was in Aubin consulting a doctor that she was presented with the possibility of founding a daughter house. For legal reasons, Abbé Marty was not altogether in favour of the plan, but Emily went ahead anyway. There followed a period of spiritual desolation. She reproached herself for lack of docility in the matter of the Aubin house, and she lost the direct support of Marty when he was appointed vicar general for the Rodez diocese. Nevertheless, the new Congregation began to expand, with enclosed as well as unenclosed houses. The unenclosed Sisters, who at Emily's insistence lived rigorously simple lives, now did nursing as well as teaching. Later they added prison visiting to their activities and in 1847 opened their first rescue home for women. All this activity was supported by the prayers of the enclosed Sisters.

There was an uncompromising—some said headstrong—side to Emily's personality, which occasionally led to misunderstandings, even with those who, like Abbé Marty, were fundamentally on her side. She became accustomed to receiving abusive letters, and from time to time slanders were circulated about her. But to the astonishment of her secretary, she always found the strength to reply courteously to her critics. From such sayings of hers as have survived she comes across as serious, single-minded, and somewhat austere, with a sharp wit. Her efforts to overcome what she saw as her besetting sin of pride led in later life to what some saw as an exaggerated disregard for appearances, especially in the matter of clothes. What struck all who met her was the strength of her inner life and the authenticity of her prayer. She always said that her greatest debt to Abbé Marty was for the appreciation he had given her of the abiding presence of the Holy Spirit.

In April 1852 a cancerous growth appeared in her left eye. Realizing that she probably did not have much longer to live, she resigned as superior general of the Congregation. For the next five months she suffered patiently, growing weaker by the day. On the evening of 18 September she told the Sisters: "The wall is crumbling." On the following day she died. She was canonized in 1950.

For a useful and readable Life see M. Savigny-Vesco, *Marie-Emilie de Rodat* (1940). Other French Lives: L. Aubineau (1891); L. Raylet (1897); A. Barthe (1897); E. Ricard (1912); M. Arnal (1951). For an English Life see D. Burton, *St Emilie de Rodat* (1951). See also *Bibl.SS.*, 4, 1181.

ST MATTHEW (p. 199)
The Angel of St Matthew, *wood engraving by Eric Gill,*
from The Four Gospels *(1931)*

20

SS ANDREW KIM, PAUL CHONG, AND
COMPANIONS, *Martyrs of Korea* (from 1839 to 1867)

In the 1938 edition of *Butler's Lives of the Saints* these martyrs were originally listed as BB Laurence Imbert and His Companions. In a manifestation of cultural, or more probably clerical, bias, which was not unusual for the time, the entry revolves round Bishop Imbert and two French priests, Pierre Philibert Mauban and Jacques Honoré Chastan. The contribution of these undeniably dedicated and brave men should not be played down. They gave their lives for the Korean Church. But Christianity had been brought to the country fifty years before they arrived, and not by foreign missionaries but by a Korean layman. To make matters worse, the Founding Fathers, as they are known, many of whom died for the Faith, are not represented among the 103 martyrs who were canonized in 1984. All these died between 1839 and 1867, in other words, after the arrival of the missionaries and the establishment in 1831 of the Choson vicariate. The suggestion that the Korean Church did not officially begin until then is a source of disappointment for many Korean Catholics, who are proud of the lay origins of their Church.

In the fourth and fifth centuries, when Korea was still divided into three separate states, Buddhism was the official religion. During the period of unification, from the tenth century to the end of the fourteenth, Confucianism, which is not strictly speaking a religion, became the predominant political philosophy, although Buddhism remained as the major spiritual force. Then, when Buddhism became corrupt and oppressive, Neo-Confucianism asserted itself as an instrument of reform. Inevitably, Neo-Confucianism too became corrupted, and by the seventeenth century Korean thinkers, who called themselves Neo-Confucian Pragmatists, were looking for new cultural values. It was at this stage that, thanks to books brought in from China, Catholicism first began to excite interest.

It is true that during the Japanese invasion at the end of the sixteenth century a Jesuit, Gregorio de Céspedes, and an unnamed monk did enter the country. But they came as chaplains in the Japanese army and had no contact with the Koreans. Real contact began in China in the eighteenth century. While they were in Beijing some Korean diplomats were introduced to Jesuits, who welcomed them to their churches and lent them books. Back in Korea, these books aroused great interest, especially among scholars. Not content to read about it, one of these scholars, a young man named Yi Sung-hun, began to promote this new faith among his friends. Then in 1784 he went with his father to Beijing and while he was there was baptized by a French missionary, Louis de Grammont, who gave him the name Peter.

When he returned to Seoul loaded with books, rosaries, crosses, and statues, Peter baptized a number of his friends and associates, who together formed the first Catholic community in Korea. The house of a man named Kim Bom-u (on the present site of Myongdong Cathedral) became their church, and they met there every week to celebrate Sunday. But this Catholic church community, the first in the world to be founded not by missionaries but by local laypeople, soon attracted the attention of the authorities. In March 1785 the group was dispersed. And since he had allowed it to meet in his house, Kim Bom-u was arrested and tortured. He died shortly afterwards in exile.

When Peter succeeded in reorganizing the community two years later, four members made themselves priests and started to celebrate the Eucharist and administer the sacraments. However, they soon felt that this was a mistake, and in 1789 a member of the community went to Beijing to consult the bishop and ask him to send priests to Korea. Eventually the bishop commissioned a Chinese priest, but the latter missed his guide and never arrived. A Chinese priest did finally reach the country on 23 December 1794, but not before several Korean Catholics had died for their faith, which members of the nobility had denounced to the king as heresy in 1791.

In the forty years between 1791 and 1831, when the vicariate apostolic of Korea was established, Catholics experienced waves of persecution. The worst was under Queen Chong-sun, who became regent for her great-grandson, Sun-jo, in 1800. She saw Catholicism as a threat to Korean customs and traditions, and about three hundred Catholics, including the Chinese priest, died in 1801 alone as a result of her determination to eradicate it. Throughout this period, Catholics who escaped death fled into the mountainous areas, where they formed new communities and kept the Faith alive. It is hard to say exactly how many Catholics there were in the country at this time. The figure of ten thousand mentioned in a letter written by a group of them to Pope Pius VII (1800-23) may be an exaggeration, but there were clearly many from all walks of life, and of those hundreds died for their faith.

Throughout the years of persecution Korean Catholics went on making the journey to Beijing to appeal for priests. One of the most active in this respect was a nobleman, Chong Ha-sang Paul, whose father and elder brother were among those who died for their faith at the beginning of the century—his mother and sister suffered shortly after he did in 1839. From the age of twenty Paul spent all his energy trying to revitalize the Church. He and some friends of his were responsible for the letter to Pius VII mentioned above, and he made the journey to Beijing no less than nine times in an effort to get priests.

At last, on 9 September 1831, the vicariate apostolic of Korea was formally established, and the Societé des Missions Etrangères in Paris was asked to take charge of it. The first vicar apostolic, Bishop Barthélemy Brugière, never managed to enter Korea and died in Mongolia on 20 October 1835. However, his successor, Bishop Laurent Marie Joseph Imbert (in English, Laurence), had better luck, crossing the Yalu river to enter the country on 31 December 1837. He avoided detection by wearing the traditional mourning dress, the principal item of which was a huge basket worn over the head and hiding it completely. Anyone wearing such a basket was not to be stopped or in any way disturbed by the police, so missionaries found them useful. By 1838 the Korean Church had a bishop, two priests—Pierre Philibert Mauban, from Vassy, south-west of Caen, who managed to get into the country sometime in 1836, and Jacques Honoré Chastan, from Marcoux in the Basses-Alpes—and about nine thousand lay members.

From the official accounts of the individual martyrs it is possible to build up a picture of what life was like for Catholics in Korea in the mid-nineteenth century. We know that Chong Ha-sang Paul used to go to Uiji on the border to meet any missionaries who managed to get that far. Once they were inside the country the missionaries were entirely dependent on the charity of local people. Among the many who welcomed them into their homes were Chong Ha-sang Paul himself; Kwon Hui Barbara, wife, mother, and sister-in-law of martyrs; Cho Chung-i Barbara, many of whose relatives had died in the 1801 persecution; and two brothers, Hong Pyong-ju Peter and Hong Yong-ju Paul, who were the grandsons and nephews of martyrs. These and others risked their lives giving the missionaries somewhere to stay, to celebrate the sacraments, or simply to hide.

The lay Catholics, who came from all levels of society, formed an extraordinarily close-knit community, or rather, a group of closely-knit communities. Many, like Hong Pyong-ju Peter, Pak Chong-won Augustine, and Hyon Song-mun Charles, worked actively for the Church as catechists. But there were several farmers among them as well as a translator, an interpreter, three court ladies, a provincial governor, and a royal chamberlain, three merchants, a pharmacist, a sailor, and a soldier, not to mention the wives, widows, and consecrated single women who account for almost half the group. The oldest, Yu So-sa, was seventy-nine when she died, the youngest, Yu Tae-ch'ol Peter, only thirteen. From the list of names it is clear that many were related to one another. A widow, Yi Chong-hui Barbara, for example, was the daughter of Ho Kye-im Magdalene, the sister of Yi Yong-hui Magdalene, the niece of Yi Mae-im Teresa, and the aunt of Yi Barbara (who was only fifteen when she died in prison). The members of this family and others like it were able to give one another much-needed support, but things would have been more difficult for Catholics who came from pagan families or, like Pak Hui-sun Lucy, worked at court. Lucy was a highly intelligent, well-educated woman who taught Korean and Chinese literature to a number of court ladies. The fact that she was liked and valued by the queen made it difficult for her to leave the court, but she managed to do so in the end by feigning illness.

The signs are that individuals remained where they were, doing what they normally did, for as long as possible. Once the persecution began to bite, one option was to move from place to place. This is what Yi Kwang-hon Augustine did. In fact, he moved around so much that he was eventually reduced to poverty. But once his fellow-Catholics became aware of this, they, like their early counterparts in Jerusalem, shared what they had so that he could buy a house near the city wall. He responded in kind by allowing it to be used as a chapel, while he worked hard as a catechist. Not surprisingly, Seoul was the main centre of Catholic activity. Many individuals in the rural areas, especially those from pagan families, gravitated to the city in search of support.

In 1839, when the anti-Catholics were once again in the ascendant politically, informers alerted them to the presence of the French missionaries. This sparked off a severe wave of persecution, and the bishop told the two priests to give themselves up in the hope of deflecting attention from the laity. On 21 September of that year, having refused to deny their God, Laurence Imbert and his two French companions were beheaded by the military at Saenamt'o, on the Han River. They were buried on Samsongsan mountain, though their remains were later transferred to Myongdong Cathedral. Laurence was forty-three, both priests were thirty-six. Between 20 May 1839 and 29 April 1841 sixty-seven of the ninety-two lay Catholics among the 103 also died for their faith after being held for weeks and sometimes months in filthy, overcrowded prison huts. In prison their constant fear would have been that they would not survive long enough to be officially sentenced to death for the Faith (eleven of the 103 did not, but died in prison). Those who did survive the extraordinarily cruel forms of torture meted out to Catholic prisoners would have been tied to a cross and taken on an ox-cart to the place of execution. There they would have been stripped naked and beheaded (the ritual was more elaborate in the case of those who, like the missionaries, were executed by the military at Saenamt'o).

The great legacy of Laurence Imbert, Pierre Mauban, and Jacques Chastan to the Korean Church, apart from the example of their dedication and their courage, was a more organized structure and the makings of an indigenous clergy. In 1837 three young men had been sent to Macao to complete their seminary training. In January 1845 one of the three, Kim Tae-gon Andrew, returned to Korea, where he made contact with a few catechists. He then left again in order to escort Laurence Imbert's successor, Bishop Joseph Ferréol, and a French priest, Antoine Daveluy, into the country. On 17 August, in Shanghai, Bishop Ferréol ordained him, the first native-born Korean priest. Andrew's ministry was short. After his return to Korea with the two Frenchmen at the end of August, he began making arrangements for another group of French missionaries and one of the other Korean seminarians, now ordained,

194

to be led into the country. But he was arrested in June 1846. Reluctant at first to sentence him because of his impressive personality, great learning, and knowledge of languages, the authorities finally condemned him to death. From prison, where he spent three months, he wrote a letter of encouragement to his people. He was only twenty-six when he was beheaded, also at Saenamt'o, on 16 September 1846.

Between 1846 and 1874, seven more French missionaries—including two bishops, Siméon Berneux and Antoine Daveluy—and twenty-five named Koreans were to die for their faith. But at least ten times that number are known to have died. With the treaty between Korea and France in 1886 a century of persecution came to an end, although there have been sporadic outbursts since then—in 1901, for example, when more than seven hundred Catholics were killed on Cheju island in the course of a few days; and during the Korean War (1950-3), when many bishops, priests, nuns, and laypeople were killed or expelled. In North Korea today the Church remains underground.

The following is a list of the 103 martyrs, in the order in which they died: Yi Ho-yong Peter (25 Nov. 1838); Chong Kuk-bo Protasius (20 May 1839); Kim Ob-i Magdalene, Pak A-gi Anne, Yi So-sa Agatha, Kim A-gi Agatha, Yi Kwang-hon Augustine, Han A-gi Barbara, Pak Hui-sun Lucy, Nam Myong-hyok Damian, Kwon Tug-in Peter (24 May 1839); Chang Song-jib Joseph (26 May 1839); Kim Barbara, Yi Barbara (27 May 1839); Kim No-sa Rose, Kim Song-im Martha, Yi Mae-im Teresa, Kim Chang-gum Anne, Yi Kwang-nyol John Baptist, Yi Yong-hui Magdalene, Kim Nusia Lucy, Won Kwi-im Mary (20 July 1839); Pak K'un-agi Mary, Kwon Hui Barbara, Pak Hu-jae John, Yi Chong-hui Barbara, Yi Yon-hui Mary, Kim Hyo-jui Agnes (3 Sept. 1839); Ch'oe Kyong-hwan Francis (12 Sept. 1839); Laurent Imbert, Pierre Maubant, Jacques Chastan (21 Sept. 1839); Chong Ha-sang Paul, Yu Chin-gil Augustine (22 Sept. 1839); Ho Kye-im Magdalene, Nam I-gwan Sebastian, Kim Yuridae Julitta, Chon Kyong-hyob Agatha, Cho Shin-ch'ol Charles, Kim Che-jun Ignatius, Pak Pong-son Magdalene, Hong Kum-ju Perpetua, Kim Hyo-im Columba (26 Sept. 1839); Kim "Kop-ch'u" (Hunchback) Lucy, Yi Catherine, Cho Magdalene (Sept. 1839); Yu Tae-ch'ol Peter (21 Oct. 1839); Yu So-sa Cecilia (23 Nov. 1839); Cho Chung-i Barbara, Han Yong-i Magdalene, Ch'oe Ch'ang-hub Peter, Hyon Kyong-nyon Benedicta, Chong Chong-hye Elizabeth, Ko Sun-i Barbara, Yi Yong-dok Magdalene (29 Dec. 1839); Kim Teresa, Yi Agatha (9 Jan. 1840); Chong Hwa-gyong Andrew (23 Jan. 1840); Min Kuk-ka Stephen, Ho Hyob Paul (30 Jan. 1840); Pak Chong-won Augustine, Hong Pyong-ju Peter, Son So-byok Magdalene, Yi Kyong-i Agatha, Yi In-dok Mary, Kwon Chin-i Agatha (31 Jan. 1840); Hong Yong-ju Paul, Yi Mun-i John, Ch'oe Yong-i Barbara (1 Feb. 1840); Hyon Song-mun Charles (19 Sept. 1840); Kim Song-u (29 Apr. 1841); Kim Tae-gon Andrew (16 Sept. 1846); Nam Kyong-mun Peter, Han I-hyong Laurence, U Sur-im Susanna, Im Ch'i-baek Joseph, Kim Im-i Teresa, Yi Kan-nan Agatha, Chong Ch'or-yom Catharine

(20 Sept. 1846); Yu Chong-nyul Peter (17 Feb. 1866); Siméon Berneux, Just Ranfer de Bretenières, Pierre Dorie, Louis Beaulieu, Nam Chong-sam John Baptist (7 Mar. 1866); Chon Chang-un John Baptist, Ch'oe Hyong Peter (9 Mar. 1866); Chong Ui-bae Mark, U Se-yong Alexius (11 Mar. 1866); Antoine Daveluy, Martin Huin, Pierre Aumaitre, Chang Chu-gi Joseph Hwang Sok-tu Luke (30 Mar. 1866); Son Cha-son Thomas (18 May 1866); Cho Hwa-so Peter, Son Son-ji Peter, Yi Myong-so Peter, Han Won-so Joseph, Chong Won-ji Peter (13 Dec. 1866); Cho Yun-ho Joseph (23 Dec. 1866); Yi Yun-il John (21 Jan. 1867). These 103 were canonized by Pope John Paul II in Seoul Cathedral on 6 May 1984.

For an excellent overview of the history of the Catholic Church in Korea with a short account of each of the 103 martyrs, see Kim C. T. and Ch'oe S. A., *Lives of 103 Martyr Saints of Korea* (1984). See also C. Dallet, *L'Histoire de l'Eglise de Corée* (1874); A. Launay, *Martyrs français et coréens* (1925); Coreanus, "Le préhistoire de l'Eglise de Corée," in *Revue d'histoire des missions* 11 (1934), pp. 203-20; Choi A., "L'Erection du premier vicariat apostolique et les origines du Catholicisme en Corée, 1592-1837," in *Nouvelle Revue de science missionaire* (1961); Kim D.-W., *A History of Religions in Korea* (1988); J. H. Grayson, *Korea: a religious history* (1989).

St Methodius of Olympus, Bishop and Martyr (311)

Very little information has survived either about St Methodius' life or about his death. According to St Jerome (30 Sept.) he was bishop first of Olympus in Lycia and then of Tyre and died a martyr at the end of the last persecution. But Jerome's view of the date and place of his death differs from that of other commentators. It is almost certain that he was never bishop of Tyre, though Greek writers mention him as bishop of Patra in Lycia. His claim to fame rests almost entirely on his writings, which include a dialogue, *On the Resurrection*, to refute Origen's teaching that the risen body is not the same as the earthly body, and a treatise on free will against the Valentinians. This prompted St Jerome to describe him as "most renowned for the brilliance of his preaching and his learning." His best-known work is the *Symposium*, or *Banquet of the Ten Virgins*, which he wrote in imitation of Plato's *Symposium*. As an imitation it is not very successful, but it ends with a hymn to Christ as Bridegroom of the Church, part of which forms one of the earliest Christian hymns.

The available data are in *AA.SS.*, Sept., 5, pp. 768-73. See also *Methodius von Olympus* (1891); O. Bardenhewer, *Altkirchliche Literatur* (1913), 2, p. 334ff.; *Bibl.SS.*, 9, 380-2; *D.T.C.*, 10, 1606-14.

Bd Thomas Johnson, Martyr (1534)

Thomas was a priest of the London charterhouse, which has the honour of having provided the first martyrs of the Tudor persecution. They were victims of the Act of Succession of 1533, which required every person over the age of sixteen to recognize Anne Boleyn as lawful queen and her children as heirs to the throne. The prestige of the monks decided King Henry to demand their overt assent, which the prior eventually gave with the proviso, "as far as the law of God permits." In February 1534 the Act of Supremacy made it high treason to deny that the king was the sole and supreme head of the Church in England. The prior warned his monks that this was a very different matter and that they could not possibly assent to it and should prepare themselves to face death. The prior and three others monks were arrested and executed on 4 May 1534, followed by three others on 19 June.

There was then a lull in executions, but constant pressure was brought to bear on the remaining Carthusians. Nineteen took the oath, but ten, including Thomas Johnson, refused. They were imprisoned in the Marshalsea, tied to posts, and left to starve to death. For a time they were kept alive by the heroic actions of the adopted daughter of Thomas More (22 June), Margaret Clement, who bribed the gaoler to let her in disguised as a milkmaid and brought them food. But she was forbidden further access when the monks appeared to be remaining alive for a surprisingly long time, and one by one they died. Thomas died on 20 September 1534. The collective cult of the Carthusian martyrs was recognized by Pope Leo XIII in 1886, and their collective feast is kept by the Carthusians and in the diocese of Westminster on 11 May.

The primary sources are in the *Letters and Papers, Foreign and Domestic: the Reign of Henry VIII*, published by the Public Record Office. See the bibliographies under the general entries for The Martyrs of England and Wales, 4 May, and The Forty Martyrs of England and Wales, 25 October.

Bd Francis de Posadas (1644-1713)

Francis (Francisco) de Posadas was born on 5 November 1644 in Córdoba, where his parents, Stéfano Martín Losada and María Fernández Posadas, earned a living as greengrocers. He was educated by Antonio Mogano, O.P., and the Jesuits, with a view to his becoming a Dominican, an idea which he himself found attractive. He was therefore disappointed when, after his father's death and his mother's remarriage, his stepfather decided his studies were a waste of time and apprenticed him to one Juan de Góngora. At first his master treated him roughly, but he was eventually won over by the young man's patience, good nature, and hard work and made it possible for him to continue his studies in his spare time. This meant that, when his stepfather died in 1662, Francis was able, having cared for a time for his mother, to think once more of becoming a Dominican. Although the convent of San Pablo in Córdoba would not accept him, the convent of Scala Coeli was happy to do so. He in fact received the habit on 23 November 1662 at the convent of Santa Caterina in Jaén, but he returned to Scala Coeli a year later, once he was professed

The first few years, during which his companions, who did not understand him, subjected him to ridicule and petty persecution, were not particularly happy. But he persevered and was in due course ordained to the priesthood.

Although he was known for his prayerfulness and for the extraordinary phenomena, including levitation, that sometimes accompanied his prayer, it was as a preacher that he immediately made his mark. He was soon conducting missions throughout the south-west of Spain, where he was hailed a second Vincent Ferrer (5 Apr.). Not content with the hard work of preaching and hearing confessions, he travelled everywhere he could on foot and practised rigorous voluntary penances. His contact with the poor made him humble, and he avoided all forms of high office, both within the Order and on the occasions when he was offered a bishopric. Yet because people could see that he lived according to his preaching, his influence was enormous. In Córdoba itself he helped to raise the standards of public and private morality to the point where brothels were having to shut down for want of business. He also wrote several books, including Lives of St Dominic (8 Aug.) and other holy members of his Order, *The Triumph of Chastity*, and numerous moral exhortations. He died at Scala Caeli on 20 September 1713 and was beatified in 1818.

See P. de Alcalá, *Vida* (1728); V. Sopena, *Vita del B. Francesco de Posadas* (1818), which deals interestingly with the question of his levitations. See also *Bibl.SS.*, 10, 1052-3; Martínez-Vígil, *La Orden de Predicadores* (1884), p. 352ff.; J. Procter, *Short Lives of the Dominican Saints* (1901), pp. 263-5; I. Taurisano, *Catalogus Hagiographicus O.P.*

St John Charles Cornay (1809-1837)

Jean-Charles Cornay was born in Poitiers on 27 February 1809. He joined the Foreign Mission Society of Paris and after his ordination was sent on the mission to Vietnam. He was one of a number of French missionaries arrested in 1835, during the wave of persecution initiated three years earlier by the emperor, Minh Mang, who had ordered the arrest of all priests. The authorities manufactured a charge of treason against him, having buried weapons on the plot of land he cultivated. He was imprisoned in a series of the brutal bamboo cages that were a normal form of torture in Vietnam at the time, and because he was young and had a fine voice he was forced to sing to his captors. He was eventually sentenced to death by the supreme tribunal, and on 20 September 1837 he was beheaded. His body was then, according to the terms of the sentence, "hewn in pieces and . . . his head, after being exposed for three days, . . . thrown in the river." He was canonized as one of the 117 Martyrs of Vietnam by Pope John Paul II on 19 June 1988.

For the bibliography see the general entry for the Martyrs of Vietnam, 2 Feb.

21

ST MATTHEW, *Apostle and Evangelist* (First Century)

In the lists of the twelve apostles given in the three Synoptic Gospels (Matt. 10:2-5; Mark 3:16-9; Luke 6:13-6) he appears simply as Matthew, though in his own Gospel he adds "the tax-collector." And he is Matthew in his own account of his call by Jesus (Matt. 9:9). However Mark and Luke in their accounts of his call (Mark 2:13-4; Luke 5:27-8) refer to him as Levi, and Mark specifies "son of Alpheus." Many Jews who dealt frequently with Gentiles had a Greek as well as a Jewish name. Matthew would have been unusual only in that both his names are Jewish. A possible explanation is that Levi was his original name, and that he took or was given the name Matthew ("gift of Yahweh") when he left his job to follow Jesus.

This he did in Capernaum, a Roman garrison town and customs post, where as a tax-collector he would have been despised by Jews and non-Jews alike. Jesus had just cured a paralyzed man and was walking past the customs house when he saw Matthew. "And he said to him, 'Follow me.' And he got up and followed him." This is the only time that Matthew is mentioned individually, although he appears consistently in all lists of the apostles, including the one in the opening chapter of the Acts of the Apostles (Acts 1:13-4).

From a very early date one of the four Gospels was attributed to Matthew—although there is nothing in the text to indicate that it is by him, and the words "according to Matthew" start appearing only in the fourth century. Whether or not it was the first to be written is still a matter of dispute. The material was certainly "gathered" and "put in order" in the second half of the first century and appears to have been written down in Greek in Syria or Phoenicia in about A.D. 80. There is a widely-held view, based on second-century witnesses quoted by Eusebius, that Matthew depended for material on Mark's Gospel or used Aramaic and Hebrew sources also known to Mark and Luke. The style is individual, however, and the author, assuming it was Matthew, was clearly writing for a specifically Jewish audience. He is familiar with the scriptures, and the Jesus he portrays fulfills them. As an evangelist the symbol of the man is usually attributed to him because he started his Gospel with the genealogy of Christ, thus emphasizing his human origins and connections.

Nothing is known for certain about what Matthew did after the resurrection. According to one tradition he preached the gospel in Judea and then went off to the east, but Ethiopia, Persia, Syria, Macedonia, and Ireland have all been put forward as possible destinations. He is venerated as a martyr, but the manner and circumstances of his death are in fact unknown. The Gnostic writer Heracleon said he died a natural death, and this seems to have been taken for granted by St Clement of Rome (23 Nov.). One tradition, followed by earlier versions of the Roman Martyrology, has it that he died in Ethiopia; according to another, followed in the *Hieronymianum*, it was at Tarrium in Persia, though this is said by some to be a misreading for Tarsuana, in the region to the east of the Persian Gulf. Relics supposed to be his were taken from Ethiopia to Finistère in Brittany and from there, by the Norman adventurer Robert Guiscard (1015-85), to Salerno. They disappeared during the invasions of the tenth century, but a letter has survived from Pope St Gregory VII (1073-85; 25 May) to the archbishop of Salerno that mentions their rediscovery. The fact that four different churches in France claimed to have his head suggests that none of the assertions made about his relics is very reliable.

St Matthew is the patron of the diocese and city of Salerno, as well as of tax-collectors, accountants, customs officials, and money-changers, and less obviously of alcoholics, hospitals, and ships. There are countless representations of him in painting, sculpture, and other forms of art. When he appears as an evangelist he is either identified by his symbol, or else he is shown sitting at a desk writing his Gospel with an angel to guide the pen or hold the inkwell. In the East his feast is celebrated on 16 November, but in the West it has been consistently celebrated on this day.

See: *AA.SS.*, Sept., 6, pp. 194-227; B. de Gaiffier, "Hagiographie salernitaine: la translation de S. Matthieu," in *Anal.Boll.* 80 (1961), pp. 82-110. Commentaries by St Jerome, and in modern times by M. J. Lagrange (1948); F. W. Filson (1960); J. C. Fenton (1963); J. D. Kingsbury (1986). See also *Bibl.SS.*, 9, 110-45; *H.S.S.C.*, 1, pp. 251-3; Jöckle, pp. 315-7.

Artists in the later Middle Ages sometimes gave him reading glasses. When he appears as an apostle he can be recognized by the instrument of his supposed martyrdom (a sword, a spear, or a halberd) or by a money bag or money box, in reference to his original profession. Frequently represented are the two incidents with which Matthew is connected in the Gospels: his call by Jesus (as in a powerful painting by Caravaggio in the church of San Luigi dei Francesi in Rome) and the "great feast" he gave in Jesus' honour at his house (famously depicted by Veronese in a painting now in the Accademia in Venice).

St Cadoc, *Abbot (c. 575)*

Cadoc (Cadog, Catwg) was one of the most celebrated of the Welsh saints. Unfortunately the earliest accounts of his life, one by Lifris, the other by Caradoc, both monks of Llancarfan, were not written until more than five hundred years after his death. Relying to a great extent on legends pieced together in a rather haphazard way, they give a powerful impression of the high regard in which Cadoc was held, but factually they are not entirely reliable.

The account they give is that Cadoc, born toward the end of the fifth century, was the son of St Gundleus (Gwynllyw; 29 Mar.), king of southern

Wales, and St Gwladys, and that he was educated in Caerwent at the school of an Irishman, St Tatheus. Fairly early on in his career he is supposed to have founded the monastery at Llancarfan, between Cardiff and Llantwit Major. This, however, is disputed by some scholars, who believe it was founded by St Dubricius (14 Nov.). In any case, he is said to have spent three years studying in Ireland and then, anxious to master the seven liberal arts, to have done a further period of study with a rhetor named Bachan, outside Brecon. The church dedicated to him at nearby Llanspyddid is said to stand on land given him by his uncle or grandfather, St Brychan. It was here that he was said to have relieved a famine by miraculously discovering a store of wheat (in fact, it was probably there all the time, as it was common practice at this period to store grain in cellars). He eventually returned to Llancarfan, which had by now attracted many monks because of its reputation for holiness and learning.

Caradoc's account of Cadoc's teaching methods probably tells us more about his own practice in the twelfth century, but Cadoc does seem to have taught by example as well as by word. He would tell his disciples—among whom is said to have been St Gildas (29 Jan.)—that they must work for their living, constantly reminding them that "he who does not work shall not eat." The monastery, in fact, provided food for about five hundred people every day, and its abbot had authority over the surrounding region. During Lent Cadoc would retire to the solitude of Barry and Flatholm, or to a place now called Cadoxton, near Neath, but he was always back at Llancarfan for Easter. There is some evidence that he visited Brittany, Cornwall, and Scotland, and he may have attended the Synod of Llandewi Brefi.

The circumstances of his death, as described in the Lives, are not a little surprising. According to Lifris, he was transported in a white cloud to Benevento in Italy, where he became a bishop and died a martyr's death. Caradoc's version is less dramatic: Cadoc travelled in the normal way to Benevento, where he died peacefully and the people accompanied him to his grave "with hymns and songs and lights." It is more likely that he died at Llansannor, a few miles from Llancarfan. Modern scholars have suggested that the Welsh had hidden his remains and that the Benevento story was an attempt by representatives of the Anglo-Norman Conquest of Glamorgan to explain away the absence of relics.

For the Life by Lifris see A. W. Wade-Evans, *Vitae Sanctorum Britanniae* (1944), pp. 24-141. For the Life by Caradoc see P. Grosjean, "Vie de S. Cadoc par Caradoc de Llancarfan," in *Anal. Boll.* 60 (1941), pp. 35-67. See also G. H. Doble, *St Cadoc in Cornwall and Brittany* (1937); C. N. L. Brooke, "St Peter of Gloucester and St Cadoc of Llancarfan," in *Celt and Saxon* (ed. N. K. Chadwick, 1963); H. D. Emanuel, "An analysis of the *Vita Cadoci*," in *National Library of Wales Journal* 7 (1952), pp. 217-27; *Bibl.SS.*, 3, 632-3.

St Maura of Troyes (827-50)

There is a short but reliable contemporary life of St Maura written by St Prudentius of Troyes (6 Apr.), who based his account on conversations he had with her mother. He tells us that from a very early age Maura, who was born in 827, had an intense prayer life and was completely focused on God. While she was still a child she obtained through her prayers and example the conversion of her father, Mauranus. And her charity and prayerfulness were said to have influenced her brother, Eutropius, who became a priest and subsequently bishop of Troyes. Maura herself continued to live at home, where she divided her time between prayer, looking after her mother Sedulia, and working through the Church for the poor and needy. Her life was carefully structured to make room for everything and regularly punctuated by acts of penance. She fasted every Wednesday and Friday, for example, and sometimes she would walk barefoot the two or three miles to the abbey of Mantenay, the abbot of which was her spiritual director. Although miracles were said to have occurred as a result of her prayers, she herself took great care not to draw attention to her gifts. She died on 21 September 850, when she was only twenty-three, and was buried in the village of Château-Nore-de-Troyes.

For the Life see *AA.SS.*, Sept., 6, pp. 271-8. See also E. Socard, *Ste Maure de Troyes* (1867); R. Breyer, *Les Vies de St Prudence et Ste Maure* (1725); *Bibl.SS.*, 9, 168-9.

SS Michael of Chernigov and Theodore, *Martyrs* (1246)

Strictly speaking, the Church in Russia had no martyrs before the Tartar invasions in the thirteenth century. At this time, however, numerous people gave their lives for Christ. The first to be venerated popularly and liturgically were the nobles and military men who led the resistance against the invaders. They were honoured less as aggressive "crusaders against the infidels" and more as selfless warriors ready to give their lives in defence of their people.

Outstanding among these nobles was Michael, duke of Chernigov. He was the son of Vsevolod Oljgovic Cerimnoj, of the Rurikids, who governed Novgorod in the early thirteenth century. One version of his story has it that when the Tartars attacked and destroyed Kiev in 1240 he made a rather unpromising start by abandoning the city and its people to their fate when he saw the enemy advancing. Soon, however, he recovered his courage and with a small party made his way to the Tartar camp in the hope that this would distract their attention from the city. A second, more credible version says that he was away at the time trying to obtain help from the Hungarian king. Returning from Hungary with empty hands, he established himself at Chernigov, which was destroyed by the Tartars in its turn in the following year, 1241. In 1245 Khan Bati, the Tartar leader, ordered him to present himself at Saraj on the lower Volga. Michael made his way there, accompanied by his cousin, Boris of Rostov, and a *boyar* named Theodore. On condition that Michael deny his faith, Bati, who insisted on using his own interpreters in case Michael tried to deceive him, made various grandiose promises. These Michael refused to accept and, fearing that they would suffer reprisals, refused also to go along with plans made by his friends to get him out of the Tartar camp. On 20 September 1246, having received Communion, he and Theodore were tortured and beheaded by the Tartars. Their bodies, which were thrown to the dogs, are said to have been miraculously preserved until some Christians arrived to remove them. They were taken to Vladimir and later to Chernigov.

The cult, which sprang up immediately after their death, was approved in 1547. When Chernigov was occupied by the Poles in 1578, Ivan IV the Terrible (1533-84) had the relics of the two saints taken to Moscow, where they were placed in the cathedral of St Michael the Archangel. In times of oppression particularly, these martyrs, and others like them, have been regarded by Russians as their special representatives before God.

Bibl.SS., 9, 464-5; C. Dawson, *The Mongol Mission* (1955), p. 10. And see the bibliography for St Sergius of Radonezh (25 Sept.).

Bd Mark of Modena (1498)

Mark was born into the Scalabrini family, probably at Mocogno, near Modena, some time in the first half of the fifteenth century. He joined the Dominicans in Modena and became famous as a preacher throughout northern Italy. For many years he was prior of the Dominican house in Pesaro, and during this period many miracles were attributed to him. The best known was the cure, attested by many serious witnesses, of the son of a local doctor. When he died in Pesaro on 21 September 1498, his body was buried in the Dominican church, but it was subsequently transferred to the chapel of Our Lady of the Rosary, where it was venerated each year on Whitmonday. When the chapel was destroyed after the suppression of the religious Orders, the reliquary was placed in the Franciscan church. It was in the cathedral between 1912 and 1949, when Modena asked for it. It is now in the Dominican church in Modena. The cult of Bd Mark was approved in 1857.

AA.SS., Sept., 6, p. 288; L. Alberti, *De Illustribus O.P.*, p. 248; L. Vedriani, *Vita* (1663); *Année Dominicaine*, 7, p. 49; L. Rosa, *Il beato Marco di Modena, Domenicano* (1949); *Bibl.SS.*, 8, 738-9.

22

St Phocas of Sinope, *Martyr* (? Fourth Century)

St Asterius (30 Oct.) wrote a panegyric in honour of this famous martyr, otherwise known as St Phocas the Gardener, but unfortunately gave no dates. The name appears four times in the *Hieronymianum* and once in the Old English martyrology, and there are still those who maintain that there are three saints with the same name: Phocas of Antioch; Phocas, bishop of Sinope; and Phocas the Gardener. However, according to another school of thought, the hagiographers made three saints out of one and that one is Phocas the Gardener, who was known for his extraordinary hospitality and generosity and died a martyr at Sinope on the Black Sea.

According to the legend, Phocas (who was never a bishop) lived as a hermit near the city gate. As a gifted and enthusiastic gardener he was able not only to support himself but to feed the many pilgrims and other visitors for whom he kept an open house, and even then there was always something left over for the poor. When persecution broke out in the area, Phocas was named as a Christian, and soldiers were dispatched to kill him there and then without the formality of a trial. Arriving at Sinope when the gates were already closed, they lodged with Phocas, unaware of who he was. When they revealed the name of the man they were looking for, Phocas said he knew him and would let him know in the morning. While the men were asleep, he dug a grave and made other necessary preparations for his burial, and then spent the rest of the night in prayer. In the morning he disclosed his identity to the astonished soldiers, who were at a loss to know what to do in the face of this extraordinary courage and determination. Only when Phocas had assured them that he regarded martyrdom as the highest honour did they overcome their scruples and behead him. He was buried by other Christians from the city, and eventually an imposing church was built and dedicated to him.

Asterius notes that pilgrims travelled great distances to visit the church, and he bears witness to the popularity of the cult:

> Phocas from the time of his death has become a pillar and support of the churches on earth. He draws all men to his house; the highways are filled with persons resorting from every country to this place of prayer. The magnificent church which is possessed of his body is the comfort and ease of the afflicted, the health of the sick, the storehouse plentifully supplying the wants of the poor. If in any other place, as in this, some small portion of his relics be found, it also becomes admirable and most desired by Christians.

He adds that some relics were taken to Rome, and there was certainly a cult at Antioch as well as in Sidon. St John Chrysostom (13 Sept.) is known to have preached a sermon when some of the relics arrived there. For some reason, possibly because his name resembles the Greek word (*phoke*) for seal, Phocas became the patron saint of sailors, and he is invoked against insect bites.

For St Asterius' panegyric see *AA.SS.*, Sept., 6, pp. 294-9; *P.G.*, 40, 300-13. See also *C.M.H.*, pp. 374-5; G. Herzfeld, *An Old English Martyrology* (E.E.T.S., 1900); *O.D.S.*, pp. 398-9. *Bibl.SS.*, 5, 948-50; *O.D.C.C.*, p. 1282. He features in a thirteenth-century mosaic in the basilica of San Marco in Venice.

St Maurice and Companions, Martyrs (? c. 287)

The principal source for our knowledge of St Maurice and the so-called Theban Legion is the *Passio martyrum Acaunensium* of St Eucherius of Lyon. The version that has survived dates from the ninth century, but Eucherius mentions it in a letter to another bishop named Salvius in about 440, by which time the oral tradition had been extant for over a century. A German scholar, D. van Berchem, who analyzed the *passio* between 1944 and 1949, came to the conclusion that the source of the oral account was Theodore, a fourth-century bishop of Octodurum, who brought the legend from the East. In his version, Maurice suffered with seventy of his soldiers, who, van Berchem argues, were neither Theban nor an entire legion.

According to Eucherius' much-embellished version the emperor, Maximian (286-305, 306-10), led an army against a group of rebellious Gauls—the Bagaudae. When he reached Octodurum (now Martigny), south-east of the lake of Geneva, he ordered his men to sacrifice to the gods for the success of the expedition. One of the units was the Theban Legion, whose members had been recruited in Upper Egypt and were without exception Christian. Rather than sacrifice to gods in whom they did not believe, they withdrew, led by their *primicerius* and spokesman, Maurice, to nearby Agaunum (now Saint-Maurice-en-Valais). When his repeated orders failed to breach their unanimity, Maximian gave orders that the legion should be decimated—every tenth man would be killed, then the order would be given again and the process repeated.

This is the point where the story loses something of its credibility. The soldiers, we are told, encouraged by their officers and in particular by Maurice, stood firm to the last man. By the time it was all over 6,600 (or according to another source 6,666) are supposed to have been killed, presumably by their companions in arms. Maurice's named companions were Candidus, Exuperius, and Vitalis, and the group is said to have included a soldier from another legion named Victor who happened to be passing and confessed his faith. Another difficulty is that Eucherius, who probably made up the words of their protest himself, states that they objected to killing other Christians who were not really the emperor's enemies and does not mention the rebellious Bagaudae.

But even if the numbers are a gross exaggeration and many of the details were added in the fifth century, there does seem to be a genuine martyrdom at the base of the story.

The cult dates from the fourth century, during which a bishop in the Valais had a basilica built to house the relics. Eucherius agrees that the relics were preserved at Agaunum and that "many come from divers provinces devoutly to honour these saints, and offer presents of gold, silver, and other things." They are now held in Brzeg in Poland and in Turin. Eucherius also mentions the miracles that were reported at the shrine. In time these saints became very popular in the West, and not a few other saints became associated with their legend (SS Felix and Regula on the 11th of this month are an example). Maurice is among the patrons of Austria, Piedmont, Savoy, and Sardinia as well as of hatters, weavers, and dyers (especially of Gobelin tapestries) and soldiers (especially the Swiss Guard).

The church built at Agaunum later became the centre of an abbey, which was the first in the West to recite the divine office round the clock by means of a cycle of choirs. This *laus perennis* became a tradition which is still followed there today. There were church dedications in France and Germany as well as in Switzerland, and as many as eight in England. Fifty-two towns and villages in France are named after St Maurice.

For Eucherius' text see *AA.SS.*, Sept., 6, pp. 308-404, 895-926; *M.G.H.*, *Scriptores Merov.*, 3, pp. 32-41. See also D. van Berchem, *Le Martyre de la légion thébane* (1956); *Bibl.SS.*, 9, 193-205; *H.S.S.C.*, 2, p. 279; Jöckle, pp. 318-9; L. Dupraz, *Les Passions de S. Maurice d'Agaune* (1961); M. Besson, *Monasterium Acaunense* (1913); H. Leclercq in *D.A.C.L.*, 10, 2699-729.

The iconography is large. Maurice is variously represented as dark or fair skinned, a foot soldier or an equestrian knight, or else in scenes from the martyrdom. A painting in the National Gallery, London, by the Master of Liesborn shows him as a knight with St Gregory the Great (3 Nov.) and St Augustine (28 Aug.). One of the most striking and individual works is *St Maurice and his Companions* by El Greco, which hangs in the Escorial, outside Madrid.

St Felix IV, *Pope* (530)

Apart from the fact that he was a Samnite by birth, nothing is known of Felix's early life. As a deacon he was a member of the delegation sent by Pope St Hormisdas (6 Aug.) to Constantinople in 519 to resolve the Acacian schism. When Pope St John I (18 May) died in 526, the see remained vacant for fifty-eight days, and then on 12 July Felix was elected to succeed him. Because of the posthumous inclusion of the antipope Felix II (355-65) in the list of legitimate popes he was styled Felix IV, but strictly speaking he should be listed as Felix III. According to the *Liber Pontificalis* he was consecrated by order of the Arian Ostrogoth king, Theodoric the Great (474-526), who had ruled Italy since 493. This somewhat bald statement fits in with evidence that the long delay between the death of John I and the election of Felix was due to a power struggle then going on in Rome between two separate factions, the Goths and the Byzantines, and that this was eventually resolved when Theodoric came down on the side of the candidate he believed would support, if not favour, the Goths.

By the end of August 526 Theodoric was dead, but Felix's position was secure. He was respected by the clergy and people of Rome as a person of integrity, and his relations with Theodoric's grandson and heir, Athalaric (526-34), and his widow, Amalasuntha, who acted as regent while Athalaric was still a minor, were good. He took advantage of this to promote the interests of the Church, obtaining, for example, a decree that the pope should judge in all proceedings, civil and criminal, against members of the clergy. Anyone who disregarded this ruling would have to pay a fine, which the Holy See could distribute to the poor. The last detail was characteristic of Felix, who was known for his concern for the poor as well as for his simplicity and humility.

Felix is known to have corresponded in particular with St Caesarius of Arles (27 Aug.)—letters have survived in which he approves a suggestion that laymen should undergo some sort of examination before being ordained to the priesthood and regrets the fact that some ordained men have been returning to secular life. He also gave Caesarius his wholehearted support in the struggle against Semi-Pelagianism. When Caesarius' views on grace were attacked at a synod in Valence, he sent him twenty-five propositions based on St Augustine's writings on grace. These were taken up at the Council of Orange in 529 and helped to bring this controversy to an end. His other great contribution was in the field of church building. He restored the basilica of St Saturninus, which had been damaged by fire, and converted a number of buildings in the Forum for Christian use. Most notable in this context was the library of Vespasian, which became the church of SS Cosmas and Damian. Here, amid some of the most spectacular mosaics in the city, is a full-length portrayal of Felix carrying a model of the church. It is important not because of any likeness to the subject but because this was the first time a living pope had been represented with saints. Popular prints generally show Felix giving to the poor, and it is this generosity of spirit and concern for human suffering that is picked up in his epitaph: *pauperibus largus, miseris solacia praestans.*

Felix's last action before his death in 530 was controversial. Having called his supporters among the clergy and in the Senate to his bedside, he issued a "precept" naming his archdeacon Boniface as his successor and had copies of the precept circulated in Rome and Ravenna. Inevitably perhaps, this essentially unconstitutional manoeuvre led, after Felix's death, to the election of another antipope; but it also provoked a ruling that banned any discussion of a pope's successor during his lifetime.

Liber Pontificalis, 1, p. 270ff.; *O.D.P.*, pp. 55-6; *Bibl.SS.*, 5, 580-2; *M.G.H., Auctores Antiquissimi*, 12, pp. 246, 255; L. Duchesne, "La succession du pape Félix IV," in *Mélanges d'archéologie et d'histoire* 3 (1883), pp. 239-66; *D.H.G.E.*, 16, 895ff.; *N.C.E.*, 5, p. 879ff.

St Sadalberga (*c.* 665)

The sources of information are piecemeal and full of contradictions. Research has shown that a Life of Sadalberga which was supposed to have been written by a contemporary dates in fact from the ninth century and is a compilation rather than a single account. The most trustworthy source is thought to be Jonas of Bobbio's Life of St Columbanus (23 Nov.). Also, Sadalberga is the correct form of the name, not Salaberga, as she was previously known.

According to the Life, which offers the more detailed and colourful account of the two, Sadalberga was born into an influential family in the outskirts of Laon. She had two brothers, Leudovinus (Bodo; 11 Sept.) and Fulcrus, with whom she was educated at home. One tradition, preferred by Jonas of Bobbio, says she was blind, possibly from birth, another that she suffered from metrorrhagia (bleeding from the womb); both agree that she was cured by St Eustace of Luxeuil (29 Mar.), who had been visiting Bavaria and stopped at her home on his way back to his monastery.

According to Jonas she remained unmarried, but the Life maintains that she married twice. Her first husband, according to this account, was a young man named Richraen, who died two months after the wedding. Sadalberga took this as a sign that she should enter a monastery, and for two years she lived a life of prayer and fasting under the guidance of Eustace. However, at the insistence of her father, who was afraid of offending the king, Dagobert I, she abandoned this project and married one of the king's counsellors, a nobleman named Blandinus. For her sake he became a Christian and together they did much charitable work. At first it seemed as though they would have no children, but after a pilgrimage to the tomb of St Remigius (1 Oct.) in Reims they had five, two of whom, Bauduin and Anstrudis (17 Oct.), have been venerated as saints. The marriage is said to have been a singularly happy one, but after some years they decided mutually to separate and enter the religious life. Blandinus became a hermit and is venerated as a saint in the diocese of Meaux. Sadalberga went first to a monastery she had founded at Poulangey. Then in about 650, following the advice of the then abbot of Luxeuil, St Gualbert, she went back to Laon and founded a new monastery, over which she presided as abbess following the Rules of St Benedict (11 July) and St Columbanus (21 Nov.). When this eventually became a double monastery, Blandinus is said to have left his cell to live in the community. During the last two years of her life Sadalberga suffered severe and continuous pain, which she bore with courage and patience. When she died, on 22 September in about 665, she was buried in the abbey church, and her daughter Anstrudis succeeded her as abbess. Already in her lifetime she had a reputation for miracles, and her cult became widespread in north-west France, Belgium, and Luxembourg.

Jonas of Bobbio's *Vita Sancti Columbani* is in *M.G.H., Rerum merov.*, 4, p. 122; there is a critical edition of the ninth-century Life of Sadalberga in *M.G.H., Scriptores merov.*, 5, pp. 41-66.

St Emmeramus, *Bishop* (Seventh Century)

Although there are at least three Lives of St Emmeramus, of which one, by Bishop Aribo of Freising, dates from the eighth century, little of what they contain is historically useful. In fact, Aribo's account has been described as "a characteristic example of hagiographical invention, exaggeration, embroidery, or all three, for the sake of popular edification." Emmeramus (or, more correctly perhaps, Haimhrammus) was said, for example, to have been the first bishop of Poitiers. This, however, is unlikely, since his name does not appear in any of the episcopal lists of that see—or, indeed, of any other see. On the other hand, it can safely be said that he was for some years a zealous and indefatigable missionary in the Poitiers area before moving on to preach the gospel in Bavaria. He got as far as Regensburg, where he was pressured by Duke Theodo into staying and ministering to his subjects. After three years, during which he made a number of converts, he decided to make the pilgrimage to Rome. He set off and had reached Kleinhelfendorf, south of Munich, when he was brutally attacked by a group of men, said to have been agents of Duke Theodo. He managed to reach Feldkirchen but there died of his injuries. His body was taken first to St Peter's church in Ascheim, then to Regensburg, where it was buried in St George's church, and finally to the church of the abbey there that bore his name. The tomb was identified in 1895.

The full circumstances of Emmeramus' death are far from clear, although it seems to be generally accepted that he was murdered. The Roman Martyrology said that "he patiently suffered a most cruel death for Christ's sake that he might set others free," but did not explain what this meant. Aribo has a complicated story involving Theodo's daughter, Oda. Having conceived a child from one of the courtiers, she feared her father's reaction both for herself and for her lover, so Emmeramus told her to say he was the father (presumably the reader was supposed to admire this display of magnanimity, though it is difficult to see how such a lie would help). In this version it was Oda's brother, Lambert, who set off with his men in pursuit of Emmeramus. When they found him they tortured him and left him to die, to an outbreak of supernatural phenomena. He was immediately acclaimed a martyr by the people.

For Aribo's Life see *M.G.H., Scriptores Merov.*, 4, pp. 452-526. Modern references include A. Bigelmair, "Die Anfänge des Christentums in Bayern" in *Festgabe A. Knöpfler* (1907); J. A. Endres in *Römische Quartalschrift* (1895, 1903). On the tomb see J. A. Endres, *Beitrage zur Geschichte des M. A. Regensburgs* (1924). See also *Bibl.SS.*, 4, 1200-2; Künstle, 2, pp. 208ff; Jöckle, p. 143

The earliest representation of St Emmeramus in art is in the sacramentary of the emperor Henry IV (1056-1105), where he is shown in bishop's vestments with the ladder on which he was supposed to have been stretched by his murderers. There are also a number of sculptures, and a seventeenth-century cycle of frescoes in the church of St Emmeramus in Regensburg.

Bd Ignatius of Santhià (1686-1770)

Lorenzo Maurizio Belvisotti, son of Pierpaolo Belvisotti and Maria Elisabetta Balocco, was born on 5 June 1686 at Santhià in the diocese of Vercelli. Little is known about his childhood apart from the fact that his father died while he, Lorenzo, was still very young. For the rest, much early material is stereotypical hagiography and does not disclose much about him as a person. More revealing is the simple account of the events of his life. His mother entrusted his education, particularly in the Faith, to a local priest, and before long the boy had decided that he too would become a priest. He attended the local seminary and was ordained there. Shortly after his ordination he became a canon of the collegiate church in Santhià and was invited to take up the post of parish priest.

To the surprise and dismay of his relatives, who had visions of him rapidly ascending the ecclesiastical ladder, Lorenzo declined. Instead he joined the Friars Minor Capuchin, taking the name Ignatius, and was professed in 1717. For the next twenty-five years he devoted most of his time to spiritual direction, becoming a much sought-after confessor of people from all walks of life. He next spent fourteen years as novice-master, finding time during the war that broke out in the area in 1743 to bring spiritual comfort to the soldiers in the military hospitals. In about 1756 he went to live at the Capuchin convent, del Monte, in Turin. Here he spent the rest of his life teaching the catechism and giving retreats for religious. How much of his teaching he wrote down is not known, but one book, *Meditazioni per un corso di esercizi spirituali*, survived and was finally published in Rome in 1912. Ignatius died peacefully in Turin on 22 September 1770. His cause was introduced in 1782, and he was beatified by Pope Paul VI (1963-78) on 17 April 1966.

There are several Italian Lives, the earliest of which, by P. da Castiglione d'Asti, dates from 1790. See others by C. F. Poirino (1889); V. da Loano (1913); A. da Bra (1945); C. de Chaux de Fonds (1950). See also *Bibl.SS.*, 7, 606-7.

23

St Linus, *Pope* (*c*. 78)

In the early episcopal lists Linus is named as Bishop of Rome after St Peter (29 June), but the exact date and the length of his episcopate are uncertain. The *Catalogus Liberianus* and the *Liber Pontificalis* say 56 to 67, but Eusebius favours 69 to 81. This is thought to reflect differences in the interpretation of texts which say that Peter and Paul nominated Linus, Anacletus, and Clement as auxiliaries or vicars. It is not entirely clear what their role would have been, since at that early stage the monarchical episcopate was a thing of the future. Virtually nothing else is known about Linus, though St Irenaeus (28 June) identifies him with the Linus mentioned by St Paul (25 Jan. and 29 June) in his second letter to Timothy (4:21), and the *Liber Pontificalis* says he was Tuscan. Later tradition, filling in the gaps, said he came from Volterra, went to Rome to study, and was converted by Peter. Although Linus was entrusted with the leadership of the Church of Rome, and this can be said to have made him the first Bishop of Rome and therefore the first pope, from the late second or early third century that distinction was traditionally accorded to St Peter. Linus is believed to have reigned for about twelve years altogether. In the West he was venerated as a martyr, but there is no evidence at all to support this. In 1969 his feast was removed from the universal Calendar. His name is still mentioned, however, in the Roman Canon of the Mass after those of SS Peter and Paul. Evidence of a cult exists in certain places, notably Volterra.

Irenaeus, *Adversus haereses*, 3, 3, 2; Eusebius, *Hist. eccl.*, 3,13; 3,15; 3, 21; 5, 6. See also E. Caspar, *Geschichte des Papstums von den Anfangen bis zur Hohe der Weltherrschaft* (1930-3), 1, pp. 11-4; *D.C.B.*, 3, pp. 726-9; *Bibl.SS.*, 8, 56; *O.D.P.*, pp. 6-7; *O.D.S.*, p. 300.

There is a fine reliquary bust dating from the seventeenth century in Volterra and a "portrait" of Linus in the basilica of St Paul-outside-the-Walls, and he is shown burying St Peter in an eleventh-century fresco in the church of San Piero a Grado, near Pisa.

St Adomnán of Iona, *Abbot* (*c*. 627-704)

Adomnán (Adamnan, Eunan) was described by Bede (25 May) as "a good and wise man, remarkably learned in the Holy Scriptures." Born at Drumhome in Co. Donegal in about 627, he was related through his father, Rónán, to the clan of Cenél Conaill and was therefore of the same lineage as St Columba (9 June). The Cenél Conaill desired one member in each generation to become a monk of St Columba. Adomnán joined, possibly at Drumhome, although the exact date is not known. What is certain is that he eventually went to the monastery of Iona, of which he was elected abbot in 679.

211

For some time between 670 and 685 Iona may have had a royal guest in the person of Aldfrith, who was to reign as king of Northumbria from 685 to 704. As a young man his father, Oswiu (642-70), had spent some time in exile in Ireland, and Aldfrith was born there of an Irish mother. He liked to retain his links with the country and was a friend of Adomnán—he later became known as *Dalta Adamnáin* (foster-son of Adomnán). So it is not improbable that he was on Iona in 685 when his half-brother Ecgfrith was killed in battle and he himself came to the throne. In any case, it made sense for Adomnán to be chosen when, in 686, someone was needed to negotiate with the Northumbrians for the release of sixty Irish prisoners who had been taken captive during Ecgfrith's reign.

Encouraged by the success of this mission, Adomnán returned to Northumbria two years later. This time he visited the monasteries of Wearmouth and Jarrow, where he met the then thirteen-year-old Bede and, more significantly at this stage, St Ceolfrith (25 Sept.). For it was Ceolfrith who persuaded him to accept the use of the tonsure and the Roman method of calculating the date of Easter, which had been adopted in Northumbria in preference to the Irish method, at the Synod of Whitby a quarter of a century earlier. Unfortunately, back in Iona, his monks were less open to persuasion. They and the monks of Iona's dependent monasteries held out and did not in fact capitulate until 716, twelve years after Adomnán's death.

In other respects, Adomnán was more immediately successful. At the Council of Birr in 697 he was responsible for a decision that was subsequently enforced all over Ireland. Known as the Law of the Innocents, or Adomnán's Law (Cáin Adomnáin), its aim was to protect women and children in time of war. Women, it ruled, should not go into battle, and they and their children should be treated as non-combatants. In other words, they were not to be killed or taken prisoner, and the same was to apply to boys and clerics.

Adomnán was Iona's most accomplished scholar. Suitably enough, his greatest work was a Life of Columba that remains one of the most important examples of the genre. Written, in Latin, at the request of his monks, it is also, with its vivid portrayal of the great pioneer of Irish monasticism, one of the most historically useful hagiographies of the early Middle Ages. It provides, in addition to a particular theology of Christian kingship, details that are crucial to our understanding of the Irish monasticism of the period. Adomnán's other important work was *De Locis Sanctis*. This was a description of the Holy Places based on the account given him by a Frankish bishop named Arculf, who made the pilgrimage to Jerusalem and in 686 found himself, "after many adventures," at Iona. Bede, who does not seem to have known the Life of St Columba, described this work as "beneficial to many and particularly to those who, being far from those places where the patriarchs and apostles lived, know no more of them than they can learn by reading."

After his death in 704 Adomnán's cult flourished both in Ireland and in

Scotland. There are dedications in Derry, Donegal, and Sligo as well as in Aberdeenshire and the Western Isles. In 727 his relics were brought from Iona, where he had been buried, to Ireland. Here they were carried round for three years before returning to Iona. Everywhere they went, people promised to obey Adomnán's Law.

Bede, *H.E.*, 5, pp. 15-7, 21-2; tenth-century Irish Life of Adomnán, ed. M. Herbert and P. O'Riain (Irish Texts Society 54, 1988). For Adomnán's own works see R. Sharpe, *Adomnán of Iona. Life of Columba* (1995); A. O. and M. O. Anderson, *Adomnán's Life of Columba* (1990); *De Locis Sanctis* (ed. P. Geyer) in *Itinera Hierosolymitana* (*C.S.E.L*, 39, [1898], pp. 219-97); *ibid.*, (ed. D. Meehan, 1958). See also *H.S.S.C.*, 4, p. 266; *Bibl.SS.*, 1, 199-201; K. Meyer, *Cain Adomnáin* (1905); D. A. Bullough, "Columba, Adomnán and the achievement of Iona," in *Scottish Historical Review* 43 (1964), pp. 111-30, and 44 (1965), pp. 17-33; J. M. Picard, "The purpose of Adomnán's Vita Columbae," in *Peritia* (1982), pp. 160-77; M. N. Dhonnchadha, "The guarantor list of Cain Adomnáin," in *ibid.*, pp. 178-215.

Bd Helen of Bologna (1520)

The known facts of Helen's life are remarkably few, given the popular devotion she inspired. Helen (Elena) Duglioli was born in Bologna in 1472. Her parents, Silverio Duglioli, a notary, and his wife, Pentisilea Boccaferri, gave her a good Christian education but were not happy when she announced that she wanted to become a nun. Their will prevailed, and when she was about seventeen she married a man of about forty named Benedetto Dall'Olio, with whom she lived happily for some thirty years. We are told that they constantly loved and supported each other and encouraged each other in the Christian way of life. Benedetto died before Helen, who followed him on 23 September 1520.

The people of Bologna, who had recognized her instinctively as a saint, now acclaimed her as such, and her cult, which was confirmed in 1828, became widespread and popular. In *De Servorum dei beatificatione* (1734-8), which he wrote when he was archbishop of Bologna, Prosper Lambertini (Pope Benedict XIV, 1740-58) cited the tributes paid to Bd Helen as an almost typical case of a spontaneous and immemorial cult. A rather more ambiguous reference, which says more about contemporary customs than it does about Helen, appears in the *Ragionamenti* of the satirist Pietro Aretino, of all people. A contemporary of Helen, he speaks satirically of the masses of candles, pictures, and ex votos deposited "*alla sapoltura do santa Beata Lena dall'Olio a Bologna.*"

See *AA.SS.*, Sept., 6, pp. 655-9; *De servorum Dei beatificatione et beatorum canonizatione*, 1/2, 18 (1839); *Bibl.SS.*, 4, 853-5; Baudot et Chaussin, 9, p. 476. Also P. Aretino, *Ragionamenti*, 1/2, p. 103.

An anonymous painting in Bologna shows a rather serious looking middle-aged Helen and Andrea Giustiniani.

BB Christopher, Antony, and John, *Martyrs* (1527/9)

The Spanish adventurer Hernán Cortés landed in Mexico in March 1519 with about five hundred soldiers and one hundred sailors. He quickly realized that his best hope of conquering the country lay in exploiting the political crisis within the Aztec empire. With a mixture of force and good public relations, plus the help of his Indian mistress, "La Malinche," he eventually won himself allies among the subject peoples, notably the Tlaxcaltecs, who hated their Aztec oppressors. When, later in the same year, in the company of his small Spanish force and about one thousand Tlaxcaltecs, Cortés started his advance on the great island city of Tenochtitlán, the Aztec king, Montezuma, played for time. However, he soon decided that Cortés was, if not the incarnation of the Aztec god Quetzalcoatl, at least his messenger. Receiving him peaceably if warily, he offered the Spaniard hospitality. Cortés, who also knew how to bide his time, gradually, with the help of La Malinche, created a situation in which Montezuma became his prisoner. He finally took Tenochtitlán on 13 August 1521.

It is easy to argue that by organizing "New Spain," as they called it, strictly along Spanish, Christian lines, the new rulers were merely introducing another form of domination. But perhaps it is not so simple. Even Cortés believed that the Spaniards should bring Christianity to the Indians, because this would be to do them a great favour. What no one thought—and perhaps the thought would have been unthinkable at the time—was that this might be done with respect for their culture—political, social, economic, and religious. As it was, the territory was quickly divided up into a number of administrative units, each under a viceroy, and the way was paved for the missionaries. Three Franciscans had already arrived to evangelize the Indian people when in May 1522, at the request of the emperor Charles V, Pope Hadrian VI issued the Bull *Exponi nobis*, authorizing the departure of twelve more. These arrived in May 1524 and were soon followed by groups of Dominicans (1526) and Augustinians (1533). The territory was divided for missionary purposes among the three Mendicant Orders. Parishes were created, and before long schools, hospitals, and convents had been established.

Inevitably some Indians, and in particular their leaders, regarded the new form of subjection with some resentment. But many of the missionaries behaved with sufficient sensitivity, and once they had learned to get by in the native languages they began to make converts. Among the latter was a local chief who gave the Franciscans houses from which to conduct their mission. In one of these the friars opened a boarding school for the sons of the upper classes, their idea being that through them they would be able to reach their parents.

One of those who sent his sons to the school was Axotecatl, a powerful chieftain in Tlaxcala. The eldest of the three, who was born at Atlihuetzia, near Tlaxcala, in 1514 or 1515, was about twelve when he was baptized and took the name Christopher (Cristóbal). He began to accompany the missionaries on their visits to the villages, while at the same time trying, unsuccessfully, to interest his father in his new beliefs. He also dared to warn his father about the evils of idolatry and to condemn the drunken orgies in which he participated. When he realized that he was being ignored, he smashed the idols in his father's presence and then did the same to the jugs that held the wine for the orgies. Encouraged by one of his wives, who wanted Christopher's inheritance for her own son, the enraged Axotecatl beat the boy until he was a mass of wounds and broken bones. When his mother tried to intervene, Axotecatl beat her too. Then, seeing that Christopher was still alive, he had him placed for a while over a blazing fire. The boy spent the night in agony and in the morning asked for his father. "Don't think that I am angry with you," he told him. "I am truly very happy because your action has brought me greater honour than your fatherhood did." He then asked for a drink but died as they gave it to him. His father had him buried under the floor of the house, but news of his bravery soon leaked out. The body, which was found to be incorrupt when it was exhumed, was reburied in the Franciscan church at Tlaxcala—now the cathedral of the oldest diocese in Mexico.

Antony and John (Antonio and Juan) were a year or two younger than Christopher. Both were born at Tizatlán, near Tlaxcala, in 1516 or 1517. Antony came from one of the ruling families; John's origins were humbler, and he frequently accompanied Antony as a servant or page. Together they attended the Franciscan school. In 1529, two years after Christopher's death, two Dominican missionaries passed through Tlaxcala on their way to Oaxaquena, a part of the country as yet untouched by Christianity. They came to the Franciscan school in the hope of recruiting some helpers for their mission. Fully aware of the risks involved, Antony, John, and one other boy volunteered.

The friars' technique, which would be regarded as unacceptable today, was to enter the houses of the Indians and destroy the statues of their gods—and only then to start talking seriously about Christianity. One day, in Cuauhtinchán, the two boys came to a house that appeared to be empty. John went inside to destroy the idols while Antony remained outside talking to a local boy who happened to be standing there. They had walked straight into a trap. Two Indians armed with clubs went into the house and beat John to death. When Antony confronted them they killed him too and threw both bodies into a ravine. Sometime later they were apprehended, tried, and sentenced to death. Both repented and asked for Baptism before they were executed.

Christopher, John, and Antony, the proto-martyrs of Mexico and certainly among the youngest martyrs anywhere, were beatified by Pope John Paul II in the basilica of Our Lady of Guadalupe in Mexico City on 6 May 1990.

F. Holböck, *Die neuen Heiligen der katholischen Kirche*, 3 (1994), pp. 189-94; "Cristóbal, Antonio und Juan, drei Märtyrknaben von Tlaxcala, Mexiko," in *Information des*

Freundeskreises Maria Goretti 43 (Mar. 1991); A. Puente, "The Church in Mexico," in E. Dussel (ed.), *The Church in Latin America: 1492-1992* (1992), pp. 218-9.

Bd William Way, *Martyr* (1562-88)

Because he was in the habit of using aliases, William Way has been confused with others who died for their faith at this time , among them Richard Flower (30 Aug.). He was born at Exeter in August 1562. Having studied for the priesthood at the English College of Douai, which was then at Reims, he was ordained at Laon on 20 September 1586. On 9 December of that year he joined the English mission, but he was not active for long. Some six months later he was arrested in Lambeth and put in the Clink Street prison in the London borough of Southwark. Eventually he was charged with being a priest ordained abroad who had returned to England against the law to exercise his ministry and was taken before a magistrate. When he refused to be tried by a lay judge the case was referred to the bishop of London, but William refused to recognize him as a bishop. He was finally condemned to death for high treason at Newgate sessions and was hanged, drawn, and quartered at Kingston-on-Thames on 9 September 1588. He is one of the Eighty-five Martyrs of England, Scotland, and Wales who are celebrated collectively on 22 November.

Anstruther, 1, pp. 374-5; T. F. Knox (ed.), *The first and second diaries of the English College, Douai* (1878), pp. 201, 209ff.; *Bibl.SS.*, 12, 1397-8.

Bd Pius of Pietrelcina (Padre Pio) (1887-1968)

The most famous stigmatist since St Francis of Assisi (4 Oct.) was born into a family of agricultural labourers in Pietrelcina, in the Benevento region northeast of Naples, on 25 May 1887. His father's name was Grazio Forgione; his mother, Maria Giuseppina Di Nunzio, was generally known as "Mamma Peppa." He was christened Francesco in the village church of Santa Anna on the day following his birth and at the age of twelve was confirmed by Mgr Donato Maria Dell'Olio, archbishop of Benevento. In 1903, at the convent in Morcone, he received the Capuchin habit, taking the name Br Pius (Fra Pio). Seven years later he was ordained to the priesthood, returning to Pietrelcina to celebrate his first Mass. Not long after this he began to experience pains in his hands and feet, and on 11 September 1911 he confessed to his spiritual director that he "had had invisible stigmata for over a year." In the following month he was transferred to Venafro, where he underwent various medical tests, having meanwhile admitted that he also suffered the pains of Christ's crown of thorns and scourging.

He had a rather disrupted couple of years during the First World War. He should have been called up for military service in 1916 but was exempted on health grounds (his lungs, not the stigmata, which still could not be seen) and allowed to return to Pietrelcina to convalesce in the pure mountain air. Then, in 1917, he served as a medical orderly for some three months, until he was again released on account of his health. He returned to do a further stint early in 1918, but he suffered an attack of double pneumonia and was sent to the convent of San Giovanni Rotondo, where he was to stay for the rest of his life.

On 5 August 1918 he underwent the further mystical experience of "transverberation" (piercing with the lance), which left him with a wound in his side that bled continually. A month later the stigmata in his hands and feet became visible and remained so until he celebrated his last Mass on the day before he died. The experience of a stigmatic in a world dominated by mass media and widespread use of photography is undoubtedly very different from that of a stigmatic in the thirteenth century. The Capuchins made no attempt to conceal Padre Pio's condition, which soon became widely known all over Italy and was the main cause of both his celebrity and the controversy that surrounded him. As people started flocking to his convent in their thousands, the Vatican, cautious as ever when faced with "private" favours and revelations, had him examined by a succession of doctors. The physical manifestations, clear from numerous photographs, were undeniable. But were they from God, the psychosomatic effect of a disturbed personality, or even a fraudulent attempt on his part or that of the convent to achieve notoriety?—he lived, after all, in a part of Italy where "miracles" tend to be associated with blood. His beatification seems to suggest that the Church has made up its mind, but it has not stilled the wider debate between sceptics and believers.

Huge crowds attended his Masses, during which he went into ecstatic states that could last for two hours and more. In July 1923 he received an order to say Mass in private, but so real was the threat of a violent popular reaction that it was rescinded the following day. A fortnight later a second order that he should move to a convent in Ancona (on the Adriatic coast, well away from the febrile atmosphere of his native region) was withdrawn after a week. While both incidents may be seen as a victory for popular over official religion, Padre Pio himself made no comment on his condition other than that he was "a mystery to himself" but his gifts should produce benefits for others. He (or his community) was able to ensure that they were so used when money offerings started coming in from his penitents and admirers. In January 1925, in a disused convent, he opened a twenty-bed hospital that was named after St Francis and remained in operation for thirteen years.

Throughout this period apostolic visitations continued, as the church authorities attempted to establish the "genuineness" of his stigmata and of his ever-growing ministry. In 1931 he was suspended from all his priestly functions apart from that of saying Mass, which he was required to do in private. However, after two years official doubt again yielded to popular enthusiasm, and the restrictions were lifted—though he was not allowed to hear women's Confessions for a full a year after he was once again allowed to hear those of men.

In 1940, with the particular support of Maria Pyle, a wealthy American woman to whose mother he had ministered as she was dying in 1929, Padre Pio was in a position to undertake a far more ambitious hospital project in the remote country area around San Giovanni Rotondo. Medical and administrative committees were soon set up, but the Second World War delayed further implementation of the project until 1946, when a limited company was formed to carry the work forward. Despite objections that San Giovanni Rotondo was not the place for such a project, building work on what came to be known as the *Casa Sollievo della Sofferenza* (House for the Relief of Suffering) began in 1947. In the same year a Capuchin convent was opened in Padre Pio's birthplace, Pietrelcina.

By 1948, when the number of would-be penitents was such that Padre Pio was obliged to establish an advance booking system, Pope Pius XII (1939-58) and the Vatican were taking a more favourable line. Padre Pio was invited to visit the pope, who suggested the formation of prayer groups, in Italy and elsewhere, to support the work of the hospital. When the latter was inaugurated in 1956 high officials of Church and State attended the ceremony, along with a crowd of fifteen thousand, and in the same year the foundation stone of a church for the Capuchins was laid. In the following year Pius XII named Padre Pio director for life of the Third Order of St Francis "of Graces," and he was given personal control of the hospital. His vision here was ambitious and entirely original: the schedule for each day was divided into "times for prayer and times for science," and he declared that he wanted the foundation to include an international study centre, a hospice for old people, and a cenacle for spiritual exercises, all to be run by a "new militia" in the service of the sick.

In 1959 Padre Pio's own health deteriorated, and it was at this time that he began broadcasting his spiritual thoughts on the hospital radio after the midday and evening Angelus. Then, in August, he recovered, apparently miraculously, when a statue of Our Lady of Fatima was brought into the hospital for two days. There does not appear to have been an inquiry at this time, and no action was taken four years later after a widely reported apostolic visitation by Mgr Carlo Maccari. Indeed the tenth anniversary of the foundation was celebrated in 1966 with an international convention of the prayer groups, and on 20 September 1968 huge crowds gathered to mark the fiftieth anniversary of Padre Pio's stigmata.

Two days later, as he raised his hands during what would turn out to be his last Mass, some membrs of the congregation noticed that the stigmata had vanished. He died on the following day, 23 September, and doctors who examined his body found his hands and feet unmarked and "as fresh as those of a child." The cause of his beatification was set in motion in November 1969. Pope John Paul II (1978-), who set up an investigation of the charges levelled against Padre Pio during his lifetime (fraudulent behaviour, improper relations with women, financial irregularities—all of which were proved false), visited

San Giovanni Rotondo and prayed at his tomb in 1987. The diocesan process was finally closed in 1990, when 104 volumes of evidence were delivered to the Congregation for the Causes of Saints. The beatification ceremony, which was conducted by Pope John Paul II on 2 May 1999, was attended by so many people that St Peter's Square could not contain them and 200,000—almost half their number—had to watch the proceedings on huge television screens in the square outside the Lateran basilica. In his address the pope spoke not so much of Padre Pio's extraordinary experiences but of the long hours the friar would spend in the confessional and of his extraordinary charity, which, he said, "was poured like balm on the sufferings of his brothers and sisters."

Despite criticism of its "gloomy" architecture and its luxury, the *Casa Sollievo della Sofferenza* has gone from strength to strength. It belongs to the Holy See, to which Padre Pio bequeathed it, but it operates as a public hospital within the Italian national health system, with the high rank of Institute for Recovery and Care of a Scientific Character. It will probably be many years before an objective assessment of Padre Pio's spirituality and "special gifts" is made. In the meantime it seems clear that he, like so many recipients of apparently supernatural favours (or burdens), used the fame and the financial resources they brought him to alleviate the sufferings of others. His own sharing in the suffering of Christ—whatever its origin—led him, as Cardinal Agostino Casaroli stated in 1981 when he looked back over the hospital's first twent-five years, "to see Christ in the sufferings of others."

The above is based largely on Various, *Il grande livro di Padre Pio* (1998). See also C. M. Carty, *Padre Pio, The Stigmatist* (1956); N. de Robeck, *Padre Pio* (1960); O. de Liso, *Padre Pio: The Priest who bears the Wounds of Christ* (Eng. trans., 1961); J. McCaffrey, *The Friar of San Giovanni: Tales of Padre Pio* (1978); A. Pandiscia, *For God and Neighbour: The Life and Work of Padre Pio* (Eng. trans., 1991); J. Gallagher, *Padre Pio: The Pierced Priest* (1995); *The Tablet*, 8 May 1999, p. 635.

24

St Geremarus, *Abbot* (*c.* 658)

There are several Lives of St Geremarus, dating from the ninth to the eleventh century. Of these, one, while not completely reliable as a source, has more to offer than the rest, which tend to be purely legendary. From it we learn that Geremarus (or Germer) was born at Vardes (Seine-Maritime) at the beginning of the seventh century. He was one of the many Frankish noblemen who, having married, raised a family, and pursued a secular career, went on to become distinguished in the ecclesiastical or monastic life of their time. He came from the area round Beauvais, and while he was young he served at the court of Dagobert I (629-39). Here he met his wife, Domana, who is herself venerated as a saint in the diocese of Evreux. They had three children, two daughters, both of whom died in childhood, and a son, Amalbert. Amalbert was educated by St Audoenus (24 Aug.), another former nobleman, by then bishop of Rouen.

It was in 649, when Amalbert announced his decision to become a monk, that Geremarus made up his mind to do the same, leaving the court and giving all his possessions to his wife—there is no record of what happened to her. He did not enter the monastery he had founded himself at Isle-sur-Epte (now Saint Pierre-au-Bois), near his birthplace. He chose instead to go to Pentale, near Brionne, where he became known for his devotion and his observance of the Rule, and was soon elected abbot. But some of the less observant among the monks did not appreciate his qualities and set out to get rid of him. Whether or not they in fact resorted to the methods described by Geremarus' biographers—for example, placing a sharp knife so that it pointed upward through the boards of his bed—their harassment had the effect they desired. Geremarus resigned his office and went to live as a hermit in a cave on the banks of the nearby river Risle. For five years he remained there contentedly, dividing his time between prayer, manual work, and ministering to the people of the neighbourhood. Then the news reached him that his son had died and that the young man's estate had reverted to him. He used the proceeds to found a monastery at Flay (subsequently named Saint-Germer-de-Flay), on the river Epte between Beauvais and Rouen. Abandoning his solitary life, he served here as abbot until his death, which came in about 658. In 906 his relics were translated to Beauvais, but they disappeared during the Revolution and have never been recovered.

The earlier of the two more reliable Lives, edited by B. Krusch, is in *M.G.H., Scriptores merov.*, 4, pp. 626-33; the later is in *AA.SS.*, Sept., 6, pp. 698-703, and in *AA.SS. O.S.B.*, 2, pp. 475-82.

St Gerard of Csanad, *Bishop and Martyr* (1046)

According to a sixteenth-century tradition Gerard (Gellért, Gerhard), who is sometimes given the Dalmatian surname Sagredo, was born in Venice at the beginning of the eleventh century. The earliest biography gives 23 April as the date of his birth, on which he was also baptized. When he was about five years old he fell seriously ill. However, thanks to the prayers of the monks at the Benedictine monastery of San Giorgio Maggiore, he recovered and entered the monastery himself when he was still quite young. He may or may not have been there long enough to become prior and abbot, as some have suggested. What is certain is that after he had been there for a while he left again in order to make the pilgrimage to Jerusalem.

Although he set off by sea, he seems to have abandoned his ship fairly quickly and ended up travelling through Hungary. There he attracted the attention of the king, St Stephen (997-1038; 16 Aug.), who offered him the post of tutor to his son, Bd Emeric (4 Nov.). Gerard accepted, and soon added to his list of duties preaching, for which he had a particular talent. When Stephen established the see of Csanad, he appointed Gerard as its first bishop. The majority of the people in the diocese were not Christian, and the majority of those who were tended to be rough and uneducated, but this did not deter Gerard. Relying on the strength he obtained from constant prayer, he worked hard and tirelessly to spread the Faith among them. He also found time to write, and although most of his works have been lost, an unfinished dissertation on the hymn of the three young men (Dan. 3) survives. His pastoral activity continued well as long as Stephen was alive, but when the king died in 1038 rival claimants began competing for the crown, and there was a backlash against Christianity.

For several years Gerard struggled to hold his flock together. Then, on 24 September 1046 while he was celebrating Mass in a little place called Giod on the Danube, he had a premonition that he would die that day. It probably came as no surprise, therefore, that as he and his party arrived at Buda and prepared to cross the river, they were attacked by the soldiers of one of the anti-Christian claimants to the throne. As they showered him with stones, Gerard prayed with the earlier St Stephen (26 Dec.): "Lord, do not lay this sin to their charge. They know not what they do." Scarcely had he spoken, when he was run through with a lance, dragged to the edge of a cliff known as Mount Kelen, and hurled into the seething waters of the Danube far below. He was immediately revered as a martyr, and Mount Kelen was renamed Gellért. His relics were enshrined in the cathedral of Buda in 1083, along with those of St Stephen and Bd Emeric. However, in 1333 the Republic of Venice, with the permission of the Hungarians, brought most of them to the church of Our Lady of Murano, where he is now venerated as the proto-martyr of Venice. He is also the patron of tutors.

The most reliable source is printed in *AA.SS.*, Sept., 6, pp. 722-4. It is not, as some have said, the summary of longer life but dates from the twelfth, or possibly the late eleventh, century. See also *Bibl.SS.*, 6, 184-6; C. Juhasz in *Studien und Mittheilungen O.S.B.* (1929), pp. 139-45, (1930), pp. 1-35; C. A. McCartney in *Archivum Europae centro-orientalis*, 4 (1938), pp. 456-90; *ibid.*, *Mediaeval Hungarian Historians* (1953).

In art Gerard is variously represented as a bishop, as a Benedictine, or at the moment of his martyrdom. There is a cycle of his life in the Vatican Library.

Bd Robert of Knaresborough (*c.* 1160-1218)

Like his fellow-hermit and fellow-Yorkshireman Richard Rolle (29 Sept.), Robert Flower, "the holy hermit of Knaresborough," was the object of a considerable popular cult that was never confirmed by canonization. It was tacitly approved, though, and Matthew Paris mentions him, along with St Edmund of Abingdon (16 Nov.) and St Elizabeth of Hungary (17 Nov.), as one of the outstandingly holy people of the late twelfth and early thirteenth centuries.

He was born in York, where his father was a prominent citizen, in about 1160. Convinced from an early age that God was calling him to some sort of dedicated life, he started training for the priesthood. However, when he reached the subdiaconate he decided, for whatever reason, to change tack and followed his brother into the Cistercian abbey at Morpeth. It took no more than four and a half months to establish that he was not called to the cenobitical life, but his desire to dedicate his life entirely to God was as strong as ever. So waiving his right to inherit as eldest son, he went to live in a cave adjoining a chapel dedicated to St Giles (1 Sept.) close to the river Nidd near Knaresborough, fifteen miles from York.

For a while Robert had to share the cave with a knight who was on the run from Richard I (1189-99), but he gained sole occupancy in 1199 when Richard died and the knight returned to his wife. After some years a wealthy widow named Helen offered him a cell and chapel dedicated to St Hilda (17 Nov.) at Rudfarlington. Richard accepted, delighted at this opportunity to move further into the forest of Knaresborough. When this hermitage was raided and destroyed by bandits, he went first to Spofforth, where he spent a few months living by the church wall under the protection of the Percys; then, to avoid the attention he was attracting as a man of God, to the priory at Hedley, where he made himself unpopular by criticizing the monks' lax interpretation of the Benedictine Rule; and finally back to Rudfarlington. Here his patroness gave him a barn and some other buildings, some land, and four deer to help him work it.

For a while things went smoothly. But he then came to the attention of William de Stuteville, constable of Knaresborough Castle, who accused him of harbouring thieves and outlaws. The accusation may have been well founded, since Robert was known for his charity to those in need; William certainly believed it was. He had Robert's buildings pulled down around him, and when Robert fled to his original hermitage by St Giles's chapel he pursued him there. He would certainly have driven Robert out again had it not been for a terrifying dream in which his life was threatened because of his treatment of the hermit. Instead he gave Robert all the land between the hermitage and Grimbald's Crag, as well as two horses, two oxen, and two cows. The hermit's task was to farm the land to support himself and provide relief for the poor. By and large Robert was left in peace now, apart from the visits made by people from all walks of life in search of advice. His brother Walter, a prosperous businessman and mayor of York, perhaps feeling that Robert's way of life somehow compromised his own dignity, tried to persuade him to go into a monastery. When Robert refused, he sent workmen to build a chapel of the Holy Cross, traces of which still remain beside the cave.

After an early attempt to run away, during which he broke a leg, one of Robert's disciples, a man named Yves, shared his eremitical life and inherited the hermitage after his death. From Robert he learned that a hermit's first duty, apart from his own sanctification, is to care for the poor. Robert, who helped all who came to him, "deserving" or not, and worked hard on his land to provide for them, refused to pay tithes of corn and hay to the parson of Knaresborough: his land, he argued, was already the patrimony of the poor. This land was enlarged by forty acres in 1216 when King John (1199-1216), who was staying at Knaresborough Castle, paid him a visit.

As he lay dying in 1218, Robert had to fend off attempts on the part of the Cistercians of nearby Fountains Abbey to affiliate him with their Order, and he warned Yves to be prepared for more of this sort of thing after he was dead. When he eventually died on 24 September of that year, the monks duly came, suggesting that he be buried in their abbey church. But Robert had arranged to be buried in his own chapel, and soldiers from the castle guarded the body until this was done in the presence of crowds mourning this "devout, debonair and discreet man, than whom a milder could not be met." Later, after Yves' death the hermitage, which according to Matthew Paris became a place of pilgrimage, came into the hands of the Trinitarian house at Knaresborough, and the canons there eventually moved Robert's body to their own church. Proceedings for the canonization were started, but it never took place.

Although his name has not been found in any calendars, there is a church at Knaresborough called St Robert's and another church dedicated to him at Pannall in North Yorkshire. Seven stained glass panels depicting his life survive at Morley in Derbyshire.

For the prose Life see *Anal. Boll.* 57 (1938), pp. 364-400. Also J. Bazire (ed.), *The Metrical Life of St Robert of Knaresborough* (E.E.T.S., 1953); J. I. Cummins, *The Legends, Saints and Shrines of Knaresborough* (1928); R. M. Clay, *Hermits and Anchorites of England* (1914); *Bibl.SS.*, 11, 234-5.

Bd Dalmatius Moner (1291-1341)

Our knowledge of this self-effacing Dominican is based on a Latin Life by his contemporary and fellow-Dominican, the famous inquisitor Nicholas Eymeric. Although it was written within ten years of Dalmatius' death and is particularly valuable for that reason, it was not identified until the beginning of the twentieth century. Earlier scholars knew of its existence but had to rely on a Spanish adaptation of the original.

Dalmatius was born in the Catalonian village of Santa Coloma de Farnés, near Gerona. He went to university not in Spain but in France, at Montpellier. When he was twenty-five and had completed his studies he applied to and was accepted by the Dominicans in Gerona. After his profession he lived unobtrusively, quietly getting on with his ordinary duties. These involved mainly teaching, which he did for many years; he also became master of novices. He added voluntary mortifications to those prescribed by the Rule (sleeping in an old armchair, for example) and prayed constantly—he particularly loved to pray outdoors in places where the beauty of nature spoke to him of the glory of God. According to the lessons of his Office he was known as "the brother who talks with the angels" and on at least one occasion was discovered levitating.

According to Nicholas Eymeric, whose description is convincing in its detail, Dalmatius was "not naturally attractive." He was "unpolished in appearance, tall, shrivelled, bald, and intense." He spoke little and when he did his voice was "high-pitched and sharp," and he had a very slow gait. Whether out of shyness or modesty or for some other reason, he would not talk to women except over his shoulder. On the other hand, he had a great devotion to St Mary Magdalene (22 July), patroness of the Dominican Order. His great desire was to die at La Sainte Baume, where, according to the legend, she had spent thirty years. This was not to be, although it is possible that he spent three years there in what was said to be Mary Magdalene's grotto. On his return to Gerona he was given permission to hollow out a cave for himself in the grounds of the friary. He lived in this uncomfortable place for four years, leaving it only to attend choir, chapter, and meals in the refectory. He died on 24 September 1341, and his cult was confirmed in 1721.

Nicholas Eymeric's Life, ed. F. van Otroy, is in *Anal.Boll.* 31 (1912), pp. 49-81. The account in *AA.SS.*, Sept., 6, pp. 157-60, is based on the adaptation. See also J. M. Gill, *El beato Dalmacio Moner, O.P., y los hombres de su tiempo* (1948); *Bibl.SS.*, 9, 546-7.

BB William Spencer and Robert Hardesty, *Martyrs* (1589)

William Spencer was born in Gisburn in the West Riding of Yorkshire in about 1555. He was educated at Trinity College, Oxford, and it was possibly while he was there that he converted to Roman Catholicism. From Oxford he went to Douai College at Reims to study for the priesthood. He was ordained there on 24 September 1583, six years to the day before his death, and was sent on the English mission the following August. He had been given permission to establish the Confraternities of the Rosary and of the Holy Name there. Nothing is known of his activities before his execution, but there is a description of him: "His countenance like his mind was cheerful, his eyes vivacious, his face was long and freckled; his hands were also covered with freckles. He had a yellowish beard and his cheeks were sparsely covered with hair. In other respects he was robust, squarely built and of moderate height." Five years later, in 1589, he was arrested for treason and tried in York, where he was hanged, drawn, and quartered on 24 September. Robert Hardesty, a layman who had been arrested for harbouring him, suffered with him. Both are numbered among the Eighty-Five Martyrs of England, Scotland, and Wales, who were beatified on 22 November 1987.

M.M.P., p. 159; Anstruther, 1, p. 329, with above description. A letter written by William at Reims to William Claxton is printed in the Publications of the Catholic Record Society, 5 (1906), p. 35.

St Pacifico of San Severino (1653-1721)

Carlo Antonio Divini was born at San Severino in the March of Ancona on 1 March 1653, the youngest of thirteen children. His parents, Antonio Divini and Maria Bruni, died when he was about five years old, leaving him in the care of his maternal uncle, Luzizio Bruni, prior of the cathedral of San Severino Marche. Luzizio was a good and cultivated man, but he was too austere and intolerant to care for a small child and, if the biographies are to be believed, reacted badly to the sudden and unwanted burden. Carlo is said to have borne his uncle's bouts of harshness and irritability with patience in spite of being used as a servant in the house. When he was not quite seventeen he applied to join the Friars Minor of the Observance. He was accepted and on 28 December 1670 was clothed, with the name Pacifico, in the friary at Forano. Having followed the usual course of studies, he was ordained on 4 June 1678, when he was twenty-five.

For the next six years he combined teaching philosophy to the younger friars at Montalboddosso and Fossombrone with travelling about doing mission work in the villages and hamlets of the region. The picture we have of him is of a tall, spare figure with pale skin, an aquiline nose, a light voice and an unassuming, friendly manner. His success was due in part to the directness and simplicity of his preaching and in part to his gift for reading the consciences of those who came to him to confess their sins—he had an uncanny way of reminding them of sins they had failed, consciously or unconsciously, to confess. But this apostolate was to be brief. In 1684 his health gave way, and by the time he was thirty-five he had begun to go deaf and blind. At the same time he suffered from chronic leg ulcers that nearly crippled him.

Despite his chronic ill health he moved between the friaries of San Severino and Forano, in both of which he held positions of responsibility. In September

1705 he was transferred for the last time to San Severino, where he would remain until he died. Here his disabilities and illness grew progressively worse, and in his last years he found it difficult to celebrate Mass or hear confessions. As if that were not enough, he fasted and practised other mortifications to the point where his superiors had to intervene; and when he attended Mass he was frequently in ecstasy. He also had the gift of foretelling. On 11 June 1721 he told the bishop of San Severino, Alessandro Calvi, who came to visit him, that he would die shortly and that he, Pacifico, would follow soon after. The bishop died within a fortnight, and Pacifico himself died on 24 September 1721. A huge crowd turned out for his funeral, and miracles were soon being reported at his tomb.

His remains were first exhumed in 1725, when they were placed in a wooden coffin near the altar of Our Lady in the friary church. Later they were transferred to a chapel that had been built in his honour. By 1752 his cause had begun, with Cardinal Henry of York as *ponente* and Mgr (afterwards Cardinal) Erskine as Promoter of the Faith. He was canonized by Pope Gregory XVI (1831-46) in 1839.

There are biographies by S. Melchiorri (1839; n.e.,1896); B. da Gaiole (1889; n.e., 1939); Diotallevi (1910); O. Marcaccini (1954). See also Léon, *Auréole*, 3, pp. 224-9; *Bibl.SS.*, 10, 7-9.

The iconography is small, and such portraits as do exist—by Nicola Monti, in his chapel (1786), and by Tommaso Corea for his beatification (nineteenth century)—are not true likenesses.

25

St Aunacharius, *Bishop* (605)

Aunacharius (in French, Aunaire) was one of the most influential and respected bishops of his time in France. He was born into a distinguished family of the Orléanais—his sister, St Austregildis, was the mother of St Lupus of Sens (1 Sept.)—and grew up at the royal court of Burgundy. His ambition, however, was to become a priest, so when the occasion presented itself he left the court and placed himself under the direction of the bishop of Autun, St Syagrius (2 Aug.). Syagrius ordained him to the priesthood, and in 561 he was appointed to the see of Auxerre. He was influential in civil as well as religious affairs, but his main area of expertise was church discipline. He was present at the Synods of Paris (573) and Mâcon (583 and 585), which among other things forbade clerics to take one another to the civil courts and enforced Sunday observance and the payment of tithes. Anxious to establish good discipline in his own diocese, he held two synods in Auxerre. His aim was partly to explain to his clergy and people how the rulings of the Paris and Mâcon synods applied locally and partly to tighten up local discipline. The forty-five canons enacted by the first of these two synods are interesting for the light they throw on contemporary beliefs and customs. People were forbidden to use churches for dancing or as a place for entertainment, dress up as stags or calves on New Year's Day, exchange "evil gifts," practise sympathetic magic, or meet in private houses to celebrate the vigils of feasts.

To inspire the faithful, Aunacharius had the biographies of his predecessors, St Amator (1 May) and St Germanus (3 Aug.), copied and made available. He also increased the revenues of his church so that the liturgy could be conducted more appropriately. Secular clergy as well as monks were expected to be present at the divine office each day, and responsibility for the solemn litanies rotated among the monasteries. His name appears as one of the bishops who tried to repress a revolt by monks at the abbey of Saint-Croix in Poitiers. Aunacharius died on 25 September 605. In 1567 his relics were hidden so that they could be kept safe from the Calvinists. They were later brought out and authenticated.

For two short Lives see *AA.SS.*, Sept., 7, pp. 106-11. See also Cochard, *Les Saints d'Orléans*, pp. 272-7; *F.E.*, 2, pp. 435-7; R. Louis in *St Germain d'Auxerre et son temps* (1948), p. 39ff.; *Bibl.SS.*, 2, 592-3.

St Finnbarr, *Bishop* (*c*. 560-*c*. 610)

Founder and patron of the city of Cork, Finnbarr (Findbarr, Bairre) belonged to the West Connacht clan of Uí Briúin Rátha. It is sometimes difficult to disentangle fact from legend in the accounts of his life, especially the early part, about which nothing definite is known. There is a Scottish legend that he was born in Caithness, but this is unlikely. The suggestion that he was born at Lisnacaheragh (Co. Cork) to a metal worker and a slave girl is more credible. He clearly received an education, probably from a bishop named MacCuirp at Achad Durbchon (Macroom), though an alternative version has it that he was educated by the monks at Kilmacahill. There is a tradition that the monks changed his name from Lochan to Finnbarr (Whitecrest) because of his blonde hair. He preached for a while in various parts of southern Ireland and then became a hermit on a small island on Lough Eiroe. When disciples began to gather around him, he founded a monastery at Etargabail on the east bank of the lake. This eventually became famous as a school, drawing its students from all over southern Ireland.

Other churches in this area claim to have been founded by him, but his greatest achievement was the foundation of another monastery on low marshy ground on the south side of the river Lee—the *corcagh mor*, from which Cork derives its name. He is said to have been consecrated bishop in about 600. When he died, greatly revered for his learning and holiness, in 610 (or 623, or 630), he was buried in Cork, and according to the legend the sun did not set for a fortnight. The centre of his cult, which has been mainly local to Ireland, is the monastery at Lough Eiroe, which is still a place of pilgrimage. Calendars and place names indicate that there was a cult in Scotland, but there is no literature connected with it. It is now thought that his connection with Barra in the Outer Hebrides probably stems from journeys made by his monks, not by him. His cult was approved in 1903.

Some of the legendary material is full of charm and poetry. Having been educated by a disciple of Pope St Gregory the Great (3 Sept.), he decided to make the pilgrimage to Rome. On the return journey, he went via Pembrokeshire to visit St David (1 Mar.). Seeing he had no means of getting back to Ireland, David lent him a horse, on which he headed out into Cardigan Bay. Fortunately, this method of transport did not have to last for long, for he soon sighted and signalled to St Brendan the Navigator (16 May), who happened to be coming his way in a boat. Another story tells how he and St Laserian (18 Apr.) were sitting under a hazel bush discussing spiritual matters. After a while Laserian asked Finnbarr for a sign that God was with him. As Finnbarr prayed the catkins on the bush above them fell off and nuts formed. When they had ripened he gathered them up in handfuls and poured them into Laserian's lap.

C. Plummer has edited the Irish Life in *Bethada Náem nErenn* (1922), with trans., in 2, pp. 11-21, and the Latin Life in *V.S.H.*, 1, pp. 65-74. See also *AA.SS.*, Sept., 7, p. 132; T. A.

Lunham, "The Life of St Finbarre," in *Journal of the Cork Historical and Archaeological Society* (1906), pp. 105-20; P. O'Riain, *Beatha Bharra. Saint Finbarr of Cork. The Complete Life*, (1994); *idem, The Making of a Saint: Finbarr of Cork 600-1200* (1997).

St Ceolfrith, *Abbot* (716)

Our knowledge of this great abbot is based on two contemporary sources. One, most probably the earlier of the two, is Bede's *Lives of the Abbots of Wearmouth and Jarrow*. The other, devoted specifically to Ceolfrith (Ceolfrid) is anonymous, although it has been suggested that the author may have been one of the monks who accompanied him on his last journey.

Ceolfrith was born into a noble Northumbrian family sometime in the middle of the seventh century, probably in Northumbria itself. When he was about eighteen he became a monk in the monastery at Gilling in North Yorkshire, where a relative, Tunbert, was abbot and the Rule was almost certainly Irish. He had been there for only a short time when he moved to the newly-founded monastery at Ripon. Here St Wilfrid (12 Oct.) was abbot and the Rule of St Benedict was observed. Ceolfrith was not the only one to join Wilfrid at this time, and the move could well have had something to do with the Synod of Whitby (663/4), where the Celtic-Roman question had come to a head. After his ordination he seems to have travelled fairly extensively. He visited two communities, those of Christ Church and SS Peter and Paul, in Canterbury, and then spent some time with St Botulf (17 June) at Icanho (now possibly Iken in Suffolk). He returned to Ripon "so well instructed that no one could be found more learned than he in either ecclesiastical or monastic traditions." On this account and because of his personal qualities, he was appointed novice-master. Whether the two ran simultaneously is not clear, but he also had practical skills for which he was made "baker" (perhaps caterer) for the monastery.

It was not long before his reputation for learning, practicality, and holiness came to the attention of the abbot of St Peter's, Wearmouth, St Benedict Biscop (12 Jan.). Perhaps with a view to increasing the Benedictine influence at Wearmouth, Benedict invited Ceolfrith to join him there. Released by Wilfrid from his obedience at Ripon, Ceolfrith went to Wearmouth, where he was soon appointed prior. That seems to have worked well until Benedict, who needed to make the long journey to Rome, left the reluctant Ceolfrith in sole charge in his absence. Ceolfrith succeeded in antagonizing some of the monks, who thought his administration too strict, and after a while he returned to Ripon. Benedict eventually managed to persuade him back to Wearmouth and in about 678 took him with him to Rome. The Roman influence at Wearmouth was strong, and Ceolfrith is known to have written a treatise to persuade the Pictish king Naiton to adopt the Roman Calendar and tonsure.

In 685 Benedict founded another monastery, dedicated to St Paul, at Jarrow, on the Tyne about six miles from Wearmouth. Strictly speaking, the two houses were one abbey, presided over by Benedict himself. But a local superior was needed at Jarrow, and Benedict sent Ceolfrith there as deputy abbot with a community of seventeen monks from Wearmouth. Benedict was absent in Rome yet again when the area was ravaged by an epidemic, probably the plague. The deputy abbot at Wearmouth, St Eosterwine (6 Mar.), and almost all the community there died, while at Jarrow the entire community was wiped out except for Ceolfrith and a young boy named Bede (25 May) who was being educated at the monastery. We are told, perhaps by Bede himself, that Ceolfrith was so anxious to keep the divine office going that he and the boy used to sing it together in choir by themselves until the numbers began to grow again. After things had returned to normal, Ceolfrith continued to teach Bede, taking a personal interest in him and encouraging and promoting him.

Before he died in 690 Benedict, with the agreement of the community, had nominated Ceolfrith as his successor. Bede, who joined the community when he was old enough, has left a fine description of the personality of this great abbot. He was "a man of acute mind, conscientious in everything he did, energetic, of mature judgment, fervent and zealous for his faith." Bede also mentions his love of the scriptures and his enthusiasm for learning. To encourage a love of learning in his monks—whose number in both monasteries rose to 600 while he was abbot—he vastly increased the size of the library. He had three copies made of a precious manuscript of the Vulgate version of the Bible, which Benedict Biscop had brought from Rome. One went to Wearmouth, one to Jarrow, and the third he kept to present to the pope when he went to Rome.

This he planned to do in 716. By then he was old and his health was failing; he felt unable to give the community what it needed from him as abbot. He resigned, and when the protesting monks had finally elected his successor he set off for Rome. Early in the morning of 4 May the six hundred monks attended Mass and then assembled in the church at Wearmouth. Ceolfrith kindled the incense, sang a prayer, and gave them his blessing from the altar steps. Then, in the chapel of St Laurence, he spoke to them for the last time, urging them to show true charity toward one another and to deal lovingly with any who needed to be corrected. For himself, he added, he forgave any wrong that might have been done him and asked forgiveness in return. When he had finished, they all followed him to the river, weeping to see him go. Having given them the kiss of peace and said another prayer, he boarded a boat, preceded by ministers carrying lighted candles and a crucifix. Then he crossed the river, kissed the cross, mounted his horse, and was gone.

In spite of his physical weakness, he relaxed none of his customary discipline. He recited the divine office daily and celebrated Mass even when he had to be carried in a litter, "except one day which was passed at sea and the three days before his death." On 25 September, when he had already been travelling for more than four months, he reached Langres in Burgundy. He died there that same day and was buried on the following day before his companions continued their journey, some on to Rome, some back to break the news to the community at Wearmouth and Jarrow. Ceolfrith's relics were later translated to Wearmouth, where they were venerated until the Viking invasions of around 800. The monks of Glastonbury claim that they were taken there in the tenth century.

For the contemporary Lives see *Baedae Opera Historica* (ed. C. Plummer, 1956); with Eng. trans., J. F. Webb and D. H. Farmer, *The Age of Bede* (1998); *E.H.D.*, 1, pp. 697-708; D. S. Boutflower, *The Life of Ceolfrid, Abbot of the Monastery of Wearmouth and Jarrow* (1991). For a modern Life see I. Wood, *The Most Holy Abbot Ceolfrid* (1995). See also J. McClure, "Bede and the Life of Ceolfrid," in *Peritia* 3 (1984), pp. 71-84; *H.S.S.C.*, 4, pp. 84, 269; *O.D.S.*, p. 93.

For a long time, the immediate fate of the single-volume Bible (*pandect*) Ceolfrith was taking to Pope Gregory II (715-31) was not known. However, it is now clear that the monks of Northumbria did in fact present it to the pope. Later on, in the twelfth century, it was offered by another pope to the monastery of St Saviour on Monte Amiato, near Siena, finally ending its journey at the Biblioteca Laurenziana in Florence. The *Codex Amiatinus*, the oldest surviving complete Latin Bible in one volume, is the very book that Ceolfrith set off with that May morning nearly 1,300 years ago. Dramatic proof of its authenticity came in the nineteenth century when ultra-violet light was used to show that the inscription at the beginning had been altered—only slightly, but in a manner described exactly by Bede. See R. L. S. Bruce-Mitford, *The Art of the Codex Amiatinus* (Jarrow Lecture, 1969); E. A. Lowe, *English Uncials* (1960).

Bd Herman "Contractus" (1013-54)

Herman was born in Swabia on 18 July 1013. His father was Count Wolfrat of Althausen, and his mother, Hiltrerd, came from Burgundy. He was severely disabled physically, possibly from birth, although his fine mind was completely unaffected. The fact that he was unable to move and could scarcely speak suggests that he suffered either from cerebral palsy or from some form of infantile paralysis. From the age of nine he was cared for at the monastery of Reichenau on Lake Constance, where he achieved much despite his total dependence. He made his profession as a member of the community when he was thirty and eventually became a priest, and he even managed to do a certain amount of travelling. His disciple Berthold described him as a warm and loving man with great reserves of wisdom and patience who worked hard and prayed constantly and was gentle and compassionate toward others.

Most of his life as a monk was devoted to study and to writing. He had an exceptional openness of mind and spirit, and although his prose works are largely forgotten now except by scholars, at the time he was in the vanguard of thought. People enjoyed coming to consult him and discuss matters of mutual interest with him, and among his many visitors were the emperor Henry III (1039-56) and Pope Leo IX (1049-54). Herman's widely-ranging curiosity is reflected in his works, which reveal a continuing interest in astronomy, history, poetry, liturgy, and music. He wrote numerous treatises on music, especially in the context of the liturgy, and modified the system of notation, introducing a new way of writing the notes themselves. His other works include a mathematico-astronomical treatise, a long poem, unfinished, on the seven deadly sins, and one of the earliest medieval world chronicles. In the latter he draws on monastic and imperial annals, episcopal lists, saints' Lives, and other sources to produce a universal history, precise, objective, and elegantly written, from the death of Christ to the middle of the eleventh century. Herman is best remembered as the author of two popular hymns that the Church has incorporated into the liturgy: *Alma redemptoris mater* and (probably) *Salve, regina*. He is also said to have made astronomical and musical instruments. Admired by his contemporaries as "the wonder of the age," he died on 24 September 1054. He was buried at Althausen, but it is no longer possible to identify the tomb.

The status of Herman's cult is sufficiently problematic for him to be excluded from the new draft Roman Martyrology. From relatively early on he featured among the *beati* in the Benedictine calendar. However, a bishop of Freiburg subsequently declared his cult inadmissible, although he did allow it to continue in the area.

See *Die Kultur der Abtei Reichenau* (1925). Herman's chronicle is in *M.G.H., Scriptores*, 6, pp. 67-133. For an article on his fraction tables see F. A. Yeldham in *Speculum*, 3 (1928), p. 240ff. See also H. Hansjakob, *Herimann der Lahme* (1954); *Bibl.SS.*, 5, 21-2; C. C. Martindale, *What are Saints?* (1939); *idem*, *From Bye-ways and Hedges* (1935); H. Thurston, *Familiar Prayers* (1953), pp. 119-25.

There are representations of Herman in the choir of the churches at Andechs and Zweihalten.

St Sergius of Radonezh, *Abbot* (*c.* 1315-92)

In 1940 the Holy See authorized a liturgical calendar for the use of Russian Christians in communion with Rome. This included the feasts of about thirty Russian saints, twenty-one of whom had never before been listed on a Latin calendar. Of the twenty-one, the best known was a monk, St Sergius of Radonezh. He was the most outstanding and most important of the *pustiniky*, or men of the wilderness, who helped breathe new life back into Russia after the Tartar invasions of the thirteenth century, which had destroyed the urban culture in the south, undermined the monasteries, and left the people wretched and demoralized.

Sergius, who was christened Bartholomew, was born in about 1315 into a family of wealthy boyars near Rostov. His father was private secretary to the last independent ruler. He does not appear to have been intellectually gifted, and the fact that he was less bright than his two brothers worried him for a while. But although he had no real enthusiasm for study, he did manage to achieve his one ambition in this respect, which was to become literate enough to study the Bible. His parents, Kiril and Marya, fell victim to the expansionist policies of the principality of Moscow, which included the destruction of the power and influence of Rostov. When Bartholomew was about fifteen, the whole family was forced to flee the area. They settled eventually in a small village named Radonezh, about fifty miles north-east of Moscow, where they lived as peasant farmers, working in the fields. Then in 1335, when his parents were dead and he himself was about twenty, Bartholomew went with his widowed brother Istvan, who was already a monk at Khotkhovo, to realize his long-held ambition to become a solitary.

They chose for their hermitage a location called Makovka, which is now known as Troike-Sergievskaya Lavra. This was a piece of rising ground in a forest several miles from the nearest human habitation. There they prepared the ground and set to work immediately to build a wooden hut and a chapel. When both were ready the metropolitan of Kiev, at their request, sent a priest to dedicate the chapel to the Most Holy Trinity—*Svetaya Troika*—an unusual dedication in Russia in those days. They had not been there long when Istvan, presumably finding that the solitary life did not suit him, went to join a monastic community in Moscow. Bartholomew remained in his hermitage, and virtually nothing was heard of him for a while. His biographer mentions demonic temptations, nights spent in prayer, threatening wild beasts, and other phenomena reminiscent of the Desert Fathers. There was, of course, one obvious difference: Sergius as he now was, having received the habit and that name from Metrophanes of Khotkhovo probably in October 1337, was being shaped not by an Egyptian desert but by a harsh environment of which wind, rain, and cold were the salient features.

Inevitably, as Sergius' reputation spread, disciples gathered round him. Each built a hut for himself, and the monastery of the Holy Trinity had come into being. When there were twelve of them, Sergius agreed to be their abbot and was ordained priest at Pereyaslav Zalesky. "Pray for me," he told them. "I am completely ignorant, and I have received a talent from on high for which I shall have to give an account and of the flock committed to me." As the number of monks increased they began to discuss which form of monastic life should be followed at Holy Trinity. There were two forms then current in the East: the eremitical and "idiorhythmic," where each monk had a separate cell on its own plot of ground and was entirely responsible for his own spiritual life, and the cenobitical, where the life of the monks was fully communal. Sergius favoured the latter, for practical as well as spiritual reasons. The monastery had attracted an influx of peasants, and with the growth of a town food supplies had become scarce. In 1354, encouraged by the ecumenical patriarch of Constantinople, he moved the monastery definitively in this direction, choosing for it the Rule of St Theodore the Studite (11 Nov.).

Unfortunately this led, as change so often does, to trouble. Some of the monks, who resented what was happening, looked for leadership to Sergius' brother Istvan, who had returned to the monastery bringing their other brother with him. Matters came to a head in 1358, when there was an incident involving the two groups one Saturday after Vespers. Preferring not to quarrel with his brothers, Sergius slipped quietly away and settled down alone by the river Kerzhach, near the monastery of Makrish. Soon, however, some of his supporters at Holy Trinity followed him there, and Holy Trinity itself began to decline. Fearing that this decline might become terminal, Metropolitan Alexis of Moscow sent a message to Sergius, who had by this time been away for four years, asking him to return. Sergius, who immediately agreed to do so, appointed a new abbot at the Kerzhach monastery and returned to Holy Trinity. There the monks were "so filled with joy that some of them kissed the father's hands, others his feet, while others caught hold of his clothing and kissed that."

Like St Bernard of Clairvaux (20 Aug.), St Hugh of Lincoln (17 Nov.), and many other holy monks before and since, Sergius was consulted by ecclesiastical and political leaders. More than one attempt was made to persuade him to become patriarch of Moscow, but he refused, preferring to mediate and reconcile from his base at Holy Trinity. One of his most famous interventions came toward the end of the struggle between the prince of Moscow, Dmitri Ivanovich Donskoy, and the Tartar leader, Khan Mamai. Faced with the choice between retreat and a final offensive, which if it failed would have disastrous consequences for Russia, Dmitri sought Sergius' advice. Sergius reminded him that he had a duty to defend the people God had entrusted to him and sent him away, accompanied by two of the monks who had formerly been soldiers and the promise, "God will be with you." The Tartars were routed on 8 September 1380 at the battle of Kulikovo Polye. Sergius, who was praying at the time, is said to have told the community about the victory an hour after it happened— "for he was a seer."

His work as mediator frequently took him away from the monastery. He is said to have undertaken all these journeys on foot despite the long distances and ignoring the hardship involved. In 1385 he made his last intervention in Russian political affairs, travelling to Riazan to reconcile Prince Oleg of Riazan with Dmitri Donskoy. It was on his return from this expedition that he resigned as abbot in favour of his chosen successor, St Nikon. Some of his other disciples are among the most celebrated figures in the Russian church: St Sava, founder of the monastery of the Nativity of Our Lady at Zvenigorod, St Methodius of Pesnoche, St Sergius of La Nouroma, St Sylvester of Obnorsk, and St Abraham of Galitch.

Sergius' biographers speak of his "many incomprehensible miracles" and of a vision of the Mother of God that is the earliest recorded in Russian hagiography, but there is little in the way of ecstasies and other unusual supernatural states. In some ways he must have seemed rather ordinary. He enjoyed and was good at carpentry and gardening and, although in no way opposed to intellectual activity, thought manual work was necessary to create a balanced person. He was certainly not learned himself, nor did he preach particularly eloquently, and although some people claimed to have been cured by his prayers, he was not a "healer." People were attracted to him and sought him out for something else: the presence of the Spirit in him, which shone through as a special warmth, as a way of concentrating all his attention on the individual to whom he was talking.

In April 1392, sensing that he was soon to die, Sergius resigned as abbot and appointed a successor. He was then taken ill for the first time in his life. Surrounded by his brethren, he received the sacraments for the last time and died peacefully on 25 September. He was buried in the principal church of the monastery (now the central feature of the town of Sergievo Posad, formerly Zagorsk), which became important in Russian history as the place where the tsar's heir was baptized. Immediately after Sergius' death it became the popular place of pilgrimage it still is today. When the monastery was forced to close during the Revolution of 1917, his relics were deposited in the local "anti-religion museum." They were restored, however, in 1945, when the monastery was given permission to reopen. Sergius, who was canonized before 1449, remains the most popular of the Russian saints, and his name is mentioned during the preparation of the Holy Things in the Russian Orthodox liturgy.

The manuscript literature of Russian saints' Lives is large. The medieval ones belong to three distinct areas. Those from Kiev and the Ukraine are the earliest and concentrate on "holy princes" and "holy monks." The first *paterik* or collection of short Lives of saints connected with a particular district or monastery was produced at the monastery of the Caves at Kiev. After the Tartar conquest a new hagiographical school developed in the north, one of its centres being Novgorod. These Lives were characterized by brevity and by the austerity of their style. The third school, which grew up in the central area around Moscow, went for the opposite effect, dressing up the facts with devotional rhetoric and edifying details. The Lives that emerged from all three areas tended to be conventional and uninformative, making it difficult to get at the person behind the stock details. Most were studied and printed during the nineteenth century, but because they were in Russian remained almost unknown in the West. The Western contribution to Russian hagiology is negligible. Even *Annus ecclesiasticus graeco-slavicus*, volume 11 of the *Acta Sanctorum* for October, has been criticized and compared unfavourably with L. Götz, *Das kiewer Höhenkloster als Kulturzentrum des vormongolischen Russlands* (1904).

The Life of St Sergius was written by Epiphanius the Wise, one of his own monks, then shortened and rewritten in the fifteenth century by a Serbian monk named Pakhomius. This can be found in G. P. Fedotov (ed.), *A Treasury of Russian Spirituality* (1950, 1981). St Sergius is discussed at length in *idem, The Russian Religious Mind: the Middle Ages* (1966). See also P. Kovalevsky, *St Serge et la spiritualité russe* (1958; Eng. trans., 1976); *Bibl.SS.*, 11, 871-3; *H.S.S.C.*, 7, pp. 225-30; *O.D.S.*, pp. 431-2. For Russian saints in general see E. Behr-Sigel, *Prière et Sainteté dans l'Eglise russe* (1950); A. Maltsev, *Menologium der Orthodox-Katholischen Kirche des Morgenlands* (1900); I. N. Danzas in *Russie et Chrétienté* 3 (1937); N. S. Arseniev in *Der christliche Osten* (1939); G. P. Fedotov, *The Russian Religious Mind: Kievan Christianity* (1946); I. Kologrivov, *Essai sur la Sainteté en Russie* (1953); E. Benz et al. (eds.) *Russische Heiligenlegenden* (1953); St Demetrius of Rostov, *Great Collection of the Lives of the Saints* (1994); J. Fennell, *History of the Russian Church to 1448* (1995).

There are many icons in which St Sergius appears either alone or with other saints. The museum of the monastery in Zagorsk has a life-size silk embroidered portrait, and there is a full-length mid-seventeenth-century icon by the Master of the Volga in the Rublev

Museum in Moscow—Andrei Rublev was one of the glories of the monastery of the Holy Trinity. See G. Gharib, *Icone di Santi* (1990), p. 251.

Bd Mark Criado, *Martyr* (1522-69)

Mark (Marco) was born at Andújar, north-east of Córdoba in southern Spain, on 25 April 1522. He seems to have been a gifted, not to say precocious, child, with a strongly developed religious sense. When he was still only fourteen he applied to and was accepted by the Trinitarian Order, which had a house in his home town. After the normal courses of study he was ordained and then sent to preach in Jaén and Ubeda as well as in Andújar. He had not been doing this for long when he was sent as a missionary to the diocese of Gualix. The entire area was a Muslim stronghold, but this did not deter Mark, who worked tirelessly to spread the gospel. For a while he served as a chaplain at La Peza, but that was to be his last taste of stability. Leaving La Peza, he travelled about on foot, alone and a great risk to himself, bringing help and encouragement to the Christians of the towns and villages of the Alpujarra, the remote region on the southern slopes of the Sierra Nevada.

It was not easy. Even in La Peza he was verbally and physically abused; in La Sierra de los Filabres they tied him to a tree and left him there for two days; and in Cadiar he would have suffered a worse fate had his hosts not enabled him to escape through one of their windows in a basket. In 1569 there was a Muslim uprising in the Alpujarra, and Mark was their first victim. Having left him tied to a tree for three days, during which he sang hymns and prayed for his torturers, they finally stoned him to death on 25 September. A cult developed immediately, and he was made patron of La Peza. The cult was confirmed by Pope Leo XIII (1878-1903) on 24 July 1899.

There are biographies by J. de Salas (1658); Silvestro dell'Addolorata (1899); Antonino de la Asunción (1900). See also J. Chirinos, *Sumario de las persecuciones de la Iglesia* (1593); *Bibl.SS.*, 4, 299-300.

St Vincent Strambi, Bishop (1745-1824)

Vincent (Vincenzo) is included here rather than on the actual date of his death—1 January—at the request of the Passionist Congregation, which commemorates him on this day.

He was the son of Giuseppe Strambi, a pharmacist, and was born at Civitavecchia on 1 January 1745. He was a happy and particularly lively child with a strong religious sense, which developed early and was much encouraged by his parents, whose ambition for him was that he should become a diocesan priest. When he was fifteen he overcame their objection that he was still too young and received the tonsure and minor orders. He entered the seminary at Montefiascone on 4 November 1762 and had progressed as far as his pre-ordination retreat when he met St Paul of the Cross (19 Oct.), the founder of the Congregation of the Passion. After a painful struggle with his disappointed parents, Vincent entered the Passionist novitiate on 20 September 1768, about a year after his ordination. Having completed two years of biblical and patristic studies, he began his career as a preacher. Soon he was receiving serious responsibilities as well, first as professor of theology within the Congregation and subsequently as provincial (1781) and consultor (1784-96). In 1801, much against his will, he was made bishop of Macerata and Tolentino in the March of Ancona.

For seven years he led his diocese in a programme of renewal that started with the priests, whom he encouraged to celebrate Mass daily and wear ecclesiastical dress. In a symbolic gesture he built a new seminary at Macerata with money raised from the sale of the old one. He made himself responsible for the choice of professors in the seminary and—unusual for the time—even appointed one or two laymen. He gave the seminarians one lecture each week himself and saw to it that in addition to their regular courses they had two lectures a week on Gregorian chant. The result was a genuine, liturgically-based renewal of fervour in the diocese. Vincent encouraged catechetics to the same end, and the cathedral-based catechetical school offered courses for adults and for catechists as well as for children. He also established a library so that people could do their own reading. To help the poor he acquired quantities of hemp, from the spinning of which they could earn good money. He also gave generous support to the school at Tolentino and the Somaschi orphanage.

This period came to an end in 1808 when, like many other bishops, he refused to take the Oath of Allegiance to Napoleon. He was expelled from the diocese, going first to Novara, where he stayed until October 1809, and then on to Milan. Here, as the guest of the Barnabites and later of Marchese G. A. Zitta Modigniani, he carried on the administration of his diocese as best he could by letter. When Napoleon abdicated in April 1814, Vincent returned to Macerata amid great rejoicing. But there was more trouble to come when Napoleon escaped from Elba in February of the following year. General Joachim Murat, who had been king of Naples since 1808 and was anxious to protect his position against the Austrians, came with an army of thirty thousand and made Macerata his headquarters. When his men were defeated by the Austrians at the battle of Tolentino in 1815, they would have sacked Macerata as they retreated had it not been for Vincent. He went out and appealed personally both to Murat and to the Austrians, with the result that the town was spared.

Peace did not bring with it freedom from adversity. During the next few years Vincent had to contend with a typhoid epidemic as well as with a food shortage verging on famine, during both of which he worked heroically to bring relief to those in need. At the same time he was pursuing his reforms despite resentment and opposition from some quarters—at least one attempt is said to have been made on his life on this account. When Pope Pius VII (1800-23) died, Vincent resigned his see and went to Rome as a special adviser to

Pope Leo XII (1823-9). He was also much sought after as a spiritual director, numbering the Ven. Luisa Maurizi and Bd Anna Maria Taigi (9 June) among his disciples. But by this time he was exhausted from the stress of his public life and the austerity of his personal life. As Anna Maria Taigi had foretold, he received the Eucharist for the last time on 31 December 1823 and died on the following day, his seventy-ninth birthday. He was buried in the basilica of SS Giovanni e Paolo, but his remains were taken from Rome to Macerata, of which he is patron and protector, on 12 November 1957. Most of his written works are lost, but a few have survived, including a Life of St Paul of the Cross. Vincent was beatified on 26 April 1925 and canonized in 1950.

There are biographies in Italian by Fr Stanislaus (1925); F. Cento (1950). See also *Bibl.SS.*, 12, 1178-80; *O.D.S.*, pp. 444-5.

There is an anonymous portrait of Vincent, painted in the nineteenth century, in the collection of the basilica of SS Giovanni e Paolo in Rome. The strength of the face with its high forehead, large nose, and wide mouth is concentrated in the intensity of the eyes.

26

SS COSMAS AND DAMIAN, *Martyrs* (? 287)

Cosmas and Damian are pre-eminent among those saints whose legend extends far beyond anything that can ever be known about them for certain. They are the best known of the *anargyroi*, or moneyless ones—saints venerated in the East for their refusal to accept money for their services. When and why they were martyred is not known, but the earliest references indicate that they suffered at Cyrrhus, north of Antioch, in Syria. Bishop Theodoret of Cyrrhus (d. 458) referred to them as "illustrious athletes and generous martyrs." A basilica built there in their honour was the centre from which their enormously popular cult spread throughout the Christian world. A wealthy pagan named Rabboula is known to have prayed there in about 400, providing a useful reference date. Churches were also built in the martyrs' honour in, among other places, Constantinople (fifth century) and Rome (sixth century).

From this slender base there developed an enormous hagiographical literature with accompanying iconography that gathered strength with time. The *passio* was reworked and translations were made, along with collections of the miracles associated with the two men. It is not clear exactly how the sources relate to one another, and the situation is further confused by the fact at least three pairs of martyrs with these names are commemorated in the East, on 1 November, 1 July, and 17 October, though it is now generally accepted by critics that these three pairs are in fact one and the same. According to the detailed and colourful legend Cosmas and Damian were twin brothers born in Arabia who went to study the sciences in Syria. Once qualified they went to Aegeae on the bay of Alexandretta in Cilicia. Here they practised medicine without accepting fees from their patients and were widely known and respected for their charity and for their integrity as Christians. As they made no secret of their faith—indeed, they did all they could to pass it on—they were an obvious target once persecution broke out. They were arrested and brought before the governor of Cilicia, who ordered that they be tortured and then beheaded. According to the Roman Martyrology their three brothers, Anthimus, Leontius, and Euprepius, suffered with them during the persecution of Diocletian.

The legend is further enhanced by numerous accounts of miracles and other marvels, some of which are also recorded of other martyrs. Not surprisingly, many of the miracles have to do with healing. Their principal church in Constantinople originated the rite of "incubation," in which sick people spent the night and slept in the church. The saints came to them in dreams and cured them by operating, applying poultices, or other means. The first collected account of such miracles dates from the sixth century. They are contrasted favourably with the pool of Bethesda in Jerusalem, which "heals only one person each year," while at the shrine of Cosmas and Damian "the whole crowd of sick are healed: the richness, then, of these Saints is great and inexhaustible." Cosmas and Damian are the patron saints, along with St Luke (18 Oct.) and St Pantaleon (27 July), of doctors, and they feature on various guild emblems and seals.

The cult of SS Cosmas and Damian first reached Rome during the pontificate of St Symmachus (498-514; 19 July), who introduced it into an oratory near the basilica of Santa Maria Maggiore. But it was Pope St Felix III (526-30; 22 Sept.) who translated their relics and built the basilica dedicated to them. From there the cult spread, and there are many dedications outside Italy, particularly in Greece and eastern Europe. Cosmas and Damian are mentioned in the Roman Canon of the Mass (the first Eucharistic Prayer). They are the patrons of not only of doctors but of nurses, surgeons, pharmacists, dentists, barbers, and—rather unexpectedly—confectioners.

AA.SS., Sept., 7, pp. 430-77. Also H. Delehaye, "Les recueils antiques de miracles des saints," in *Anal.Boll.* 43 (1924), pp. 8-18; M. L. David-Danel, *Iconographie des saints médecins Côme et Damien* (1958); A. Wittmann, *Kosmas und Damian* (1967). *H.S.S.C.*, 2, pp. 114-20; *Bibl.SS.*, 4, 223-37; Jöckle, pp. 117-9.

Cosmas and Damian seem to have captured the imagination of artists. There are many individual representations of these two saints, starting with the mosaics in the church dedicated to them in Rome, and a number of cycles. The paintings especially have much to tell us about medieval medical practice. One of the cycles, in San Marco in Florence, is by Fra Angelico. He was helped by a donation from Cosimo de'Medici (1389-1464), who had a great devotion to his namesake. Another, anonymous, cycle is in an antiphoner from north Italy, which is now at the Society of Antiquaries in London. There is an early-fourteenth-century, probably Polish, icon in the Museum of Popular Architecture in Sarok in Poland showing the saints full length with scenes from their lives down each side: see G. Gharib, *Icone di Santi* (1990), pp. 148-53.

St Colmán Elo, *Abbot* (*c.* 555-611)

The name Colman was a very common one in the early Irish Church, and literally dozens of St Colmans have been or are still venerated in Ireland— twelve are mentioned in various calendars for the month of September alone. Of the many, Colmán Elo is one of the most important, and two Lives have survived, one in Latin, the other in Irish. The former, best preserved in the *Codex Salmanticensis*, may date from as early as the end of the seventh century. It gives him the patronymic *mac Beugne* but supports the claim of the southern Uí Néill, the group of ruling dynasties in the province (as opposed to the much less extensive county) of Meath, that he belonged to them. In fact, the family is now thought to have originated in Antrim, and Colmán himself was born in about 555. He came under the influence of St Columba (or Colmcille; 9 June), who may have been a relative although the evidence for this is late and slight (the Irish Life mentions a woman named Uanach who is described as the sister of Columba and Colmán's mother, who is not named here or, it seems, anywhere else).

Colmán does appear to have visited Columba in Iona, and from there he is believed to have gone on to preach in Scotland before returning to Ireland. The next mention of him is in 590, when he founded a monastery on a site given to him at Lann Elo (now Lynally) in Offaly, not far from Columba's monastery at Durrow. According to the early Life, which makes various attempts to link Colmán with Columba, the donor was Aed Sláine, over-king of the southern Uí Néill, who gave Colmán the monastery at Columba's request. In any case, the foundation of the monastery was taken as the fulfillment of a prophecy made sixty years earlier by St Macanisius (3 Sept.)—Colmán is sometimes referred to as "*combráthair* [kinsman] of Mac Nisse," who is buried at Connor in Antrim.

Llan Elo was Colmán's most significant and best-known foundation. It attracted people from outside as well as inside Ireland and flourished long after his death. he is also associated with Muchamore and with Connor, of which he is the second patron, after St Macanisius. The link with Muchamore, the ruins of which survive, is either unlikely or the foundation was later than 550: when Colmán died in 610 he was still in his early fifties.

As is the case with so many saints of the period, it is not easy to say what sort of personality Colmán had. The fact that he is said to have suffered the temporary loss of his memory as a punishment for intellectual pride may be some sort of indicator. On the other hand, the legends associated with him tend to be gentler, with fewer punitive elements, than those of some other Celtic saints. They tell, for example, of a British member of the community who was reprimanded by Colmán for some breach of the Rule. When he raised his hand to strike the abbot it remained there, stiff and paralyzed, until he asked for and received the latter's forgiveness. There are several occasions on which Colmán is supposed miraculously to have recovered lost or stolen articles in order to save someone inconvenience or embarrassment. And he is credited with foreknowledge of future events. One day when he was working in the fields, he is said to have fallen to the ground weeping. When the other monks asked what the trouble was he replied that he had had a vision of angels visiting Earth. At first he thought this was a sign that the day of judgment had come, but then he saw them taking the soul of Pope St Gregory the Great (3 Sept.) to heaven on a golden altar. A year later to the day he predicted that a messenger would soon arrive to confirm what he had seen. The monks soon learned, from a pilgrim who arrived from Rome, that Gregory had died a year earlier, on 3 September 604. Toward the end of his life Colmán made a pilgrimage to Clonard, where he had a vision of St Finnian (12 Dec.) and a premonition of his own death. This was said to have taken place in 620 or 611, traditionally when he was fifty-five, though he could have been as young as fifty-two or as old as fifty-six. After his death miracles were attributed to his intercession.

Colmán is credited with the authorship of a devotional work entitled *Apgitir Chrábaid* (Alphabet of Piety), although the attribution is questioned by modern scholars.

C. Plummer has edited both Lives, the Latin in *V.S.H.*, 1, pp. 258-73, the Irish in *Bethada Naem nErenn* (Eng. trans. in 2, pp. 162-76). See also *Bibl.SS.*, 4, 93-4; Baudot et Chaussin, 9, pp. 535-6. J. O'Hanlon provides a digest of the legends in *Lives of the Irish Saints*, 9 (1901). The *Apgitir Chrábaid* is ed. and trans. V. E. Hull, in *Celtica* 8 (1968), pp. 44-89. See also P. P. O'Néill, "The date and authorship of *Apgitir Chrábaid*: some internal evidence," in P. Ní Chatháin and M. Richter (eds.), *Ireland und die Christenheit* (1987), pp. 203-15.

St Nilus of Rossano, *Abbot* (*c.* 910-1004)

Sometimes called "the Younger" to distinguish him from St Nilus the Elder (12 Nov.), this Nilus was born of Greek parents, who named him Nicholas, at Rossano in Calabria in about 910. This part of Calabria had remained Byzantine throughout the upheavals of the ninth century. It was Greek, and that Greekness had merely been reinforced when Greeks fleeing the Arab invaders poured in from Sicily. But when Nilus was born it had just been reunited, for administrative purposes, with the rest of the region, which had until then been in the hands of the Lombards. Rossano was at the point where the two cultures met, and Nilus, who was familiar with Latin as well as with Greek, served throughout his life as a bridge between them.

Alban Butler says that as a youth he was "fervent in religious duties and in the practice of all virtues," but it seems that this was not the case. He was irresponsible and no more than lukewarm in his attitude to religion, and the previous revision of Butler points out, rather primly, that "it has even been questioned whether the lady with whom he lived, and who bore him a daughter, was married to him." However, when he was thirty both she and the child died, presumably in an epidemic, and he himself was seriously ill. The double loss forced him to take stock of himself, and he underwent a profound conversion. His first step was to join one of the Byzantine-rite monasteries, of which there were quite a number in southern Italy at that time, taking the name Nilus. He in fact lived in several of them at different times, both as a hermit and as a cenobite.

Eventually he became abbot of Sant'Adriano, near San Demétrio Corone, which he founded himself in 953. He had a strong feeling for the ties of loyalty that bound him to his family, his teachers, and his first disciples, and he was to remain at Sant'Adriano for nearly thirty years. As abbot he gained a reputation for learning and holiness, and people came from throughout the region to seek his advice. Although he apparently accepted theories about salvation and the number of the elect that even his contemporaries found extreme and which would certainly seem so today, he did not see the monastic life as the only route to salvation. He told a nobleman who wished to join the monastery as a sign of repentance: "Your baptismal promises are enough. Repentance calls not for new promises but for a whole-hearted change in your way of life."

Throughout Nilus' life peace in southern Italy was constantly being threatened by Arab raids and marauding mercenaries. In 981 an Arab incursion forced him and his monks to flee from Sant'Adriano. They travelled northwest and were taken in at Monte Cassino, where the monks received them "as if St Antony had come from Alexandria, or their own great St Benedict from the dead." They lived in the house for a while, celebrating their Greek liturgy in the church, until the abbot, Aligern, gave them a monastery at Valleluce, which happened to be standing empty. After fifteen years they moved on again to Serperi, near Gaeta. Nilus' monasteries would not have been the cenobitical type familiar in the West. He himself preferred solitude to community life, and his monks would have lived like hermits alongside one another according to the Eastern model. There was no single Rule, and Nilus, who earned his living by copying manuscripts, would frequently go off alone to fast and pray.

In 998 he had an opportunity to show his tolerant and compassionate side. The emperor, Otto III (996-1002), came to Rome to expel Philagathos, bishop of Piacenza, who as John XVI (997-8) had been set up as an antipope to Gregory V (996-9). Philagathos was a fellow-Calabrian and native of Rossano, and Nilus had already tried, by letter, to shift him from the disastrous path he was taking. Now he travelled to Rome with a view to persuading the pope and the emperor to deal gently with the old man. The pope and the emperor allowed Nilus to have his say, but it seems they took no notice, and there was nothing he could do to mitigate the atrociously cruel and humiliating way in which Philagathos was treated. After he had been blinded and otherwise mutilated, a prelate was sent to explain to Nilus why this had been necessary. Nilus, who had already made his protest about what amounted to torture, was so angry that he pretended to be asleep in order not to have to speak to the man. Some time later, Otto had the gall to visit Nilus at his monastery. Surprised by the primitive simplicity of the monks' life, he offered Nilus a plot of land in his own dominions on which a new monastery could be built and promised to endow it. Nilus refused, and when the emperor asked him to accept at least something, Nilus replied: "The only thing I ask of you is that you save your soul. You may be the emperor, but you must die and give and account of your life to God, just like everyone else."

In 1004 Nilus set off to visit a monastery south of Tusculum but was taken ill in the Alban Hills. While waiting to recover sufficiently to continue his journey he had a vision in which Our Lady is said to have told him that this was to be a permanent home for his community. He duly obtained land rights from Gregorio, count of Tusculum, on the slopes of Monte Cavo, eleven miles from Rome, and sent for his monks. Plans were drawn up, but before building could commence he died. Work on what became the great abbey of Grottaferrata was carried on by Nilus's successor, St Bartholomew (11 Nov.), but Nilus is regarded as the founder and first abbot. He was buried at Grottaferrata and still enjoys a cult in southern Italy, where he is invoked especially against epilepsy.

The Eastern-rite abbey still flourishes as a centre of holiness and learning. Today instead of creating manuscripts the monks use the most up-to-date techniques to preserve them. Some of Nilus' manuscripts still survive.

An historically reliable Greek Life, printed in *AA.SS.*, Sept., 7, pp. 262-319, has been translated into Italian by G. Minasi (1893) and A. Rocchi (1904). See also biography by G. Giovanelli (1966); D. Attwater, *Saints of the East* (1963), pp. 118-24; *H.S.S.C.*, 5, pp. 209-14; *Bibl.SS.*, 9, 995-1008; *O.D.S.*, p. 357; T. Minisci, *Santa Maria di Grottaferrata* (1966).

Bd Lucy of Caltagirone (Thirteenth Century)

Very little is known about Bd Lucy, and the available information is not reliable. She was born at Caltagirone in Sicily, a town later associated more with Don Luigi Sturzo, the priest, politician, and social reformer who was born there in 1871, but she spent most of her life in a convent of regular Franciscan tertiaries in Salerno. There she was appointed mistress of novices and is best remembered for her fidelity to the Rule and her devotion to the Five Wounds of Christ. Miracles were attributed to her before as well as after her death, the date of which is unknown. Despite the fact that she was a Franciscan, her body ended up at the Benedictine monastery of Santa Maria Maddalena in Salerno, although it is not clear how this happened. Her cult seems to have been approved by Pope Callistus II (1455-8) and Pope Leo X (1513-21).

AA.SS., Sept., 7, pp. 361-74; *Bibl.SS.*, 8, 239; Baudot et Chaussin, 9, p. 529.

St Teresa Couderc, *Foundress* (1805-85)

Marie-Victoire Couderc was born into a comfortably-off farming family at Le Mas-de-Sablières, in the Ardèche, on 1 February 1805. As a child she received little formal education. She could read, however, and she learned much in that way and from the practical Christianity of her parents, particularly her mother. From her early teenage years it was her ambition to join a religious community in order to bring the Faith back to the people of the countryside. Her father disapproved of this idea, but he did allow her to go and board with the Sisters of St Joseph so that she could acquire some extra education. She was still there when, in Lent 1825, a mission was announced in Sablières, the first since the Revolution. She went home to take part in it.

One of the priests who preached the mission was a man named Jean Terme who had recently founded a community of Sisters to teach in the parochial school at Aps, where he was parish priest. Marie-Victoire eventually overcame her father's resistance, and in January 1826 she became one of the first to join, taking the religious name Teresa (Thérèse). Six months later Fr Terme invited her and two other Sisters to take part in a project in which he was involved in nearby La Louvesc. In 1824 he and a number of other priests had been sent to the area by their bishop to do missionary work among the peasants and to look after the shrine of St John Francis Regis (31 Dec.), which was a popular place of pilgrimage. It soon became obvious that accommodation was badly needed for the women pilgrims. So a hostel was opened, and it was this that Teresa and her companions came to look after.

Things went well at first. Despite the sort of difficulties that attend most beginnings, not to mention the climate, which at four thousand feet could be fierce, the community began to grow. In 1828, recognizing that she had "a sound head, sound judgment and a power of spiritual discrimination" (adding, characteristically for the time, "rare in a woman"), Fr Terme made Teresa, who was still only twenty-three, superior of the community. Then, in the following year came an important turning-point. Fr Terme went to make a retreat at the Jesuit house near Le Puy and came back with his head full of a new idea. In addition to their other work, the Daughters of St Regis (as the Sisters were then called) should start giving retreats for women. Even though this did not involve giving spiritual direction, which was still the preserve of priests, it was a remarkably novel idea for the time. And it was an immediate success, especially among the country women. But on 12 December 1834 Fr Terme died. This was a serious blow for the community and in particular for Teresa, who lost not only a valued friend and counsellor but also the guardian of the community's finances.

In the person of Jean Terme's successor, Fr François Renault, the Jesuits, who had taken over the shrine and parish of La Louvesc, separated the work of teaching from that of retreat-giving. Twelve Sisters, headed by Teresa, were withdrawn from the Daughters of St Regis to form a separate community, with a new Rule and a distinct habit. They were known as the Sisters of the Retreat, and later as Religious of the Cenacle. They began immediately to give retreats according to the method of St Ignatius (31 July), receiving such a positive response that it soon became necessary to build a new house and church. All went well until the community's source of funds for these and other works failed, leaving the Sisters with enormous debts and no means of paying them. In October 1837, accepting the word of a member of the community who exaggerated the extent of the debts, Fr Renault humiliated Teresa by handing her a sheaf of bills as "a bouquet" on her feast-day. Blaming herself for what had happened and accepting the humiliation, Teresa resigned as superior. With the approval of the bishop of Viviers, Fr Renault appointed in her place a wealthy widow, Vicomtesse de La Villeurnoy, who was styled "superior general, foundress." She had joined the community less than a month before.

From this point the development of the Congregation of Our Lady of the Cenacle, as it soon came to be called, did not run entirely smoothly. Mme de La Villeurnoy, who seems to have understood little about the religious life and less about finance, dug the community even further into debt and was removed from her post eleven months later. In her place the community elected Charlotte Contenet, a good religious, more experienced and with many fine qualities, who had visions of taking the Congregation into the major cities of France. She also had ideas about the type of religious needed for this, and no fewer than nine of the original Sisters were dismissed. Teresa could not conveniently be dismissed because, under the terms of Jean Terme's will, she was joint-owner with one other Sister of the house in which they were all living. But for the next thirteen years she was given, and quietly accepted, mainly manual work in the house or garden that had nothing to do with the chosen apostolate of the Congregation. She was sent to Lyons in 1842 when the Congregation wanted to make a foundation there, but only to help with the heavy cleaning and then, when the project failed, to look after the house. In 1843, in the face of competition and at half the asking price, she managed to purchase another property at La Fourvière, above the city. Charlotte Contenet's surprise was obviously genuine, but it suggests that she really had no idea of Teresa's capabilities.

There was trouble of a different kind when Charlotte died in 1851. Mother de Larochenégly was elected superior general, but her assistant, Mother Anaïs de Saint-Privat, refused to accept this and effectively led the Sisters at the recently founded Paris house into schism. In March 1854 Teresa was sent to Paris to bring about a reconciliation. Although Anaïs and four of the Sisters preferred to leave the Congregation others stayed, and three of the four later returned. Teresa remained in charge of the community for a while and then returned to her place in the background, emerging only on one or two occasions to help with a new foundation. The difference was that she was respected now, and the bishop of Viviers finally confirmed that the two and only founders of the Congregation were Jean Terme and Teresa Couderc.

She was happy to further the work of the Congregation in this way from a hidden vantage point. All that she had suffered during the middle years of her life had left her not embittered but with a powerful sense of the meaning of suffering and of her place in the redemptive scheme of things. "God has always given me peace of soul," she once said, "the grace to leave myself in his hands and to want nothing but to love him and be ever closer to him." She could not hide what she was, however, and those who knew her recognized her *bonté*—her innate goodness. A photograph taken of her in the mid-1870s when she was about seventy shows a strong, intelligent face with a generous mouth, intense, penetrating eyes, and a gently astute expression.

Toward the end of her life she was very deaf, and rheumatism and arthritis left her in constant pain and discomfort. And to failing health was added the sorrow caused her by the Franco-Prussian war of 1870-1. She had to bear spiritual dryness and depression but never asked to be released from them. Her life was based on acceptance, and she united her suffering to that of the souls in purgatory, of whom she became intensely aware toward the end. She died at Fourvière on 26 September 1885, surrounded by members of the community, and was buried, at her request, in the cemetery at La Louvesc. In 1885 there were twelve Cenacles, nine in France and three in Italy. Today there are more than sixty in fourteen countries. Teresa Couderc was beatified in 1951 and canonized in 1970.

English biographies by C. C. Martindale (1921); E. Surles (1951); A. Wainewright (n.d.). In French see "E. M. I." (1911); H. Perroy (1928; Eng. trans., 1960); S. Dehin (1947). See also P. Vernion, *Le Cénacle et son message* (1948); E. Hugon, *The Spirituality of Mother Thérèse Couderc* (n.d.); G. Longhaye, *La Société de Notre Dame du Cénacle* (1898); M. de Sailly, *J. P. E. Terme* (1913).

Bd Caspar Stanggassinger (1871-99)

Caspar, the second of sixteen children, was born at Berchtesgaden in Bavaria on 12 January 1871. As a child he manifested an unusual degree of religious awareness, combined with extraordinary singlemindedness. From a very young age he announced that he was going to be a priest, and he was only ten when he entered the junior seminary at Freising. Study did not come easily to him, and his father warned him that unless he did well he would have to leave. He took this to heart, and those who taught him, as well as his companions, were impressed by his determination and by the dedication with which he followed the régime of prayer and study. When he was sixteen, having discussed the matter with his confessor, he made a vow of perpetual chastity. Two years later, in 1889, he consecrated himself to the Sacred Heart of Jesus in thanksgiving for his quick and complete recovery from a serious illness. Then, in 1890 he entered the seminary of Munich-Freising and on 2 April 1892 received the tonsure and the four minor orders. All seemed set for his ordination. That summer, however, he went on a pilgrimage to the Marian shrine at Altötting. While he was there he felt a strong call to join the Redemptorists, inspired, no doubt, by his spiritual director, who was himself a Redemptorist.

With characteristic decisiveness and despite the opposition of his father, Caspar went immediately to the Redemptorist novitiate at Gars. Following a self-imposed programme reminiscent of that of St John Berchmans (13 Aug.), who told himself, "I can, I will, I must be a saint," he was professed on 16 October 1893 and ordained on 16 June 1895. His great desire was to join the first band of Redemptorist missionaries in Brazil, but he was sent instead to teach future missionaries at the minor seminary and missionary school in Dürrnberg. If he was disappointed he did not show it. Instead he threw himself into a heavy schedule of teaching and counselling in the seminary and pastoral work in the surrounding villages, living all the while an intense prayer life centred on the Eucharist. He remained in Dürrnberg until the summer of 1899, when he was sent to be director of the Redemptorists' newly-opened seminary at Gars. Two months later, he suffered an acute attack of peritonitis, which, in those pre-penicillin days, proved fatal. He died, aged twenty-eight, on 26 September. He was beatified by Pope John Paul II on 24 April 1988.

See *Bibl.SS.*, 11, 1361-2; D. M. Cummings, *A Shining Light* (1963); K. Büche, *Kaspar Stanggassinger* (1968); O. Weiss, *Sel. Kaspar Stanggassinger* (1988); F. Baumann in *Lexikon für Theologie und Kirche*, 11, 1017.

27

ST VINCENT DE PAUL, *Founder* (1581-1660)

Vincent was born at Pouy (now Saint-Vincent-de Paul), in the Landes of south-western France near Dax, in 1581. He was the third of six children in a family of Gascon peasants (the particle *de* is not a sign of any connection with the nobility, and in fact the name is more correctly spelled not de Paul but Depaul, which is how Vincent always signed himself). As a boy he spent much of his time working in the fields, but in 1595 he went to train for the priesthood at the Franciscan college in Dax. As things turned out he did not spend long at the college. A judge in Pouy named De Comet noticed the extraordinary progress he was making in his studies and engaged him as a resident tutor for his children. Vincent nevertheless continued his training somehow and on 20 December 1596 received the tonsure and minor orders. He went next to the university of Toulouse for his theological studies and was ordained at the unusually young age of not quite twenty on 23 September 1600. After his ordination he continued to study theology in Toulouse, obtaining his degree as bachelor of theology in 1604.

There is still disagreement about exactly what happened next. Early in his career he was a court chaplain, living on the revenues from a commendatory abbey until he was falsely accused of stealing and underwent some sort of religious conversion. Chronologically that would present no problem in itself. However, two letters survive in which Vincent describes how he was travelling from Marseilles to Narbonne in July 1605 when the ship was attacked by pirates, who took the passengers prisoner. Having spent two years as a slave in Tunisia, Vincent escaped with his third and last master, whom he had converted to Christianity. The two managed to cross the Mediterranean in a rowing boat, arriving at Aigues-Mortes in Provence on 28 April 1607. From there they went to Rome, where Vincent remained for a year. There is no doubt that the account poses problems, and many critics dismiss it as legendary. But if it is, there is no really satisfactory explanation as to why it was invented, presumably by Vincent—the letters are universally accepted as authentic.

What does seem certain is that Vincent spent a year in Rome, possibly studying, before he returned somewhat disappointed to France. Back in Paris he joined the priests who had gathered round his friend and mentor Pierre (later Cardinal) de Bérulle, one of the major figures of the French religious renaissance of the seventeenth century, who in 1611 established the Congregation of the Oratory in France. Following Bérulle's advice, in May 1612 Vincent became parish priest of Clichy on the northern outskirts of Paris. And in the following year, again guided by Bérulle, he entered the employ of the powerful Gondi family as tutor to their eldest son, Pierre, whose brother Paul was to become well known as the ambitious Cardinal de Retz.

At this point it becomes difficult to continue with a strictly chronological account of Vincent's life. The numerous charitable works for which he is now remembered were not the fruit of long consideration and careful planning. With immense energy and with selfless commitment to those he wished to help he responded to the needs of the moment. And, which is as important if not more so, he inspired others to respond. There seems to have been a cooling off in his relationship with Bérulle in about 1618. It is not clear why, but perhaps the two men did not see eye to eye on the direction Vincent felt his life should take. In any case, he chose another director. It was also about this time that he came to know St Francis de Sales (24 Jan.), whose writings, especially the *Introduction à la vie dévote* and the *Traité de l'amour de Dieu*, had a strong influence on him.

Vincent remained nominally with the Gondi for twelve years, combining the duties of tutor with those of chaplain to the many peasants on their estates. But it was during a six-month period spent as parish priest at Châtillon-les-Dombes in 1617 that he established the first of the many organizations that are associated with him. He had been in Châtillon for less than a month when he was told of a local family that had no help at all at a time when all its members had fallen ill. An appeal to the parish produced an immediate response—and far more help than was needed. Vincent realized that in a few days time the offers of help would subside and the family would be back where it started. So he decided to establish a confraternity of caring individuals who would commit themselves to taking it in turns to help the sick poor of the parish. The first *Charité*, the all-female members of which were known as "Servants of the Poor," came into being on 20 August 1617. Three months later Vincent produced the Rule, which had the approval of the archbishop of Lyons. Into it he wove the fundamental principles of his own spirituality: to see Christ in the poor and to become holy through the practice of a personal charity that takes a person spiritually and materially into the very hovels of the poor. Once he had returned to Paris, he began to found *Charités* in the many villages on the Gondi estates.

Vincent had hoped to have male and female *Charités* working side by side, but in the end he had to settle, in his lifetime at least, for women only. (The men's branch was reconstituted in 1833 by Emanuel Bailly, with the writer and historian Frédéric Ozanam [beatified in 1997; 8 Sept.] as one of its founder members. Frédéric was the prime mover when what is today called the Society of St Vincent de Paul was established later in the same year.) But men were not, as a result, left out of Vincent's scheme of things. In 1625 he founded a society of priests known variously as the Priests of the Mission, Vincentians, and Lazarists. He had first seen the need some years before when a sermon he preached at Folleville made such an impact that there were not enough confessors to handle the mass of penitents. Mme Gondi offered financial support for any community that would undertake to preach regularly to the peasants on the Gondi estates. At first Vincent was reluctant to accept, but by 1618 he and a small group of like-minded priests were going from village to village conducting regular missions.

The venture was so successful that within seven years the Gondi were willing to put up enough capital to place it on a permanent footing. The archbishop of Paris provided an empty building in the rue St Victor, and on 17 April 1625 Vincent signed a contract with the Gondi. This required the priests to live a common life, forgo ecclesiastical dignities and responsibilities, and preach in country villages only; in addition they were expected to look after the spiritual welfare of convicts and in the summer, when the peasants were out in the fields, to teach the catechism in the parish churches. One of the very earliest Congregations whose members did not take vows, the Congregation of the Mission was approved by the archbishop of Paris on 26 April 1626. By the time it was approved by Pope Urban VIII (1623-44) on 12 January 1632, the community had been given larger accommodation in the priory of Saint-Lazare, which became one the great centres of spiritual renewal in France. Realizing how important the training of priests was, Vincent agreed when the archbishop of Paris asked him to train the diocesan seminarians at Saint-Lazare. And as the community grew the work diversified. Vincent accepted calls from abroad, and work was undertaken with slaves and convicts as well as with ordinary workers. For the latter he persuaded Philippe-Emmanuel de Gondi, who was *général des galères*, to build a hospice in Marseilles for galley-workers.

Meanwhile the *Charités* had begun to multiply as parishes took up the idea. When they reached Paris, as they did in 1629, and other cities, the membership multiplied, and the Servants of the Poor became *Dames de Charité*, or Ladies of Charity. The most significant of the urban associations was that of the Hôtel-Dieu in Paris, for which Vincent waived the principle of parochiality. Founded in 1634, this was the organization from which he received the most solid support for his many charitable projects. Its members were women from all walks of life, including many members of the Parisian nobility.

For a variety of reasons, not all the middle-class Parisian women who joined the *Dames de Charité* were able to carry out personally the work to which their association was committed. So, acting once again to fill a need, Vincent founded yet another group, the *Filles de Charité* (Daughters of Charity). Initially these were young women from the country whose experience of life was closer to that of the poor and the sick to whom they wished to devote themselves. At first Vincent simply assigned them to the various urban *Charités*. Then in 1633 he decided they should have some training and invited an aristocratic widow, Louise de Marillac (15 Mar.), to collaborate with him. In November 1633 she took four young women into her home. By the following July there were twelve of them, and at this point Vincent and Louise began to think in terms of a new Order.

Vincent was adamant that the Sisters should not be religious, with all that meant in terms of vows, enclosure, and so on. This was a bold step at a time when all women religious were enclosed. But he had seen the restrictions enclosure placed on Francis de Sales's Visitation Sisters and was in no doubt: "When you leave your prayer to care for a sick person, you leave God for God: to care for a sick person *is* to pray." And he would remind the Sisters: "For a monastery you have the homes of the sick and that of your superior; for your cell, a rented room; for your chapel, the parish church; for a cloister, the streets of the city; for enclosure, obedience. . . . Fear of God is your grill, and modesty your veil." Even today, the Sisters of Charity make private vows, which they renew each year. The young Congregation flourished, and as it expanded it found new fields of activity—in hospitals, with foundlings and orphans, in prisons, with the old, with the war-wounded. It was approved by the archbishop of Paris in 1646 and by the Holy See in 1668, eight years after Vincent's death.

Vincent personally made an enormous contribution to the renewal of the clergy in seventeenth-century France. Young ordinands were so inspired by the spiritual exercises he led for them, first in the diocese of Beauvais and later in Paris, that they asked for weekly follow-up meetings once they were ordained. The first of Vincent's Tuesday conferences took place in 1633, and they continued until his death. During this time he influenced the spiritual development of more than 250 young priests, including Jean-Jacques Olier, founder of the seminary of Saint-Sulpice. In particular, he was concerned to encourage a simpler, more practically oriented style of preaching. With the Priests of the Mission he also became involved in work for seminarians. And in a wider context, at the request of Anne of Austria, who was regent from 1643 to 1661 during the minority of her son, Louis XIV (1643-1715), he became a member of the so-called Council of Conscience. Established in 1643 and presided over by Anne's prime minister, Cardinal Jules Mazarin, this five-member commission was concerned with such matters as the appointment of worthy and suitable bishops and the bestowal and transfer of certain benefices. Vincent clashed openly with Mazarin, who frequently made decisions with purely political ends in view. Mazarin retaliated by increasing the length of time between council meetings, while continuing to promote his *protégés*. Vincent made matters worse for himself in 1649 when he suggested to the queen that for the sake of the country she should distance herself from Mazarin. In 1652 he was dropped from the council.

During the same period Vincent actively opposed the teaching of the Jansenists. Basing his ideas on a narrow reading of St Augustine (28 Aug.) on the subject of grace, the bishop of Ypres, Cornelius Jansen, taught that all human beings are predestined to heaven or hell and that only a chosen few are saved. Introduced into France by the abbot of Saint-Cyran, Jean Duvergier de Hauranne, and by his *protégé*, Antoine Arnauld, this teaching with its coldly austere piety and morality found its spiritual home at the convent of Port-Royal-des-Champs, outside Paris. The issue split the country down the middle, and it is not surprising that Vincent became involved. He and the abbot of Saint-Cyran had met thirty years earlier at the house of Bérulle, where they had become close friends. But Vincent could not allow friendship to blind him to the dangerously élitist character of Jansenist teaching. He always distinguished between a man and his ideas, but having failed to bring the abbot round by means of discussion and friendly persuasion, he went on the offensive. He was one of the moving spirits behind the petition the French bishops sent to Pope Innocent X (1644-55) asking him to condemn five particular propositions taken from Jansen's *Augustinus*. The pope complied on 13 May 1653, and the condemnation was confirmed three years later by Alexander VII (1655-67). The affair dragged on into the next century, but for the next few years Vincent was mainly concerned, in a spirit of charity, to win acceptance for the papal decision.

In Vincent's own teaching it is possible to recognize a number of influences. Strongest are the Christian humanism of his great friend St Francis de Sales, the contemplative spirituality of Bérulle, and the asceticism of St Ignatius (31 July). But together they emerge from the prism of his personality and experience as something new: simple, practical, and directed to the salvation of souls.

In 1656 Vincent was attacked by a fever that he could not shake off. He developed pains and then ulcers in his legs, so that he was unable to walk. The ulcers worsened toward the end of 1659, and on 27 September 1660 he died. The bishop who preached at his funeral said of Vincent that although he came from the country he was far from being a "simple rustic" and that in his lifetime he "changed the face of the Church." A cult developed almost immediately, and Vincent was beatified in 1729; he was canonized in 1737, and on 12 May 1885 Pope Leo XIII (1878-1903) named him universal patron of all works of charity. By the time of his death he had established a pattern for practical charitable work at parish level that is still being followed three hundred years later. His legacy continues in two worldwide orders, the Vincentians and the Daughters of Charity of St Vincent de Paul, and at parish level in the lay confraternity known as the Society of St Vincent de Paul.

The earliest biography is L. Abelly, *La Vie du Vénérable Serviteur de Dieu, Vincent de Paul* (1664; n.e., 1891). By 1986 there were four hundred; among the most recent are those by P. Coste (1932; Eng. trans., 1934-5); J. Calvet (1948; Eng. trans., 1952); L. von Matt (1959; Eng. trans., 1960); L. Chierotti (1960); H. Daniel-Rops (1961); J.-F. Six (1980). For St Vincent's works see P. Coste (ed.), *Correspondance, Entretiens, Documents* (1920-5—a final, fifteenth volume is in preparation); J. Leonard (ed.), *The Conferences of St Vincent de Paul to the Sisters of Charity* (1938-40); *idem.*, *St Vincent de Paul and Mental Prayer* (1925). See also *Bibl.SS.*, 12, 1155-68 (which has a good bibliography of specific aspects of St Vincent's life, including the question of the captivity in Tunisia); *H.S.S.C.*, 8, pp. 275-84; *O.D.S.*, pp. 481-2; J. E. Rybolt and F. Ryan, *Vincent de Paul and Louise de Marillac: rules, conferences, writings* (1995).

Unfortunately there is no portrait of Vincent as a young or middle-aged man. However, the one executed at the end of his life by Simon François of Tours (the original is thought to be in the convent of the Daughters of Charity at Moutier-Saint-Jean) fits well with the description of him given by his first biographer, Louis Abelly. "He was of medium height and well made. His slightly balding head was large but in proportion with the rest of his body; he had a broad, imposing forehead, and his face was neither too full nor too bony. His expression was gentle, . . . his bearing dignified and his dignity full of kindness. He was simple and frank, always very friendly and approachable, with a natural goodness and warmth. Sanguine and quick-tempered, he had a strong, robust complexion."

Monsieur Vincent, a screen version of Vincent's life directed by Maurice Cloche, was first released in France in 1947.

St Sigebert, *Martyr* (637)

Sigebert was the name of several East Anglian and East Saxon kings during the seventh century. Not to be confused with Sigebert Sanctus (the Good), who ruled the East Saxons, brought St Cedd (26 Oct.) to Essex, and died sometime between 653 and 664, this Sigebert is thought to have been the stepson of Redwald, king of East Anglia. There was constant friction between the two men, and eventually Sigebert was driven into exile. He spent his years of exile in Gaul, remaining there not only for the rest of Redwald's reign but also during that of his brother, Earpwald. During this time he was baptized and became a fervent and committed Christian.

Earpwald was assassinated in 629. There followed a three-year interregnum, at the end of which Sigebert was asked to accept the throne as Earpwald's successor. He did, and for the next several years he worked hard to convert his people to Christianity. This was not easy, but he enjoyed the cooperation of St Felix of Dunwich (8 Mar.) and of the Irish missionary St Fursey (16 Jan.). With Sigebert's support the latter established a monastery at Cnobheresburg (perhaps Burgh Castle in Suffolk). After some years Sigebert decided to abdicate in favour of a relative (possibly a brother-in-law) named Ecgric. He then entered the monastery at Betrichsworth (later Bury St Edmunds).

In 636 East Anglia was attacked by Penda, the pagan king of Mercia. Sigebert was asked to leave his monastery in order to lead an East Anglian army against Penda. Reluctantly, he agreed to do so, but only on condition, according to one account, that he himself would go into battle unarmed—"he did not wish," as Bede put it, "to carry so much as a stick in his hand." The inevitable happened, and on 27 September 637 Sigebert died on the battlefield, together with Ecgric. His former subjects acclaimed him as a martyr, and he was commemorated on 27 September, although some English menologies mention him on 25 January. A series of letters to St Desiderius of Cahors (15 Nov.) has been wrongly attributed to him. The writer was almost certainly Sigebert III of Austrasia (631-56).

AA.SS., Oct., 12, pp. 892-904; F. M. Stenton, *Anglo-Saxon England* (1950); Bede, *H.E.*, p. 116; W. Hunt, *The English Church from its Foundation to the Norman Conquest, 597-1066* (1931), pp. 64-6; *Bibl.SS.*, 11, 1035.

Bd Laurence of Ripafratta (*c.* 1373-1457)

With the removal of the papacy from Rome to something like siege conditions in Avignon, and the Great Schism of the West, during which two and some-times three individuals vied with one another for the papal office, the four-teenth century was a difficult one for the Church. Its various institutions inevi-tably suffered, and for the religious Orders the malaise was compounded, espe-cially in Italy, by outbreaks of plague, which decimated their communities. But despite the decline there were signs of reform. In Bd Raymund of Capua (5 Oct.) the Dominicans found a strong reforming master general, and among those who, along with Bd John Dominici (10 June), supported him in his work was Laurence of Ripafratta.

Little information has survived about Laurence's background and early life. He seems to have been born on 23 March 1373 (or 1374) at Ripafratta, near Pisa. He started training for the priesthood and was already a deacon when he entered the Dominican Order in Pisa. From there he went to Cortona, where he did his novitiate, and then to Fabriano for a brief spell, but most of his life was spent at Pistoia. After he had completed his studies he preached for some years, although this was not something for which he had any particular talent. On the other hand, he was a good teacher and had exactly the balance of qualities needed in a prior or a master of novices in the priory at Cortona. He served more than once in both capacities, upholding rigorous observance while recognizing and making use of the adaptability of the Order's Constitutions. If for nothing else he deserves our gratitude for encouraging Fra Angelico (18 Feb.) to paint—on the ground that preaching can be done as well through pictures as through the spoken word: "The most persuasive tongue becomes silent in death," he told him, "but your heavenly pictures will go on speaking of religion and virtue throughout the ages." Eventually he was made vicar general of the priories that had adopted the reform. Almost immediately there was a serious outbreak of plague, and his administrative duties were allowed to wait while he turned his attention to the needs of the sick and their families.

When he died at an advanced age he was widely and genuinely mourned. The commune asked if it could do the funeral at its own expense, and a fine marble tomb was erected in Pistoia. One of Laurence's former novices, St Antoninus (10 May), who was by then bishop of Florence, spoke of the power of his words and example, adding: "I weep also for my own loss, for never again shall I receive those tender letters with which he used to stir up my fervour in the duties of this pastoral office." Miracles were reported at his tomb, and his cult was confirmed by Pope Pius IX in 1851.

V. Marchese, *Cenni storici del beato Lorenzo di Ripafratta* (1851); a short Life by M. de Waresquiel (1907); J. Procter, *Short Lives of the Dominican Saints* (1902), pp. 38-41; S. Orlandi, *Il beato Lorenzo da Ripafratta, campione della riforma domenicana* (1956); I. P.Grossi, *Il beato Lorenzo da Ripafratta, domenicano* (1957); *Bibl.SS.*, 8, 144-5.

ST WENCESLAS (over page)
Red banner with gold staff and white eagle, on silver field.
Also shown as a king or warrior in armour; with Boleslas kneeling to beg his pardon;
reaping corn for altar-bread.

255

28

ST WENCESLAS, Martyr (c. 907-29)

When Wenceslas (Václav—the name means "greater glory") became duke of Bohemia in 922, Christianity was still not firmly established in the country. Sixty years earlier the brothers SS Cyril and Methodius (14 Feb.) had laid the foundations for a distinctly Slav Christianity, but a Latin strain emanating from the Regensburg diocese also had some influence. And meanwhile paganism still survived under the surface. Wenceslas' grandparents, Borivoy and St Ludmila (16 Sept.), had converted, and his father, Ratislav, had married a nominally Christian woman named Drahomíra, who belonged to the western Slav Stodorané in present-day Brandenburg. But this did not automatically attract all their subjects to the Church, and when Wenceslas succeeded his father there were powerful interests, supported if not led by his mother, who actively opposed the new religion.

Wenceslas, the eldest son, was born near Prague in about 907. His grandmother, Ludmila, made herself responsible for his education, enlisting the help of her chaplain, a personal disciple of St Methodius. Although this made for bad relations with Drahomíra it did secure Wenceslas a good moral and scholastic education. By the time he was sent to study with a Slav priest at Budec he is said to have "understood Latin as if he were a bishop and read Slavonic with ease." He was only fourteen when his father died in battle against the Magyars in February 921. Drahomíra, backed by anti-Christian elements in the nobility and no doubt inspired to some extent by her jealousy of Ludmila, assumed the regency and pursued a secularist policy.

When Ludmila, fearing that religion might be completely wiped out, began to encourage Wenceslas to grasp the reins of government himself, two of the nobles murdered her in her palace at Tetín. But if they hoped that this would deprive Wenceslas of support, they were disappointed. The reliablility of the details in accounts of what happened next is uncertain, but there is no doubt that Wenceslas had some backing. In about 922, by which time he was gaining support from people alienated by Drahomíra's extravagant behaviour, he was proclaimed duke, and some eighteen months after that Drahomíra was banished to Budec. In 925, as if confirming his independence and his authority, he brought the body of his grandmother back from Tetín to St George's church in Prague. At this point he had full control of western Bohemia, the western part of central Bohemia, and southern Bohemia. Unfortunately his brother Boleslas was trying to create a power base for himself in the east, with its centre at Stará Boleslav.

Young as he was, Wenceslas proved to be an upright and decisive ruler. And although he relied much on the clergy for advice, his mother, whom he recalled from her banishment in Budec, seems to have made no further attempt to oppose him. His domestic policy was based on a determination to establish the rule of law, to improve educational standards, and to build up the religious faith of his people. His foreign policies reflected a strong desire to open Bohemia up to the West and at the same time to protect it from Western aggression. But it was his acknowledgment of the German king, Henry I the Fowler (919-36), as the successor of Charlemagne and his own overlord, that provoked some of the nobles, especially those who resented his reliance on the clergy and the severity with which he dealt with disorders among the nobility. When Wenceslas married and had a son, this party found a natural supporter in his brother Boleslas, who had just lost his place in the line of succession to the dukedom.

In September 929 (according to the earliest local sources, although the Saxon chronicler Widukind says 935), Boleslas invited Wenceslas to go to Stará Boleslav to celebrate the feast of SS Cosmas and Damian (now 26, but then 27 Sept.) and the dedication of the church there. After the celebrations Wenceslas was warned that he was in danger but refused to take any notice, instead proposing a toast to "St Michael, whom we pray to guide us to peace and eternal joy." Next morning, on his way to Matins, he met Boleslas and thanked him for his hospitality. In response, Boleslas struck him and while the brothers struggled friends of Boleslas ran up and killed Wenceslas. As he fell at the chapel door, he murmured, "Brother, may God forgive you."

Although his death had nothing directly to do with religion, he was immediately venerated as a martyr. Initially his mother, who was not involved in his death, took charge of the body. Eventually, however, his relics were translated, possibly by Boleslas himself, to St Vitus' church in Prague. There is evidence that his feast was celebrated from 985. The shrine became a place of pilgrimage, and from the beginning of the eleventh century Svaty Václav was regarded as the patron saint of Bohemia. The legends that attached themselves to him at this time are typical of the hagiography of the period, but for all their exaggeration they describe the epitome of the Christian prince. More recently, as patron of the modern state of Czechoslovakia (now the Czech Republic and Slovakia), Wenceslas became a focus for Czech and Slovak nationalism. A series of wall paintings in the castle at Karlstejn, south-west of Prague, emphasises this side of his cult, as does the sixteenth-century series in the chapel dedicated to him in the metropolitan church at Prague Castle (see below).

Despite the popular Christmas carol "Good King Wenceslas" there has been no widespread popular devotion to St Wenceslas in England. His feast was introduced with the Roman Missal. The words of the carol were written by the nineteenth-century hymn-writer J. M. Neale to fit the tune of a thirteenth-century spring carol, *Tempus adest floridum*; they do not relate to any known incident in the saint's life and exemplify the Christian ideals of the nineteenth century rather than of the tenth.

The *First Old Slavonic Legend* was composed shortly after his death, as was the Latin *Crescente fide christiana*, the probable source of the late-tenth-century *Christian's Legend*, and a *Second Old Slavonic Legend*, dwelling more on miracles, dates from the eleventh century. A new account in rhyming prose for monastic use, *Oportet nos fratres* dates from the end of the eleventh century, and the popular hymn *Svaty Václave* from the twelfth. See *AA.SS.*, Sept., 7, pp. 770-844; *Propylaeum*, pp. 421-2. In *Anal.Boll.* 48 (1929), pp. 218-21, where he discusses the available literature in Czech, P. Peeters points out that much of it is racially and politically biased. See also P. Devos, "Le dossier de S. Wenceslas dans un manuscrit du XIIIᵉ siècle," in *Anal.Boll.* 72 (1953), pp. 87-131; F. Dvornik, *St Wenceslas of Bohemia* (Eng. trans., 1929); C. Parrott, "St Wenceslas of Bohemia," in *History Today* 16 (1966), pp. 225-33; *O.D.S.*, pp. 490-1; *Bibl.SS.*, 12, 991-1000; *H.S.S.C.*, 5, pp. 248-55 (the last two have substantial biographies in Czech); Jöckle, pp. 469-70.

The iconography is huge and tied directly to the growth of the cult. From very early on St Wenceslas was depicted on coins, and then, in the twelfth and thirteenth centuries, his face—bearded as well as beardless—began to appear on official seals. Later he was shown as an armed knight, a tradition that culminated in the huge twentieth-century equestrian statue that stands at the top of Wenceslas Square in Prague. The series of wall paintings referred to above is on the upper walls of the Gothic chapel of St Vitus. Recently restored, the twenty-four paintings were executed in two stages, begun in the 1470s and finished in the 1500s; the later phase is identified as the work of the Master of the Leitmeritz Altarpiece. A codex with copies of the paintings, written and drawn by Matthias Hutsky of Krivoklát, who called himself "master painter of Prague," was dedicated in 1585 to Archduke Ferdinand II of Tyrol and is now in the Austrian National Library, Vienna (Cod. Ser. n. 2633). The accompanying text is based on the work of the Czech humanist, historian, and bishop Jan Dubravius (? 1486-1553). The codex has been published in facsimile as *The Life and Martyrdom of St Wenceslas, Prince of Bohemia, in Historic Pictures: Prague 1585* (1997).

ST LAURENCE RUIZ AND FIFTEEN COMPANIONS,
Martyrs (from 1633 to 1637)

A general account of the persecutions in Japan will be found as the first entry under 6 February in the present work. The sixteen martyrs celebrated on this day suffered there between 1633 and 1637 and were beatified by Pope John Paul II in Manila in 1981, the venue reflecting the fact that Lorenzo Ruiz came from the Philippines and is the first Filipino saint. They were canonized on Mission Sunday 1987 and now have their own feast in the universal Calendar; their names and brief details are given separately here.

Laurence (Lorenzo) Ruiz was born to Christian parents in Manila but fled to Japan to escape an unjust charge in July 1636. As a Christian he and all the others were subject to the edict issued by Tokugawa Ieyasu in 1603. This banned Christianity and was followed in 1623 by another edict forcing all Japanese to make a public declaration of their adherence to the official state religion. Christians were required to trample on *fumie* (plaques imprinted with an image of the Virgin and Child). Refusal was punished by death, in the early stages generally by slow burning and then by the form of torture known as "the pit," followed by decapitation if the victims were still alive after some days. Laurence died in this manner on 28 September 1637.

The fifteen others were, in order of date of death:

Fr Dominic (Domingo) Ibañez de Erquicia, Spanish Dominican, 14 August 1633, with Francis Soyemon, Japanese Dominican auxiliary;

Fr James Kyushei Gorubioye Tomanga, Japanese Dominican, 17 August 1633, with Michael Kuribioye, Japanese lay catechist;

Fr Luke (Lucas) del Espíritu Santo, Spanish Dominican, 19 October 1633, with Matthew Kohioye, Japanese Dominican auxiliary;

Magdalene of Nagasaki, Japanese Augustinian tertiary, 15 October 1634;

Fr Giordano Ansalone, Italian Dominican, between 11 and 17 November 1634, with Fr Thomas Hioji Rokuzayemon, Japanese Dominican, and Marina of Omura, Japanese Dominican Tertiary;

Fr Antony (Antonio) González, Spanish Dominican, between 24 and 29 September 1637, with Fr Michael (Miguel) de Aozoaza, Spanish Dominican; Fr William (Guillaume) Courtet, French Dominican; Fr Vincent Shiwozuka, Japanese Dominican; Lazaro of Ktoto, Japanese layman.

These saints join the 231 other Catholics martyred in Japan in the sixteenth and seventeenth centuries and previously canonized.

For the bibliography see the general entry on the Martyrs of Japan, 6 Feb.

St Exsuperius of Toulouse, *Bishop* (*c.* 412)

A contemporary, St Paulinus of Nola (22 June), described Exsuperius as one of the most illustrious bishops of the Church in Gaul, and by the middle of the sixth century he was held in equal honour with St Saturninus (Sernin, 29 Nov.) in Toulouse. He was born probably sometime in the fourth century at Arreau, in the Hautes-Pyrénées, where there is a chapel dedicated to him. Few details of his career have survived. All that is known for certain is that he succeeded to the see of Toulouse in about 405 and that he completed the great church of Saint-Sernin begun by his predecessor, St Silvius. What has survived is a strong impression of his personality and particularly of the generosity that seems to have been its salient characteristic. His charity found ample scope not only at home—Gaul was overrun by the Vandals while he was bishop—but also abroad. St Jerome (30 Sept.), who dedicated his commentary on the book of Zechariah to Exsuperius in gratitude for gifts sent to monks in Egypt and Palestine, wrote of him: "To relieve the hunger of the poor he suffered it himself. . . . He gave his all to the poor of Christ. . . . His charity knew no bounds. It sought for objects in the most distant parts, and the solitaries of Egypt felt its effects." He is known to have sought the advice of Pope St Innocent I (401-17; 28 July) on a number of matters, including the canon of scripture. The list the pope sent him in reply was identical to the list as we know it today. Where and when Exsuperius died is not known for certain, though he may have been forced into exile toward the end of his life.

Strangely, St Exsuperius is not mentioned in the *Hieronymianum*, but the available details are in *AA.SS.*, Sept., 7, p. 623. See also *Bibl.SS.*, 5, 104; *D.T.C.*, 5, 2022-37; *F.E.*, 1, p. 307.

St Eustochium (*c.* 367-*c.* 419)

All that is known of Eustochium Julia comes from the letters of St Jerome (30 Sept.). The third of the four daughters of St Paula (26 Jan.) and her husband, Toxotius, she was about twelve when her father died in 379. After a period of profound mourning, Paula, who was herself only thirty-two, experienced a religious conversion. She joined the cenacle of a redoubtable Christian widow named Marcella (31 Jan.)—"the glory of the ladies of Rome," Jerome called her—and began to devote her life exclusively to prayer, penance, and works of charity. Eustochium was the only one of the four daughters to emulate her mother's new way of life, and as things turned out they were to remain together until Paula died.

The event that determined the course of their lives was the arrival in Rome in 382 of Jerome, under whose spiritual direction they placed themselves. Relatives were concerned that the austerities he encouraged were too severe for Eustochium. She was still only about fourteen or fifteen, and an uncle and aunt, Hymettius and Praetextata, tried to persuade her to take part in some of the ordinary pleasures of life. They were unsuccessful, and before long Eustochium had made a vow of perpetual virginity. She was the first young Roman noblewoman to do this, and to mark the occasion Jerome addressed to her his famous letter, "Concerning the Preservation of Virginity"—though with its passages of satire and its merciless criticism of certain consecrated virgins and priests, this letter was clearly intended for a wider audience. Another, more strictly personal letter, dated 29 June 384, has survived. In it Jerome reprimands her sharply for sending him some cherries, doves, and other items, which he clearly regarded as trivia.

Eustochium does not seem to have been permanently cast down by this. Her training had been entrusted to Marcella, who helped Paula through her grief and exercised a strong influence on her as well as on her daughter. But when Paula, along with a number of other women who aspired to the religious life, decided to accompany Jerome to Palestine, Eustochium opted to go with her mother. The group travelled to Antioch to meet up with Jerome, who was to prove a stimulating leader, giving learned disquisitions on all the places they visited. After a peripatetic period during which they went to Jerusalem and even as far as Egypt to visit the monks in the Nitrian desert, they settled down in Bethlehem in 386. Three communities of women were established, and Eustochium assisted Paula in the direction of these. She, like her mother, learned both Greek and Hebrew, and when Jerome's eyesight began to fail she was able to help him with his translation of the Bible. At their request he wrote commentaries on Paul's Epistles to the Galatians, the Ephesians, Titus, and Philemon, and he acknowledged their genuine learning by dedicating some of his other works to them—they were, he said, "more capable of forming a judgment on them than most men."

In 403 Paula fell ill, and Eustochium divided her time between caring for her and praying for her in the cave of the Nativity. When her mother eventually died on 26 January 404, the pain of separation and loss was terrible for Eustochium. Jerome said she was like "a baby weaned from her nurse," adding that she "could scarcely be drawn away from her mother." She did survive her grief, however, and assumed her mother's role as director of the communities, only to find them in serious debt. The situation was resolved thanks in part to the encouragement she received from Jerome, in part to her own quiet courage, and in part to funds brought by her niece, also named Paula, who had arrived from Rome to join the community. In 416 the monasteries were burned down and the inmates attacked by a group of thugs. Jerome, Eustochium, and Paula wrote to alert Pope St Innocent I (401-17; 28 July), and he in his turn reprimanded the bishop of Jerusalem for his failure to provide better security. But for Eustochium the damage was done. She did not really get over the shock, and she died in about 419. She was buried in the same tomb as her mother, near the cave of the Nativity. Jerome's grief is evident from at least three of his letters. The tomb is still there, but it is now empty. There was no early cult, and Eustochium's name features in only a few martyrologies. There was a renewal of interest in the sixteenth century when St Angela Merici (27 Jan.) founded the Ursuline Congregation—Paula and Eustochium are portrayed on the walls of the oratory of the Ursuline convent in Rome.

The relevant material is in *AA.SS.*, Sept., 7, pp. 630-45. See also F. Lagrange, *Histoire de Ste Paule* (1868); R. Genier, Ste Paule (1917); J. N. D. Kelly, *Jerome* (1975); *Bibl.SS.*, 5, 302-4. For the relevant letters of St Jerome, 22, 66, 108, 143, 151, 153, 154, see H. Hilberg (ed.) in *C.S.E.L.*, 54-6.

St Faustus of Riez, Bishop (*c.* 405-*c.* 490)

Faustus was born, perhaps in Britain as his contemporaries St Avitus and St Sidonius Apollinaris (21 Aug.) say but more proably in Brittany, in the early years of the fifth century. He is said to have begun his adult life as a lawyer, but he cannot have gone far in that profession because he became a monk at Lérins before its founder, St Honoratus (16 Jan.), left, and that was in 426. He was ordained to the priesthood and having lived an uneventful monastic life for about eight years was elected abbot in place of Honoratus' successor, St Maximus (27 Nov.), who had been made bishop of Riez. It was probably during this period that he defended the autonomy of the abbot in his own monastery against Theodore, bishop of Fréjus. Faustus was distinguished for his observance of the Rule, which won him the respect of many, including Honoratus and Sidonius Apollinaris. He was also known as a brilliant extempore preacher. In one of his letters Sidonius tells how he used to shout himself hoarse during Faustus' sermons—vocal approval and dissent were common in church in those days. After he had been abbot of Lérins for about twenty-five years Faustus replaced Maximus in the see of Riez. He was as diligent a bishop as he had been an abbot, continuing his austere way of life while tending to the needs of his diocese. He was particularly concerned for purity of doctrine and vigorously opposed both Arianism and the teachings of "that pestiferous teacher, Pelagius," who denied the existence of original sin and taught that human beings could attain salvation without the help of grace or the Church.

Faustus became involved in theological controversy himself in connection with heretical assertions made by a priest named Lucidus. Lucidus argued that salvation and damnation depend entirely on God's will regardless of anything the individual might do. When Faustus persuaded Lucidus of the flaws in his position, the bishops, who had assembled at Arles and then Lyons in 475 to deal with the problem, invited Faustus to write a treatise against predestinationism. Faustus in fact produced two treatises on free will and grace. While refuting Pelagianism and predestinationism, he ended up putting forward the so-called Semi-Pelagian error that although we need grace to accomplish good works we do not need it to initiate them. As soon as his treatises were published he was vehemently attacked, though the views they contain were not condemned until the Council of Orange in 529.

Opposition of a different, cruder kind came from Euric, king of the Arian Visigoths, who objected to Faustus' condemnation of Arianism. Although he had given Euric a certain amount of political support, Faustus was driven from his see in 478 and forced to live in exile until Euric died some years later. He then returned and took up his pastoral duties where he had left off. When he died, aged about ninety, he was genuinely mourned by his people, and a large basilica was built in his honour. He was one of the writers who helped to make Lérins famous, and some of his letters, sermons, and other works survive. He is not listed in the Roman Martyrology, but his cult is recognized as being very ancient.

AA.SS., Sept., 7, pp. 651-714; A. Koch, *Der hl. Faustus von Riez* (1895). For the works see *Vienna Corpus Scriptorum* (ed. A. Engelbrecht)—this edition is criticized by G. Morin in *Revue Bénédictine* 9 (1892), pp. 49-64, and 10 (1893), pp. 62-78. See also *Bibl.SS.*, 5, 495-6; *D.T.C.*, 5, 2101-5; *F.E.*, 1, p. 284.

St Annemund, *Bishop* (658)

Annemund belonged to a Gallo-Roman family, and his father, Sigon, was prefect in Lyons. He himself trained at the court of the Frankish king Dagobert I (629-39) and was an adviser to Dagobert's son, Clovis II (639-57). At some stage he became a priest, and he is next heard of as bishop of Lyons. He was already there when St Benedict Biscop (12 Jan.) came through the city on his first journey to Rome, accompanied by a young man who, according to Bede, pleased Annemund with his "wise conversation, the grace of his appearance, his eager manner and the maturity of his thoughts." This was Wilfrid (12 Oct.), later bishop of York. Annemund, who opened his house to the pair while they were in Lyons, even offered to adopt Wilfrid, give him his niece in marriage, and find him work of some kind. Wilfrid thanked him, but explained that he wanted to be a priest and was travelling to Rome with this in mind. At this Annemund gave the party all they needed for the remainder of their journey and begged Wilfrid to return through Lyons. Not only did Wilfrid do this, but he stayed for three years, during which he received the tonsure from Annemund. He might well have remained and become Annemund's successor had it not been for the bishop's sudden death. On 29 September 658, Annemund was killed by soldiers at Mâcon, or possibly Châlon-sur-Saône, in the disturbances that followed the death of Clovis II. Wilfrid, who was with him, offered to die with him, but when they heard he was a foreigner the soldiers let him go. According to Wilfrid's biographer, Eddius, the person ultimately responsible for the death of Annemund and nine other French bishops was the queen-regent, St Bathild (30 Jan.). There is no evidence for this, and it is highly improbable. Wilfrid helped to bury Annemund's body in Lyons and then left for England. Annemund was immediately venerated as a martyr.

The principal sources are Eddius' Life of St Wilfrid, and Bede. For a brief *passio* see *AA.SS.*, Sept., 7, pp. 720–48; *M.G.H., Scriptores merov.*, 6, p. 197ff. See also *Bibl.SS.*, 1, 1311.

St Lioba (782)

The Life by Rudolf of Fulda, on which much of our knowledge of St Lioba is based, was compiled from the recollections of four of her closest companions, Agatha, Thecla, Mary, and Eoliba. It paints a vivid and attractive portrait, free of many of the exaggerations that are normally found in hagiographical writings of this period. And it should conclusively demolish any idea that the involvement of women religious in missionary work is a purely nineteenth- and twentieth-century phenomenon. Lioba was born into a good Wessex family, and her mother, Aebba, was related to St Boniface (5 Jun.). She was baptized Trhûtgeba but came to be known as Liobgetha (Leofgyth), which was abbreviated to Lioba (the dear one). From an early age she went to be educated by the nuns, first at Minster-in-Thanet and then at Wimborne in Dorset, where she was eventually accepted, at her request, as a full member of the community. The two things that most impressed people about her at this stage were her single-mindedness and her enthusiasm for books and learning.

It is not known exactly how old she was in 722 or for how long she had been professed, but that was the year in which Boniface was consecrated bishop by Pope Gregory II (715–31) and sent to preach the gospel among the Saxons and

Thuringians. When news of his work filtered back to Wimborne, Lioba felt inspired to write to him as her kinsman:

I beg you of your kindness to remember your early friendship in the west country with my father, Dynna, who died eight years ago and from whose soul, therefore, I ask you not to withhold your prayers. I also commend to your memory my mother Aebba, who still lives, but painfully; she is, as you know, related to you. I am the only child of my parents and, unworthy though I be, I should like to look on you as my brother, for I can trust you more than anyone else of my kinsfolk. I send you this little gift [the letter itself or one of her own poems which she sends with it?] not because it is worth your consideration but simply so that you may have something to remind you of my humble self, and so not forget me when you are so far away; may it draw tighter the bond of true love between us for ever. I beseech you, dear brother, help me with your prayers against the attacks of the hidden enemy. I would ask you, too, if you would be so good as to correct this unlearned letter and not to refuse to send me a few kind words, which I eagerly look forward to as a token of your good will.

Clearly touched by her appeal, Boniface entered into a correspondence with Lioba, which continued over the years. Then in 748 he wrote to the abbess of Wimborne, St Tetta (12 Aug./12 Dec.), asking her if Lioba and a number of companions could come to help with the evangelization of Germany by founding some monasteries for women. Tetta sent no less than thirty nuns, among them St Thecla (15 Oct.), also related to Lioba, St Walburga (25 Feb.), and Lioba herself. Boniface settled them in a monastery to which they gave the name Tauberbischofsheim, which suggests that he may have given up his own house for them. Under Lioba's leadership it flourished, and she was soon sending out groups of nuns to found new houses. Even houses not founded directly from Tauberbischofsheim would ask for one of Lioba's nuns as abbess.

Rudolf of Fulda describes her at this time as so absorbed in her work that she appeared to have forgotten Wessex altogether. Physically she seems to have been very striking, and her personality was equally attractive—her patience, her intelligence, and her enormous warmth and kindness are mentioned in particular. The Rule followed in all her monasteries was that of St Benedict. Each day was a balanced mixture of prayer, especially the public prayer of the Church, manual work in the kitchen, bakehouse, brewery, or garden, and intellectual activity—all the nuns had to learn Latin, and the *scriptorium* was always busy. No Sister was allowed to engage in imprudent austerities, and Lioba insisted that all take the midday rest prescribed by the Rule, "for she said that by loss of sleep understanding was lost, especially in reading." She herself would spend the hour lying down while a novice read to her from the Bible, always remaining alert enough to correct any novice who, thinking she had gone to sleep, became careless about her pronunciation.

In all this the main purpose of the community was to provide spiritual support for the monks who worked in the countryside round about. But once people got to know Lioba she had a constant stream of people coming to her for help and advice, those with influence in both Church and State as well as men and women from the locality.

Before setting out on what turned out to be his last mission, to Holland in 754, Boniface, who must have been aware of the dangers he faced, came to say goodbye to Lioba and gave her his cowl. He had already recommended her to St Lull (16 Oct.), a monk of Malmesbury who was his right-hand man and would succeed him as bishop, and to the monks of Fulda. In particular he had asked the monks to bury her near him when she died so that they could await the resurrection together. After Boniface's death she was given the special permission to enter the abbey in order to visit his tomb and to attend services and conferences.

When, by now very old, she had been abbess of Tauberbischofsheim for twenty-eight years, she made sure that everything was in order in the monasteries under her care and then retired to the monastery of Schornsheim, four miles from Mainz. She went briefly to Aachen to visit her friend Bd Hildegard (30 April), Charlemagne's wife. As she left to return to Schornsheim, she said to the queen: "Farewell, precious part of my soul! May Christ our Creator and Redeemer grant that we may see each other without confusion of face in the day of judgment, for in this life we shall never more see each other." Shortly after this, in 782, she died and was buried in the abbey church at Fulda. Her relics were translated in 819 and again in 838, this time to the church of Mount St Peter. Her name appears in the martyrology of Rabanus Maurus as well as in certain ninth-century litanies. Despite her English origins her cult has always been greatest in Germany.

Rudolf of Fulda's Life is in *AA.SS.*, Sept., 7, pp. 748-69; for an English translation see C. H. Talbot, *Anglo-Saxon Missionaries in Germany* (1954); D. Whitelock, *English Historical Documents*, 1 (1968), p. 719. For Boniface's correspondence with St Lull see *Die Briefe des heiligen Bonifatius und Lullus* in *M.G.H.* (1916). See also W. Levison, *England and the Continent in the Eighth Century* (1946); *O.D.S.*, pp. 300-1, *H.S.S.C.*, 4, p. 97; *Bibl.SS.*, 8, 60-1.

Bd Bernardino of Feltre (1439-94)

Bernardino of Feltre was one of the great preachers of the fifteenth century and a practical if controversial economist. Born Martino Tomitani in Feltre near Venice in 1439, he was the eldest of ten children. His intellectual gifts were quickly recognized, and he received a good education, going in 1456 to the university of Padua to study law and philosophy. Almost immediately he came into contact with the Franciscan preacher and disciple of St Bernardino of Siena (13 May), St James of the March (28 Nov.). In May of the same year he joined the Friars Minor of the Observance, taking the name Bernardino after the recently canonized Sienese. The radical, uncompromising commitment that remained characteristic of him throughout his life is typified by a comment he made at this time about one of his great loves, music. It was, he said, "not suitable for those consecrated to God." He was ordained in 1463 and spent the next six years peacefully studying and praying. Then in 1469 the Venice chapter of the Order appointed him one of their preachers.

Bernardino was horrified. He had never preached in public before, he lacked self-confidence, and—which did not help—he was very short of stature: he used to sign himself "*piccolino e poverello*." However, making the sign of the cross on the young friar's lips, his spiritual director told him: "God will unlock your tongue, to show you that the gift of preaching is from him alone." When, carefully prepared, he went into the pulpit for the first time before a large congregation in Mantua, he was seized by panic and forgot everything he had planned to say. Remembering his patron St Bernardino, he abandoned his prepared ideas and began to preach eloquently about him. From then on he never prepared his sermons in the conventional way. He trusted instead to prayer, which he said was "a better preparation than study because it is both more efficacious and quicker."

For the next twenty-five years Bernardino travelled up and down Italy preaching as he went. At least 120 of his sermons have survived, so we know that his style was straightforward, unadorned—"ostentation never does any good," he said—and lively. In time he attracted an enormous following. In Florence and Pavia the congregation would overflow into the main *piazza*; in Padua and Feltre all the available accommodation would be booked far in advance of his coming; and on one occasion three thousand people walked through the night from Crema to Lodi, a distance of about twelve miles, in order to hear two of his sermons in succession. He was uncompromising, harsh even, in his denunciation of the failures of a society torn apart by war, political rivalries, violence, and corruption. Indeed, so vehement did this frail man, threatened by tuberculosis, become that there are at least two recorded instances of his breaking a blood vessel.

The fact that he soon made enemies among those, particularly in positions of power, who felt threatened by the accuracy of his criticisms, did not deter him. Nor did the attempts that were made on his life. Laws were soon being repealed or enacted as a result of his intervention. It was because of him, for example, that men and women were separated for the first time in the prisons; that, in anticipation of the Married Women's Property Act, it was made illegal for a husband to waste his wife's money; that the races at Brescia on 15 August were abolished because of the abuses they encouraged; and that public gaming establishments were closed down in several cities. Like Bernardino of Siena and his own Florentine contemporary, the Dominican Girolamo Savonarola, he used to organize huge bonfires on which what he called "the devil's stronghold"—anything from cards, dice, and pornographic literature to the badges of the rival factions that were causing such strife in Italian cities at the time and unnecessary and frivolous articles of dress—was burned. The people loved it, and if their leaders were less enthusiastic most of them learned to respect him, and even to use him as a mediator when it suited them. Only with the constantly warring Oddi and Baglioni factions in Perugia did he fail to make any impression at all.

One of the most serious disorders with which Bernardino felt he needed to deal was the practice of usury. Money was being lent at exorbitant rates of interest by individual moneylenders, most of whom happened to be Jews, and by the rapacious Lombard bankers. Aware of the prevailing atmosphere of anti-Semitism, Bernardino made it clear that he was not attacking the Jews as Jews:

> Jews must not be harmed either in their persons or in their property. . . . Justice and charity must be extended to them, for they are of the same nature as ourselves. I say this everywhere . . . because good order, the sovereign pontiffs and Christian charity alike require it. But it is not less true that canon law expressly forbids too frequent dealings, too great familiarity with them. Today no one has any scruples in this matter, and I cannot be silent about it: Jewish usurers exceed all bounds; they ruin the poor and get fat at their expense. I, who live on alms and myself eat the bread of poverty, cannot be a dumb dog before such outrageous injustice.

It sounds patronizing and in some respects offensive today, but it was relatively enlightened at the time.

In 1484, making good his word and despite the opposition of some of the friars, he started his first *monte di pietà*. The original *mons pietatis* (compassionate fund, perhaps—it is hard to translate but the meaning is clear) was probably founded in the previous century by a bishop of London, Michael of Northborough. He left one thousand silver marks to be lent without interest to the poor, who were to deposit one or more of their possessions as security. A Franciscan, Barnaba da Terni, founded a similar "pawnshop" in Perugia in 1462, and others were opened subsequently in Tuscany, the Marches, and the Papal States. But it was Bernardino who took the idea and used it to form an effective organization. The Mantuan *monte di pietà* met with such opposition from local moneylenders that it folded, but between 1484 and 1492 Bernardino founded no less that twenty. Each was administered by a committee of friars and laymen (representative of the different trades), and some were municipally controlled. The initial capital fund came in part from voluntary subscriptions, in part from loans from the moneylenders themselves. Profits were added to the capital, and this in turn meant the small interest rate could be reduced. Bernardino was attacked on all sides—by the moneylenders and bankers who succeeded in closing some of the *monti di pietà*, and by canon lawyers, who argued that to charge any interest, however little, was tantamount to usury. Bernardino stood his ground, pointing out that unless they charged a small rate of interest the funds would not exist at all. The matter was never settled in his lifetime, but in 1515 the Fifth Lateran Council decreed that the *monti di pietà* were not only lawful but to be encouraged. After this they became common throughout Europe, except in the British Isles.

At the end of August 1494 Bernardino, whose precarious health was finally beginning to give way, dragged himself to Pavia, where he was due to preach. He warned the people that he could hear the French "shoeing their horses for the invasion of Italy." The invasion in fact went ahead under Charles VIII a few months later. But Bernardino had died by then, in Pavia on 28 September, at the relatively early age of fifty-five. He was immediately acclaimed a saint, and his cult was confirmed in 1654.

See *AA.SS.*, Sept., 7; *Bibl.SS.*, 2, 1289-94; *Archivum Franciscanum Historicum*, 19 (1926), pp. 226-46. The most complete modern biography is L. de Besse, *Le bienheureux Bernardin de Feltre et son oeuvre* (1902). See also Léon, *Auréole* (Eng. trans.), 3, pp. 243-66; F. Casolini, *Il martello degli usurai* (1939).

Bd Simon de Rojas (1552-1624)

Simon was born at Valladolid on 28 October 1552 to Gregorio Ruiz de Navamuel and Costanza de Rojas. He is said to have been precociously religious as a child, and when he was sixteen (some sources say twelve) he entered the Trinitarian Order. In 1579, with his studies and his ordination to the priesthood behind him, he went to teach philosophy and theology in Toledo. By this time his reputation for learning and holiness was spreading, and in the next few years he served as superior of several different houses of the Order. Eventually the Spanish king, Philip III (1598-1621), came to hear of him and called him to court as confessor to his wife, Margaret.

Like Bd Alphonsus de Orozco (19 Sept.) in a similar situation, Simon had a significant influence on the values and customs of the court. But although he was loyal to the king he remained his own man. While he was in Madrid there was a serious outbreak of the plague. His instinct was to go out immediately and help the victims and their families, but the king, fearing that infection would enter the palace, forbade him to do so. Simon replied: "Sick beds are more fitting places for me that royal palaces, and if I must give up one I will give up the court." In addition to his work at court he conducted missions very successfully, founded a confraternity dedicated to Our Lady, and wrote an Office for the feast of the Holy Name of Mary, to which his Order had a special devotion. Refusing the bishoprics of Jaén and Valladolid, he eventually returned to Valladolid. In 1624, having held a series of other responsible positions in the Order, he was made provincial for Castile. When he died on 29 September of that same year, his funeral ceremonies are said to have lasted for thirteen days. He was beatified in 1766.

Prospero Lambertini (Pope Benedict XIV) mentions Bd Simon in his great work, *De servorum Dei beatificatione et beatorum canonizatione* (1734-8), 2. See also *Compendio della Vita del B. Simone de Roxas* (1767); P. Deslandres, *L'Ordre des Trinitaires* (1903), 1, p. 618; *Bibl.SS.*, 11, 298-9; Pierre de la Nativité, *L'Histoire merveilleuse du b. Simon de Rojas* (1949).

29

Bd Richard of Hampole (*c.* 1300-1349)

Although the cult of Richard Rolle of Hampole has never been officially confirmed, the attribution to him of the title "Blessed" is justified by the popular devotion he inspired after his death. Miracles had been reported at his tomb and preparations for his canonization were set in train. In York an Office for his feast had even been prepared, although it was published with a warning: "The Office of St Richard, hermit, after he shall be canonized by the Church, because in the meantime it is not allowed to sing the canonical hours *de eo* in public, nor to solemnize his feast. Nevertheless, having evidence of the extreme sanctity of his life, we may venerate him and in our private devotions seek his intercession, and commend ourselves to his prayers." Although for some reason the canonization never took place, the lessons for Matins in this Office remain, together with his writings, as the principal source of information about this important figure in the English mystical tradition.

Richard was born in about 1300 at Thornton—traditionally identified as Thornton-le-Dale, near Pickering—in North Yorkshire. With the help of Master Thomas Neville, who was later archdeacon of Durham, his parents were able to send him to Oxford. He pursued his studies for a while, but when he was eighteen or nineteen he abandoned them and left the university without graduating. According to the account given in the lessons for his Office, at this point he went home immediately. There he asked his sister for two of her gowns, out of which he made a garment that roughly resembled the habits worn by hermits. His sister made it quite clear that she thought he was mad, so Richard, fearing his father's reaction, decided to slip quietly away from home. He is said to have gone to the church of a neighbouring parish (Topcliffe?), where he knelt in the pew reserved for the squire, John of Dalton, and was recognized by the latter's sons, who had been at Oxford with him. The next day was the feast of the Assumption (15 Aug.). Richard appeared again, this time vested in a surplice, and with the priest's permission "gave the people a sermon of wonderful edification, in so much that the crowd that heard it was moved to tears, and they all said that they had never before heard a sermon of such virtue and power." After Mass John of Dalton invited Richard to dinner and, having assured himself of his good faith, gave him a place to live on his own estate, as well as food, proper clothing, and whatever else he needed. Richard then "began with all diligence by day and night to seek how to perfect his life and to take every opportunity to advance in contemplation and to be fervent in divine love."

This account presents a number of problems, and it is more than likely that the author has given an abridged and expurgated version of events in order to make the story more edifying for his readers. In his own works Richard speaks of his "unclean and sinful" youth, which, even allowing for his humility, does not fit in with what the lessons say. What is more probable is that the events described took place not when he was just out of Oxford but about ten years later, when he was already about twenty-eight and had had some experience of life. He may even have been a doctor of theology, although not a priest—it is generally agreed now that he was never ordained. This would fit in with what an English martyrology published in 1608 by a priest, John Wilson, says of him: "He was first a Doctor, and then leaving the world became an Eremite."

For some years Richard carried on his solitary but not enclosed life on the Dalton estate. At first he suffered greatly as a result of the extremes to which he exposed himself: "I have so weakened my body and suffer so from head-aches that I cannot stand, so bad are they, unless I am strengthened by wholesome food." Gradually he realized that there might be greater virtue in moderation: "It behoves him truly to be strong that will manfully use the love of God. The flesh being enfeebled with great disease oft-times a man cannot pray, and then much more he cannot lift himself to high things with hot desire. I would rather therefore that man failed for the greatness of love than for too much fasting." For years he bore cheerfully the hostility and malicious criticism of people—some of whom he had "trusted before as faithful friends"—who decided that anyone who lived even in the grounds of a rich landowner could not possibly be close to God.

When John of Dalton's wife died, Richard, "for most urgent and practical reasons," moved away and into the Richmond area. He seems to have had no fixed residence at this stage, "so that dwelling in many places he might benefit many unto salvation." One Maundy Thursday he was called to the bedside of a recluse and close friend, Dame Margaret Kirkby, who for a fortnight had been ill and unable to speak. While he was there, she fell into a heavy sleep, during which she had a violent convulsion. When she woke up to find her speech restored her first words were, "*Gloria tibi, Domine*," to which Richard replied with the second half of the verse—"*qui natus es de Virgine*"—and reminded her to use her speech "as a woman whose speech is for good." Eventually Richard settled at Hampole, on the Wakefield road four miles from Doncaster. His cell was near the priory of the Cistercian nuns, but it is not clear whether he was their chaplain or simply a counsellor and friend.

Whatever time he did not spend praying or counselling others Richard would devote to writing. His best-known work is *Incendium Amoris* (The Fire of Love), of which he said: "I here stir all manner of folk to love, and am busy to show the hottest and supernatural desire of love." Some think he wrote it at Hampole, but it seems more likely that it dates from an earlier period—by the time he went to Hampole he was writing only or mostly in English. He had translated and commented on the psalms for Margaret Kirkby—a chained copy of this was kept at Hampole priory; he had written a small book in English for a Benedictine nun at Yedingham; and now he wrote *Commandment of Love to God* for one of the Hampole nuns. Much of what he says is based directly on his own experience, and earlier it could be described as self-absorbed. Although writers on mysticism have tried to match what he says about progress in the spiritual life with the classic scheme of the purgative, illuminative, and unitive ways, it never quite fits. What is more, although he speaks of "consolations," he claims none of the direct revelations and visions enjoyed by so many of the mystics, and as far as is known his spiritual experiences were not accompanied by any unusual physical phenomena. He seems to have been a very practical—perhaps just very English—mystic.

He was—and is—not without his critics. His near contemporaries Walter Hilton and the author of *The Cloud of Unknowing* were suspicious of his teachings. And there are still those who detect a lack of development in his writings. He can certainly sound a bit querulous at times, especially when he feels the need to justify his way of life against those who argued that hermits were lazy, inferior to priests and monks. But the keynote of his message is joy: "The holy lover of God shows himself neither too merry nor full heavy in this habitation of exile, but he has cheerfulness with maturity. . . . Laughter, therefore, which is from lightness and vanity of mind is to be reproved, but that truly which is of gladness of conscience and spiritual mirth is to be praised; the which is only in the righteous, and it is called mirth in the love of God."

See H. E. Allen, *Writings ascribed to Richard Rolle and Materials for his Biography* (1927); *ibid.* (ed.), *English Writings* (1931); S. J. Ogilvy Thompson (ed.), *Richard Rolle: Prose and Verse* (1988); F. Comper, *Life and Lyrics of Richard Rolle* (1928); R. M. Woolley, *Richard Rolle of Hampole* (1919); M. Deanesly, *Incendium Amoris* (1926); G. C. Heseltine, *Selected Works of Richard Rolle* (1930). More recently: M. L. Arntz, *Richard Rolle and the Holy Boke Gratia Dei* (1981); H. A. Allen (ed.), *English Writings of Richard Rolle, Hermit of Hampole* (1988); J. C. Dolan, *The Tractatus super psalmum vicesimum of Richard Rolle of Hampole* (1991); G. C. Miller (ed.), *The Way of the English Mystics* (1996), pp. 17–39. See also D. Knowles, *The English Mystical Tradition* (1960); *N.C.E.*, 12, p. 561.

Bd Charles of Blois (1319-64)

Charles, whose story fills a small chapter in the history of the Hundred Years War, was the son of Guy de Châtillon, count of Blois, and Margaret, sister of Philip VI of France. He was born in 1319 and in his youth was remarkable for his goodness as well as for his bravery. In 1337 he married Joan the Lame of Penthièvre, niece and heir of John III, duke of Brittany. In view of that relationship, John had designated Charles as his heir. But when he died in 1341 and Charles claimed the dukedom, the claim was disputed by the late duke's stepbrother, Jean de Montfort. This led to a war between the two men, which continued for the remainder of Charles' life. Although he and his wife did not, as they might have done, resolve the problem by withdrawing the claim, Charles did offer to settle the matter himself in single combat. And when that offer was refused and the war went ahead, he did all in his power to minimize its effects on his subjects. After the capture of Nantes, for example, his first act was to make sure that the poor had food and the injured were adequately cared for, and the same was true after the battles of Rennes, Guincamp, and others.

Meanwhile he founded religious houses so that the monks could pray for his cause and for the souls of those who died as a result of the fighting; and he went barefooted on pilgrimage to the shrine of St Ivo (19 May) at Tréguier for the same purpose. Some of his followers felt he might have done better to become a monk himself, and when he suspended the siege of Hennebont so that the troops could go to Mass, one of the officers protested openly. But Charles replied, "We can always have towns and castles. If they are taken away from us, God will help us to get them back again. But we cannot afford to miss Mass."

Eventually, despite help from the French king, Philip IV of Valois (1328-50), Charles was defeated by Jean de Montfort, who had the support of Edward III of England (1327-77). He had managed to hold out for a while, but in January 1347, after the battle of Crécy and the sacking of Poitiers, he was defeated at the battle of La Roche-Derrien near Tréguier, taken prisoner, and shipped over to England. The sum of money demanded for his ransom was so large that he had to spend nine years in the Tower of London before regaining his liberty. During his captivity, he wrote a biography of St Ivo, whose canonization he helped to procure, while his patience and prayerfulness earned him the ungrudging admiration of his gaolers.

Having at last purchased his release, on 12 July 1363 he agreed to a partition of the dukedom. Unfortunately this did not please his wife, and, having broken the agreement, Charles pursued their claim for another nine years, with varying fortunes. The last battle took place at Auray on 29 September 1364. Arrayed against Charles was an army of British soldiers commanded by Sir John Chandos. Bertrand du Guesclin was taken prisoner, and Charles was killed on the battlefield. He was buried at Guincamp. Miracles were reported at his tomb, and there was a strong movement in favour of his canonization in spite of opposition from Jean V de Montfort, who feared this might damage his own cause in Brittany. It seems that Pope Gregory XI (1370-8) did in fact authorize the canonization, but in the turmoil of his departure for Avignon in 1376 the Bull was never drawn up. People nevertheless continued to venerate Charles, and the cult was confirmed by Pope St Pius X (26 Aug.) in 1904.

See A de Sérent, *Monuments du procès de canonisation du bx Charles de Blois* (1921); G. Lobineau, *Histoire de Bretagne* (1744), 2, pp. 540-70; N. Maurice-Denis-Boulet, "La canonisation de Charles de Blois," in *Revue d'histoire de l'Eglise de France* 28, (1942), pp. 216-24; *Bibl.SS.*, 3, 793-4; *H.S.S.C.*, 7, p. 274; Baudot et Chausson, 9, pp. 615-9.

Bd John of Dukla (*c.* 1414-84)

John was born at Dukla near the Carpathian mountains in Poland in about 1414. Having joined the Friars Minor Conventual, he was one of the many Polish members of the Order who were inspired by the preaching of St John Capistrano (23 Oct.) to adopt the stricter Constitutions of the Observant friars. He lived for some time more or less as a recluse, but this inevitably changed when he was appointed guardian of the friary at Lvov. It was at this point that, with permission from his superiors, he moved over to the Bernardines, an offshoot of the Friars Minor, so called because their churches were dedicated to St Bernard (20 Aug.). He now threw himself into apostolic work, concentrating on the pulpit and the confessional. When he went blind in his old age he continued undaunted, simply employing a novice to read the biblical texts to him so that he could prepare his sermons. Many people, including members of the Hussite and other sects, came into or returned to the Church as a result of his preaching and example.

Throughout his life his particular combination of enthusiasm and prudence led to his being placed in positions of responsibility. He served several terms as guardian at Krosno and Lvov and was at one stage custodian of the province. This was significant because of the proximity of the Orthodox and of the missionary nature of the houses under his jurisdiction. When he died at Lvov on 29 September 1484, there was an immediate upsurge of veneration, and miracles were reported at his tomb. His cult as a principal patron of Poland and Lithuania was approved by Pope Clement XII (1730-40) in 1739, and in 1984 the Sacred Congregation of Rites declared the cause for his canonization open.

The *Archivum Franciscanum Historicum*, 22 (1929), pp. 434-7, contains a tolerably full account by K. Kantak, who complains of the shortage of historical sources. For the chronicle of Jan Komorowski on which he draws, see Liske and Lorkiewicz, *Monumenta Poloniae Historica* (1888), 5, pp. 246-9. Also *Bibl.SS.*, 6, 749, which lists works in Polish; Léon, *Auréole*, 2, pp. 507-9.

ST JEROME (over page)
Red cross on silver field

30

ST JEROME, *Doctor* (*c.* 345-420)

Eusebius Hieronymus Sophronius, known to the English-speaking world as Jerome, was one of the most learned, most difficult, and most restless and combative of all the saints in the Church's Calendar. He was born into a well-to-do and probably Christian family at Stridon, a small town near Aquileia, sometime between 340 and 347. His father, having himself made sure that Jerome had a thorough grounding in the Christian faith as well as in the basic secular subjects, soon sent him to pursue his education in Rome. There his tutor was the great grammarian Aelius Donatus, whose *Ars minor* was used as a textbook throughout the Middle Ages.

Jerome applied himself with purpose and enthusiasm to his studies. His mother tongue was Illyrian, but he soon became fluent in both Latin and Greek and was able to read and familiarize himself with the best authors in both languages. He also studied rhetoric to great effect, as his writings would subsequently show. He was later to say regretfully that the one thing he neglected at this stage was his religious education. However, although Alban Butler describes him as leaving Donatus' school "unhappily a stranger to the Christian spirit," things cannot have been as bad as this implies. Jerome himself recalls that on Sundays he was in the habit of going with like-minded friends to visit "the tombs of the martyrs and apostles" in the catacombs. And sometime before 366, having deferred it as people did at the time, he was baptized.

When he had been in Rome for about three years, he decided that what he needed to further his education and gain some experience was travel. With his childhood friend and fellow-student, Bonosus, he spent the next few years in Gaul, Dalmatia, and Italy. While they were in Trier, which is where the emperor then resided, Jerome seems to have undergone some sort of religious conversion and decided to become a monk. This he did in about 370, together with several other friends, while they were in Aquileia. At the end of the fourth century Aquileia was a lively Christian centre with a clergy that came from far and wide, attracted by the energy and commitment with which it was run. Here Jerome met many of the men whose names appear in his writings— St Chromatius (2 Dec.), who eventually became bishop of Aquileia; his brothers Jovinian and Eusebius, both deacons; St Heliodorus (3 July) and his nephew Nepotian; and above all Rufinus, for many years Jerome's great friend but in the end his bitter opponent.

Even at this stage, however, the difficult, confrontational side of Jerome's personality was at work, making him enemies as easily as his energy and enthusiasm made him friends. He became involved in some sort of quarrel that had the effect of splitting the group. When they decided to leave Aquileia, Bonosus went to an island in the Adriatic, but Jerome resolved to move further afield. While he was still making up his mind exactly where this was to be, a chance meeting with a priest from Antioch named Evagrius influenced him in favour of the East. He set off with three friends and reached Antioch sometime in 374. They had not been there long when two of his friends died and he himself fell seriously ill. In a letter written much later to St Eustochium (28 Sept.), he described how the fever induced a delirious state in which he seemed to be standing before the judgment seat of Christ. Asked who he was, he replied, "I am a Christian." "Liar!" came the answer. "You are a Ciceronian, not a Christian; for where your treasure is there also is your heart." Deeply affected by this and by his meeting with St Malchus (21 Oct.), which happened about this time, he retired to the desert of Chalcis, a barren region south-east of Antioch.

Despite recurrent ill health and severe temptations of the flesh Jerome remained in the desert for at least four years. He described his extraordinary fasts and the possibly hallucinatory experiences they induced in a letter, again to Eustochium: "In the remotest part of a wild and stony desert, burnt by the heat of the sun which is so scorching that it frightens even the monks who spend their lives there, I seemed to be surrounded by the attractions and the crowds of Rome. . . . In this exile and prison, to which, in fear of hell, I had voluntarily condemned myself, with no other company but scorpions and wild beasts, I frequently imagined I could see young Roman women dancing, and it was as if I was there in the midst of them. . . . In my cold body and my parched flesh, which seemed dead before its time, passion was able to live."

To ward off the temptations of the flesh he resorted to a method that was certainly more useful and probably more effective than his extreme austerities: he gave up the classics, at least temporarily, and began to learn Hebrew from a converted Jew who had become a monk. His long familiarity with the classics and their polished style made it difficult for him at first to put up with the stylistically rougher Hebrew of the Bible. "From the judicious rules of Quintilian," he wrote to a monk named Rusticus in 411, "from the full and flowing elegance of Cicero, from the grave style of Fronto and from the smoothness of Pliny, I turned to this language of hissing and broken-winded words. The effort it cost me, the difficulties I went through and the number of times I gave up in despair only to take it up again, are things to which those who lived with me can bear witness as well as I. I thank Our Lord that I now gather such sweet fruit from the bitter sowing of those studies." With the Hebrew he was now fully equipped for his work as biblical scholar, translator, and writer.

The church of Antioch was plagued throughout this period by doctrinal and disciplinary disputes. The monks in the desert of Chalcis were not slow to take sides, and they tried to persuade Jerome to do the same. Uncharacteristically he refused, preferring to remain unaligned, although he twice consulted Pope St Damasus I (366-84; 11 Dec.) as to which of the three claimants to the see of Antioch he should support. When the pope failed to reply promptly to his first letter, in which he had spoken of church unity in terms of communion with the Bishop of Rome, Jerome wrote again. Damasus' reply has not survived, but he must have named Paulinus as the rightful claimant, because it was Paulinus who, as bishop of Antioch, ordained Jerome when he eventually returned from the desert. It is not easy to understand why he was ordained. He believed he was called to be a monk and had no wish to be a priest as well. That idea came from others, and he seems to have consented on condition that he did not have to serve as a priest in Antioch or anywhere else. He is not known ever to have celebrated Mass.

Whatever the truth about this, Jerome left soon afterwards for Constantinople, where he studied the scriptures for a time under St Gregory Nazianzen (2 Jan.). In later years he spoke and wrote gratefully of this invaluable opportunity to work with one of the great biblical scholars of the period. It was while he was in Constantinople that, in addition to translations of some of Origen's works and of Eusebius's *Chronicles* (from Greek to Latin), he published his first original biblical commentary, on the Vision of Isaiah (Isa. 6:1-13).

This happy and fulfilling period came to an end when Gregory left Constantinople in 382. Jerome went to Rome as interpreter for Paulinus of Antioch and St Epiphanius of Salamis (12 May) at a council called by Pope Damasus to discuss the schism in Antioch. Once the council was over, Damasus asked him to remain in Rome as his secretary. As part of his official duties over the course of the next three years Jerome wrote a number of significant biblical commentaries. At the same time, with a view to publishing a standard Latin text, he embarked on a complete revision of the Bible based on the original texts. This was a monumental task, which eventually produced what came to be known as the Vulgate version of the Bible.

Despite these official calls on his time Jerome still had the energy for other activities. In Rome there was a group of Christian women, all of them from noble families and most of them widows, who were living a quasi-monastic life. Among them were St Marcella (31 Jan.) and St Fabiola (27 Dec.) as well as St Paula (26 Jan.) and her daughter St Eustochium (28 Sept.), who were to play such a large part in Jerome's life. He undertook to be their spiritual director and to help them with their study of the scriptures. Things went relatively well as long as Damasus was alive. However, when the pope died in 384 Jerome, who had made himself thoroughly unpopular in some circles, was left without a protector. People admired his learning and his obvious integrity, but many found what they experienced as unnecessarily blunt outspokenness and biting sarcasm difficult to take. His defence of St Blesilla's decision to abandon the world of Roman society is sharply witty, but it is easy to see how it offended those at whose expense he made fun—"those who paint their cheeks with rouge and their eyelids with antimony; whose plastered faces, too white to be human, look like idols, and if they forget and shed a tear it makes a furrow as it rolls down the painted cheek; who . . . enamel a lost youth on the wrinkles of age, and affect a maidenly timidity in the midst of a troupe of grandchildren." Nor did he reserve his comments for the members of fashionable society. He could be equally hard on priests: "The only thing they worry about is their clothes—you would think they were bridegrooms rather than clerics; and their one concern is to know about the names, the houses and the activities of rich women." And some of his more personal comments verged on cruelty: "If he would conceal his nose and keep his mouth shut," he remarked of one unfortunate man, "he might be taken for both handsome and learned." So it is not surprising that people took advantage of his exposed position and sought revenge. Despite the austerity of the women whose direction he had undertaken and his own reserve, rumours were circulated about his relationship with them and in particular with Paula. He was justifiably indignant about the calumny but, rather than stay and fight, decided to look for peace and quiet in the Holy Land. However, before he left in August 385 he did make his position clear in a letter to Marcella's sister, St Asella (6 Dec.). Asking her to pass on his greetings to Paula and Eustochium—"mine in Christ, whether the world likes it or not"—he added: "Tell them that we shall all stand before the judgment seat of Christ, and then the spirit in which each of us has lived will be plain for all to see."

Jerome was still in Antioch nine months later when he was joined by several of the Roman ladies, including Paula and Eustochium, who had decided to share his exile. The party travelled first to Jerusalem but soon went on to Egypt to consult the monks of Nitria and a famous blind teacher named Didymus at the school of Alexandria. They then returned to the Holy Land and settled in Bethlehem. Here, with generous financial support from Paula, they established a monastery for men and three communities of women. Jerome himself lived and worked in a cell hewn from the rock near the traditional birthplace of Jesus. He immediately began to work on commentaries on the Epistles of St Paul and on the book of Ecclesiastes. At the same time he opened a free school and a hospice, which, if he is to be taken literally, were frequented by people from far and wide: "The illustrious Gauls gather here, and no sooner has the Briton, so remote from our world, made some progress in religion than he leaves his early-setting sun for a land which he knows by reputation and from the Scriptures. And what of the Armenians, the Persians, the people of India and Ethiopia, of Egypt, of Pontus, Cappadocia, Syria and Mesopotamia? . . . They throng here and set us the example of every virtue. The languages differ but the religion is the same; there are as many different choirs singing the psalms as there are nations." The same letter contains an attractive description of their life there: "Bread, our own vegetables, and milk—country fare—provide us with a plain but healthy diet. In summer the trees give us shade; in autumn the air is cool and the fallen leaves are restful; in spring our chanting of the psalms is made sweeter by the singing of the birds; and in winter, when it is cold and the snow falls, there is no lack of wood."

But even in these peaceful rural surroundings Jerome could not resist becoming involved in controversy. While he was last in Rome he had written a treatise on the perpetual virginity of Mary in answer to Helvidius, who said she had children by St Joseph after the birth of Jesus. When Helvidius' view was taken up and developed by a man named Jovinian, St Pammachius (30 Aug.), Paula's son-in-law, and a number of other laymen were shocked and sent his writings to Jerome. Jerome responded robustly with two books, one on the value of virginity freely chosen, one in answer to the other points Jovinian made. His forthright style predictably offended some people in Rome, who felt that what he said belittled marriage. Pammachius informed him of this, whereupon Jerome wrote a third treatise, the tone of which cannot have made matters any better. A few years later he turned his fire on a man named Vigilantius (Jerome liked to call him Dormantius, sleepy), a Gallo-Roman priest who denounced both celibacy and the veneration of relics. Vigilantius called the latter idolatry and the worshipping of ashes, but Jerome, who had a strong feeling for the intercessory power of the saints, used vehement language to convince him that while Christians honour the saints they do not worship them.

Between 395 and 400 Jerome became involved in a controversy over the teachings of Origen that was to have sad personal consequences for him. As a great admirer of Origen he had made extensive use of his works. But when he discovered that Eastern Christians were being led into error by some of Origen's opinions, he went into battle against what he saw as a pernicious evil. It so happened that Rufinus, who was living at a monastery in Jerusalem, had translated some of Origen's works, of which he was an enthusiastic advocate. There is no evidence that Rufinus intended to uphold what were judged to be Origen's heretical views, but Jerome failed to distinguish between attributed views and views actually held and insisted on attacking the man rather than his opinions. Unfortunately, moderation and compromise were foreign to his nature, and he had a way of assuming that his view and the Truth were one and the same. For the most part, the unsparing polemicist in him did not get in the way of the loyal and tenacious friend. But in this case he allowed what was essentially no more than an intellectual argument to destroy an old friendship. Nor was Rufinus the only friend who managed to upset him. He was provoked by St Augustine (28 Aug.) during a debate on the second chapter of the Epistle to the Galatians, and it took all Augustine's tact to restore tranquility to the situation.

Jerome's greatest claim to fame is as a scholar, in particular as a translator of and commentator on the Bible. While in Rome he had produced a revised edition of the Psalms and of the Gospels and the rest of the New Testament. In Bethlehem he began to work on the Old Testament, eventually translating most of the books into Latin directly from the Hebrew—Wisdom, Ecclesiasticus, Baruch, and Maccabees I and II are the only ones he did not translate, or at least work on. The results were a stumbling-block at first because they cast doubt on the version that had been in use until then. But his version gradually won acceptance, and the so-called Vulgate edition was formally recognized in 1942 as the authoritative Latin biblical text of the Catholic Church. (The sixteenth-century Douai and the twentieth-century Knox English translations were both made from the Vulgate.) He also had much to say about the monastic life, which he believed should be based on *lectio divina*—a prayerful study of the scriptures and the writings of the Fathers of the Church. He himself is one of the greatest of these Fathers, and he is honoured as one of the four Latin Doctors.

Some of his expressed views on celibacy and marriage would today be regarded as extreme. Apparently unable to praise the former without denigrating the latter, he once said: "Marriage, I praise it because it produces virgins; from the thorns I pluck the rose." Yet he had a great gift for friendship, especially with women. We know from his letters and other writings that he kept in touch with his friends in Rome, and felt their misfortunes keenly. "All of a sudden," he once wrote, "I was told about the deaths of Pammachius and Marcella, the sack of Rome and the end of many brothers and sisters. I was overwhelmed—quite stunned in fact—and did nothing all day but think of the safety of each and every one." The attempts made to cast doubt on his integrity, especially where his relationship with Paula was concerned, never held. What is certain is that he was devoted to her, and when she died in 404 he was inconsolable.

Rome was sacked by Alaric, king of the Visigoths (395-410), in 410. Jerome was forced to interrupt his scholarly activities in order to help the many refugees who fled eastward. "I cannot help them all," he wrote, "but I grieve and weep with them. Completely involved in the activities charity imposes on me, I have set aside my commentary on Ezekiel and almost all study. For today we must translate the words of the Scriptures into deeds, and instead of speaking saintly words we must act them." His studies were similarly interrupted once again in 416. On that occasion a gang of ruffians, apparently sent by the Pelagians, attacked the monastic complex. They beat the monks and nuns, killing at least one person, and set fire to the buildings. Eustochium never recovered, and in the following year she died. Jerome, too, was failing. He was worn out by his austerities and his hard work, and his sight, so essential to him as a scholar, was poor. He died peacefully in Bethlehem on 30 September 420 and was buried in the church of the Nativity, close to Paula and Eustochium. His remains were later taken to Santa Maria Maggiore in Rome. As he left no Rule—he had simply taken and applied that of Pachomius—the monasteries did not effectively survive him for long. However, in the fourteenth century various groups adopted his particular brand of asceticism, taking names such as the Hermits of St Jerome of the Congregation of Fiesole or the Poor Hermits of St Jerome.

For St Jerome's works see *P.L.*, 22-30; *C.S.E.L.*, 54-6, 59; *Corpus Christianorum*, 72, 78. For translations see *S.C.* and Ancient Christian Writers. Erasmus wrote a brief Life and edited his works, published in nine folio volumes by Johann Frobel in Basle in 1516 and several times revised: selected Eng. trans. by J. F. Brady and J. C. Olin, *Collected Works of Erasmus*, 61, *The Edition of St Jerome* (1992). There is no worthwhile early account of his life and work—his own letters and writings remain the best source—but there are many valuable modern studies: G. Grutzmacher, *Hieronymus: Eine biographische Studie* (1901-8); F. Cavallera, *Saint Jérôme, sa vie et son oeuvre* (1922); *Saint Jérôme et les dames de l'Aventin* (1938); A. Penna, *S. Gerolamo* (1949); *idem, Principi e carattere dell'esegesi di S. Gerolamo* (1952); D. Gorce, *Saint Jérôme et la Lectio Divina* (1952); F. X. Murphy (ed.), *A Monument to St Jerome* (1952); H. F. D. Sparks, "Jerome as Biblical Scholar," in *The Cambridge History of the Bible*, 1 (1970), pp. 510-41; J. N. D. Kelly, *Jerome* (1975). See also E. D. Hunt, *Holy Land Pilgrimage in the Later Roman Empire* (1982); *O.D.S.*, pp. 252-3; *O.D.C.C.* (1997), p. 867; *H.S.S.C.*, 3, pp. 250-8; *Bibl.SS.*, 6, 1109-37; Jöckle, pp. 231-4.

The iconography is enormous. Jerome is variously represented as cardinal (probably because of his connection with Pope Damasus I), scholar, and ascetic. Not only was he never a cardinal, but the idea is anachronistic anyway: the first cardinals were bishops who lost their dioceses during the barbarian invasions and were reassigned by the pope; then the title was given to the pastors of certain parish churches in Rome; only in the eleventh century did the latter become organized as a "college." But scholar and ascetic he certainly was (one Renaissance pope, seeing a painting of him holding the stone that symbolized his voluntary penance, remarked that it was just as well he had that, for without it he would hardly be considered a saint). There are many representations dating mainly from the fifteenth to the seventeenth century of him in a study, or else in or near his cave, often with a lion at his feet. This is a reference to the legend (borrowed from that of St Gerasimus, 5 Mar.) that a lion with a thorn in its paw came limping to him for help; having drawn the thorn, Jerome tamed the lion, which then minded his donkey. The earliest representation of him is probably the painting on the seventh-century ivory diptych of Boethius (in Brescia Museum), followed by the one in the ninth-century Bible of Charles the Bald. Here he is shown setting out for the Holy Land and explaining the scriptures to Paula and Eustochium. He appears as one of the four Latin Doctors on rood screens in East Anglia. Later representations with various attributes include Andrea da Messina (1460-5; Reggio di Calabria); Cima da Conegliano (1504/10; National Gallery, London); Hieronymus Bosch (*c.* 1505; Doge's Palace, Venice); Parmigianino, *The Vision of St Jerome of the Virgin and Child with St John the Baptist* (1527; National Gallery, London); Domenichino, *The Last Communion of St Jerome* (1614; Vatican Gallery); Zurbarán, *The Temptation of St Jerome* and other subjects (Jeronymite Monastery, Guadalupe, Spain). See P. and L. Murray, *The Oxford Companion to Christian Art and Architecture* (1996), p. 250.

St Gregory the Enlightener, *Bishop* (*c.* 260-*c.* 330)

Accounts of how and through whom Christianity first came to Armenia vary, especially locally, where legends abound. What now seems certain is that it was brought during the second or third century, probably by missionaries from Syria and Persia. However, Gregory of Ashtishat, the "Illuminator" or "Enlightener," is the one whom the Armenians venerate as their national saint and patron. According to the available information, which is at best patchily reliable, he was born in Armenia in about 260, when the country was occupied by the Persians. Exactly where or in what circumstances is not known. There is a dubious tradition that he was the son of a Parthian prince named Anak, who murdered Khosrov I of Armenia, and that when the dying Khosrov ordered the extermination of Anak's family he was smuggled away, Moses-like, to Caesarea in Cappadocia. He seems to have been baptized and educated in Caesarea, where he also married and had two sons, SS Aristakes and Vardanes.

When Khosrov's son, Tiridates, returned from exile with an army and successfully claimed his father's throne, Gregory, who had probably been ordained by this stage, was given a position at court. Soon, however, he had alienated the king with his zeal in making converts and his general encouragement of Armenian Christians. Once Tiridates began actively to persecute Christians, Gregory was among the first to suffer. But then Tiridates himself was converted—he is venerated as a saint—and things changed. In 314, when Gregory was consecrated bishop, Christianity was proclaimed the official religion of Armenia, which thus became the first Christian State.

Gregory's consecration took place in Caesarea, but he quickly moved on to Ashtishat, where he established his see. Here, it seems, it was necessary to start from scratch, which he did with energy and enthusiasm. There was no clergy, so he recruited some young men, gave them a good if basic grounding in the scriptures and Christian morality, and taught them Greek and Syriac. Meanwhile, with the help of Greek and Syrian missionaries he organized his Church and set about the work of instructing converts. When the Council of Nicaea took place in 325, Gregory sent his son Aristakes to represent him and shortly afterwards consecrated Aristakes bishop in his place. The see in fact remained hereditary until well into the next century, when St Isaac I (9 Sept.) ruled that married priests could not become bishops. In about 330 Gregory himself withdrew to a hermitage on Mount Manyea. He was found dead by a shepherd sometime between 330 and 332 and was buried at Thortan.

Legends of Gregory abound. There is a notable collection in a "history" that purports to have been written by a secretary of Tiridates named Agathangelos, though in fact it dates from the second half of the fifth century. This tells that, having displeased Tiridates, Gregory was tortured then left in a stinking dungeon or pit for fifteen years, forgotten by all except a kindly widow, whose support kept him alive. Then, after the martyrdom of St Rhipsime (5 Oct.), Tiridates was turned into a wild boar, so Gregory, whose prayers were needed to restore him to his natural state, was released from the pit. Having fasted, prayed, and preached for seventy days, Gregory had a vision at Valarsharpat, near Mount Ararat, and was told to build the cathedral church of Armenia there (this story was probably invented to support the Armenian Church's claim to independence from Caesarea). The Armenians celebrate the incidents liturgically as the Twelve Torments, the Casting into the Pit, the Release from the Pit, and the Vision, along with other feasts of the saint. The wild boar story may be less fantastical than it seems. Tiridates is said to have converted to Christianity after Gregory cured him from a serious illness, and it has been suggested that the illness may have been lycanthropy, a form of mental illness in which the sufferer believes he is a wolf or some other wild beast.

St Gregory is sometimes venerated as a martyr, but this is a mistake. There is evidence of devotion to him in southern Italy, where it was probably introduced by Armenian "colonists." A church in Naples even claims to have some of his relics, but it is unlikely that they ever left Armenia. He is commemorated in the Canon of the Armenian Mass.

Sources are second-hand for all but Oriental Language specialists. See *AA.SS.*, Sept., 8, pp. 295-405. On the narrative of Agathangelos see G. Garitte, *Documents pour l'étude du livre d'Agathange* (1946); G. Winkler, "Our present knowledge of the *History* of Agat'angelos and its oriental versions," in *Revue des Etudes Arméniennes*, 14 (1980); P. Peeters in *Anal.Boll.* 26 (1907), pp. 117-20, and 50 (1931), pp. 3-58; S. Weber, *Die Katholische Kirche in Armenien* (1903); L. Duchesne, *Histoire ancienne de l'Eglise*, 3 (1911), pp. 528-36; D. Attwater, *The Christian Churches of the East* (1963). See also *O.D.C.C.*, pp. 27, 106, 711.

St Honorius of Canterbury, *Bishop* (653)

Honorius, a Roman by birth, was the fifth archbishop of Canterbury. He was living as a monk at Sant' Andrea on the Coelian Hill in Rome when he came to the attention of Pope St Gregory the Great (590-604; 3 Sept.), who was looking for men he could send as missionaries to convert the English. Honorius probably travelled over, not with St Augustine (26 May) in the first band of missionaries but in 601, as a member of the second band. On the death of the fourth archbishop, St Justus (10 Nov.), in 627, Honorius was chosen to succeed him and was consecrated in Lincoln Cathedral by the bishop of York, St Paulinus (10 Oct.). When Pope Honorius I (625-38) sent the *pallium* to "the two metropolitans, Honorius and Paulinus," there was an accompanying letter in which the pope effectively established a relationship of equality between the two sees. To both archbishops was given the power "to ordain the person that should be duly elected" should either see become vacant. This delegation of power was made, the pope explained, "because of the great distance of sea and land that lies between us and you."

Honorius' chief contribution was to consolidate the work of his predecessors. He occupied the see of Canterbury for twenty-five years, during which many new converts were made throughout the country. In this connection one of his most important acts was to send St Felix of Dunwich (8 Mar.), a Burgundian by birth and education, to evangelize the East Angles. When Paulinus was forced to flee after the battle of Hatfield Chase (634), in which King Edwin of Northumbria died fighting against the pagan Penda of Mercia and his Welsh Christian ally Cadwallon, he appointed him to the vacant see of Rochester.

And when Paulinus died Honorius consecrated the first English-born bishop, St Ithamar (10 June), a man of Kent, as his successor. Nothing is known about the private life or character of Honorius, who died on 30 September 653. He was buried in the abbey church of SS Peter and Paul (later St Augustine) in Canterbury, which became the centre of his cult.

Bede, *H.E.*, 2, 15, 17, 18, 20, and 3, 20; *AA.SS.*, Sept., 7, pp. 698-811; *Bibl.SS.*, 9, 1213-4; *O.D.S.*, p. 234. See also N. Brooks, *The Early History of the Church of Canterbury* (1984), pp. 65-7.

St Simon of Crépy (1048-82)

Simon was well known during his lifetime, and there are many contemporary tributes to his qualities. Knowledge of him depends on these and on an anonymous Life written shortly after his death. He was born at the castle of Crépy, near Senlis, in 1048. As count of Crépy-en-Valois, he was related to Matilda, the wife of William of Normandy, the "Conqueror" (1035-87), at whose court he was brought up after his mother died. His family, which claimed descent from Charlemagne, was one of the most powerful in France, and when his father, Raoul III, died in 1072, he became the owner of vast territories around Amiens, Bar-sur-Aube, Crépy, and the Vexin. Philip I of France (1060-1108), taking advantage of the youth of his vassal, tried to annex this land, but Simon, with William's help, managed to withstand him. Despite this and the fact that he fought for William against Philip in order to retain the Vexin for Normandy, Simon's real desire was to become a monk.

There is a story that he persuaded his fiancée, a daughter of Hildebert, count of Auvergne, to become a nun and planned their flight from their respective homes just before the wedding. This may or may not be true. What is certain is that at some stage William frustrated Simon's ambition to become a monk because he wanted him to marry his own daughter, Adela. Reluctant to refuse William directly, Simon set off to Rome in 1077 on the pretext of finding out if the proposed marriage would be lawful—Adela was in some way related to him—and to deal with some business left over by his father. On the way he stopped at the abbey of Saint-Claude at Condat in the Jura, and there he received the habit.

Although this ruled out the idea that he might marry, it did not prevent relatives and friends from seeking his advice and asking him to use his influence on their behalf. St Hugh of Cluny (29 Apr.) sent him to the French king to recover lands that had been taken from the monastery; he acted as a mediator between William of Normandy and his sons; and during the Investiture Controversy he helped Pope St Gregory VII (1073-85; 25 May) in his negotiations with Robert Guiscard: when these were successfully concluded at Aquino in 1080 Gregory retained Simon in Rome as an adviser. In 1082, still only in his thirties, Simon died in Rome, having received the Last Sacraments from Gregory himself. He was buried in St Peter's Basilica, and his epitaph was written by Eudes of Châtillon (later Pope Urban II, 1088-99). His remains were later moved to the abbey of Saint-Claude.

The testimonies to St Simon and the anonymous Life are in *AA.SS.*, Sept., 8, pp. 711-51. See also *Bibl.SS.*, 11, 1179-80; G. Corblet, *Hagiographie du diocèse d'Amiens*, 3, pp. 491-519; P. Benoît, *Histoire de l'abbaye de la terre de Saint-Claude*, 1 (1890).

Bd Frederick Albert (1820-76)

Frederick (Federico) was born on 16 October 1820 in Turin, where his father was serving as a high-ranking officer in the Sardinian army. As the eldest son, he was himself preparing to take up a place at the city's military academy when he went to pray one day at the tomb of Bd Sebastian Valfré (30 Jan.), the so-called "apostle of Turin." Whatever it was that happened on that day, he turned his back on the army and went instead to train as a priest. After his ordination on 10 June 1843 his first post, which he held for about nine years, was that of royal chaplain. It may seem strange that it was given to someone so young, but Frederick clearly did not allow this to worry him. There was a famous occasion in 1852 when Victor Emanuel II, accompanied by his family and the entire court, attended one of Frederick's Lenten sermons. The text of the day happened to be St John's account of the woman taken in adultery. Frederick did not mince his words, and there was anxious muttering among the alarmed courtiers, who were well aware of the king's lapses in this respect. But the king admired his honesty and said as he was leaving: "Thank you. You have always told me the truth."

A brief spell in the Turin parish of San Callo made Frederick determined not to remain at court all his life. He asked and received permission to leave and was given charge of a large, heavily populated, and demanding parish at Lanzo Torinese, in the mountains outside the city. The contrast with what he had become used to could not have been more complete, and for a while he found life difficult. But he persevered, starting with the church, which had fallen into serious disrepair. Assisted by his parishioners, who with him formed a human chain to bring large stones up from the dry bed of a seasonal stream in the valley, he set to work to restore it.

If he put the restoration of the church first this was no doubt as a way of getting to know his parishioners. But he was interested in more than parish buildings. Using his considerable gifts as a preacher, he conducted spiritual exercises both for the laity and for the clergy, and he organized public missions. During the latter, which sometimes lasted as long as a month, he would disregard his own physical needs in order to devote all his energies to the spiritual needs of his people. Having decided to found a school for boys, he turned to his close friend St John Bosco (31 Jan.) for practical support. In order to provide shelter and care for orphans and other needy persons he built the Ospizio di Maria Immacolata and subsequently founded the Suore Vincenziane di Maria Immacolata (known as the Albertines) to run it.

In 1873, much to his dismay, he was chosen to be bishop of Pinerolo, south-east of Turin. After much pleading and many prayers he managed to persuade Pope Pius IX (1846-78) to appoint someone else. So grateful was he for what was to him a lucky escape that he decided to make a pilgrimage to Rome to thank the pope personally—until, that is, his confessor pointed out that this was a luxury that the priest of a large and busy parish could not afford.

Frederick's life was cut short suddenly in 1876, when he was not quite fifty-six. He was busy creating a farming settlement—a sort of kibbutz where young people would be employed to cultivate church land. While he was painting the ceiling of the chapel—a task he had typically chosen for himself rather than place one of the young people in danger—he lost his balance and crashed to the floor. For two days, during which he was in excruciating pain, John Bosco and another Salesian, Bd Michael Rua (6 Apr.), were among those who cared for him. But there was nothing anyone could do, and on 30 September he died, much mourned by his parishioners. People remembered him above all for his tireless practical charity, his tolerant and compassionate approach to people, and his patient, equable temperament. His cause was introduced at the diocesan level in 1929, and he was beatified by Pope John Paul II on 30 September 1984.

M. P. Albert, *Il teologo, Federico Albert* (1296); J. Cottino, *Il Venerabile Federico Albert* (1954).

Alphabetical List of Entries

(Names are listed for those saints and blessed who have entries in the main body of the text. Those listed in the RM paragraph at the end of each day are omitted.)